# DECISION AND ORGANIZATION

A VOLUME IN HONOR OF JACOB MARSCHAK

# STUDIES IN MATHEMATICAL AND MANAGERIAL ECONOMICS

*editor*

HENRI THEIL

VOLUME 12

NORTH-HOLLAND PUBLISHING COMPANY
AMSTERDAM · LONDON

# DECISION AND ORGANIZATION

*A Volume in Honor of Jacob Marschak*

*edited by*

C. B. McGUIRE and ROY RADNER

*Contributors*

KENNETH J. ARROW
MARTIN J. BECKMANN
GERARD DEBREU
LEONID HURWICZ
TJALLING C. KOOPMANS
THOMAS A. MARSCHAK
C.B. McGUIRE
ROY RADNER
HERBERT SCARF
HERBERT A. SIMON

1972

NORTH-HOLLAND PUBLISHING COMPANY
AMSTERDAM · LONDON

Library of Congress Catalog Card Number: 77-157021
North-Holland ISBN: 0 7204 3313 4
American Elsevier ISBN: 0 444 10120 9

PUBLISHERS:

NORTH-HOLLAND PUBLISHING COMPANY—AMSTERDAM
NORTH-HOLLAND PUBLISHING COMPANY, LTD.—LONDON

SOLE DISTRIBUTORS FOR THE U.S.A. AND CANADA:

AMERICAN ELSEVIER PUBLISHING CO., INC.
52 VANDERBILT AVENUE, NEW YORK, N.Y. 10017

PRINTED IN BELGIUM

## INTRODUCTION TO THE SERIES

This is a series of books concerned with the quantitative approach to problems in the behavioural science field. The studies are in particular in the overlapping areas of mathematical economics, econometrics, operational research, and management science. Also, the mathematical and statistical techniques which belong to the apparatus of modern behavioural science have their place in this series. A well-balanced mixture of pure theory and practical applications is envisaged, which ought to be useful for universities and for research workers in business and government.

The Editor hopes that the volumes of this series, all of which relate to such a young and vigorous field of research activity, will contribute to the exchange of scientific information at a truly international level.

THE EDITOR

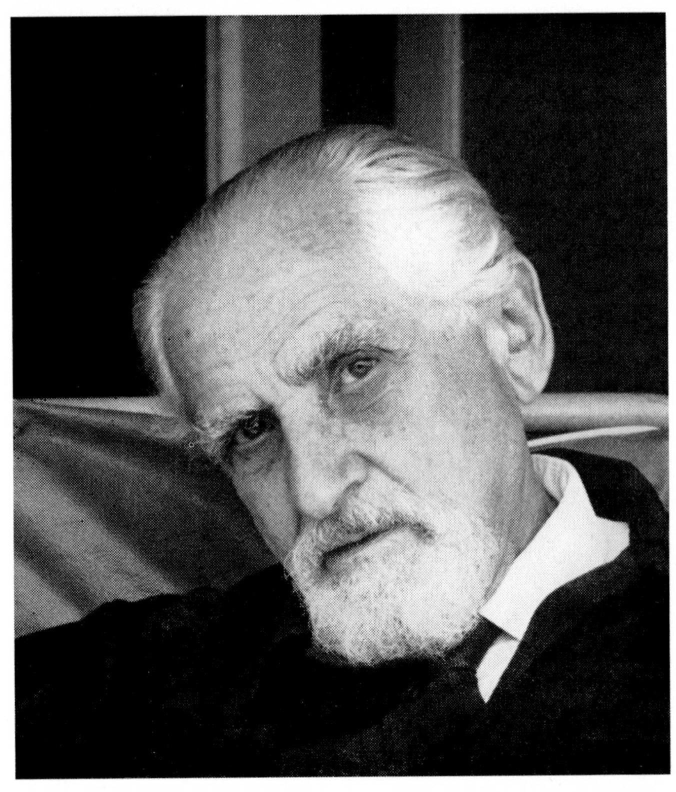

*Photograph by Marcia Roltner*

## PREFACE

We gather here in print to honor our colleague, critic, mentor – friend – Jacob Marschak, and to display to him our wish to share in his long enthusiastic concern with communicating to both students and professionals the exciting (or so he has always made it seem) margin of theoretical development. With anyone else it would be quite appropriate here to express the hope that he find something of interest in the chapters that follow. In this case, we needn't worry. Working in our favor are both his well-known propensity to find *something* interesting in almost any paper, and the fact that many of the chapters survey theoretical topics that Marschak himself was instrumental in initiating – and his interest seldom flags.

The essays in this volume have been designed to complement each other in providing a fairly comprehensive picture of current economic theory in the area most recently the focus of Jacob Marschak's own work, namely, that of the "rational" decision maker and the organization in which he and others like him reside. All of the authors participated in the work of coordinating and criticizing the related presentations in the different chapters. The result is a book that we hope will serve (perhaps uniquely) to bridge that theoretical territory between graduate price theory courses (as conducted in any of the large doctoral programs in the United States) and current theoretical investigations on decision and organization.

The authors have been at some pains to maintain *both* rigor *and* accessibility, a combination so characteristic of Jacob Marschak's own writings. The mathematical prerequisites for reading the book have been kept down at the occasional cost of some generality. In addition to his preparation in economics, the reader will need a *good* grounding in calculus, a *slight* acquaintance with the elements of linear algebra, *some* facility with elementary (and, for the most part, finite) probability, and – above all – the patience and interest that mathematical exposition always asks of its readers. All but the last of these prerequisites have come to be standard demands in all graduate economics programs.

We wish to thank the Office of Naval Research and the National Science Foundation for their support of the editorial work involved in assembling this volume. Both of these organizations will, in addition, be found among those generous organizations acknowledged separately in the chapters for their support of the research described. The Center for Research in Management Science at the University of California in Berkeley housed the editorial work from the beginning.

To Mrs. Ikuko Workman we are indebted for her skillful and patient typing, retyping, and general management of the manuscript. Mrs. Barbara Ellis Tryfos attended to most of the early editorial work and correspondence. Mrs. Julia Rubalcava did much of the early typing in her usual exacting fashion. Miss Alice Kwong supplied valuable bibliographic help. Most of the drawings were done by Mrs. Katherine C. Eardley; Miss Iao Katagiri and Mrs. Lois Robertson helped with proofreading and indexing. For all of this indispensable support so graciously provided, the editors express their thanks.

C. B. M.
R. R.

## TABLE OF CONTENTS

CHAPTER 1

# NORMATIVE THEORY OF INDIVIDUAL DECISION: AN INTRODUCTION

ROY RADNER



Rational choice among alternatives has sometimes been taken to be the defining characteristic of "economic man". The past thirty years has seen an especially intense exploration of the theory of rational choice, an effort in which economists have been joined by statisticians, mathematicians, logicians, psychologists, and others. The purpose of this volume is to give an account of different aspects of this theory, as it applies to both individuals and groups.

In the case of individuals, rational choice is usually related to an ordering of the alternatives in the available set; the individual is assumed to choose a most preferred alternative from among those available. [1] Complications in the theory arise as we consider various special structures of the set of alternatives, and various special characteristics of the ordering. In the present volume we shall concentrate on complications associated with the consideration of uncertainty and time.

In the case of a group, the explanation of choice in terms of a single ordering of alternatives by the group has not, on the whole, been found acceptable. It would seem that the very definition of group rationality may have to depend on the particular alternatives available to each group member, on each member's information about the environment and about the other members of the group, on the possibilities for communication among group members, and on the degree and nature of the differences among the ways different group members order the consequences of group action.

[1] See, however, A. K. SEN (1971), and references given there, in which patterns of choice are considered that may not be consistent with an ordering of the available alternatives.

The introductory material for this volume has been divided between the present chapter and Chapter 9. This division corresponds, more or less, to the two subject matter groups, (1) individual preference and decision, and (2) group decision. We hope that the reader will find this introductory material useful, not only as a first look at the topics to be treated in detail in later chapters, but also as a common frame of reference to which the various discussions can be related.[2]

## 1. The Theory of Choice under Uncertainty

We first turn our attention, in Chapter 2, to an exposition of the theory of (individual) choice under uncertainty. As K. J. Arrow says in his introduction to Chapter 2, "the immediate basis for a special theory of behaviour under uncertainty is the subjective sensation that an *action* may not uniquely determine the consequence to the agent. It follows that a structure of choices among sets of consequences is not sufficient to determine choices among actions, unlike the situation under (subjective) certainty, where actions imply unique consequences, and therefore, choices among consequences imply choices among actions."

"To formalize the theory of choice under uncertainty, it is convenient to introduce the concept of the *state of the world* (environment), a description of the world so complete that, if true and known, the consequences of every action would be known. ... The meaning of uncertainty is that the agent does not know the state of the world." By definition, the consequences of any given action would be known if the state of the world were known; "...in the description of a consequence is included all that the agent values, so that he will be indifferent between two actions which yield the same consequences for each state of the world. ... From this description it is clear that any choice function for actions must be synthesized out of two components, the valuation of the consequences, and the relative strength of belief in the occurrence of the different states of the world."

The concept of *rationality* is embodied in a number of postulates that require various types of "consistency" in the ordering of actions by the decision maker. Three of these are of particular interest, and we shall give a rough description of them at this point. The first, which has been called by SAVAGE (1954) the "Sure-thing Principle," states that if, of two actions, the consequences of the first action in each state of the world are at least as

[2] See also the Preface.

highly valued as the corresponding consequences of the second action, then the first action is at least as good as the second action. This postulate is closely related to the requirement of "admissibility" in the theory of statistics. Once one accepts the idea of relating choice among alternative actions to an ordering of those actions, the Sure-thing Principle does not seem to be controversial.

A second postulate has been called by J. Marschak the requirement of "the independence of tastes and beliefs." Here "tastes" refer to the ordering of consequences by preference, and "beliefs" to the ordering of states of the world by (subjective) likelihood. Roughly speaking, we require an agent's ranking of consequences to be independent of the states of the world in which they might occur, and his ranking of the likelihoods of states to be independent of the consequences that might be associated with them. Thus, for example, we require the agent to be free of "wishful thinking."

(In paraphrasing the first two postulates, we have referred to rankings of consequences [tastes] and of likelihoods of states [beliefs], whereas we started the discussion in terms of a ranking [ordering] of actions. In the formal development of the theory in Chapter 2, the postulates are formulated in a way that permits one to define tastes and beliefs, in terms of the ranking of actions, and guarantees their independence.)

A third postulate, which is implicit in the theory, requires the agent to be logical, and to have (potentially) unlimited capacity for computation. We shall return below to this important requirement.

A basic proposition that follows from these postulates (together with a "continuity" postulate, which we have not stated) is the Expected Utility Theorem. This theorem states that the individual agent's ordering of actions can be represented, or scaled, by a numerical function called expected utility, which itself is synthesized from two other numerical scales: (1) a *utility* scale, representing the agent's ranking of consequences, and (2) a *subjective probability* scale, representing his ranking of the likelihoods of alternative states of the environment.

In order to give a mathematical formulation of expected utility, we formally introduce the concept of an *act*; an act is a function from the set $S$ of states of the environment (world) to the set $C$ of consequences. Such a function provides a simple way of expressing the fact that the consequences of action are uncertain. Thus, for any act $\boldsymbol{a}$ and any state $s$ let $\boldsymbol{a}(s)$ denote the corresponding consequence that follows from the choice of $\boldsymbol{a}$ and the occurrence of $s$. The acts are the objects of choice. An act may be a simple action, such as betting on the outcome of a race, or it may be a complicated strategy that determines the individual's behavior over an extended period of time.[3]

The postulates on the individual's ordering of acts imply the existence of a function $u$ on the set of consequences, called the *utility* function, and a function $\phi$ on the set of states of the world, called the *subjective probability* function, such that the *expected utility* function $U$ defined on acts by

$$U(\boldsymbol{a}) = \sum_{s} u[\boldsymbol{a}(s)]\, \phi(s) \tag{1}$$

represents the ordering of acts, i.e. act $a^1$ is preferred to act $a^2$ if and only if $U(a^1) > U(a^2)$. The utility function $u$ is defined up to a positive linear transformation, and thus may be said to be "cardinal". The probability function $\phi$ has all of the usual properties of a probability measure on the set of states of the environment.[4]

It can be shown that the utility function represents, not only the individual's preference ordering of consequences, but also his "attitude towards risk." (Since this last topic is not explicitly discussed in this volume, the interested reader must consult other sources, such as ARROW (1965) and RADNER (1964).)

## 2. Dynamic Aspects of Choice

Many problems of economic choice have a dynamic aspect. This may introduce one or more of the following complications: (1) the "consequence" of action may unfold through time, and thus, the over-all consequence of action may itself be a sequence $(c_1, c_2, \ldots)$ of dated consequences; (2) similarly, the over-all action of an agent may itself be a sequence of dated actions; (3) future actions may depend on information that will become available before the actions are to be taken, so that the agent must choose a *rule of action* (strategy, decision rule) that specifies what actions will be taken in response to alternative information signals received. From a formal point of view, a dynamic decision problem can be made to fit into the general abstract framework already described by (1) identifying the "consequence" in the general formulation with the sequence $(c_1, c_2, \ldots)$ of dated consequences in the dynamic formulation, (2) identifying the act in

---

[3] In Chapter 2, Arrow uses the term "action" to describe what we have here called an "act". The term "act" was introduced by SAVAGE (1954); we have retained it here because the word "action" is sometimes used in other chapters it its informal, every-day sense.

[4] In the precise development of the theory, the set of states is uncountably infinite, so the "sum" in the formula for expected utility must be replaced by a generalized integral.

the general formulation with the *strategy* or *decision rule* in the dynamic problem, and (3) interpreting the *state of the world* in the general problem as a complete history of the relevant environment in the dynamic problem. But the additional structure in the dynamic case makes possible further analysis, which is crucial for a good understanding of the nature of rational decision making in a dynamic context.

## 3. Independence and Separability

In the case in which the over-all consequence of action is itself a sequence $(c_1, c_2, \ldots)$ of dated consequences, $c_t$, it is common to represent the utility of the over-all consequence as a sum of utilities of dated consequences:

$$u(c_1, c_2, \ldots) = u_1(c_1)+u_2(c_2)+\ldots \tag{2}$$

One often meets this formulation in analyses of problems of optimal economic growth and saving; especially in the particular form

$$u(c_1, c_2, \ldots) = v(c_1)+\alpha v(c_2)+\alpha^2 v(c_3)+ \ \ldots, \tag{3}$$

i.e., the particular form in which

$$u_t(c_t) = \alpha^t v(c_t).$$

A utility function of the form (2) is said to be (additively) *separable*. An implication of separability is that *it is possible to define, for each date, a preference ordering of consequences at that date, which is independent of the particular consequences that are realized at other dates.* This independence condition can be formulated as a property of the *preference ordering* on the set of over-all consequences, rather than as a property of the particular numerical utility function $u$ that is used to represent that ordering. In fact, it is shown in Chapter 3 that, roughly speaking, this independence condition *characterizes* those orderings of over-all consequences that can be represented by a separable utility function.

The relation between independence and separability has more general applicability than just the analysis of preferences in a dynamic decision problem. Indeed, we have already met an example of this relationship in the theory of choice under uncertainty. The representation (1) of preferences under uncertainty in terms of expected utility is a special case of (2); this is easily seen if we make a simple change of notation. In the problem of choice under uncertainty, let us label the alternative states with the numbers 1, 2,

3, ..., etc. (the particular association of states with labels is unimportant), and let $s$ denote the label of the corresponding state. A particular action associates a consequence, say $c_s$, to each state $s$, so that each action can be represented by a sequence, $(c_1, c_2, c_3, \ldots)$, of consequences. The expected utility representation (1) can be rewritten in the form

$$\phi(1)\,u(c_1)+\phi(2)\,u(c_2)+\phi(3)\,u(c_3)+\ldots \tag{4}$$

The representation (4) is, of course, a special case of (2) with

$$u_s(c_s) = \phi(s)\,u(c_s)\,. \tag{5}$$

The proposition that independence implies separability is, in fact, used in Chapter 2 in the derivation of the expected utility representation. However, the "independence of tastes and beliefs" is a stronger condition than the general independence condition associated with (2), which accounts for the fact that we can derive the more special form (5).

Chapter 3 gives a proof of the general proposition that independence (together with certain other conditions) implies separability. Chapter 3 also analyzes the circumstances in which a preference ordering can at all be represented by a continuous utility function (separable or not). This last question is important for the theory of decision under certainty, in which we typically do not have a natural procedure for constructing a numerical scale of preferences (i.e., "utility" is inherently "ordinal" rather than "cardinal").

In Chapter 4, the propositions on the numerical representation of an ordering are applied to the case of dated consequences. In particular, it is shown that, roughly speaking, if a condition of *stationarity* of preferences is added to the independence condition, then the preference ordering can be represented by a numerical utility function of the special form (3).

## 4. Information and Decision Functions

We have already mentioned the fact that in a typical dynamic decision problem one's actions are made in response to information signals. In the simplest situation of this type, the decision maker first receives one of a set of alternative signals, and then takes a decision. To formulate this situation in a precise manner, we must describe how the information signals are generated, i.e., how they are related to the state of the enivornment.

A simple formalism, which also turns out to be quite general, is the characterization of an information signal in terms of the set of states of the environment that give rise to that signal. Thus, let $Y$ denote the set of alternative information signals that the decision maker could receive, and suppose that there is a function, say, $\eta$, that associates to each state $s$ an information signal $y=\eta(s)$. The decision maker must now make a decision, which will be some function of the signal received. Let $D$ denote the set of alternative decisions available to the decision maker, and let $\rho(s, d)$ be the consequence of decision $d$ if state $s$ obtains. If the decision is chosen according to a function $\delta$, then if state $s$ obtains, the signal received will be $\eta(s)$, the decision taken will be $\delta[\eta(s)]$, and the consequence will be $\rho(s, \delta[\eta(s)])$. The function $\eta$ will be called the information function, and $\delta$ the decision function. Thus, to each information function $\eta$ and decision function $\delta$ corresponds an *act* (in the sense we have used already), defined by

$$\mathbf{a}(s) = \rho(s, \delta[\eta(s)]). \tag{6}$$

The set of acts available to the decision maker will depend upon the set of available information and decision functions. The expected utility of a given pair $(\eta, \delta)$ is simply the expected utility of the corresponding act.

In many decision problems, the information function is given, and the problem is to choose an optimal decision function from the set of all possible functions from the set $Y$ of signals to the set $D$ of decisions. For the simple situation we have described, there is a correspondingly simple condition that characterizes optimal decision functions: *for each signal, an optimal decision maximizes the conditional expected utility of the consequence, given the signal.* We shall call this the principle of maximizing conditional expected utility.

The proof of this characterization of optimal decision functions is quite easy, and illuminates the description of information that we have introduced. First, we need an expression for the expected utility of any information-function – decision-function pair, $(\eta, \delta)$. For any state $s$ and decision $d$, define the *payoff* $w(s, d)$ to be the utility of the resulting consequence:

$$w(s, d) = u[\rho(s, d)]; \tag{7}$$

we shall call $w$ the *payoff function*. In terms of the payoff function, the expected utility of an information function $\eta$ and a decision function $\delta$ can be expressed as

$$U(\eta, \delta) = \sum_s \phi(s)\, w(s, \delta[\eta(s)]). \tag{8}$$

For the given information function, to each signal $y$ is associated the set $S_y$ of all states that give rise to the signal $y$, i.e., the set of all $s$ such that

$\eta(s)=y$. For any decision function $\delta$ that uses the information function $\eta$, all states in the same set $S_y$ must lead to the same decision. Therefore, we can rewrite the expected utility of $(\eta, \delta)$ as

$$U(\eta, \delta) = \sum_s \phi(s)\, w(s, \delta[\eta(s)]) \tag{9}$$

$$= \sum_y P(y) \sum_{s \text{ in } S_y} P(s|y)\, w(s, \delta[y]),$$

where $P(y)$ is the probability of the signal $y$, and $P(s|y)$ is the conditional probability of the state $s$, given the signal $y$, i.e.,

$$P(y) = \sum_{s \text{ in } S_y} \phi(s), \tag{10}$$

$$P(s|y) = \phi(s)/P(y), \quad \text{for } s \text{ in } S_y$$

(we can assume, without loss of generality, that $P(y) \neq 0$ for every signal $y$ in $Y$). Since we are free to choose any decision $d$ in $D$ as the value of $\delta(y)$, it follows from (9) that maximizing the expected utility $U(\eta, \delta)$ is equivalent to choosing, for each signal $y$, a decision $d$ that maximizes the conditional expectation

$$\sum_{s \text{ in } S_y} P(s|y)\, w(s, d). \tag{11}$$

## 5. Comparison of Information

If two decision functions use the same information function, we can say that the first is better than the second if (with the given information function) it gives a higher expected utility than the second.

The comparison of information functions is not as straightforward, since any one information function can be used with a number of alternative decision functions. However, a natural extension of the above comparison is the one that says that one information function is better than another if the maximum expected utility achievable with the first is greater than the maximum expected utility achievable with the second. In other words, we compare the expected utility of information functions when used with their corresponding *optimal* decision functions.

Now the maximum expected utility of an information function depends upon the payoff function, $w$, and the probability distribution, $\phi$, on the set of states. (Recall, too, that the payoff function is itself a composition of the utility function with the function, $\rho$, that relates consequences to states and decisions.) Is it possible that of two information functions, $\eta_1$ and $\eta_2$, one of them, say, $\eta_1$, might be as good as or better than the other *for all combinations of payoff function and probability distribution*? In such a case we would be justified in saying that $\eta_1$ *is generally as informative as* $\eta_2$. We might also be interested in weaker comparisons, in which we only ask that $\eta_1$ be as good as $\eta_2$ for some selected set of combinations of payoff function and probability distribution.

Comparisons of this type form the subject matter of Chapter 5. In order to illustrate the results presented in that chapter, we shall present here a simple condition for one information structure to be generally as informative as another.

For a given information function, the corresponding sets $S_y$ form a *partition* of the set $S$ of states of the environment. If $\mathscr{P}_1$ and $\mathscr{P}_2$ are two partitions of $S$, we shall say that $\mathscr{P}_1$ is *as fine as* $\mathscr{P}_2$ if every member of $\mathscr{P}_1$ is contained in some member of $\mathscr{P}_2$. (Keep in mind that the members of $\mathscr{P}_1$ and $\mathscr{P}_2$ are subsets of $S$.) A simple example will illustrate the comparison of fineness. Let $S$ have three elements, labeled 1, 2, and 3, respectively; there are five possible partitions of $S$:

| | | |
|---|---|---|
| (1)(2)(3) | (12) (3) | (123) |
| | (13) (2) | |
| | (23) (1) | |

The partition (1) (2) (3) is as fine as every partition, and every partition is as fine as (123). However, the three partitions in the middle column are not comparable with respect to fineness. Thus, the relation "as fine as" is only a partial ordering of partitions.

The relevance of fineness in the present context is the following proposition, which we shall call (for the purposes of this discussion) the Fineness Theorem for the Comparison of Information Functions: If $\eta_1$ and $\eta_2$ are two information functions on the same set of states of the environment, then $\eta_1$ is generally as informative as $\eta_2$ if and only if the partition associated with $\eta_1$ is as fine as the partition associated with $\eta_2$.

We shall not prove the Fineness Theorem here (although the proof is elementary), but the following discussion will, we hope, make the theorem plausible. We have already indicated in (6) how an information function and decision function generate an act. Therefore, for a given information function $\eta$, the set of all decision functions that use the given information function (i.e., the set of all functions from the set $Y$ of signals to the set $D$ of decisions) generates a corresponding set of acts, say, $A(\eta)$. The Fineness

Theorem is essentially based on the observation that the partition associated with $\eta_1$ is as fine as the partition associated with $\eta_2$, if and only if $A(\eta_1)$ contains $A(\eta_2)$.

In particular, if two information functions generate the same partition, they are equivalent from the point of view of information. Another way of saying this is that the "names" or "labels" attached to the signals are not important in themselves; the significance of a signal is the set of states that give rise to that signal.

Notice that, since the relation "as fine as" among partitions is only a partial ordering, the Fineness Theorem shows that *the relation "generally as informative as" is only a partial ordering among information functions*. This shows that it is not possible to define a "measure of information" on information functions such that, of two information functions, the one with the higher "measure of information" is better, from the point of view of expected utility, for every payoff function and probability distribution. (For, if such a measure were possible, then every pair of information functions would be comparable with respect to the relation "generally as informative as.")

## 6. Noisy Information

The analysis in Chapter 5 uses a concept of information that is somewhat more sophisticated than the one we have just presented, in that the relation between state of environment and signal is allowed to be probabilistic. Thus, for each state $s$ let $p_{sy}$ be the conditional probability that signal $y$ is received, given that state $s$ obtains. A matrix $(p_{sy})$ of such probabilities will be called an *information structure*. An information function may be regarded as a special case of an information structure, in which for each state $s$ there is some signal $y$ for which $p_{sy}=1$ (in other words, it is a deterministic information structure). An information structure that is not a (deterministic) function is sometimes called *noisy*.

The Fineness Theorem can be generalized to cover the case of noisy information (Chapter 5, Theorem 1), and can also be generalized to apply to the comparison of information structures relative to an arbitrary set of combinations of payoff function and probability distribution on $S$ (Chapter 5, Theorem 6).

It might be objected that in formulating the concept of noisy information we have introduced a new element of uncertainty that has not been captured in the specification of the "state of the environment," and that we have, therefore, departed from our original model of choice under uncertainty.

However, by a suitable reformulation of the set of states, any decision problem with noisy information can be reformulated as a problem with noiseless (deterministic) information. For example, if the state of the environment is originally defined to be the temperature of an object, and the information signal is the reading on a (possibly inaccurate) thermometer, then the "environment" can be redefined to include both the temperature of the object and the state (or error) of the thermometer. Indeed, a purist might insist that the "environment" for this decision problem *should* be so defined. He might go on to point out that this example illustrates the general principle that a proper formulation of the state of the environment in any decision problem should include not only those aspects of the environment that directly affect the payoff function, but also the behavior of the processes that produce the information signals for the decision maker.

Thus, we see that the concept of noisy information is really an interesting special case of our original concept of information; the "noise" in the signal reflects aspects of the environment that are not "payoff relevant" (a term introduced by J. MARSCHAK (1963).) Furthermore, the special features of noisy information enable one to provide sharper conditions for the comparability of information structures.

## 7. Value of Information

Thus far, we have assumed, at least implicitly, that those information functions (or structures) actually available to the decision maker are costless. Formally, the consequence to the decision maker is determined by the state and the decision, and does not depend on which particular information and decision functions led to that particular decision in that state.

However, nothing in our formal model of the decision problem prevents us from considering costs (consequences) that depend directly on the information function used. We typically think of a "cost" as something that is subtracted from a "gross return." Thus, the "net consequence" might be represented as the difference between a "gross return," $r = \rho(s, d)$, and a "cost", $\gamma(\eta)$:

$$c = \rho(s, \delta[\eta(s)]) - \gamma(\eta),$$

where, as before, the decision, $d$, is determined by $d = \delta[\eta(s)]$. The expected utility for an information function would now be the maximum expected utility of the *net* consequence that could be achieved with the set of decision functions for the given information function. Note that, unless the utility were a linear function of the consequence, the optimal *decision* function for a given information function would typically depend on *the cost of the information function.* Note, too, that for this formulation to be meaningful, returns and costs must be something, like numbers or vectors, that can be added and subtracted.

The cost of information can also enter the problem by affecting the set of decisions available to the decision maker. Thus, the more an investor spends on getting information about prospective investments, the less he will have to invest when he makes his eventual choice.

The *value* of an information function will be related to the increase in expected utility that can be achieved by using that information function instead of some particular alternative one. However, the value cannot in general be identified with that increase in expected utility (unless the utility function is linear in the consequence). One way to define the value is that it equals that cost which would just make the expected utility for the information function in question equal to the expected utility of the alternative information function. A natural alternative to use for comparison purposes is the *constant function*, for which the signal received is the same for all states.

In Chapter 6 the concept of value of information is analyzed in the context of a decision problem in which the decisions available are bets on the occurrences of states of the environment. Chapter 6 also explores the relationship between value of information and the "quantity of information" in the sense of Shannon.

## 8. Sequential Decision Making

We turn next, in Chapter 7, to the consideration of problems in which there is a sequence of dated decisions, each such decision depending upon information that has been received up to that date. We shall illustrate this type of problem with a simple example of inventory control.

Suppose that one starts out with an initial stock of $z_0$ units of a commodity, and buys $d_1$ units to add to the stock before the beginning of period 1. During period 1 there is a demand for $x_1$ units. This demand is satisfied if it does not exceed the quantity available $(z_0+d_1)$; otherwise, the quantity sold is only equal to $(z_0+d_1)$. Any remaining stock is carried over to the next period, and the process begins again. Thus, at any given period $t$, let

$z_{t-1}$ be the stock carried over from the previous period,

$d_t$ be the amount bought at the beginning of the period,

$x_t$ be the demand during the period,
$q_t$ be the amount sold during the period.
These variables satisfy the relations:

(12) $$q_t = \min(x_t, z_{t-1}+d_t),$$

$$z_t = z_{t-1}+d_t-q_t.$$

Suppose that the per unit buying price, selling price, and holding (inventory) costs are, respectively, $f$, $g$, $h$. The net revenue for period $t$ is then equal to

(13) $$c_t = fq_t-gd_t-hz_{t-1}.$$

Suppose further, that the demands form a sequence of independent, identically distributed random variables, with

(14) $$p_i = \text{Prob}(x_t = i), \qquad i = 0,1,2, \ldots,$$

and that the initial stock (given) and the amounts to be bought at each period (to be chosen) are nonnegative integers. Finally, suppose that the objective is to maximize the sum of the discounted expected values of the one-period net revenues, with discount factor $\alpha$ $(0<\alpha<1)$.

We can relate this example to our general decision problem formulation as follows. A state of the environment is a particular sequence $(x_1, x_2, \ldots)$ of demands. The sequence of decisions is the sequence $(d_1, d_2, \ldots)$ of amounts bought. The overall consequence is the sequence $(c_1, c_2, \ldots)$ of one-period net revenues. The utility of such a consequence (sequence) is

(15) $$\sum_{t \geqq 1} \alpha^{t-1} c_t.$$

Note that we have here a separable utility function in the form of (3). The information signal available to the decision maker at date $t$ is the past history $(x_1, \ldots, x_{t-1})$ of demands. The parameters of the problem (also known to the decision maker), are $z_0$, $f$, $g$, $h$, $(p_i)$, and $\alpha$. The problem is to determine a sequence of decision functions that maximizes the expected value of the utility (15).

This example belongs to the important class of *Markovian decision problems*; for problems in this class one can apply the powerful tool of *recursive optimization* or *dynamic programming*. (In fact, one of the first uses of the method of dynamic programming was in a problem of optimal inventory control; see ARROW, HARRIS, and MARSCHAK (1951)). We shall use our present example to illustrate the use of this tool.

First, we note that the net revenue of any period $t$ can be expressed in terms of $z_{t-1}$, $z_t$, and $d_t$, since, from (12)

$$q_t = z_{t-1} + d_t - z_t,$$

and, therefore, from (13),

$$c_t = (f-h)z_{t-1} + (f-g)d_t - fz_t. \tag{16}$$

Second, the conditional distribution of $z_t$, given the previous values of all the variables, i.e., given $x_1, \ldots, x_{t-1}, z_0, \ldots, z_{t-1}, d_1, \ldots, d_t$, *depends only on* $z_{t-1}$ *and* $d_t$, since

$$z_t = \max(0, z_{t-1} + d_t - x_t). \tag{17}$$

Let us deal first with the case of a finite number of periods, $t = 1, \ldots, T$. The basic idea of the method of dynamic programming is to solve successively for the optimal decision functions, $\delta_t$, *beginning with the last*, $\delta_T$, and working backwards. Consider the situation facing the decision maker at the last period, $T$. The net revenues $c_1, \ldots, c_{T-1}$, have already been determined; hence, the decision function $\delta_T$ should be chosen to maximize the expected value of $\alpha^{T-1} c_T$, or equivalently, to maximize the expected value of $c_T$. By the principle of maximizing conditional expected utility, the optimal decision at $T$ should maximize the conditional expectation of $c_T$, given the information signal $y_T = (x_1, \ldots, x_{T-1})$. Recall that we have just shown that $c_T$ depends only on $z_{T-1}$, $z_T$, and $d_T$. Furthermore, for any given decision functions $\delta_1, \ldots, \delta_{T-1}$, the previous demands determine $z_{T-1}$; hence, by the previous paragraph, the conditional distribution of $z_T$, given the previous demands and $d_T$, depends only on $z_{T-1}$ and $d_T$. *It follows that an optimal decision function for period T can be chosen so that the optimal decision depends only on* $z_{T-1}$. Call this optimal decision function $\hat{\delta}_T$, and denote the conditional expectation of $c_T$, given $z_{T-1}$ and given that $\hat{\delta}_T$ is used, by $V_1(z_{T-1})$.

Now consider the situation facing the decision maker at the next-to-last period, $T-1$. The net revenues $c_1, \ldots, c_{T-2}$, have already been determined, and an optimal decision function, $\hat{\delta}_T$, for period $T$ has also been chosen. Hence, the decision function $\delta_{T-1}$ should be chosen to maximize the expected value of $\alpha^{T-2} c_{T-1} + \alpha^{T-1} c_T$, *given that* $\hat{\delta}_T$ *will be used in period T*. But, if $\hat{\delta}_T$ is used in period $T$, then the expected value of $c_T$ equals the expected value of $V_1(z_{T-1})$, so that $\delta_{T-1}$ should be chosen to maximize the expected value of $\alpha^{T-2} c_{T-1} + \alpha^{T-1} V_1(z_{T-1})$, or equivalently, to maximize the expected value of

$$c_{T-1} + \alpha V_1(z_{T-1}). \tag{18}$$

An argument similar to that used for period $T$ shows that we can choose an optimal decision function, $\hat{\delta}_{T-1}$, for period $(T-1)$ to be a function of $z_{T-2}$ only. Correspondingly, let $V_2(z_{T-2})$ denote the conditional expectation of expression (18), given $z_{T-2}$ and given that the decision functions $\hat{\delta}_{T-1}$ and $\hat{\delta}_T$ are used.

Proceeding backwards, we obtain the recursive relation

$$V_{T-t+1}(z_{t-1}) = \max_d E[c_t + \alpha V_{T-t}(z_t) | z_{t-1}]. \tag{19}$$

This relation also determines optimal decision functions; for every $t$ and $z_{t-1}$, let $\hat{\delta}_t(z_{t-1})$ be a value of $d$ that achieves the maximum in (19).

Two points are noteworthy about relations (19) and the corresponding optimal decision functions. First, at each period $t$ the variable $z_{t-1}$ carries all the information needed to determine the optimal decision at that period. We are, therefore, justified in calling $z_{t-1}$ *the state of the system at the beginning of period t*. Notice that, whereas the state of the environment is not affected by decisions, the state of the system is; in other words, the state of the environment is exogenous, but the state of the system is endogenous. Nevertheless, the system state variable contains information about the environment that is sufficient to enable the taking of optimal decisions. Second, $V_k(z)$ can be interpreted as *the maximum expected utility achievable in a problem with k periods, given that the initial system state (initial stock) is z*.

The functions $V_k$ are called the *state evaluation functions*, or *value functions*, and equation (19) is called the *principle of optimality for dynamic programming*.

Under certain conditions, as the number of periods, $T$, increases, the functions $V_t$ approach a limit function, say, $V$, and this limit function satisfies an equation corresponding to (19),

$$V(z_{t-1}) = \max_d E[c_t + \alpha V(z_t) | z_{t-1}]. \tag{20}$$

Notice that the function $V$ appears on both sides of (20), so that (20) is a functional equation; under certain conditions this functional equation characterizes $V$, in which case, it may be a useful tool for solving the infinite horizon decision problem.

In the present example, we can use the functional equation (20) to show that, for the case in which $T$ is infinite (the "infinite horizon" case), the optimal decision function is the same in each period, and has the form of a "one bin inventory policy": there is a number, say $\hat{D}$, the "desired inventory level," such that if the quantity of stock carried over from the previous period is $z$, then the optimal quantity to buy is $d=(\hat{D}-z)$. To see why this is so, first note that, for our example, equation (20) takes the following form if we use (16) and (17):

$$V(z) = \max_{d \geqq 0} E[(f-h)z+(f-g)d-fZ+\alpha V(Z)\,z], \tag{21}$$

where $Z=\max(0, z+d-X)$, and $X$ is a random variable with probability frequency function $(p_x)$. If we define a new variable $D=(z+d)$, then $Z=\max(0, D-X)$, and equation (21) takes the form

$$V(z) = (g-h)z+\max_{D \geqq z} E[(f-g)D-fZ+\alpha V(Z)|z]. \tag{22}$$

The variable $D$ can be interpreted as the desired beginning-of-period inventory level; $z$ is the stock carried over from the previous period, and $Z$ is the stock that will be carried over to the next period (a random variable). The conditional distribution of $Z$, given $z$ and $d$, actually depends on $z$ and $d$ through $D$, and (22) shows that the problem of finding the optimal order, $d$, given $z$, reduces to one of finding a $D$ that maximizes the conditional expectation in (22) subject to the constraint that $D$ be no smaller than $z$. Let $\hat{D}$ denote the value of $D$ that maximizes the conditional expectation in (22) subject only to the constraint that $D$ be nonnegative; then the optimal $D$ will be equal to $\hat{D}$ if $z \leqslant \hat{D}$. It is not difficult to show that the optimal $D$ equals $z$ if $z > \hat{D}$, i.e., the optimal order is zero if the stock carried over from the previous period exceeds the desired inventory level. Of course, if one starts with no inventory, and follows an optimal policy, then $z$ will never exceed $\hat{D}$. The functional equation (22) can also be used as the basis for an iterative procedure for calculating the optimal level $\hat{D}$. This iterative procedure is in fact basic to the general theory of dynamic programming as explained in Chapter 7.

## 9. Bounded Rationality

We have thus far outlined a theory of rational choice, and have discussed some of the complications due to the presence of uncertainty, the need to take account of information as it becomes available, the dynamic aspect of consequences of decision, and the sequential nature of decision making in a dynamic context. A serious consideration of these complications leads us to face up to a further complication that they imply, namely, that the very *complexity* of a real-world decision problem will typically prevent the decision maker from satisfying the criteria for rational choice that we have presented. To put it another way, we have not taken account of the limited capacities of an individual decision maker for imagination and computation.

The existence of these limitations raises serious problems for the concept of rational choice as we have presented it in terms of *optimizing behavior*. A mode of behavior that is not even *feasible* can hardly qualify as *rational*! Although a satisfactory resolution of these problems has not yet been discovered, a number of interesting approaches are being studied, and these are discussed in Chapter 8. Of particular importance is the concept of *satisficing behavior* as an alternative to optimizing.

### 10. Group Decision

The last part of this volume is devoted to various problems of rational decision making in groups. The interaction among several decision makers introduces the possibility of uncertainty about other group members' actions as well as about the state of the environment. Furthermore, differences among individuals with respect to their preferences for the consequences of group action lead to a new problem of definition of rationality or optimality, both for the group as a whole and for individual group members.

The study of rationality in group decision making is generally known as the *theory of games*, although this term actually covers a variety of theoretical approaches. A special case, which concentrates on difference of information among group members, is called the theory of *teams*. The study of decision making in groups is, of course, basic to a theory of *optimal organization*.[5] A detailed introduction to theories of rational group decision and organization is postponed to Chapter 9.

### 11. Stochastic Choice

One topic not treated in this volume is that of stochastic choice (J. MARSCHAK (1960)). In one sense, this topic falls outside the normative approach to decision making; the perfectly rational decision maker should have no uncertainty about his own choice of decision rule. (Uncertainty about the choice of a decision rule should be distinguished from uncertainty about one's own future action. The latter can occur because (1) a future action may depend, according to a chosen decision rule, upon information

[5] See J. MARSCHAK (1959).

to be acquired in the future, or because (2) that action will be the result of deliberate randomization, according to a "mixed strategy," as in the theory of games.) On the other hand, if we are prepared to admit into consideration limitations on the capacity of a (rational) decision maker to envisage alternatives and/or to do computations, then we might also be prepared to admit that uncertainty about choice could well play a significant role in rational decision making. However, the integration of this topic into the theory of rational choice will have to await the results of current and future research.

## References

ARROW, K. J. (1965), *Aspects of the Theory of Risk Bearing*, Yrjö Jahnsson Lecture Series, Helsinki.

ARROW, K. J., T. HARRIS, and J. MARSCHAK (1951), "Optimal Inventory Policy," *Econometrica*, **19**, 250-272.

MARSCHAK, J. (1959), "Efficient and Viable Organizational Forms," Chapter 11 in M. HAIRE (ed.), *Modern Organization Theory*, Wiley, New York, pp. 307-320.

MARSCHAK, J. (1960), "Binary Choice Constraints and Random Utility Indicators," Chapter 21 in K. J. ARROW, S. KARLIN, and P. SUPPES (eds.), *Mathematical Methods in the Social Sciences*, Stanford University Press, Stanford, pp. 312-329.

MARSCHAK, J. (1963), "The Payoff-Relevant Description of States and Acts," *Econometrica*, **31**, 719-725.

RADNER, R. (1964), "Mathematical Specifications of Goals for Decision Problems", Chapter 11 in M. W. SHELLY and G. L. BRYAN (eds.), *Human Judgments and Optimality*, Wiley, New York, pp. 178-216.

SAVAGE, L. J. (1954), *The Foundations of Statistics*, Wiley, New York.

SEN, A. K. (1971), "Choice Functions and Revealed Preference", *Review of Economic Studies* (forthcoming).

CHAPTER 2

# EXPOSITION OF THE THEORY OF CHOICE UNDER UNCERTAINTY[1]

KENNETH J. ARROW



## 1. Structure of a Theory of Behavior under Uncertainty

The basic need for a special theory to explain behavior under conditions of uncertainty arises from two considerations: (1) subjective feelings of imperfect knowledge when certain types of choices, typically involving commitments over time, are made; (2) the existence of certain observed phenomena, of which insurance is the most conspicuous example, which cannot be explained on the assumption that individuals act with subjective certainty.

A theory of choice is a set of propositions about choice rules, rules which indicate for each set of available actions that action which will in fact be chosen. It is assumed in general that certain consistency relations hold among the choices from different sets of possible actions and also that these sets belong to some restricted class; from these assumptions, which may be stronger or weaker, it is possible to deduce some propositions about the observable behavior of the individual agents. In the case of the theory of consumer's demand under certainty, for example, an action is the choice of a consumption bundle; the set of possible actions, for any given income and set of prices, is the set of consumption bundles satisfying the budget constraint; and the choice rule is maximization in accordance with the ordering expressing the individual's preference pattern. This theory, though certainly not very strong, implies the well-known Slutzky relations, which are statements about the functional relation between the action taken and the price-income parameters defining the set of possible actions.

---

[1] Part of this paper has already been published as Lecture 1 in K. J. Arrow (1970), *Essays in the Theory of Risk-Bearing*, North-Holland, Amsterdam.

The immediate basis for a special theory of behavior under uncertainty is the subjective sensation that an *action* may not uniquely determine the consequences to the agent. It follows that a structure of choices among sets of consequences is not sufficient to determine choices among actions unlike the situation under (subjective) certainty, where actions imply unique consequences, and therefore choices among consequences imply choices among actions.

To formalize the theory of choice under uncertainty, it is convenient to introduce the concept of the *state of the world*, a description of the world so complete that, if true and known, the consequences of every action would be known. In what follows, the symbol $s$ will stand for a state of the world, and $\boldsymbol{a}$ for an action.

The meaning of uncertainty is that the agent does not know the state of the world. By definition, the consequences would be known if both the action and the state of the world are known; that is, there is a function mapping ordered pairs $(\boldsymbol{a}, s)$ of actions and states of the world into consequences. We will understand that in the description of a consequence is included all that the agent values, so that he will be indifferent between two actions which yield the same consequence for each state of the world.

From this description it is clear that any choice function for actions must be synthesized out of two components, the valuation of the consequences and the relative strength of belief in the occurrence of the different states of the world. Just as in the theory of consumer's demand, choice is subjective; in choice among actions, both the values and the beliefs are subjective in the sense that only the values and the beliefs of the economic agent are relevant to explaining his choice, regardless of how these might differ from values or beliefs "objectively" given in some sense.

But it is of the utmost importance to observe that the subjectivity of beliefs does not exclude their being influenced by experience. Let us define an *event* as some set of the states of the world. Beliefs about different events are necessarily interrelated if only because of the logical relations among them; hence, knowledge that some event has occurred, i.e., that the states of the world are now known to lie in some restricted range, will lead to a revaluation of beliefs about the remaining possible states of the world. When beliefs are represented by probabilities, then the observation of an event causes the agent to act in accordance with the conditional probabilities given that event rather than with the probabilities held before the observation.

The influence of experience on beliefs is of the utmost importance for a rational theory of behavior under uncertainty, and failure to account for it must be taken as a strong objection to theories such as SHACKLE'S (1952).

## 2. A Set of Postulates

*Events* are statements about states of the world, or, in a different language, they are sets of states of the world (i.e., an event consists of all states of the world which satisfy some given condition). It is not feasible, in general, to consider all sets of states of the world if we wish to assign probabilities to those events which satisfy the usual assumptions of probability theory. We do assume as usual that various sets derived from other events are also events. Thus, if $E_1$ and $E_2$ are events, the *union* of the two events, denoted by $E_1 \cup E_2$ and defined to be the set of all states of the world in either $E_1$ or $E_2$ or both, is also an event. More generally, let $\{E_i\}$ $(i = 1, \ldots, \infty)$ be an infinite sequence of events; the union, here denoted by $\bigcup_{i=1}^{\infty} E_i$, is the set of all states of the world in at least one of the events $E_i$; again we assume the union of a sequence of events to be an event. For any event $E$, the *complement*, denoted by $\tilde{E}$ and defined to be the set of all states of the world not in $E$, is assumed to be an event. Finally, the set of all possible states of the world is assumed to be an event. In technical terms, the set of events is assumed to be $\sigma$-algebra.[2]

In the present case, it will also be assumed that sets consisting of a single state of the world are events. As a matter of notation we will let $s$ denote, where appropriate, the event consisting of the single state $s$; the ambiguity of notation whereby $s$ sometimes represents a state of the world and sometimes the event which consists only of that state will occasion no difficulty.

We now specify in more detail a set of assumptions designed to characterize reasonable behavior under conditions of uncertainty. The history of these assumptions is long, dating back indeed, in some respects, to the classical paper of Daniel BERNOULLI (1738) but owing special debt to Frank RAMSEY (1926), Bruno DE FINETTI (1937), John VON NEUMANN and Oskar MORGENSTERN (1944; detailed proofs in 1953), and Leonard J. SAVAGE (1954).

The most primitive assumption is that which is basic to the theory of rationality in consumer demand.

---

[2] In the text, the concept "states of the world" is assumed to be primitive and events described in terms of them. It is alternatively possible and perhaps more elegant to start with the concept "event" as primitive; see VILLEGAS (1964, 1787-8).

*Ordering:* The individual's choice among actions can be represented by an ordering.

By this is meant the following two statements: (1) Given any two actions, the agent prefers one to the other or else regards them as indifferent; this property is termed *connectedness*; (2) given three actions, $\boldsymbol{a}^1$, $\boldsymbol{a}^2$, and $\boldsymbol{a}^3$, if the agent prefers $\boldsymbol{a}^1$ to $\boldsymbol{a}^2$ or is indifferent between them and if the same holds as between $\boldsymbol{a}^2$ and $\boldsymbol{a}^3$, then he must prefer $\boldsymbol{a}^1$ to $\boldsymbol{a}^3$ or be indifferent between them; this property is termed *transitivity*. An ordering is usually taken to be a hallmark of rationality; in the absence of connectedness, no choice at all may be possible; in the absence of transitivity choice may whirl about in circles.

The expressions $\boldsymbol{a}^1 \succ \boldsymbol{a}^2$, $\boldsymbol{a}^1 \succsim \boldsymbol{a}^2$, $\boldsymbol{a}^1 \sim \boldsymbol{a}^2$, will denote the statements "$\boldsymbol{a}^1$ is preferred to $\boldsymbol{a}^2$," "$\boldsymbol{a}^1$ is preferred or indifferent to $\boldsymbol{a}^2$," and "$\boldsymbol{a}^1$ is indifferent to $\boldsymbol{a}^2$," respectively.

The second assumption also is a simple analogue of one used, often unthinkingly, in consumer's demand theory. We assume continuity of preferences in the sense that if one action is preferred to another, then any action sufficiently close to the first is also preferred to the second and, similarly, the first action is preferred to any action sufficiently close to the first. However, the concept "sufficiently close" has not been formally defined with respect to actions.

A complete formalization of the concept of closeness will not be attempted. Rather, a condition which is intuitively sufficient for closeness is formalized, and it is asserted only that preferences are not altered by changes from one action to another which satisfy this condition for closeness. Consider a *monotone decreasing* sequence of events $\{E_i\}$, i.e., a sequence for which $E_{i+1} \subset E_i$ (in words, every state of the world in $E_{i+1}$ is also in $E_i$). A monotone decreasing sequence of events such that there is no state of the world common to all members of the sequence will be termed a *vanishing sequence*. Clearly, an event which is far out on a vanishing sequence is "small" by any reasonable standard. If one action is derived from another by altering the consequences for states of the world on an event which is sufficiently small in this sense, the preference relation of that action with respect to any other given action should be unaltered.

*Monotone Continuity.*[3] Given $\boldsymbol{a}$ and $\boldsymbol{b}$, where $\boldsymbol{a} \succ \boldsymbol{b}$, a consequence $c$, and a vanishing sequence $\{E^i\}$, suppose the sequences of actions $\{\boldsymbol{a}^i\}$, $\{\boldsymbol{b}^i\}$

[3] This axiom was first proposed by Villegas (1964, 1789) for the restricted class of actions to be called *bets* in Section 4 below.

satisfy the conditions that $(\boldsymbol{a}^i, s)$ yield the same consequences as $(\boldsymbol{a}, s)$ for all $s$ in $\tilde{E}_i$ and the consequence $c$ for all $s$ in $E_i$, while $(\boldsymbol{b}^i, s)$ yields the same consequences as $(\boldsymbol{b}, s)$ for all $s$ in $\tilde{E}_i$ and the consequence $c$ for all $s$ in $E_i$. Then, for all $i$ sufficiently large, $\boldsymbol{a}^i \succ \boldsymbol{b}$ and $\boldsymbol{a} \succ \boldsymbol{b}^i$.

The assumption of Monotone Continuity seems, I believe correctly, to be the harmless simplification almost inevitable in the formalization of any real-life problem. It is sometimes held that certain possible consequences, such as death, are incommensurably greater than others, such as receiving one cent. Let action $\boldsymbol{a}^1$ involve receiving one cent with no risk of life, $\boldsymbol{a}^2$ receiving nothing with no risk of life, and $\boldsymbol{a}^3$ receiving one cent with an exceedingly small probability of death. Clearly, $\boldsymbol{a}^1$ is preferred to $\boldsymbol{a}^2$. Continuity would demand that $\boldsymbol{a}^3$ be preferred to $\boldsymbol{a}^2$ if the probability of death under $\boldsymbol{a}^3$ is sufficiently small. This may sound outrageous at first blush, but I think a little reflection will demonstrate the reasonableness of the result. The probability in question may be $10^{-6}$ or $10^{-10}$, inconceivably small magnitudes. Also, if in the above example, one cent were replaced by one billion dollars, one would hardly raise the same argument, and yet to go from one cent to one billion dollars certainly involves no discontinuity, however big the difference in scale may be. "Every journey, no matter how long, begins with a single step."

Blaise Pascal indeed suggested that the salvation of the soul or the avoidance of eternal damnation might be of infinitely greater value than any earthly regard; but the humble economist may be excused for regarding such choices as beyond the scope of his theories.

The assumptions of Ordering and Monotone Continuity so far made are, in spirit, common to theories of choice in a wide range of circumstances. The first assumption special to the theory of choice under uncertainty may be put this way: what might have happened under conditions that we know won't prevail should have no influence on our choice of actions. Suppose, that is, we are given the information that certain states of nature are impossible. We reform our beliefs about the remaining states of nature, and on the basis of these new beliefs we form a new ordering of the actions. The principle of Conditional Preference, which we will now introduce, asserts that the ordering will depend only on the consequences of the actions for those states of the world not ruled out by the information.

*Conditional Preference.* For any given event $E$, there is defined an ordering over actions satisfying also the condition of Monotone Continuity such that any two actions which have the same consequences for all states of the world in $E$ will be indifferent given $E$.

Preference of $\boldsymbol{a}^1$ over $\boldsymbol{a}^2$, given $E$, will be denoted by $\boldsymbol{a}^1 \succ \boldsymbol{a}^2 | E$, and similarly for the relations of indifference and preference-or-indifference.

Given the concept of conditional preference, it is now possible to introduce a very strong and yet highly acceptable postulate, relating conditional to unconditional preference.

Two definitions are needed. A *null event* is an event $E$ such that the conditional ordering given its complement $\tilde{E}$ is the same as the unconditional ordering. The intended interpretation is that null events are those deemed impossible to begin with, so that the unconditional preferences would not be altered upon being informed that $\tilde{E}$ held, i.e., that $E$ was in fact not true. A *partition* is defined as a finite or infinite collection of events which are mutually exclusive and collectively exhaustive, i.e., every state of the world belongs to one and only one event in the partition.

*Dominance.* Let $P$ be a partition. Given two actions, $\boldsymbol{a}^1$ and $\boldsymbol{a}^2$, if, for every event $E$ in the partition $P$, $\boldsymbol{a}^1 \succsim \boldsymbol{a}^2 | E$, then $\boldsymbol{a}^1 \succsim \boldsymbol{a}^2$; and if in addition there exists a collection $P'$ of events in $P$ whose union is nonnull and such that $\boldsymbol{a}^1 \succ \boldsymbol{a}^2 | E$ for all events $E$ in $P'$, then $\boldsymbol{a}^1 \succ \boldsymbol{a}^2$.

A third assumption expresses the condition that for a given state of the world actions are effectively valued solely by their consequences, together with an additional hypothesis which permits conceptually the attainment of any consequence in any state.

*Valuation of Actions by Consequences.* (a) If $\boldsymbol{a}^1$, $\boldsymbol{a}^2$, $\boldsymbol{b}^1$, $\boldsymbol{b}^2$ are actions, and $s_1$, $s_2$ states of the world, such that $(\boldsymbol{a}^1, s_1)$ and $(\boldsymbol{a}^2, s_2)$ yield the same consequence and similarly with $(\boldsymbol{b}^1, s_1)$ and $(\boldsymbol{b}^2, s_2)$, then $\boldsymbol{a}^1 \succ \boldsymbol{b}^1 | s_1$ if and only if $\boldsymbol{a}^2 \succ \boldsymbol{b}^2 | s_2$. (b) If $a(s)$ is any function which assigns to each state $s$ a consequence, then there is an action $\boldsymbol{a}$ such that $(\boldsymbol{a}, s)$ yields the consequence $a(s)$ for all $s$.

If, first of all, we set $s_1 = s_2 = s$ and $\boldsymbol{b}^1 = \boldsymbol{b}^2 = \boldsymbol{a}^1$, then $\boldsymbol{a}^1 \sim \boldsymbol{a}^1 | s$ if and only if $\boldsymbol{a}^1 \sim \boldsymbol{a}^2 | s$. But by Conditional Preference, certainly $\boldsymbol{a}^1 \sim \boldsymbol{a}^1 | s$, so that any two actions which yield the same consequence in state $s$ are indifferent, and this is true for any $s$. Further, by (b), all consequences are yielded by some action in $s$. Hence, all consequences are ordered for a given state $s$, and by (a) the ordering is the same for all $s$. Thus, we may speak unequivocally of an ordering of consequences, and we will use the same notation as for ordering actions.

It is natural and, from these assumptions, proper to identify a consequence with an action which yields that consequence for all $s$; such actions always exist by (b). Let $\boldsymbol{a}^1$ yield consequence $c_1$ for all $s$, and let $\boldsymbol{a}^2$ yield $c_2$. If $c_1 \succ c_2$, then $\boldsymbol{a}^1 \succ \boldsymbol{a}^2 | s$ for all $s$. By Dominance, $\boldsymbol{a}^1 \succ \boldsymbol{a}^2$ since the states of the world form a partition. Similar results hold if $c_1 \sim c_2$ or $c_1 \prec c_2$; hence, $\boldsymbol{a}^1 \succ \boldsymbol{a}^2$ if and only if $c_1 \succ c_2$, so that the ordering of consequences is indeed the same as that of actions which yield constant consequences.

Any action $\boldsymbol{a}$ defines a function, $a(s)$, mapping states of the world into consequences. If two actions define the same such function, they are indifferent given any $s$ and therefore are indifferent unconditionally, by Dominance; hence, it will be harmless to identify action $\boldsymbol{a}$ with the function $a(s)$. For any given action $\boldsymbol{a}$, and given consequence $c$, we will be considering such sets of states of the world as $\{s | a(s) \sim c\}$ or $\{s | a(s) \succ c\}$. It is clearly convenient to restrict the set of actions to be considered to those for which these sets are events, and this will be assumed in what follows.

The following simple consequence of these axioms will be used repeatedly in the sequel.

*Lemma 1.* If $a(s) \succsim$ (respectively, $\succ$) $b(s)$ for all $s$ in $E$, where $E$ is nonnull, then $\boldsymbol{a} \succsim$ (respectively, $\succ$) $\boldsymbol{b} | E$.

*Proof.* Let $\boldsymbol{a}^*$ be an action for which $\boldsymbol{a}^*(s) = a(s)$ for $s$ in $E$, $a^*(s) = b(s)$ for $s$ in $\tilde{E}$. From the last we conclude by conditional preference

$$\boldsymbol{a}^* \sim \boldsymbol{b} | \tilde{E} .$$

If $a(s) = a^*(s) \succsim b(s)$, all $s \in E$, then, by Dominance, $\boldsymbol{a}^* \succsim \boldsymbol{b}$. But if $\boldsymbol{a}^* \prec \boldsymbol{b} | E$, it would follow, again by Dominance, that $\boldsymbol{a}^* \prec \boldsymbol{b}$, a contradiction; hence, $\boldsymbol{a}^* \succsim \boldsymbol{b} | E$. But by Conditional Preference $\boldsymbol{a} \sim \boldsymbol{a}^* | E$; hence, $\boldsymbol{a} \succsim \boldsymbol{b} | E$. A similar argument holds when strict preference obtains.

Finally, we need an assumption about the structure of beliefs. Provisionally, the strong assumption will be made that beliefs are expressed by a probability distribution over the states of the world. In Section 4 it will be shown, following Ramsey, de Finetti, Savage, and Villegas, that it is possible to derive this conclusion from more intuitive and basic assumptions.

Since an action determines consequences as a function of the state of the world, a given action defines the probability distribution of consequences for any given probability distribution over the states of the world.

It will be assumed that there are no "indivisible" events; specifically, a probability distribution is said to be *atomless* if any event $E$ with probability greater than zero can be partitioned into two events, each with probability greater than zero. This will certainly hold if there is some indefinitely repeatable occurrence more or less independent of the rest of the state of the world, for example, a coin tossing. Imagine the coin tossed indefinitely, with independence from trial to trial, and a positive probability of head and also of tail. If $E$ is an event with positive probability, the statements defining $E$ can refer only to finitely many tosses of the coin (otherwise the probability of $E$ would be zero). Hence, $E$ can be divided into two events, each of positive probability, by considering the alternative outcomes of a coin toss not included in the definition of $E$. To say that beliefs are expressed by these probabilities has the following meaning in terms of choices among actions.

*Probabilistic Beliefs*. The probability distribution of states of the world is atomless. If the probability distribution of consequences is the same for two actions, they are indifferent.

*Remark:* In the sequel, the assumption of Probabilistic Beliefs will be applied only to actions which take on only a finite number of consequences.

## 3. The Expected Utility Theorem

With these assumptions, it can be shown that choice among actions can be represented in a remarkably simple way. It is possible to attach numbers called *utilities* to consequences in such a way that the expected value of utility measures the preference for an action. In more detail, consider any way of attaching utility numbers to consequences. For a given action, the utility then becomes a random variable. If the probability distribution of utility satisfies some additional hypotheses, for example, if utility is confined to a bounded set with probability one, then utility has a well-defined expected value or average. The proposition then is that by choosing properly the utility numbers assigned to different consequences, it will be true that one action will be preferred to another if and only if the expected value of the utility of its consequences is greater.

It is still more fruitful and general to consider utility as attached to an action; since a consequence can, as previously remarked, always be thought of as a particular form of action—namely, one that yields the same consequence regardless of the state of nature—the utility of consequences is defined as a special case of the utility of actions. The utility for actions must have the usual properties of any utility, specifically that preferences are expressed by higher utility values. We now state formally the

EXPECTED UTILITY THEOREM. *It is possible to define a real-valued utility function over actions, with the following properties:* (1) $\boldsymbol{a}^1 \succ \boldsymbol{a}^2$ *if and only if* $U(\boldsymbol{a}^1) > U(\boldsymbol{a}^2)$; (2) $U(\boldsymbol{a}) = E\{U[a(s)]\}$.

A utility function with these properties will be referred to as a *Bernoulli utility indicator*.

*Remark:* Because of (2), the utility function has the following continuity property if the range of the function is bounded with probability 1 (as will be shown to be true): Let $\{\boldsymbol{a}^i\}$ be a sequence of actions, $\boldsymbol{a}$ a particular action; suppose that, for any set $C$ of consequences for which the sets $\{s|a^i(s) \in C\}$, $\{s|a(s) \in C\}$ are all measurable, $P[a^i(s) \in C]$ converges to $P[a(s) \in C]$ uniformly in $C$; then $U(\boldsymbol{a}^i)$ approaches $U(\boldsymbol{a})$.

I want to attempt a somewhat novel presentation of the proof by relating it to the economic concept of independent goods. Suppose an individual is asked for his preferences among different combinations of amounts of two commodities. He may state that he cannot answer without knowing what he will have of some third commodity; the choice between bread and cereal may depend on how much butter is available. But it can happen that his preferences among combinations of the two commodities are in fact independent of the amounts of any third commodity; and this may be true of any pair of commodities.

More generally, if there are more than three commodities, it can happen that preferences among bundles, for which the components in any given set of commodities are constant, are independent of the levels at which they are constant. In that case, there is a well-known theorem that it is possible to represent these preferences by a utility function which adds up utilities from the different commodities; in symbols,

$$U(x_1, \ldots, x_n) = U_1(x_1) + U_2(x_2) + \ldots + U_n(x_n), \tag{3.1}$$

where $U(x_1, \ldots, x_n)$ is the utility of a bundle containing $x_1$ of the first commodity, and so forth.[4] This choice of utility function is also known to be unique up to positive linear transformations; that is, if there are two utility indicators of the form of (3.1), either can be obtained from the other by adding a constant and multiplying through by a positive constant.

With this remark we proceed to the proof proper. Because of the assumption of Probabilistic Beliefs we can speak indifferently of ordering actions

[4] See, e.g., SAMUELSON (1947, pp. 174–180). For a more general approach, see DEBREU (1960). Similar theorems arise in mathematical psychology; for a survey of recent literature on additive utility theory see FISHBURN (1966).

and of ordering probability distributions of consequences. For the time being we will confine attention to actions which yield consequences in a fixed finite set. We will start off with what seems to be a remarkably special problem, but in fact is very general: attaching utilities to probability distributions of probability distributions. More precisely, let $E_1, \ldots, E_n$ constitute a partition, each event $E_j$ having probability $l/n$. Let $\pi_1, \ldots, \pi_n$ be probability distributions over consequences in the given set. We will consider actions for which the conditional distribution of consequences, given $E_j$, is $\pi_j$, where the distributions $\pi_j$ are considered as variables which can range over all possible distributions over the fixed finite set of consequences. Any such action will be denoted by $(\pi_1, \ldots, \pi_n)$. For such an action, the unconditional probability distribution of consequences is simply the average, $\sum_{j=1}^{n} \pi_j/n$; according to our assumptions, all such distributions can be ordered, and we therefore have an ordering of the sets of $n$ probability distributions, $(\pi_1, \ldots, \pi_n)$.

Such an ordering is precisely analogous to the ordering of sets of $n$ commodities with which we are familiar from demand theory, and we will apply the theory of independent goods, sketched above, to it.

First, it is established that the ordering of these probability distributions of consequences has the continuity properties usually assumed for finite-dimensional commodity spaces; specifically, that for any given distribution $\pi^0$ the sets $\{\pi|\pi \succ \pi^0\}$ and $\{\pi|\pi^0 \succ \pi\}$ are open sets.

Let $\pi^*$ and $\pi_*$ be two distributions over the fixed finite set of consequences, and suppose $\pi^* \succ \pi_*$. Let $\{\pi^i\}$ be a sequence of probability distributions over these consequences converging to $\pi^*$. Since there are only finitely many consequences, the probability distributions are finite-dimensional vectors, and the usual definition of convergence applies. It will be shown that $\pi^i \succ \pi_*$ for $i$ sufficiently large. By a parallel argument, it can be shown that if $\pi^i \to \pi_*$, then $\pi^* \succ \pi^i$ for $i$ sufficiently large.

Choose a vanishing sequence $\{F_k\}$ such that $P(F_k) > 0$ for all $k$, where $P(F)$ is the probability of the event $F$; such a sequence exists by the assumed atomlessness of the probability distribution of states of the world. Let $\boldsymbol{a}^*$ be an action such that

$$P[a^*(s) = c|\tilde{F}_1] = \pi^*(c) \text{ for all c},$$

and also

$$P[a^*(s) = c|F_k - F_{k+1}] = \pi^*(c) \text{ for all } c \text{ and } k,$$

where $F_k - F_{k+1}$ consists of all $s$ in $F_k$ but not $F_{k+1}$. Since the sets $\tilde{F}_1$, $F_k - F_{k+1}$ constitute a partition, it follows that $P[a^*(s) = c] = \pi^*(c)$ for all $c$.

That $\boldsymbol{a}^*$ can be constructed as indicated follows again from the atomlessness of the probability distribution of states. Also choose an action $\boldsymbol{a}_*$ with probability distribution $\pi_*$ over consequences. Then the statement $\pi^* \succ \pi_*$ is equivalent to the statement $\boldsymbol{a}^* \succ \boldsymbol{a}_*$.

Let $\underline{c}$ be the least preferred of all the consequences considered. Then, by Monotone Continuity it is possible to choose $F_k$ so that the action $\boldsymbol{a}^{**}$, defined by

$$a^{**}(s) = \begin{cases} a^*(s) \text{ if } s \in \tilde{F}_k, \\ \underline{c} \quad\quad \text{if } s \in F_k, \end{cases}$$

is preferred to $\boldsymbol{a}_*$.

By construction, $P(\tilde{F}_k) = 1 - P(F_k) < 1$. Since $\pi^i(c)$ approaches $\pi^*(c)$, $\pi^i(c) \geqq \pi^*(c)P(\tilde{F}_k)$ for $i$ sufficiently large if $\pi^*(c) > 0$, and the inequality certainly holds if $\pi^*(c) = 0$. Since there are only finitely many $c$, the inequality holds for all $c$ for $i$ sufficiently large. Define

$$\bar{\pi}(c) = [\pi^i(c) - \pi^*(c)\,P(\tilde{F}_k)]/P(\tilde{F}_k);$$

then $\bar{\pi}$ is a probability distribution. Define the action $\bar{\boldsymbol{a}}$ to coincide with $\boldsymbol{a}^*$ on $\tilde{F}_k$ and such that the conditional probability distribution of $\bar{\boldsymbol{a}}$, given $F_k$, is $\bar{\pi}$. From construction, the conditional distribution of $\boldsymbol{a}^*$, given $\tilde{F}_k$, is $\pi^*$ for any $k$; hence, an easy calculation shows that the distribution of $\bar{\boldsymbol{a}}$ is $\pi^i$.

We wish to show that $\bar{\boldsymbol{a}} \succ \boldsymbol{a}_*$; this is equivalent to saying that $\pi^i \succ \pi_*$. But $\bar{\boldsymbol{a}}$ coincides with $\boldsymbol{a}^{**}$ on $\tilde{F}_k$, and hence $\bar{\boldsymbol{a}} \sim \boldsymbol{a}^{**} | \tilde{F}_k$. Since $\underline{c}$ is the least preferred consequence, it follows from Lemma 1 of Section 2 that $\bar{\pi} \succsim \underline{c}$, and therefore $\bar{\boldsymbol{a}} \succsim \boldsymbol{a}^{**} | F_k$. By Dominance again, $\bar{\boldsymbol{a}} \succsim \boldsymbol{a}^{**} \succ \boldsymbol{a}_*$, as was to be proved.

Let $E$ be the event of either $E_1$ or $E_2$, i.e., it contains all states of the world in either of these two events. By the assumption of Conditional Preference, all actions can be ordered given $E$, and the ordering depends only on the outcomes for states of the world in $E$. Together with the assumption of Probabilistic Beliefs this implies that there is a well-defined ordering of the pairs $(\pi_1, \pi_2)$. Now consider two sets of $n$ probability distributions, $(\pi_1, \pi_2, \pi_3, \ldots, \pi_n)$ and $(\pi'_1, \pi'_2, \pi_3, \ldots, \pi_n)$, which yield the same conditional probability distributions of consequences in states $E_3, \ldots, E_n$. By the Dominance axiom, then, $(\pi_1, \pi_2, \pi_3, \ldots, \pi_n) \succ (\pi'_1, \pi'_2, \pi_3, \ldots, \pi_n)$ if and only if $(\pi_1, \pi_2) \succ (\pi'_1, \pi'_2) | E$; to see this, we must take our partition to be the sets $E$, $E_3, \ldots, E_n$. The choice is thus independent of $\pi_3, \ldots, \pi_n$. Any pair or, more generally, any collection of events could have been substituted for $E_1$ and $E_2$

in this argument; thus, the preferences for varying any set of conditional probability distributions holding all others constant are in fact independent of the levels at which the others are held constant. It follows that the conditional probability distributions act as independent goods, and by the theorem of DEBREU (1960) we can express the preferences among sets of probability distributions $(\pi_1, \ldots, \pi_n)$ by a continuous additive utility function,

$$V_n(\pi_1, \ldots, \pi_n) = \sum_{j=1}^{n} W_{jn}(\pi_j). \tag{3.2}$$

The subscript $n$ is designed to remind us that we have so far considered a partition into a fixed number of events.

The assumption of Probabilistic Beliefs also assures that interchanging any pair of conditional probability distributions leads to a new action which is indifferent to the first, since only the resulting unconditional probability distribution, $\sum_{j=1}^{n} \pi_j/n$, matters as far as preference is concerned. Hence, the function $W_{jn}(\pi_j)$ must be the same for all $j$, and the subscript $j$ can be deleted.

$$V_n(\pi_1, \ldots, \pi_n) = \sum_{j=1}^{n} W_n(\pi_j). \tag{3.3}$$

The next step is to relate the utility functions for different values of $n$, i.e., different numbers of equiprobable events. For this purpose we define

$$U_n(\pi) = n W_n(\pi), \tag{3.4}$$

and (3.3) becomes

$$V_n(\pi_1, \ldots, \pi_n) = \sum_{j=1}^{n} (1/n)\, U_n(\pi_j). \tag{3.5}$$

Notice that, since the probability of $E_j$ is $l/n$ for each $j$, the right-hand side is the expected value of a utility function. We will show that $U_n(\pi)$ is in fact the same function for all $n$.

Since (3.5) holds for any $n$, it holds in particular for $mn$, where $m$ is any positive integer. When there are $mn$ equally probable events, it will be convenient to label them with pairs of subscripts; thus, $E_{jk}$, with $j$ running from 1 to $n$ and $k$ from 1 to $m$. Then (3.5) becomes

$$V_{mn}(\pi_{11}, \ldots, \pi_{mn}) = \sum_{j=1}^{n} \sum_{k=1}^{m} (1/mn)\, U_{mn}(\pi_{jk}). \tag{3.6}$$

In particular, now let us suppose that for any given index $j$ the conditional probability distribution is the same for all events $E_{jk}$; in symbols, $\pi_{jk} = \pi_j$

for $k=1, \ldots, m$. Then

$$\sum_{k=1}^{m} (1/mn)\, U_{mn}(\pi_{jk}),$$

is a sum of $m$ terms, each of which is the same, $(1/mn)\, U_{mn}(\pi_j)$, and therefore equals $(1/n)\, U_{mn}(\pi_j)$. Further, the unconditional distribution of consequences is $\sum_{j=1}^{n} \sum_{k=1}^{n} \pi_{jk}/mn = \sum_{j=1}^{n} \pi_j/n$, so that the expression (3.6) defines an ordering on the sets of $n$ conditional probability distributions $(\pi_1, \ldots, \pi_n)$. Since we have

$$V_{mn}(\pi_{11}, \ldots, \pi_{mn}) = \sum_{j=1}^{n} (1/n)\, U_{mn}(\pi_j),$$

when $\pi_{jk} = \pi_j$, we see that $V_{mn}$ constitutes an additive utility function for sets of $n$ conditional probability distributions. But additive utility functions are unique up to positive linear transformations; it follows that $U_{mn}(\pi)$ is essentially the same as $U_n(\pi)$. As $U_m(\pi)$ is also the same as $U_{mn}(\pi)$, it follows that $U_n(\pi)$ is essentially the same as $U_m(\pi)$ for any pair of integers $m$, $n$, and therefore we may drop the subscript $n$. Thus,

$$V_n(\pi_1, \ldots, \pi_n) = \sum_{j=1}^{n} (1/n)\, U(\pi_j). \tag{3.7}$$

Note that this expression can also be regarded as the utility attached to the unconditional distribution, so that

$$V\left(\sum_{j=1}^{n} \pi_j/n\right) = \sum_{j=1}^{n} (1/n)\, U(\pi_j). \tag{3.8}$$

Suppose in particular that all the $\pi_j$'s are the same: $\pi_j = \pi$. Then $\sum_{i=1}^{n} \pi_j/n = \pi$, and

$$\sum_{j=1}^{n} (1/n)\, U(\pi_j) = \sum_{j=1}^{n} (1/n)\, U(\pi) = U(\pi),$$

so that $U(\pi) = V(\pi)$. If we now substitute in (3.8), we find that

$$U\left(\sum_{j=1}^{n} \pi_j/n\right) = \sum_{j=1}^{n} (1/n)\, U(\pi_j); \tag{3.9}$$

in words, the utility of an average of probability distributions is the average of their utilities.

We have now defined a utility function, unique up to positive linear transformations, for all probability distributions with finitely many consequences, and have shown that it has the property that the utility of a random choice among any finite number of equally probable conditional probability distributions is the expected utility of the conditional probability distribution.

Next we wish to relax the condition that the partition consists of equally probable events. Suppose now we have $n$ events with probabilities which are rational numbers: we can put all these probabilities over a common denominator, say $N$. Then

$$P(E_j) = m_j/N .$$

For each $j$, let us partition $E_j$ into $m_j$ equally probable events, $E_{jk}$, $k = 1, \ldots, m_j$, so that $P(E_{jk}) = 1/N$. The events $E_{jk}$ then constitute a partition into equally probable events, and we can apply (3.9). In particular, let $\pi_{jk}$, the conditional probability distribution given event $E_{jk}$, be $\pi_j$ independent of $k$. The unconditional distribution then is clearly

$$\sum_{j=1}^{n} \sum_{k=1}^{m_j} \pi_j/N = \sum_{j=1}^{n} (m_j/N)\, \pi_j = \sum_{j=1}^{n} P(E_j)\, \pi_j .$$

The right-hand side of (3.9) becomes

$$\sum_{j=1}^{n} \sum_{k=1}^{m_j} (1/N)\, U(\pi_{jk}) = \sum_{j=1}^{n} (m_j/N)\, U(\pi_j) = \sum_{j=1}^{n} P(E_j)\, U(\pi_j),$$

so that (3.9) generalizes to

$$U\left(\sum_{j=1}^{n} P(E_j)\, \pi_j\right) = \sum_{j=1}^{n} P(E_j)\, U(\pi_j); \tag{3.10}$$

in words, the utility of a weighted mixture of probability distributions is the weighted average of their utilities.

This has been proved so far only for rational probabilities. Now suppose one or more of the probabilities $P(E_j)$ is not a rational number. We can always choose rational numbers, $p_j$, so that

$$p_j < P(E_j),$$

and indeed as close as we wish. Let $E_j'$ be a subset of $E_j$ such that

$$P(E_j') = p_j \qquad (j = 1, \ldots, n). \tag{3.11}$$

Let $E_j''$ consist of all the elements of $E_j$ not in $E_j'$. Without loss of generality, we renumber the events so that $\pi_1$ is the least preferred among the probability distributions $\pi_j$ (or a least preferred distribution if there is a tie), and similarly $\pi_n$ is a most preferred distribution among the $r_j$'s. Let $\boldsymbol{a}^1$, $\boldsymbol{a}^2$, $\boldsymbol{a}^3$ be three actions for which the conditional probability distributions of consequences given the events $E'_j$, $E''_j$ are as follows:

$a^1$: conditional distribution given $E'_j$ is $\pi_j$;
conditional distribution given $E''_j$ is $\pi_j$.

$a^2$: conditional distribution given $E'_j$ is $\pi_j$;
conditional distribution given $E''_j$ is $\pi_1$.

$a_3$: conditional distribution given $E'_j$ is $\pi_j$;
conditional distribution given $E''_j$ is $\pi_n$.

The events $E'_j$, $E''_j$ constitute a partition. The conditional distribution given $E'_j$ is the same for all three actions and so, by the postulate of Conditional Preference, the three actions are indifferent given $E'_j$ for each $j$. However, by construction, $\pi_n$ is preferred or indifferent to $\pi_j$ and the latter to $\pi_1$; hence $a_3 \succsim a^1 | E''_j$ and $a^1 \succsim a^2 | E''_j$ for each $j$. By the postulate of Dominance, $a^3 \succsim a^1 \succsim a^2$, so that

$$U(a^3) \geqq U(a^1) \geqq U(a^2).$$

Now write $E'_{n+1}$ for the set of states of the world not in any of the events $E'_1, \ldots, E'_n$, or equivalently for the set of states of the world in one of the events $E''_1, \ldots, E''_n$. Note first that

$$P(E'_{n+1}) = 1 - \sum_{j=1}^{n} P(E_j) = 1 - \sum_{j=1}^{n} p_j$$

is a rational number. For the action $a^2$, the conditional distribution given $E''_j$ is the same for each $j$, namely, $\pi_1$. Therefore, the conditional distribution given $E'_{n+1}$ must also be $\pi_1$. We can now apply (3.10) since the probabilities of the events $E'_1, \ldots, E'_n, E'_{n+1}$ are all rational.

$$U(a^2) = \sum_{j=1}^{n} P(E'_j)\, U(\pi_j) + P(E'_{n+1})\, U(\pi_1).$$

Similarly,

$$U(a^3) = \sum_{j=1}^{n} p_j U(\pi_j) + \left(1 - \sum_{j=1}^{n} p_j\right) U(\pi_n).$$

Now let the numbers $p_j$ approach $P(E_j)$ for each $j$. Then $1 - \sum_{j=1}^{n} p_j$ approaches zero. Both $U(a^2)$ and $U(a^3)$ converge to

$$\sum_{j=1}^{n} P(E_j)\, U(\pi_j),$$

which is therefore equal to $U(a^1)$. But $a^1$ is so defined that the conditional distribution given either $E'_j$ or $E''_j$ is $\pi_j$. Hence, the conditional distribution given $E_j$ is also $\pi_j$ since $E_j$ is simply divided into $E_j'$ and $E_j''$. Thus, the unconditional distribution for $\boldsymbol{a}^1$ is simply $\sum_{j=1}^{n} P(E_j)\pi_j$, and it has now been demonstrated that (3.10) also holds when the probabilities $P(E_j)$ are irrational.

Before going on, let us interpret (3.10) in terms of utilities of consequences. Consider any action which yields the finitely many different possible consequences $c_1, \ldots, c_n$. Let $E_i$ be the event that $c_i$ occurs, and let $\pi_i$ be the distribution under which $c_i$ occurs with probability 1. Then $U(\pi_i)$ may very reasonably be interpreted as the utility of the consequence $c_i$, and we will use the notation $U(c_i)$. The mixed probability distribution, $\sum_{i=1}^{n} P(E_i)\pi_i$, is now just the probability distribution of the consequence. Then (3.10) states that the utility of any action which has only a finite number of consequences is the expected utility of the consequence.

So far, attention has been confined to utility comparisons of actions which yield consequences in a fixed finite set, say $K$. Provisionally, this restriction may be symbolized by writing the utility function as $U(\boldsymbol{a}|K)$, defined for all actions $\boldsymbol{a}$ for which $a(s) \in K$, all $s$. But if $K_1 \subset K_2$, the set of actions $\boldsymbol{a}$ for which $a(s) \in K_1$, all $s$, is a subset of that for which $a(s) \in K_2$, all $s$. Hence, $U(\boldsymbol{a}|K_2)$ defines a utility indicator of the former class of actions, and this indicator satisfies (3.10). Therefore, the function $U(\boldsymbol{a}|K_2)$ is, up to a positive linear transformation, identical with the function $U(\boldsymbol{a}|K_1)$ for actions with consequences in $K_1$. It follows that the utility function is essentially the same for all $K$; for if $\boldsymbol{a}^1$ and $\boldsymbol{a}^2$ are any two actions with finitely many consequences, we need only choose $K$ to be any finite set of consequences such that both $a^1(s) \in K$ and $a^2(s) \in K$ for all $s$; than $\boldsymbol{a}^1 \succ \boldsymbol{a}^2$ if and only if $U(\boldsymbol{a}^1|K) > U(\boldsymbol{a}^2|K)$, and the function $U$ satisfies (3.10).

Thus, a Bernoulli utility indicator has been defined, with finite values, for all actions with finitely many consequences. The final step is to drop the restriction that the number of different possible consequences is finite. For most practical purposes it is easier to consider random variables which are continuous and therefore take on an infinite number of values. This last step is, however, not quite straightforward and turns out, somewhat surprisingly, to imply that the utility function must be bounded; we cannot have utilities which are indefinitely large in either the positive or the negative direction.

The argument depends interestingly on the very problem that originally gave rise to Daniel BERNOULLI's original paper (1738) and which has been given the name of the "St. Petersburg paradox" after the place where Bernoulli wrote. In its original form, a gambling game was considered in which a prize of $2^n$ was given with a probability of $(1/2)^n$ for $n = 1, \ldots,$

*ad infinitum*. The expected value in money terms was infinite, yet it is obvious to common sense that no one would pay any very large fee for the right to play the game. Bernoulli suggested that maximizing expected utility instead of expected money income was the proper criterion of action and if, for example, the utility of a quantity of money were equal to its logarithm, one could easily compute that the maximum entrance fee which an individual would be willing to pay was finite and in fact reasonably small.

But this solution is in fact incomplete. If the utility function is unbounded, one can always construct an action with an infinite utility as was first observed by the mathematician Karl MENGER (1934). To see this, suppose the utility function is unbounded above. Then we can find a consequence with a utility as large as we wish. In particular, choose consequence $c_i$ so that

$$U(c_i) \geqq 2^i \text{ and also } U(c_i) > U(c_{i-1}),$$

for each $i$. Let $\{E_i\}$ ($i=1, \ldots, ad.\ inf.$) be a partition, with $P(E_i) = (1/2)^i$. Let $\boldsymbol{a}^1$ be the action which gives rise to consequence $c_i$ when event $E_i$ occurs. Fix a positive integer $N$, and let $\boldsymbol{a}^2$ be the action which gives rise to consequence $c_i$ when $E_i$ occurs, for $i \leqq N$, and to $c_{N+1}$ when $E_i$ occurs for any $i > N$. The action $\boldsymbol{a}^2$ has only a finite number of possible consequences, and so (3.10) is valid. Note that the probability of $c_{N+1}$ under action $\boldsymbol{a}^2$ is $1 - \sum_{i=1}^{n} P(E_i)$.

$$U(\boldsymbol{a}^2) = \sum_{i=1}^{N} P(E_i)\, U(c_i) + \left[1 - \sum_{i=1}^{N} P(E_i)\right] U(c_{n+1})$$

$$\geqq \sum_{i=1}^{N} (1/2)^i\, U(c_i) \geqq \sum_{i=1}^{N} (1/2)^i\, 2^i = N.$$

On the other hand, $\boldsymbol{a}^1$ coincides with $\boldsymbol{a}^2$ on $E_i (i = 1, \ldots, N+1)$, while on $E_i (i > N+1)$ it yields $c_i$, which is preferred to $c_{N+1}$, the outcome of $\boldsymbol{a}^2$. By Lemma 1 of Section 2, $\boldsymbol{a}^1 \succ \boldsymbol{a}^2$. Now let $\boldsymbol{a}$ be any action with finitely many consequences; choose $N$ integer, $N > U(\boldsymbol{a})$. Then $U(\boldsymbol{a}^2) > U(\boldsymbol{a})$, so that $\boldsymbol{a}^2 \succ \boldsymbol{a}$, and therefore $\boldsymbol{a}^1 \succ \boldsymbol{a}$. It has thus been shown that, if the utility function is unbounded above, then $\boldsymbol{a}^1$ is preferred to any action with finitely many consequences.

But this leads to a contradiction. Let $\{\bar{c}_i\}$ be a sequence of consequences such that $\bar{c}_i \succ c_i$, each $i$, and let $\boldsymbol{a}^3$ be the action defined by $a^3(s) = \bar{c}_i$ for $s \in E_i$. Then, by Dominance, $\boldsymbol{a}^3 \succ \boldsymbol{a}^1$. Let $F_j = \bigcup_{i=j}^{\infty} E_i$; then $\{F_j\}$ is certainly a vanishing sequence. Let $c$ be any arbitrary consequence. By

Monotone Continuity it is possible to choose $j$ so that the action $\boldsymbol{a}^4$ defined by

$$a^4(s) = \begin{cases} a^3(s) \text{ for } s \in \tilde{F}_j, \\ c \quad \text{ for } s \in F_j, \end{cases}$$

is preferred to $\boldsymbol{a}^1$. By definition of $F_j$, $a^4(s) = \bar{c}_i$ for $s \in E_i$, $i<j$, $a^4(s) = c$ for $s \in F_j$. Then $\boldsymbol{a}^4$ has finitely many consequences and is preferred to $\boldsymbol{a}^1$, a contradiction.

By a similar argument the utility function must be bounded from below. It is now possible to establish the Expected Utility Theorem for any probability distribution of consequences. Since the utility function is bounded in both directions, let $\underline{u} = \inf U(c)$, $\bar{u} = \sup U(c)$. First let us assume that these bounds are actually attained, that there are consequences $\underline{c}$, $\bar{c}$ such that $\underline{c} \precsim c \precsim \bar{c}$ for all consequences $c$, and therefore $\underline{c} \precsim a(s) \precsim \bar{c}$ for all actions $\boldsymbol{a}$ and all states of the world $s$. Note that $\underline{u} = U(\underline{c})$, $\bar{u} = U(\bar{c})$.

Divide the interval from $\underline{u}$ to $\bar{u}$ into a finite number of intervals; let $u_i (i = 0, \ldots, n)$, with $u_0 = \underline{u}$ and $u_n = \bar{u}$. Given any action $\boldsymbol{a}$, the utility of the consequence, $U[a(s)]$, is a random variable with a known distribution. Let $E_i = \{s | u_i \leqq U[a(s)] < u_{i+1}\}$ $(i = 0, \ldots, n-1)$, $E_n = \{s | U[a(s)] = u_n\}$. Let $\boldsymbol{a}^{1n}$ be an action with finitely many consequences for which $E\{U[a^{1n}(s)] | E_i\} = u_i$ $(i = 0, \ldots, n)$, $\boldsymbol{a}^{2n}$ an action with finitely many consequences for which $E\{U[a^{2n}(s)] | E_i\} = u_{i+1}$ $(i = 0, \ldots, n-1)$, $E\{U[a^{2n}(s)] | E_n\} = u_n$. Such actions can always be found; for example, let $\boldsymbol{a}^{1n}$ take on only the two values $\underline{c}$, $\bar{c}$, and be so defined that the conditional probability distribution of $a^{1n}(s)$ given $E_i$ satisfies the conditions:

$$P[a^{1n}(s) = \bar{c} | E_i]\, \bar{u} + P[a^{1n}(s) = \underline{c} | E_i]\, \underline{u} = u_i, \; P[a^{1n}(s) = \bar{c} | E_i] + P[a^{1n}(s) = \underline{c} | E_i] = 1 .$$

To prove that $\boldsymbol{a} \succsim \boldsymbol{a}^{1n} | E_i$ and $\boldsymbol{a}^{2n} \succsim \boldsymbol{a} | E_i$, the following lemma is established:

LEMMA 1. *If $E$ is nonnull, $a(s) \succsim \boldsymbol{b} | E$ for all $s$ in $E$, and $\boldsymbol{b}$ has finitely many consequences, then $\boldsymbol{a} \succsim \boldsymbol{b} | E$.*

Note that in the hypothesis the *consequence* $a(s)$ is being compared with the *action* $\boldsymbol{b}$, for any given $s$.

*Proof.* The action $\boldsymbol{b}$ defines a conditional probability distribution over finitely many consequences, given $E$; this distribution then has a utility, which we may denote by $U(\boldsymbol{b} | E)$. For any given $s'$ in $E$, define $\boldsymbol{b}_{s'}$, which coincides with $\boldsymbol{b}$ on $E$, with $b_{s'}(s)=a(s')$ on $\tilde{E}$. On the one hand, $U(\boldsymbol{b}_{s'})=U(\boldsymbol{b}|E)P(E)+U[a(s')]P(\tilde{E})$; on the other, $a(s')\gtrsim \boldsymbol{b}_{s'}|E$, and $a(s')=\boldsymbol{b}_{s'}|\tilde{E}$, so that $a(s')\gtrsim \boldsymbol{b}_{s'}$, and therefore $U[a(s')]\geqq U(\boldsymbol{b}_{s'})$, from which it follows that $U[a(s')]\geqq U(\boldsymbol{b}|E)$ for all $s'$ in $E$. Let

$$u_* = \inf_{s\in E} U[a(s)] \geqq U(\boldsymbol{b}|E).$$

There are two possibilities: either the infimum is assumed or it is not. In the first case, let $s_*$ be such that $U[a(s_*)]=u_*$, and define actions $\boldsymbol{a}^*$, $\boldsymbol{b}^*$ to coincide with $\boldsymbol{a}$, $\boldsymbol{b}$ respectively, on $E$, with $a^*(s)=b^*(s)=a(s_*)$ for $s\in\tilde{E}$. Then, by construction, $a^*(s)\gtrsim a(s_*)$ for all $s$, so that $\boldsymbol{a}^*\gtrsim a(s_*)$. Also, $a(s_*)\gtrsim \boldsymbol{b}^*|E$, by hypothesis, and $a(s_*)=\boldsymbol{b}^*|\tilde{E}$, so that $a(s_*)\gtrsim \boldsymbol{b}^*$. Hence, $\boldsymbol{a}^*\gtrsim \boldsymbol{b}^*$. Since $\boldsymbol{a}^*=\boldsymbol{b}^*|\tilde{E}$, it follows from Dominance that $\boldsymbol{a}^*\gtrsim \boldsymbol{b}^*|\tilde{E}$; but since $\boldsymbol{a}^*$, $\boldsymbol{b}^*$ coincide with $\boldsymbol{a}$, $\boldsymbol{b}$, respectively, on $E$, $\boldsymbol{a}\gtrsim\boldsymbol{b}|E$, as was to be shown.

In the second case, $U[a(s)]>u_*$ for all $s$ in $E$. Let $s_i$ be a sequence of states of the world in $E$, such that $U[a(s_i)]$ decreases to $u_*$. Let $E_i=\{s|a(s_i)\succ a(s),\ s\in E\}$; then $\{E_i\}$ is a vanishing sequence. Define $\boldsymbol{a}^i$ so that $a^i(s)=a(s)$ for $s\in E-E_i$, $a^i(s)=a(s_1)$ for $s\in E_i$, $a^i(s)=a(s_i)$ for $s\in\tilde{E}$. Define $\boldsymbol{b}^i$ so that $b^i(s)=b(s)$ for $s\in E$, $b^i(s)=a(s_i)$ for $s\in\tilde{E}$. Then clearly $a^i(s)\gtrsim a(s_i)$, all $s$, so that $\boldsymbol{a}^i\gtrsim a(s_i)$. By hypothesis, $a(s_i)\gtrsim \boldsymbol{b}^i|E$; by construction, $a(s_i)=\boldsymbol{b}^i|\tilde{E}$, so that $a(s_i)\gtrsim \boldsymbol{b}^i$, and hence $\boldsymbol{a}^i\gtrsim \boldsymbol{b}^i$. Since $\boldsymbol{a}^i=\boldsymbol{b}^i|\tilde{E}$, it follows by the usual argument that $\boldsymbol{a}^i\gtrsim \boldsymbol{b}^i|E$, and therefore $\boldsymbol{a}^i\gtrsim \boldsymbol{b}|E$.

Now take any fixed consequence, $c$, and let $\underline{\boldsymbol{a}}^i$, $\underline{\boldsymbol{a}}$, $\underline{\boldsymbol{b}}$ be actions which coincide with $\boldsymbol{a}^i$, $\boldsymbol{a}$, $\boldsymbol{b}$, respectively, on $E$ and yield $c$ on $\tilde{E}$. Then by the usual Dominance argument, $\underline{\boldsymbol{a}}^i\gtrsim\underline{\boldsymbol{b}}$. But $\underline{\boldsymbol{a}}^i$ differs from $\underline{\boldsymbol{a}}$ only on a vanishing sequence; hence, $\underline{\boldsymbol{a}}\gtrsim\underline{\boldsymbol{b}}$. Finally, since $\underline{\boldsymbol{a}}=\underline{\boldsymbol{b}}|\tilde{E}$, $\underline{\boldsymbol{a}}\gtrsim\underline{\boldsymbol{b}}|E$, or $\boldsymbol{a}\gtrsim\boldsymbol{b}|E$, as was to be proved.

We now return to the proof of the Expected Utility Theorem. By the lemma, $\boldsymbol{a}\gtrsim\boldsymbol{a}^{1n}|E_i$ for any nonnull $E_i$ and, by a similar argument, $\boldsymbol{a}^{2n}\gtrsim\boldsymbol{a}|E_i$. Since these statements hold for all nonnull $E_i$, we can say that $\boldsymbol{a}^{2n}\gtrsim\boldsymbol{a}\gtrsim\boldsymbol{a}^{1n}$. But from (3.10),

$$U(\boldsymbol{a}^{1n}) = \sum_{i=0}^{n} P(E_i)\,u_i,\ U(\boldsymbol{a}^{2n}) = \sum_{i=0}^{n-1} P(E_i)\,U_{i+1}+P(E_n)\,u_n.$$

Now let the subdivision become finer so that $n$ increases and the distance between successive $u_i$'s becomes smaller. From general theorems on Lebesgue integration, it follows that $U(\boldsymbol{a}^{1n})$ and $U(\boldsymbol{a}^{2n})$ approach a common limit, which is the expected value of the utility, $E\{U[a(s)]\}=u^*$, say. Since

$\bar{u} \geqq u^* \geqq \underline{u}$, we can construct an action $\boldsymbol{a}^*$ which yields only the two consequences $\underline{c}$, $\bar{c}$, such that $U(\boldsymbol{a}^*) = u^*$. It will be shown that $\boldsymbol{a} \sim \boldsymbol{a}^*$.

Suppose $\boldsymbol{a}$ were preferred to $\boldsymbol{a}^*$. We will construct $\boldsymbol{a}^{**}$, an action with finitely many consequences, such that $\boldsymbol{a} \succ \boldsymbol{a}^{**} \succ \boldsymbol{a}^*$. This leads to a contradiction. For $U(\boldsymbol{a}^{**}) > U(\boldsymbol{a}^*)$; since $U(\boldsymbol{a}^{2n}) \to U(\boldsymbol{a}^*)$, $U(\boldsymbol{a}^{2n}) < U(\boldsymbol{a}^{**})$ for $n$ large, and therefore $\boldsymbol{a}^{**} \succ \boldsymbol{a}^{2n}$, contrary to the constructions which insure $\boldsymbol{a}^{2n} \succsim \boldsymbol{a} \succ \boldsymbol{a}^{**}$.

It remains to construct $\boldsymbol{a}^{**}$. Suppose that $P[a^*(s) = \bar{c}] = 1$. Then by Dominance, $\boldsymbol{a}^* \succsim \boldsymbol{a}$, contrary to assumption. Thus, $P[a^*(s) = \underline{c}] > 0$. Let $E_1 = \{s | a^*(s) = \underline{c}\}$, $\{E_i\}$ be a vanishing sequence with $P(E_i) > 0$. Then, by Monotone Continuity, if $\boldsymbol{a} \succ \boldsymbol{a}^*$, we can find $i$ and $\boldsymbol{a}^{**}$, with $a^{**}(s) = a^*(s)$ for $s \in \tilde{E}_i$, $a^{**}(s) = \bar{c}$ for $s \in E_i$, $\boldsymbol{a} \succ \boldsymbol{a}^{**}$. Since $E_i \subset E_1$, $a^{**}(s) = \bar{c} \succ \underline{c} = a^*(s)$ for $s \in E_i$, and therefore by Dominance $\boldsymbol{a}^{**} \succ \boldsymbol{a}^*$.

Thus, it is impossible that $\boldsymbol{a} \succ \boldsymbol{a}^*$ and similarly impossible that $\boldsymbol{a}^* \succ \boldsymbol{a}$. Then $\boldsymbol{a}$ is indifferent to an action $\boldsymbol{a}^*$ whose utility is $E\{U[a(s)]\}$. From this the Expected Utility Theorem has been shown to hold if there exist a best and a worst consequence.

Now drop the assumption that maximal and minimal consequences exist. For any fixed pair of consequences, $\underline{c}$, $\bar{c}$, with $\underline{c} \precsim \bar{c}$, consider the class of actions, $K(\underline{c}, \bar{c})$, for which $\underline{c} \precsim a(s) \precsim \bar{c}$. Within any such class, the Expected Utility Theorem holds. Define an action $\boldsymbol{a}$ to be *bounded below* if, for some consequence $\underline{c}$, $P[a(s)] \succsim \underline{c}] = 1$; define *bounded above* similarly, and say an action is *bounded* if it is bounded both above and below. By modifying the consequences of a bounded action, $\boldsymbol{a}$, on a set of probability zero, we can obtain a second action, $\boldsymbol{a}'$, such that $\boldsymbol{a} \sim \boldsymbol{a}'$, $\boldsymbol{a}' \in K(\underline{c}, \bar{c})$ for some $\underline{c}$, $\bar{c}$, and $E\{U[a(s)]\} = E\{U[a'(s)]\}$. If $\boldsymbol{a}$ and $\boldsymbol{b}$ are two bounded actions, then, we can choose $\underline{c}$, $\bar{c}$ so that both $\boldsymbol{a}'$ and $\boldsymbol{a}'$ belong to $K(\underline{c}, \bar{c})$; then $\boldsymbol{a} \succ \boldsymbol{b}$ if and only if $E\{U[a(s)]\} > E\{U[b(s)]\}$.

Now let $\boldsymbol{a}$ be any action bounded below but not necessarily above. We construct a vanishing sequence $\{E_i\}$ and a sequence of actions, $\{\boldsymbol{a}^i\}$, such that

$$a^i(s) = \begin{cases} c & \text{for } s \in E_i, \text{ for some } c, \\ a(s) & \text{for } s \in \tilde{E}_i; \end{cases} \tag{3.12}$$

$$\boldsymbol{a}^i \text{ bounded}; \tag{3.13}$$

$$\boldsymbol{a} \succ \boldsymbol{a}^i; \tag{3.14}$$

$$E\{U[a(s)]\} > E\{U[a^i(s)]\}. \tag{3.15}$$

If $\boldsymbol{a}$ is unbounded above, for any consequence $c$, $P[a(s) \succ c] > 0$, and therefore $U[a(s)] > U(c)$ with positive probability. Let $\{c_i\}$ be a sequence of consequences, with $c_{i+1} \succ c_i$ and $\lim U(c_i) = \bar{u}$, let $E_i = \{s | a(s) \succ c_i\}$, and define $a^i(s) = c_1$ for $s \in E_i$, $a^i(s) = a(s)$ for $s \in \tilde{E}_i$. Then $a^i(s) \precsim c_i$, all $s$, so that (3.12) and (3.13) are satisfied; (3.14) follows immediately from Dominance, and (3.15) by obvious integration.

If, on the other hand, $\boldsymbol{a}$ is bounded above, let $\{E_i\}$ be any vanishing sequence for which $P(E_i) > 0$, and let $c = \underline{c}$ in (3.12), where $\underline{c}$ is a lower bound for the action $\boldsymbol{a}$. Then again (3.12-3.15) are easily seen to hold.

Now let $\boldsymbol{a}$ and $\boldsymbol{b}$ be any two actions bounded below but not necessarily above, and let $\{\boldsymbol{a}^i\}$ and $\boldsymbol{b}^j\}$ be corresponding sequences satisfying (3.12-3.15). Suppose $\boldsymbol{a} \succ \boldsymbol{b}$. From (3.12) and Monotone Continuity, with $i$ sufficiently large, $\boldsymbol{a}^i \succ \boldsymbol{b}$; but $\boldsymbol{b} \succ \boldsymbol{b}^j$, by (3.14), so that $\boldsymbol{a}^i \succ \boldsymbol{b}^j$, all $j$. Since $\boldsymbol{a}^i$ and $\boldsymbol{b}^j$ are bounded,

$$E\{U[a^i(s)]\} > E\{U[b^j(s)]\}, \text{ all } j.$$

Let $j$ approach infinity; then $E\{U[a^i(s)]\} \geqq E\{U[b(s)]\}$; from (3.15), $E\{U[a(s)]\} > E\{U[b(s)]\}$.

Conversely, suppose $E\{U[a(s)]\} > E\{U[b(s)]\}$. Then for $i$ sufficiently large,

$$E\{U[a^i(s)]\} > E\{U[b(s)]\},$$

and by (3.15),

$$E\{U[a^i(s)]\} > E\{U[b^j(s)]\}.$$

Since $\boldsymbol{a}^i$ and $\boldsymbol{b}^j$ are bounded actions, and the Expected Utility Theorem has been shown to hold for such actions, $\boldsymbol{a}^i \succ \boldsymbol{b}^j$. By Monotone Continuity, $\boldsymbol{a}^i \succ \boldsymbol{b}$; by (3.14), $\boldsymbol{a} \succ \boldsymbol{b}$.

The Expected Utility Theorem has thus been shown to hold for all actions bounded below. By an exactly parallel argument, its range of applicability can be expected to all pairs of actions.

Not only have we proved the existence of an expected utility function but we have shown the following theorem:

UTILITY BOUNDEDNESS THEOREM. *Any utility function which satisfies the conditions of the Expected Utility Theorem must be bounded both from above and from below.*

## 4. Personal Probability

A particular class of actions of interest are those which yield only two possible consequences. Such an action is uniquely defined by specifying the more preferred of the two consequences, $c^*$, the less preferred, $c_*$, and the event $E$ for which the action yields the consequence $c^*$; it yields $c_*$ on $\tilde{E}$. An action of this form may, for abvious reasons, be termed a *bet* on $E$, with *prizes* $c^*$, $c_*$. (It is assumed that the two consequences are not indifferent to each other; if they were, the action so defined would also be indifferent to both of the consequences, by Dominance, and preference statements about the action would be independent of the set $E$.) To avoid a trivial case we assume that not all consequences are indifferent.

The ordering of all actions implies in particular an ordering of bets. It is reasonable to assert, in particular, that the ordering of bets with given consequences is determined exclusively by beliefs concerning the occurrence of the events bet on. If it is preferable to bet on one event rather than another with given prizes for winning and losing, then the same preference should manifest itself if the prizes are altered, as long as the prize for winning is preferred to that for losing. This conclusion is an obvious implication of the Expected Utility Theorem, for a bet on $E_1$, with prizes $c^*$, $c_*$, is preferred to a bet of $E_2$ with the same prizes if and only if

$$P(E_1)\,U(c^*)+[1-P(E_1)]\,U(c_*)>P(E_2)\,U(c^*)+[1-P(E_2)]\,U(c_*),$$

which is obviously equivalent to the statement $P(E_1)>P(E_2)$, provided $U(c^*)>U(c_*)$. Changing the prizes does not alter the ordering among bets.

Following RAMSEY (1926) and later writers, we drop the assumption of Probabilistic Beliefs and seek to show that it can in fact be derived merely from the assumption that preferences among bets are independent of the prizes plus a more technical assumption. The argument used here is a paraphrase of VILLEGAS (1964), who first showed that the probability distributions obtained are countably and not merely finitely additive.

*Ordering of Events.* If $E_1$ and $E_2$ are events, and $c^*$, $c_*$, $\underline{c}^*$, $\bar{c}_*$ are consequences for which $c^* \succ c_*$, $\bar{c}^* \succ \underline{c}_*$, then the bet on $E_1$ with prizes $c^*$, $c_*$ is preferred to the bet on $E_2$ with the same prizes if and only if the bet on $E_1$ with prizes $\bar{c}^*$, $\underline{c}_*$ is preferred to the bet on $E_2$ with the same prizes.

In view of this assumption, preferences among bets are statements only about the events involved. It is meaningful then to speak of preference or indifference among events, and we use the obvious notation: thus, $E_1 \succ E_2$ means that a bet on $E_1$ is preferred to one on $E_2$ with the same prizes. (The statement $E_1 \succ E_2$ might be read "$E_1$ is more probable than $E_2$", but for sake of uniformity the language of preference rather than that of probability judgment will be used here.)

The assumptions of Dominance and of Monotone Continuity yield interesting implications for the ordering of events. We will have occasion to single out the *universal event*, consisting of all possible states of the world and denoted by $V$, and the *empty event*, consisting of no state of the world and denoted by $\Lambda$. If $c^*$ and $c_*$ are the winning and losing prizes, a bet on $V$ is simply $c^*$ and a bet on $\Lambda$ is $c_*$; since $c^* \succ c_*$,

(4.1) $$V \succ \Lambda .$$

Recall that $E$ is termed a null event if, for all actions $\boldsymbol{a}^1$ and $\boldsymbol{a}^2$, $\boldsymbol{a}^1 \succ \boldsymbol{a}^2$ if and only if $\boldsymbol{a}^1 \succ \boldsymbol{a}^2 | \tilde{E}$. This holds trivially if $E = \Lambda$. A bet on any event $E$ loses, and therefore coincides with a bet on $\Lambda$ if $\tilde{E}$ holds; hence, $E \sim \Lambda | \tilde{E}$ for any event $E$. If, in particular, $E$ is a null event, then $E \sim \Lambda$.

(4.2) A null event is indifferent to the empty event.

(The converse of this statement is also true; see Corollary 5 below).

Dominance implies an important monotony property for preferences among events.

LEMMA 1 (Monotony). *If $E_1$ is disjoint from $E_2$, and $F_1$ from $F_2$, $E_1 \prec F_1$ (respectively, $E_1 \precsim F_1$), and $E_2 \precsim F_2$, then $E_1 \cup E_2 \prec F_1 \cup F_2$ (respectively, $E_1 \cup E_2 \precsim F_1 \cup F_2$).*

*Proof*. First assume $E_2 = F_2$. Then $E_1$ and $F_1$ are both disjoint from $F_2$; if $F_2$ occurs, both lose. Then $E_1 = F_1 | F_2$, and therefore $E_1 \sim F_1 | F_2$. If $E_1 \prec F_1$, suppose $E_1 \succsim F_1 | \tilde{F}_2$; by Dominance, $E_1 \succsim F_1$, contrary to hypothesis. Hence, $E_1 \prec F_1 | F_2$. Further, if $\tilde{F}_2$ were a null event, we would have $E_1 \sim F_1$, again contrary to hypothesis, so that $\tilde{F}_2$ is nonnull. If, on the other hand, it is hypothesized that $E_1 \precsim F_1$, suppose $E_1 \succ F_1 | \tilde{F}_2$; then, by Dominance, either $E_1 \succ F_1$, contrary to hypothesis, or $\tilde{F}_2$ is a null event. Hence, $E_1 \precsim F_1 | \tilde{F}_2$ unless $\tilde{F}_2$ is a null event. Since $E_2 = F_2$ is disjoint from $\tilde{F}_2$, we have trivially $E_1 = E_1 \cup E_2 | \tilde{F}_2$, $F_1 = F_1 \cup F_2 | \tilde{F}_2$. Then $E_1 \cup E_2 \prec F_1 \cup F_2 | \tilde{F}_2$ if $E_1 \prec F_1$, while either $E_1 \cup E_2 \precsim F_1 \cup F_2 | \tilde{F}_2$ or $\tilde{F}_2$ is null if $E_1 \precsim F_1$. Finally, $E_2$ and $F_2$ win on $F_2$, and therefore certainly $E_1 \cup E_2$ and $F_1 \cup F_2$ both win on $F_2$. Then $E_1 \cup E_2 = F_1 \cup F_2 | F_2$. By Dominance, then, $E_1 \cup E_2 \prec F_1 \cup F_2$ if $E_1 \prec F_1$. If $E_1 \precsim F_1$ and $\tilde{F}_2$ is nonnull, Dominance yields that $E_1 \cup E_2 \precsim F_1 \cup F_2$; if $\tilde{F}_2$ is null, the last holds trivially.

Now remove the hypothesis that $E_2 = F_2$. Let

$$E_2' = E_2 - F_1,\ F_1' = F_1 - E_2,\ G = E_2 \cap F_1,$$

where $E - F = \{s | s \in E, s \notin F\}$. Then $E_2' \cap F_1 = \Lambda$, $F_1' \cap E_2 = \Lambda$, $E_2' \cup G = E_2$, $F_1' \cup G = F_1$; also, $E_2' \subset E_2$ and thus $E_2' \cap E_1 = \Lambda$, $F_1' \subset F_1$ and thus $F_1' \cap F_2 = \Lambda$,

$G \subset E_2$ and therefore $E_1 \cap G = \Lambda$, $G \subset F_1$ and therefore $G \cap F_2 = \Lambda$. By construction, $E_2' \cap G = F_1' \cap G = \Lambda$. Then by use of the lemma for the special case, $E_2 = F_2$, already established,

$$E_1 \cup E_2' \prec F_1 \cup E_2' = F_1' \cup G \cup E_2' = F_1' \cup E_2 \precsim F_1' \cup F_2 \quad \text{if} \quad E_1 \prec F_1,$$

$$E_1 \cup E_2' \precsim F_1' \cup F_2 \text{ if } E_1 \precsim F_1.$$

But

$$(E_1 \cup E_2') \cap G = (E_1 \cap G) \cup (E_2' \cap G) = \Lambda, \; (F_1' \cup F_2) \cap G = \Lambda,$$

so that

$$E_1 \cup E_2 = E_1 \cup E_2' \cup G \prec F_1' \cup F_2 \cup G = (F_1' \cup G) \cup F_2 = F_1 \cup F_2 \text{ if } E_1 \prec F_1$$

$$E_1 \cup E_2 \precsim F_1 \cup F_2 \quad \text{if} \quad E_1 \precsim E_2.$$

COROLLARY 1 (Subtraction). *If $E_1$ is disjoint from $E_2$ and $F_1$ from $F_2$, $E_1 \sim F_1$ and $E_1 \cup E_2 \sim F_1 \cup F_2$, then $E_2 \sim F_2$.*

*Proof.* Suppose $E_2 \prec F_2$. Then, by Lemma 1 (with subscripts 1 and 2 interchanged), $E_1 \cup E_2 \prec F_1 \cup F_2$, contrary to hypothesis. Similarly, $E_2 \succ F_2$ leads to a contradiction.

COROLLARY 2. *If $E \subset F$, then $E \precsim F$.*

*Proof.* Let $E_1 = F_1 = E$, $E_2 = \Lambda$, $F_2 = F - E$. By Dominance, $\Lambda \precsim F - E$; by Lemma 1, $E = E \cup \Lambda = E_1 \cup E_2 \precsim F_1 \cup F_2 = E \cup (F - E) = F$.

A sequence of events $\{E_i\}$ is said to be *monotone increasing (decreasing)* if $E_i \subset E_{i+1}$, all $i$ ($E_{i+1} \subset E_i$, all $i$). A sequence is said to be *monotone* if it is either monotone increasing or monotone decreasing. For a monotone increasing sequence, define

$$\lim E_i = \bigcup_{i=1}^{\infty} E_i,$$

and for a monotone decreasing sequence, define

$$\lim E_i = \bigcap_{i=1}^{\infty} E_i.$$

In brief, the statement $\lim E_i = E$ means that either (*a*) $E_i \subset E$, all $i$, $\{E - E_i\}$ is a vanishing sequence, or (b) $E \subset E_i$, all $i$, $\{E_i - E\}$ is a vanishing sequence. In either case, a bet on $E_i$ is an action which differs from a bet on $E$ only on an element of a vanishing sequence. The assumption of Monotone Continuity then immediately yields a specialization to the case of events.

LEMMA 2 (Monotone Continuity for Events). *If* lim $E_i = E$, *then* $E \succ F$ *implies that* $E_i \succ F$ *for i sufficiently large and* $F \succ E$ *implies that* $F \succ E_i$ *for i sufficiently large.*

COROLLARY 3. *If lim* $E_i = E$, *lim* $F_i = F$ *and* $E_i \precsim F_i$, *all i, then* $E \precsim F$.

*Proof.* Suppose $E \succ F$. By Lemma 2, $E_i \succ F$ for all $i > I$, for suitably chosen $I$. For any given $i > I$, it again follows from Lemma 2 that $E_i \succ F_j$ for $j > J_i$. A contradiction to the hypothesis is achieved if $E_k \succ F_k$, some $k$. First suppose $\{E_i\}$ monotone increasing. Choose $j$ so that $E_i \succ F_j$, $i < j$. But by Corollary 2, $E_j \succsim E_i$ when $E\{_i\}$ is monotone increasing so that we can choose $k = j$. By a parallel argument, the contradiction can also be found if $\{F_i\}$ is monotone decreasing. Suppose now $\{E_i\}$ monotone decreasing, $\{F_i\}$ monotone increasing. Let $k = \min(i, j)$. Then Corollary 2 assures that $E_k \succsim E_i$, $F_j \succsim F_k$; then from $E_i \succ F_j$, some $i$ and $j$, follows $E_k \succ F_k$, a contradiction to the hypothesis.

A particularly interesting type of monotone decreasing sequence is that for which the successor, $E_{i+1}$, to any given member of the sequence, $E_i$, is obtained by partitioning $E_i$ into two subevents and choosing for $E_{i+1}$ one subevent which is not preferred to the other. As might be expected, the limit of such a sequence is indifferent to the empty event.

COROLLARY 4. *If* $\{E_i\}$ *is monotone decreasing, and* $E_{i+1} \precsim E_i - E_{i+1}$ *for all i, then lim* $E_i \sim \Lambda$.

*Proof.*

$$\lim E_i = \bigcap_i E_i \subset E_{j+1} \qquad E_j - E_{j+1} \subset \bigcup_{i=j}^{\infty} (E_i - E_{i+1}),$$

for any $j$. Since $E \subset F$ implies $E \precsim F$ by Corollary 2,

$$\lim E_i \precsim \bigcup_{i=j}^{\infty} (E_i - E_{i+1}) \text{ for all } j. \tag{4.3}$$

But since the events $E_i - E_{i+1}$ are disjoint, the right-hand expression in (4.3) is a vanishing sequence. If lim $E_i \succ \Lambda$, (4.3) could not hold for $j$ sufficiently large.

The theorem sought for is one which assigns numbers to events so as to be an indicator of preferences and also to satisfy the assumptions of probability theory. A (countably additive) *probability measure* is a real-valued function of events, $P(E)$, with the following properties:

$$P(E) \geqq 0, \text{ all } E; \; P(V) = 1; \tag{4.4}$$

(4.5) if the events in the sequence $\{E_i\}$ are mutually disjoint, then

$$P\left(\bigcup_{i=1}^{\infty} E_i\right) = \sum_{i=1}^{\infty} P(E_i).$$

If $E_i = \Lambda$ for all $i$, then $\bigcup_{i=1}^{\infty} E_i = \Lambda$, so that (4.5) implies

$$P(\Lambda) = \sum_{i=1}^{\infty} P(\Lambda),$$

which is possible only if $P(\Lambda) = 0$. Now if we set $E_i = \Lambda$ for $i > 2$ in (4.4), $\bigcup_{i=1} E_i = E_1 \cup E_2$, and $P(E_i) = 0$ for $i > 2$, so that (4.5) implies the property of finite additivity,

(4.6) if $E_1$ and $E_2$ are disjoint, then $P(E_1 \cup E_2) = P(E_1) + P(E_2)$.

A real-valued function on events satisfying (4.4) and (4.6) is termed a *finitely additive probability measure*. Since $\Lambda = \Lambda \cup \Lambda$, $P(\Lambda) = P(\Lambda) + P(\Lambda)$ or $P(\Lambda) = 0$. Also, for any event $E$, $V = E \cup \tilde{E}$, so that $1 = P(V) = P(E \cup \tilde{E})$ $= P(E) + P(\tilde{E})$, $P(E) \geqq 0$, from (4.6) and (4.4).

(4.7) If $P$ is a finitely-additive probability measure, $1 \geqq P(E)$ for all events $E$, and $P(\Lambda) = 0$.

A finitely- or countably-additive probability measure will be said to *agree* with a given ordering of events if $E \succ F$ if and only if $P(E) > P(F)$. Under the assumptions already made, particularly that of Monotone Continuity, we can show

LEMMA 3. *A finitely-additive probability measure which agrees with the ordering of events is countably additive.*

*Proof.* By induction, (4.6) implies that if the events $E_i (i = 1, \ldots, n)$ are mutually disjoint, then

$$P\left(\bigcup_{i=1}^{n} E_i\right) = \sum_{i=1}^{n} P(E_i).$$

Now let the events in the infinite sequence $\{E_i\}$ be mutually disjoint. We can write

$$\bigcup_{i=1}^{\infty} E_i = \bigcup_{i=1}^{j} E_i \cup \bigcup_{i=j+1}^{\infty} E_i.$$

The right-hand side is a finite union of mutually disjoint events, so that

$$(4.8) \qquad P\left(\bigcup_{i=1}^{\infty} E_i\right) = \sum_{i=1}^{j} P(E_i) + P\left(\bigcup_{i=j+1}^{\infty} E_i\right).$$

From (4.7) and (4.4),

$$P\left(\bigcup_{i=1}^{\infty} E_i\right) \leqq 1, \; P\left(\bigcup_{i=j+1}^{\infty} E_i\right) \geqq 0,$$

so that, from (4.8),

$$\sum_{i=1}^{j} P(E_i) \leqq 1, \text{ all } j.$$

Since $P(E_i) \geqq 0$, all $i$, $\sum_{i=1}^{j} P(E_i)$ converges as $j$ approaches infinity, and therefore $P(E_i) \to 0$ or, for any $\varepsilon$, $P(E_i) < \varepsilon$ for all $i$ sufficiently large. There are two possibilities: (a) $0 < P(E_k) < \varepsilon$ for some $k$, or (b) $P(E_i) = 0$ for all $i$ sufficiently large.

(a) Since the probability measure $P$ agrees with the ordering, $E_k \succ \Lambda$. The sequence $\{\bigcup_{i=j+1}^{\infty} E_i\}$ is a vanishing sequence (i.e., approaching $\Lambda$), so that, for all $j$ sufficiently large, $E_k > \bigcup_{i=j+1}^{\infty} E_i$, and therefore

$$P\left(\bigcup_{i=j+1}^{\infty} E_i\right) < P(E_k) < \varepsilon.$$

Countable additivity (4.5) follows by letting $j$ approach infinity in (4.8).

(b) Choose $j$ so that $P(E_i) = 0$ for all $i > j$. Then $E_i \sim \Lambda$ for $i > j$. By Corollary 3, $\bigcup_{i=j+1} E_i \sim \bigcup_{i=j+1} \Lambda = \Lambda$, so that

$$P\left(\bigcup_{i=j+1}^{\infty} E_i\right) = P(\Lambda) = 0 = \sum_{i=j+1}^{\infty} P(E_i),$$

and countable additivity again follows from (4.8).

In view of Lemma 3, it suffices to establish the existence of a finitely-additive probability measure agreeing with the ordering.

In the assumption of Probabilistic Beliefs, it was postulated that the probability measure be atomless. We now introduce an assumption on the ordering of events which has the same effect but does not presuppose the existence of a probability measure.

*Atomlessness.* If $E \succ \Lambda$, then there is a subset $E_1$ of $E$ such that $E \succ E_1 \succ \Lambda$.

To clarify the exposition, a stronger assumption will be made in this section:

*Equidivisibility*. Any event $E$ can be partitioned into disjoint subevents $E_1$, $E_2$, where $E_1 \cup E_2 = E$ and $E_1 \sim E_2$.

To see that Equidivisibility implies Atomlessness, suppose $E \succ \Lambda$. Since $\Lambda \subset E_1 \subset E$, $E \gtrsim E_1 \gtrsim \Lambda$. Suppose $E_1 \sim \Lambda$. Then $E_2 \sim \Lambda$ and, by Lemma 1, $E = E_1 \cup E_2 \sim \Lambda \cup \Lambda = \Lambda$, a contradiction. Clearly, $E = E_1|E_1$ since $E_1 \subset E$, and $E = E_1|\tilde{E}$ since both lose there; also, $E \succ E_1|E_2$ since $E$ wins and $E_1$ loses. By Dominance, $E \succ E_1$ unless $E_2$ is a null event, and therefore indifferent to $\Lambda$ by (4.2). But then $E_1 \sim \Lambda$, which has already been seen to lead to a contradiction. Hence, $E \succ E_1 \succ \Lambda$.

The converse implication, that Atomlessness implies Equidivisibility, requires relatively advanced tools, and its proof is deferred to Section 6 below.

By Equidivisibility, the universal event can be divided into two mutually indifferent disjoint events, each of them can be similarly subdivided, and so forth. Thus, there is a sequence of partitions of the universal event, where the *nth* partition, say $P_n$, consists of $2^n$ mutually indifferent events, and $P_{n+1}$ is derived from $P_n$ by splitting each member of the latter into two mutually indifferent events. Intuitively, it is reasonable to ascribe the probability $1/2^n$ to any members of $P_n$ and therefore the probability $m/2^n$ to any union of $m$ members of $P_n$ and the same probability to any event indifferent to a union of $m$ members of $P_n$. Any event not assigned a probability by this process can be assigned one as the limit of a suitable sequence of approximations.

More formally, note that it can be deduced from Lemma 1, by induction, that all unions of $m$ members of $P_n$ are indifferent to each other. For any event $E$, let $m_n(E)$ be the largest $m$ such that $E$ is preferred or indifferent to a union of $m$ members of $P_n$. Let $S_n$ be a union of $m_n$ members of $P_n$. It is also a union of $2m_n$ members of $P_{n+1}$ so that, by definition of $m_{n+1}$, $m_{n+1} \geqq 2m_n$, and therefore $m_{n+1}/2^{n+1} \geqq m_n/2^n$. Since also $m_n \leqq 2^n$, all $n$, the sequence $\{m_n/2^n\}$ is monotone increasing and bounded from above. Define

$$P(E) = \lim_{n \to \infty} m_n(E)/2^n. \tag{4.9}$$

It is to be shown that $P(E)$ is a finitely additive probability measure and agrees with the given ordering or events; it will then be a probability measure by Lemma 3.

Since $V$ is the union of all members of $P_n$, $m_n(V) = 2^n$, all $n$, and therefore $P(V) = 1$; thus, (4.4) holds.

Let $E=E_1\cup E_2$, where $E_1$ and $E_2$ are disjoint. Suppose $m_n(E_1)+m_n(E_2)\geqq 2^n$. Let $m_n'=2^n-m_n(E_1)$; then $m_n'\leqq m_n(E_2)$. Let $S_n$ be a union of $m_n(E_1)$ members of $P_n$; $\tilde{S}_n$ is the union of $m_n'$ members of $P_n$. Then $E_1\gtrsim S_n$ and $E_2\gtrsim\tilde{S}_n$, so that, by Lemma 1, $E\gtrsim V$. Obviously, then, $E\sim V$, which is possible only if $E_1\sim S_n$ and $E_2\sim\tilde{S}_n$. In this case, $P(E_1)=m_n(E_1)/2^n$, $P(E_2)=m_n'/2^n=m_n(E_2)/2^n$, and $P(E)=1=P(E_1)+P(E_2)$, so that (4.5) holds.

Now suppose that $m_n(E_1)+m_n(E_2)<2^n$. Let $S_n(E_1)$, $S_n(E_2)$ be unions of $m_n(E_1)$, $m_n(E_2)$ members of $P_n$, respectively, so chosen that $S_n(E_1)\cap S_n(E_2)=\Lambda$. Then, by Lemma 1, $E\gtrsim S_n(E_1)\cup S_n(E_2)$, so that $m_n(E)\geqq m_n(E_1)+m_n(E_2)$. Suppose

$$m_n(E)\geqq m_n(E_1)+m_n(E_2)+2\,. \tag{4.10}$$

Let $T_n(E_1)$ be a union of $m_n(E_1)+1$ members of $P_n$, $T_n(E_2)$ a union of $m_n(E_2)+1$ members of $P_n$, so chosen that $T_n(E_1)\cap T_n(E_2)=\Lambda$. Then $T_n(E_1)\cup T_n(E_2)$ has $m_n(E_1)+m_n(E_2)+2$ members, so that from the definition of $m_n(E)$ and the assumed inequality (4.10) $E\gtrsim T_n(E_1)\cup T_n(E_2)$. On the other hand, from the definitions of $m_n(E_1)$, $m_n(E_2)$, we must have $T_n(E_1)\succ E_1$, $T_n(E_2)\succ E_2$ and, by Lemma 1, $T_n(E_1)\cup T_n(E_2)\succ E_1\cup E_2=E$. The inequality (4.10) leads to a contradiction.

$$m_n(E_1)+m_n(E_2)\leqq m_n(E)\leqq m_n(E_1)+m_n(E_2)+1\,.$$

If all terms in this inequality are divided by $2^n$ and we let $n$ approach infinity, (4.6) is deduced.

It remains then to show that $P(E)$ agrees with the ordering. If $P(E_1)>P(E_2)$, then $m_n(E_1)>m_n(E_2)$ for some $n$. If $S$ is the union of $m_n(E_1)$ members of the partition $P_n$, then $E_1\gtrsim S\succ E_2$, by definition of $m_n$. It remains to establish the converse implication: that $P(E_1)=P(E_2)$ implies $E_1\sim E_2$. First consider the special case where $E_2=\Lambda$; then we seek to show that $P(E)=0$ implies $E\sim\Lambda$. In this case, $m_n=0$ for all $n$. If $E_n$ is any member of $P_n$, $E_n\succ E$. We can choose $E_{n+1}$ to be one of the two mutually indifferent subevents of $E_n$ in $P_{n+1}$. Then $E_{n+1}\subset E_n$, and $E_{n+1}\sim E_n-E_{n+1}$. By Corollary 4, $\lim E_n\sim\Lambda$. By Corollary 3, $\lim E_n\gtrsim E$; hence, $E\sim\Lambda$.

Now consider the general case where $P(E_1)=P(E_2)$. Assume $E_1\lesssim E_2$. Then $m_n(E_2)\geqq m_n(E_1)$, all $n$. Let $S_n$ be a union of $m_n(E_1)$ members of $P_n$, $T_n$ a union of $m_n(E_2)+1$ members of $P_n$. Then $S_n\lesssim E_1$, $E_2\prec T_n$. Further, we can choose $S_n$, $T_n$, so that $\{S_n\}$ is an increasing sequence, $\{T_n\}$ a decreasing sequence, and $S_n\subset T_n$ for all $n$. To see this, suppose it has already been carried out up to stage $n$. $T_n-S_n$ is the union of one or more members of $P_n$.

Also, $T_n$ is the union of $2[m_n(E_2)+1]$ members of $P_{n+1}$; then $m_{n+1}(E_2)< 2[m_n(E_2)+1]$, so that $m_{n+1}(E_2)=2m_n(E_2)$ or $=2m_n(E_2)+1$. In the latter case, let $T_{n+1}=T_n$; in the former, subtract from $T_n$ one member of $P_{n+1}$ entirely contained in $T_n-S_n$. In either case, $T_{n+1}-S_n$ is the union of one or more members of $P_{n+1}$. Similarly, $m_{n+1}(E_1)=2m_n(E_1)$ or $=2m_n(E_1)+1$. In the first case, let $S_{n+1}=S_n$; in the second, add to $S_n$ one member of $P_{n+1}$ entirely contained in $T_{n+1}-S_n$.

The sequences $\{S_n\}$ and $\{T_n\}$ converge to limits $S$ and $T$ respectively, with $S\subset T$. Since $S_n\lesssim E_1$, $S\lesssim E_1$; similarly, $E_2\lesssim T$. Also

$$P(S_n)=m_n(E_1)/2^n.$$

Since $S_n\subset S_{n+1}$, $S_{n+1}=S_n\cup(S_{n+1}-S_n)$, with the latter two sets disjoint;

$$P(S_{n+1}-S_n)=P(S_{n+1})-P(S_n).$$

$$S=\bigcup_{i=1}^{\infty} S_n=S_1\cup\bigcup_{i=1}^{\infty}(S_{i+1}-S_i)=S_1\cup\bigcup_{i=1}^{j}(S_{i+1}-S_i)+\bigcup_{i=j+1}^{\infty}(S_{i+1}-S_i)$$

so that, by finite additivity,

$$\begin{aligned} P(S) &= P(S_1)+\sum_{i=1}^{j}P(S_{i+1}-S_i)+P\left[\bigcup_{i=j+1}^{\infty}(S_{i+1}-S_i)\right] \\ &\geqq P(S_1)+\sum_{i=1}^{j}[P(S_{i+1})-P(S_i)] \\ &= P(S_{j+1}), \end{aligned}$$

and, since $\{P(S_{j+1})\}$ is a monotone increasing, bounded sequence of real numbers,

$$P(S)\geqq \lim P(S_n)=P(E_1).$$

Similarly, since $P(T_n)=[m_n(E_2)+1]/2^n$ and $V-T=\bigcup_{i=1}^{\infty}(V-T_i)$, it can be deduced that $P(V-T)\geqq \lim P(V-T_n)$, and therefore $P(T)\leqq \lim P(T_n)= P(E_2)$. Since $S\subset T$, $0\leqq P(T-S)=P(T)-P(S)\leqq \lim P(T_n)-\lim P(S_n)= P(E_2)-P(E_1)=0$ by assumption. Then, as just shown, $T-S\sim\Lambda$. Since $S\lesssim E_1$, $T=S\cup(T-S)\lesssim E_1\cup\Lambda=E_1$. Since $T\gtrsim E_2\gtrsim E_1$, it must be that $E_1\sim E_2$.

Personal Probability Theorem. *Under the assumptions of Ordering, Monotone Continuity, Conditional Preference, Ordering of Events, and Equidivisibility, there is a probability measure, $P(E)$, defined over events* *such that for any two events, $E_1$ and $E_2$, a bet on $E_1$ is preferred to a bet on $E_2$ with the same prizes if and only is $P(E_1) > P(E_2)$.*

COROLLARY 5. *An event is null if and only if its probability is zero.*

*Proof.* For any event $E$, it follows by definition and the Ordering of Events that $E = \Lambda|\tilde{E}$, $E \succ \Lambda|E$; by Dominance, if $E$ is nonnull, then $E \succ \Lambda$, and therefore $E \sim \Lambda$ implies $E$ null. The converse has already been stated as (4.2) above. But by the theorem, $E \sim \Lambda$ if and only if $P(E) = P(\Lambda) = 0$.

## 5. Probabilistic Beliefs

It remains to prove that the probabilities which reproduce the ordering of events also suffice to permit the representation of the ordering of actions in general (not merely bets) by expected utilities. In view of the analysis of Section 3, it suffices to show that the assumption of Probabilistic Beliefs follows from the assumptions used in the hypothesis of the Personal Probability Theorem; in fact, from the Remark following the assumption of Probabilistic Beliefs, it suffices to prove the

THEOREM OF PROBABILISTIC BELIEFS. *If* $\boldsymbol{a}$ *and* $\boldsymbol{b}$ *are actions which yield as possible consequences* $c_i (i = 1, \dots, n)$ *and if* $P[a(s) = c_i] = P[b(s) = c_i]$ $(i = 1, \dots, n)$, *then* $\boldsymbol{a} \sim \boldsymbol{b}$.

*Proof.* We will establish the following apparently more general theorem:

(5.1) If $c_i$ $(i = 1, \dots, n)$ are all the consequences yielded by $\boldsymbol{a}$ or $\boldsymbol{b}$ for $s \in E$, and $P[a(s) = c_i|E] = P[b(s) = c_i|E]$ for all $i$, then $\boldsymbol{a} \sim \boldsymbol{b}|E$, provided $P(E) > 0$.

First, note that if the theorem holds for any $n$, then (5.1) holds for that $n$. Suppose $\boldsymbol{a}$, $\boldsymbol{b}$ have the properties hypothesized in (5.1). Define actions $\boldsymbol{a}^*$, $\boldsymbol{b}^*$ as follows: $\boldsymbol{a}^*(s) = a(s)$, $b^*(s) = b(s)$ for $s \in E$; $a^*(s) = b^*(s) = c_1$ for $s \in \tilde{E}$. Then the conclusion, $\boldsymbol{a} \sim \boldsymbol{b}|E$, is equivalent to the statement, $\boldsymbol{a}^* \sim \boldsymbol{b}^*|E$, by Conditional Preference, and it suffices to establish the latter. Since $P(E) > 0$, $E$ is nonnull by Corollary 5 of Section 4. Since $\boldsymbol{a}^* = \boldsymbol{b}^*|\tilde{E}$, $\boldsymbol{a}^* \succ \boldsymbol{b}^*|E$ would imply $\boldsymbol{a}^* \succ \boldsymbol{b}^*$, and similarly $\boldsymbol{a}^* \prec \boldsymbol{b}^*|E$ would imply $\boldsymbol{a}^* \prec \boldsymbol{b}^*$. Therefore, $\boldsymbol{a}^* \sim \boldsymbol{b}^*$ implies that $\boldsymbol{a}^* \sim \boldsymbol{b}^*|E$. But

$$P[a^*(s) = c_i] = P[a^*(s) = c_i|E]\,P(E) + P[a^*(s) = c_i|\tilde{E}]\,P(\tilde{E}).$$

$P[a^*(s) = c_i|E] = P[a(s) = c_i|E]$; $P[a^*(s) = c_1|\tilde{E}] = 1$, $P[a^*(s) = c_i|\tilde{E}] = 0$ for

$i>1$. Similar remarks apply to $\boldsymbol{b}^*$ and $\boldsymbol{b}$. Then, clearly

$$P[a^*(s)=c_i] = P[b^*(s)=c_i] \qquad (i=1, \ldots, n),$$

so that

(5.2) If the theorem holds for any $n$, so does (5.1).

Next observe that the Personal Probability Theorem implies the Theorem of Probabilistic Beliefs for the case $n=2$; for if $c_1 \sim c_2$, the conclusion holds by Dominance, while if $c_1$ is not indifferent to $c_2$ and $c^*$ is the more preferred of the two, actions $\boldsymbol{a}$ and $\boldsymbol{b}$ are bets on the sets $\{s|a(s)=c^*\}$ and $\{s|b(s)=c^*\}$, respectively; since these are equally probable by hypothesis, the actions are indifferent by the Personal Probability Theorem.

Assume, then, the Theorem, and therefore (5.1) valid for 2 and $n-1$ consequences. Let

$$F=\{s|a(s)\neq c_n,\ b(s)=c_n\},\ G=\{s|a(s)=c_n,\ b(s)\neq c_n\},$$

$$F_i=\{s|a(s)=c_i,\ b(s)=c_n\}.$$

Note that the sets $F_i$ are disjoint and $F=\bigcup_{i=1}^{n-1} F_i$.

$$\{s|a(s)=c_n\} = G\cup\{s|a(s)=c_n,\ b(s)=c_n\},$$

$$\{s|b(s)=c_n\} = F\cup\{s|a(s)=c_n,\ b(s)=c_n\}.$$

The right-hand sides of these two expressions are unions of disjoint events, while the left-hand sides have the same probabilities, by hypothesis. Then

$$P(G)+P[a(s)=c_n, b(s)=c_n] = P(F)+P[a(s)=c_n, b(s)=c_n],$$

or

$$P(G)=P(F)=\sum_{i=1}^{n-1} P(F_i).$$

Then we can partition $G$ into mutually disjoint subevents, $G_i$ $(i=1, \ldots, n-1)$ such that $P(G_i)=P(F_i)$ $(i=1, \ldots, n-1)$. To see this, apply Equidivisibility $n$ successive times to $G$ so that $G$ is expressed as the sum of $2^m$ equally probable events. For any fixed $i$, choose $p_{im}$ as the largest integer $p$ for which $p/2^m \leqq P(F_i)/P(F)$. Let $S_{im}$ be the union of $p_{im}$ events in this partition; choose them in particular so that the different unions, $S_{im}$, for fixed $m$, are disjoint and also so that $S_{im}\subset S_{i\,m+1}$. Let $G_i=\lim_{m\to\infty} S_{im}$; then, clearly $G_i\subset G$, $P(G_i)=P(F_i)$. The union of the events $G_i$ can then differ from $G$ by at most a set of probability zero, and this can be added to one of the $G_i$ 's.

Now define a finite sequence of actions, $a^i$ $(i=1, \ldots, n)$, as follows:

$$(5.3)\qquad \boldsymbol{a}^1 = \boldsymbol{a}$$

$$a^{i+1}(s) = \begin{cases} c_n & \text{for } s \in F_i \\ c_i & \text{for } s \in G_i, \\ a^i(s) & \text{for all other } s. \end{cases}$$

Since $G$ and $F$ are disjoint by definition, $G_i$ and $F_j$ are disjoint for all $i$, $j \leqq n-1$. By induction, it is easily seen that

$$(5.4)\qquad a^i(s) = \begin{cases} c_j \text{ for } s \in F_j & (\text{all } j \geqq i), \\ c_n \text{ for } s \in G_j & (\text{all } j \geqq i). \end{cases}$$

We need to prove that

$$(5.5)\qquad \boldsymbol{a}^i \sim \boldsymbol{a}^{i+1}.$$

From (5.3), $a^{i+1}(s) = a^i(s)$ for $s \notin G_i \cup F_i$. If $G_i \cup F_i$ is null, then (5.5) holds. Otherwise, to prove (5.5) it suffices to show that

$$(5.6)\qquad \boldsymbol{a}^i \sim \boldsymbol{a}^{i+1} | G_i \cup F_i.$$

But from (5.3) and (5.4) with $j=i$, both $\boldsymbol{a}^i$ and $\boldsymbol{a}^{i+1}$ take on only the two values $c_i$ and $c_n$ on $F_i \cup G_i$; further, since $P(F_i) = P(G_i)$ and $P(G_i \cup F_i) > 0$ by Corollary 5, Section 4,

$P(F_i|F_i \cup G_i) = P(G_i|F_i \cup G_i)$ so that $P[a^{i+1}(s) = c_i|F_i \cup G_i]$
$= P[a^i(s) = c_i|F_i \cup G_i]$ and $P[a^{i+1}(s) = c_n|F_i \cup G_i] = P[a^i(s) = c_n|F_i \cup G_i]$.

Since (5.1) holds with $n=2$, (5.6) holds, and therefore (5.5).

The same calculations also show immediately that

$$(5.7)\qquad P[a^{i+1}(s) = c_j] = P[a^i(s) = c_j], \text{ all } j.$$

From (5.5), it follows by induction that $\boldsymbol{a}^1 \sim \boldsymbol{a}^n$; since $\boldsymbol{a}^1 = \boldsymbol{a}$, it remains to show that $\boldsymbol{a}^n \sim \boldsymbol{b}$, in which case the theorem has been shown to hold for $n$ consequences.

From (5.7), it follows by induction that

$$P[a^1(s) = c_j] = P[a^n(s) = c_j], \text{ all } j.$$

Since $\boldsymbol{a}^1 = \boldsymbol{a}$, it follows from the hypothesis that $\boldsymbol{a}$ and $\boldsymbol{b}$ yield the same probability distribution of consequences that

$$P[a^n(s)=c_j]=P[b(s)=c_j],\ \text{all } j. \tag{5.8}$$

From (5.3), it follows by induction that

$a^i(s)=c_n$ if and only if either $a(s)=b(s)=c_n$ or

$$s\in \bigcup_{j=1}^{i-1} F_j \cup \bigcup_{j=i}^{n-1} G_j.$$

In particular, let $i=n$; then $a^n(s)=c_n$ if and only if either $a(s)=b(s)=c_n$ or $s\in \bigcup_{j=1}^{n-1} F_j=F$. From the definition of $F$,

$$a^n(s)=c_n \text{ if and only if } b(s)=c_n. \tag{5.9}$$

If $b(s)=c_n$ with probability 1, then the set $\{s|b(s)\neq c_n\}$ is a null set, and $\boldsymbol{a}^n\sim \boldsymbol{b}$, trivially. Otherwise, it follows immediately from (5.8) and (5.9) that

$$P[a^n(s)=c_j|b(s)\neq c_n]=P[b(s)=c_j|b(s)\neq c_n],\ \text{all } j<n.$$

But from (5.9), actions $\boldsymbol{a}^n$ and $\boldsymbol{b}$ take only the $n-1$ consequences $c_j$ $(j<n)$ on the set $\{s|b(s)\neq c_n\}$; by (5.1), for $n-1$ consequences, $\boldsymbol{a}^n\sim \boldsymbol{b}|b(s)\neq c_n$. Since $a^n=b|b(s)=c_n$ by (5.9), $\boldsymbol{a}^n\sim \boldsymbol{b}$ by Dominance, and the theorem has been demonstrated.

## 6. Atomlessness Implies Equidivisibility[5]

It will now be shown, as promised in Section 4, that the assumption of Atomlessness implies that of Equidivisibility in the presence of the other assumptions. The proof is essentially that of VILLEGAS (1964). First, two implications of Atomlessness are developed.

LEMMA 1. *If* $E\succ\Lambda$, *there is a monotone decreasing sequence* $\{E_i\}$ *such that* $E_i\subset E$, $E_i\succ\Lambda$, *for all* $i$, $\lim E_i\sim\Lambda$.

*Proof.* Let $E_1=E$. If $E_i$ has been defined and $E_i\succ\Lambda$, Atomlessness permits us to choose $E'_{i+1}$ so that $E'_{i+1}\subset E_i$, $E_i\succ E'_{i+1}\succ\Lambda$. If $E_i-E'_{i+1}\sim\Lambda$, then $E_i\sim E'_{i+1}$ by Monotony, a contradiction; hence $E_i-E'_{i+1}\succ\Lambda$. Let $E_{i+1}=E'_{i+1}$ if $E'_{i+1}\precsim E_i-E'_{i+1}$ and $E_{i+1}=E_i-E'_{i+1}$ otherwise. Then $E_{i+1}\succ\Lambda$, $E_{i+1}\precsim E_i-E_{i+1}$. By Corollary 4, Section 4, $\lim E_i\sim\Lambda$.

LEMMA 2. *Any family of mutually disjoint events, each preferred to the empty event, must be finite or denumerably infinite.*

[5] I am indebted to H.L. Royden for a very helpful discussion relative to this section.

*Proof.* Let $E=V$ in Lemma 1, and construct the sequence $\{E_i\}$, with $E_i \succ \Lambda$, all $i$, $\lim E_i \sim \Lambda$. If any event is preferred to $\Lambda$, then it is preferred to $E_i$ for $i$ sufficiently large (Lemma 2, Section 4). Hence, it suffices for the proof of the lemma to show that for any given $E_i$ there are at most finitely many events in the given family which are preferred to $E_i$.

Suppose not. Then for some $i$ there is a sequence $\{F_j\}$ such that $F_j \succ E_i$, all $j$, and the sets $F_j$ are disjoint. Let $G_n = \bigcup_{j=n}^{\infty} F_j$; then $F_j \subset G_j$ so that $G_j \succ E_i$, all $j$. But the sequence $\{G_n\}$ is vanishing. By Lemma 2, Section 4, if $E_i \succ \Lambda$, then $G_j \prec E_i$, some $j$, a contradiction.

To prove that Atomlessness implies Equidivisibility, it appears necessary to appeal to one of a group of theorems in set theory closely related to the axiom of choice; typical examples are the Hausdorff maximal principle, Zorn's lemma, or the proposition that every set can be well ordered. For an excellent brief exposition, see KELLEY (1955, pp. 31-36). The particular theorem which seems simplest to use here is a lemma due to Tukey. A family of sets is said to be of *finite character* if a necessary and sufficient condition for a set to belong to the family is that every finite subset belongs to the family. A set is said to be *maximal* in a family if it belongs to the family and is not a proper subset of any member of the family.

*Tukey's Lemma.* Each family of finite character has a maximal set.

In what follows, we start with a fixed event $E$, where $E \succ \Lambda$. We seek to construct $E_1 \subset E$ so that $E_1 \sim E - E_1$. In what follows, all events to be considered are subevents of $E$. An event $F$ will be termed *minor* if $F \precsim E - F$. Tukey's lemma will be applied to a family of collections of events. Specifically, the family consists of all collections of events such that (a) each event is preferred to the null event; (b) the events in the collection are mutually disjoint; and (c) the union of all the events in any finite subcollection is a minor event. This family is obviously of finite character, so there is a maximal collection $K$ in the family.

Since $K$ satisfies (a) and (b), it can have at most denumerably many members by Lemma 2. Let the events in $K$ then be represented as the sequence $\{F_i\}$. Then by (c),

$$\bigcup_{i=1}^{n} F_i \precsim E - \bigcup_{i=1}^{n} F_i, \text{ all } n.$$

The left-hand side is a monotone increasing sequence, the right-hand side monotone decreasing; by Corollary 3, Section 4,

$$E_1 \precsim E - E_1, \tag{6.1}$$

where $E_1$ is the union of all events in $K$.

From (6.1), $E - E_1 \succ \Lambda$ (otherwise $E \sim \Lambda$). By Lemma 1 there is a sequence $\{G_i\}$, with $G_i \subset E - E_1$, $G_i \succ \Lambda$, lim $G_i \sim \Lambda$. Then $G_i$ is disjoint from any event in $K$. Let $K_i$ be the collection of events consisting of $G_i$ and all members of $K$. Then $K_i$ properly includes $K$ and satisfies conditions (a) and (b) above. Since $K$ is maximal in the family defined by (a), (b), and (c), $K_i$ must violate (c). There is a finite subcollection of $K_i$ whose union is preferred to its complement with respect to $E$. But the union of all events in $K_i$ certainly includes the union of any finite subcollection, and the complement of the larger set is included in the complement of the smaller, so that the union of events in $K_i$ is preferred to its complement. The union of events in $K_i$ is clearly $E_1 \cup G_i$.

$$E_1 \cup G_i \succ E - (E_1 \cup G_i), \text{ all } i.$$

The sequences on the two sides are both monotone; by taking limits we have

$$E_1 \succsim E - E_1,$$

which, together with (6.1), establishes Equidivisibility, as desired.

## References

BERNOULLI, D. (1738), "Specimen Theoriae Novae de Mensura Sortis," *Commentarii Academiae Scientiarum Imperialis Petropolitanae 5*, 175-192. English translation by L. Sommer (1954), "Exposition of a New Theory on the Measurement of Risk," *Econometrica*, *22*, 23-26.

DEBREU, G. (1960, "Topological Methods in Cardinal Utility Theory," Chapter 2 in K. J. ARROW, S. KARLIN, and P. SUPPES (eds.), *Mathematical Methods in the Social Sciences*, Stanford University Press, Stanford, pp. 16-26.

DE FINETTI, B. (1937), "La prévision : ses lois logiques, ses sources subjectives," *Annales de l'Institut Henri Poincaré 7*, 1–68. English translation by H. E. KYBURG (1964), in Kyburg and Smokler (eds)., *Studies in Subjective Probability*, Wiley, New York, pp. 95–158.

FISHBURN, P. C. (1966), "A Note on Recent Developments in Additive Utility Theories for Multiple-Factor Situations," *Operations Research*, *14*, 1143-1148.

KELLEY, J. L. (1955), *General Topology*, Van Nostrand, New York.

MENGER, K. (1934), "Das Unsicherheitsmoment in der Wertlehre, Betrachtungen im Anschluss an das sogenannte Petersburger Spiel," *Zeitschrift für Nationalökonomie*, *5*, 459-485.

Ramsey, F. P. (1926), "Truth and Probability," Chapter 7 in F. P. Ramsey (1950), *The Foundations of Mathematics and Other Logical Essays*, The Humanities Press, New York, pp. 156-198.

Samuelson, P. A. (1947), *Foundations of Economic Analysis*, Harvard University Press, Cambridge.

Savage, L. J. (1954), *The Foundations of Statistics*, Wiley, New York.

Shackle, G. L. S. (1952), *Expectation in Economics*, (2nd ed.), Cambridge University Press, Cambridge.

Villegas, C. (1964), "On Quantitative Probability $\sigma$-Algebras," *Annals of Mathematical Statistics*, *35*, 1787-1796.

von Neumann, J. and O. Morgenstern (1944), *Theory of Games and Economic Behavior*, (1st ed.), Princeton University Press, Princeton, (see also 3rd edition, 1953).

CHAPTER 3

# REPRESENTATION OF PREFERENCE ORDERINGS WITH INDEPENDENT COMPONENTS OF CONSUMPTION

TJALLING C. KOOPMANS

1. Introductory remarks. – 2. Preference orderings and representations thereof. – 3. Representation of a continuous preference ordering. – 4. Separable representation in the presence of two independent components of consumption. – 5. Additively separable representation in the case of three independent components of consumption. – 6. Extensions to the case of more than three independent components of consumption. – 7. Reconsideration of the case of two independent components of consumption.

## 1. Introductory Remarks

A standard model in the theory of consumer's choice assumes that the consumer maximizes a *utility function* under given budgetary constraints. Even in the case of the individual consumer planning for a single period's consumption, however, the time-honored concept of a utility function is not an entirely satisfactory primary concept. One may wish to look on it as a numerical representation of an underlying *preference ordering*, a more basic concept to be more fully defined below. Once this step is made, one will also want to know which class of preference orderings permits such a representation. Moreover, one will not want to exclude *a priori* the consideration of preference orderings that do not permit such a representation.

The present Chapter 3 presents a basic proposition stating sufficient conditions under which a given preference ordering is representable by a continuous function. It goes on to state, and supply proof for, a second proposition concerning the implications, for such a representation, of independence of different components of consumption in the given preference ordering. These propositions are presented for their own interest as well as for their application in Chapter 4. In the latter chapter, both propositions are applied in discussing the choice of a criterion for the evaluation of growth paths, starting from postulates about a preference ordering

[1] This chapter reports on research carried out under a grant from the National Science Foundation. It is a revision of Sections 1–4 of KOOPMANS (1966). I am indebted to Kenneth Arrow and Gerard Debreu for extremely valuable comments.

of such paths. The labeling of results and propositions is consecutive over the two chapters.

In both chapters, we aim for the simplest proposition of each type, capable of proof by relatively elementary mathematical methods, rather than for propositions and proofs of greatest generality.

In some sections technical parts of the reasoning are set off in starred subsections bearing the same number. These can be passed up by readers interested in results rather than proofs. Equality by definition will be denoted by $\equiv$. References to the literature for both chapters are listed at the end of Chapter 4.

## 2. Preference Orderings and Representations Thereoof

We shall now define and describe the mathematical concept of a *preference ordering* on a *prospect space*.

The prospect space $\mathscr{X}$ is the set of all alternative *prospects* between which choice may conceivably arise. The term "space" is a geometric metaphor, and the prospects will sometimes be called "points." In the static model of consumer's choice, the prospects are usually interpreted as bundles of consumption goods imagined used or used up in consumption in a stated period. (A bundle specifies the amount of each good on the list.) Instead of attaching preference to the use of goods, some authors have suggested attaching it to characteristics of goods (LANCASTER (1966a, b)), or to the levels of consuming activities each involving either the use or the disappearance of one or more goods (GALE (1967, 1968, pp. 209, 217, 218)). Everything that follows is compatible with any of these interpretations of the coordinates of the points $x$ of the prospect space. Accordingly, we shall use the term *vector* to refer either to a bundle of commodities, or to their characteristics, or to a statement of the levels of specified activities.

A complete preference ordering is a relation (to be denoted $\gtrsim$) between the prospects $x, y, \ldots$ in $\mathscr{X}$, compared pairwise, such that

(*transitivity*) if $x \gtrsim y$ and $y \gtrsim z$ then $x \gtrsim z$,

(*completeness*) for any pair of prospects $x$, $y$ of $\mathscr{X}$

either $x \gtrsim y$ or $y \gtrsim x$ or both.

The relation $x \gtrsim y$ is interpreted as "$x$ is at least as good as $y$," or synonymously "$x$ is *preferred or equivalent* to $y$." *Preference* ($\succ$) and *equivalence* ($\sim$) are again transitive relations, derived from $\gtrsim$ by saying that "$x \succ y$"

means "$x \succsim y$ but not $y \succsim x$," and is also denoted "$y \prec x$," and that "$x \sim y$" means "$x \succsim y$ and also $y \succsim x$."

A *partial* preference ordering is obtained if we substitute for the completeness requirement above

(*reflexivity*) for all $x$ of $\mathscr{X}$, $x \succsim x$.

Completeness implies reflexivity (take $x = y$), but the converse is, of course, not true. Hence, in a partially ordered space there may be pairs of prospects that are not comparable.[2]

By a numerical representation of a complete[3] preference ordering $\succsim$ we mean a function $f$, defined in all points $x$ of the prospect space $\mathscr{X}$, and whose values $f(x)$ are real numbers, such that

$$f(x) \geqq f(y) \text{ if and only if } x \succsim y. \tag{2.1}$$

Using the above definitions of preference and of equivalence, one sees readily that this is logically equivalent to (2.2a), which in turn implies (2.2b):

$$f(x) > f(y) \text{ if and only if } x \succ y, \tag{2.2a}$$

$$f(x) = f(y) \text{ if and only if } x \sim y. \tag{2.2b}$$

The usefulness of a representation by a continuous function, if one exists, lies primarily in the availability of stronger mathematical techniques in that case. There is a temptation to look on the values, and the differences between values, assumed by a representing "utility function" as numerical measures of satisfaction levels, and of differences thereof, associated with the prospects in question. Such interpretations may have heuristic usefulness because of the brevity of phrasing they make possible. However, their observational basis is not really clear. An observed choice between two prospects reveals at best the fact and the direction of preference, not its strength. A descriptive theory of choice thus stays somewhat closer to what is verifiable by observation if it is built on postulates about the underlying preference ordering.

---

[2] What is called a "preference ordering" here is called a "preordering" by DEBREU (1959, p. 7). ARROW (1963, pp. 13, 35) uses "weak ordering" for our "complete preference ordering," and "quasi-ordering" for our "partial preference ordering." In mathematical literature, the term "weak order," or "weak ordering," is used whenever (as here) equivalence ($x \sim y$) does *not* necessarily imply equality ($x = y$).

[3] If the preference ordering is not complete, a numerical representation is a function $f$ such that $f(x) > f(y)$ if $x \succ y$, and $f(x) = f(y)$ if $x \sim y$, together with a specification of the set of pairs $(x, y)$ of prospects $x$, $y$ in $\mathfrak{X}$ which are indeed comparable. Such representations have been considered by AUMANN (1964b).

A similar remark applies to normative theory. One can better inspect and appraise a recommendation couched in terms of actual choices in various situations, than one derived from measures of "satisfaction" whose operational significance is unclear.

We shall now describe the results of two postulational studies in the literature, as illustrations of the points just made, and for use in what follows. In Chapter 3 and 4 (except for Section 6 of Chapter 4), we shall discuss only complete preference orderings, without always repeating the adjective.

## 3. Representation of a Continuous Preference Ordering

Intuitively, one would call a preference ordering continuous if a small change in any prospect cannot drastically change the position of that prospect in the ranking of all other prospects. Starting from a sharp definition of this concept, Debreu (1959, Section 4.6) has shown conditions under which a *continuous preference ordering* can be represented by a continuous utility function.[4] In Subsection 3* we show that the definition used by Debreu is logically equivalent to the following one.

The notion of a "small" change in a prospect can be made precise by assuming a given *distance function* in the prospect space.[5] This is a function $d(x, y)$, defined for all pairs $(x, y)$ of points in $\mathscr{X}$, with the following properties usually associated with a distance:

$$\text{(3.1)} \qquad \begin{cases} d(x, y) = d(y, x) \geqq 0 \text{ for all } x, y, \\ d(x, y) = 0 \text{ if and only if } x = y, \\ d(x, z) \leqq d(x, y) + d(y, z) \text{ for all } x, y, z. \end{cases}$$

We shall call the preference ordering $\succsim$ continuous on $\mathscr{X}$ if (see Fig. 1)

$$\text{(3.2)} \qquad \begin{cases} \text{for any } x, y \text{ of } \mathscr{X} \text{ such that } x \succ y, \text{ there exists a number } \delta > 0 \text{ such that} \\ (a)\ z \succ y \text{ for all } z \text{ in } \mathscr{X} \text{ such that } d(z, x) \leqq \delta, \text{ and} \\ (b)\ x \succ w \text{ for all } w \text{ in } \mathscr{X} \text{ such that } d(y, w) \leqq \delta. \end{cases}$$

(Note that this is vacuously the case if all prospects in $\mathscr{X}$ are equivalent.) The same continuity concept is obtained from many, but not from all, different choices of the distance function.[6] We now have

---

[4] See also WOLD (1943).

[5] The prospect space thereby becomes a *metric space*.

[6] These include, for instance, the Euclidean distance $d(x, y) = [\Sigma_i (x_i - y_i)^2]^{\frac{1}{2}}$.

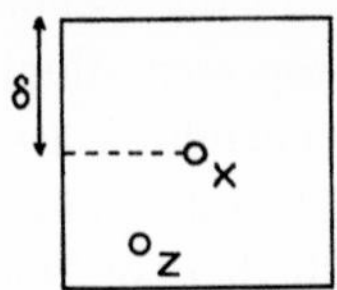


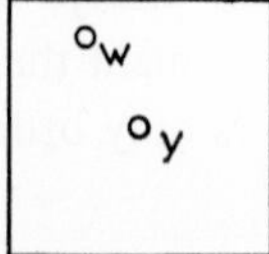


Fig. 1

PROPOSITION 1 (DEBREU (1959)). *A continuous*[7] *complete preference ordering* $\succsim$ *defined on a connected subset* $\mathscr{X}$ *of n-dimensional Euclidean space*[8] $\mathscr{E}^n$ *(n finite) can be represented by a utility function u(x) defined and continuous in* $\mathscr{X}$.

Not every conceivable preference ordering is continuous. If any increase, however small, in this year's food supply, is deemed preferable to any increase, however large, in next year's food supply, we have an example of the discontinuous *lexicographic ordering.*

If $u(x)$ is a continuous representation of $\succsim$, and if $\varphi$ is any continuous and strictly increasing function defined for all values assumed by $u(x)$ on $\mathscr{X}$, then

$$u^*(x) \equiv \varphi(u(x)) \tag{3.3}$$

[7] Continuity of $\succsim$ and of $u(x)$ is defined using the *same* distance function. Fig. 1 uses $d(x, y) = \max|x_i - y_i|$, if $x_i$, $i = 1, ..., n$, are the coordinates of $x$. While this distance function depends on the units of measurement of the amounts $x_i$, $i = 1, ..., n$, the continuity concept defined by it is again independent of these units.

[8] Depending on the interpretation, the prospect space $\mathscr{X}$ may be the set of all points $x$ with all coordinates $x_i \geqq 0$, or any other representation of the range of alternative prospects suitable in a given problem. $\mathscr{X}$ is called (arcwise) *connected* if any two points of $\mathscr{X}$ can be connected by a continuous curve contained in $\mathscr{X}$. Debreu credits a paper by EILENBERG (1941) as containing the mathematical essence of Proposition 1. For a stronger theorem establishing existence of a continuous representation without assuming connectedness or finite dimensionality see DEBREU (1954, 1964) and RADER (1963).

[9] The proof of this statement is implied in the last paragraph of Subsection 4* below: take $x = x_P$ and replace the pair $(U(x), u(x))$ of (4.4) by the pair $(u^*(x), u(x))$ of (3.3).

is likewise a continuous representation of $\succsim$. Conversely, if $u(x)$ and $u^*(x)$ are two continuous representations of $\succsim$, then such a function $\varphi$ exists for which (3.3) holds.[9] Therefore, a remark already made in Section 2 about representations in general applies equally to continuous representations: Only the notion of "higher" or "lower" among the levels of $u(x)$ has significance, not the numerical values $u(x)$ themselves or the differences thereof. In particular, even if $\succsim$ should possess a differentiable representation $u(x)$, there is no intrinsic meaning in the "marginal utility" $\partial u/dx_i$ of any single commodity. This is often expressed by the statement that $u(x)$ is an *ordinal*, not a *cardinal*, utility. However, even if $u(x)$ is only ordinal, for given units of commodities $i, j$, the ratio

$$\frac{\partial u^*(x)}{\partial x_i} \bigg/ \frac{du^*(x')}{\partial x'_j} \tag{3.4}$$

of two "marginal utilities" at the same point ($x = x'$), or at two equivalent points ($x \sim x'$), is invariant. That is, the ratio (3.4) is independent of the choice of a differentiable $\varphi$ in (3.3), hence is a quantity meaningful in terms of the given ordering $\succsim$.

Whenever $\mathscr{X}$ contains two nonequivalent points, one can by suitable choice of $\varphi$ in (3.3) make the range $\mathscr{U}^* = u^*(\mathscr{X})$ of $u^*(x)$ coincide with any interval of positive, finite or infinite, length, that includes the left and/or right endpoint depending on whether $\mathscr{X}$ contains a worst and/or best element of $\succsim$. Existence of a worst and/or best element does not preclude $\mathscr{U}^*$ being unbounded from below and/or above if the values $-\infty$ and/or $+\infty$ are adjoined to the range of $u^*$.

*3*. Equivalence of two definitions of continuity of an ordering.* The definitions to be compared are

*D* If $\lim_{n\to\infty} y_n = y$ then "$x \succsim y_n$ for all $n$" implies "$x \succsim y$," and "$y_n \succsim z$ for all $n$" implies "$y \succsim z$."

*D′* If $y \succ x$ there exists $\delta > 0$ such that (a) $d(y, w) \leqq \delta$ implies $w \succ x$, and (b) $d(w, x) \leqq \delta$ implies $y \succ w$.

Assume "*D′* and not *D*." Then there exist either $x, y_n$ with $x \succsim y_n$ for all $n$ but $\lim_{n\to\infty} y_n = y \succ x$, or $z, y_n$ with $y_n \succsim z$ for all $n$ but $z \succ y = \lim_{n\to\infty} y_n$. Taking the case $y \succ x$, we choose $\delta$ in *D′* such that $d(y, y') \leqq \delta$ implies $y' \succ x$, and $N$ in the definition of limit such that $d(y, y_N) \leqq \delta$. Then $y_N \succ x \succsim y_N$, a contradiction. The case $z \succ y$ is similar.

Assume next "$D$ and not $D'$," and take $\delta_n = 1/2^n$. Then, for some $x, y$ such that $y \succ x$, there exists either a sequence $y_n$ such that $d(y, y_n) \leqq \delta_n$ but $x \succsim y_n$, or a sequence $x_n$ such that $d(x_n, x) \leqq \delta_n$ but $x_n \succsim y$. By $D$, both cases imply $x \succsim y$, contradicting $y \succ x$.

Two statements such that the negation of either contradicts the other are equivalent.

## 4. Separable Representation in the Presence of Two Independent Components of Consumption

The problem of deriving special forms for a utility function from assumptions about independence among components of consumption has been studied by several authors, including LEONTIEF (1947a, b) and SAMUELSON (1947, Ch. 7). We shall follow DEBREU (1960) because he avoids assumptions of differentiability of the utility function that seem unrelated to the essence of the problem.

To illustrate the independence concept in terms of the traditional commodity space, one may wish to assume that preferences between food bundles are independent of the amounts of various articles of clothing and of other commodities consumed, and similarly for preferences between clothing bundles, etc.; furthermore that preferences between food-and-clothing bundles are independent of the amount of other commodities consumed, and so on.

In this section we shall derive a preliminary result for the case of two independent components of consumption. Let $\succsim$ denote a preference ordering on the space

(4.1) $$\mathscr{X} = \mathscr{X}_P \times \mathscr{X}_Q$$

of all vectors $x = (x_P, x_Q)$ such that $x_P$ is in a given space $\mathscr{X}_P$, $x_Q$ in $\mathscr{X}_Q$. In mathematical terminology, $\mathscr{X}$ is called the (Cartesian) *product* of the spaces $\mathscr{X}_P$, $\mathscr{X}_Q$, the latter *factor spaces* of $\mathscr{X}$.

To express the required independence assumption we use an arbitrary but fixed *reference vector* in $\mathscr{X}$,

(4.2) $$z = (z_P, z_Q),$$

to define two orderings, $\succsim_P^z$ on $\mathscr{X}_P$ and $\succsim_Q^z$ on $\mathscr{X}_Q$, induced by $\succsim$, as follows,

(4.3) $$\begin{aligned} x_P \succsim_P^z y_P &\text{ means } (x_P, z_Q) \succsim (y_P, z_Q), \\ x_Q \succsim_Q^z y_Q &\text{ means } (z_P, x_Q) \succsim (z_P, y_Q). \end{aligned}$$

In general, the induced orderings depend on the reference vector, in the sense that $\succsim_P^z$ depends on $z_Q$, and $\succsim_Q^z$ on $z_P$. The independence assumption will say that this dependence-in-principle is not a dependence-in-fact. In Subsection 4* we show, following DEBREU (1960),

RESULT A. *Let a preference ordering* $\succsim$ *on a product space* $\mathscr{X} = \mathscr{X}_P \times \mathscr{X}_Q$ *be representable by a utility function* $U(x)$, *and let the ordering* $\succsim_P^z$, $\succsim_Q^z$ *induced by* $\succsim$ (as defined above) *be independent of the reference vector* $z$. *Then* $U(x)$ *has the form*

$$U(x) = F(u(x_P), v(x_Q)), \tag{4.4}$$

*where* $F$ *is an increasing function of both* $u$ *and* $v$. *Moreover, if* $\mathscr{X}$ *is connected,* $U(x)$ *continuous, then* $u(x_P)$, $v(x_Q)$ *and* $F(u, v)$ *are continuous, and the ranges of* $u(x_P)$, $v(x_Q)$ *are intervals.*

A function of this form has been called a *utility tree* by STROTZ (1956, 1959), and a *separable utility function* by GORMAN (1959a, b). In the case of two independent components of consumption, therefore, instead of one function $U$ of $n_P + n_Q$ variables (there are a great many such functions!) we have a triple of functions, one ($F$) of two variables, one ($u$) of $n_P$, and one ($v$) of $n_Q$ variables. In some sense the "number" of such triples forms a much smaller infinity. The utility $U(x)$ of $x$ depends only on the utility levels $u(x_P)$, $v(x_Q)$ associated with $x_P$, $x_Q$ in their respective spaces, rather than on these vectors in their full detail.

*4*. Proof of Result A.* We define, for some fixed reference vector $z^0$,

$$u(x_P) \equiv U(x_P, z_Q^0), \qquad v(x_Q) \equiv U(z_P^0, x_Q), \tag{4.5}$$

and consider two vectors $x$, $y$ in $\mathscr{X}$ such that

$$u(x_P) = u(y_P), \qquad v(x_Q) = v(y_Q).$$

Since $U$ represents $\succsim$, we then have

$$(x_P, z_Q^0) \sim (y_P, z_Q^0), \qquad (z_P^0, x_Q) \sim (z_P^0, y_Q),$$

Since $\succsim_P$ and $\succsim_Q$ are independent of the choice of $z^0$, we have further

$$x = (x_P, x_Q) \sim (y_P, x_Q) \sim (y_P, y_Q) = y$$

(choose the alternative reference vector $z = (y_P, x_Q)$). Hence $x \sim y$, and $U(x) = U(y)$. This means that the value of $U(x)$ for any vector $x$ in $\mathscr{X}$ depends only on the values of $u(x_P)$, $v(x_Q)$ assumed for the subvectors $x_P$, $x_Q$ of $x$, respectively, confirming (4.4).

Moreover, from the independence of $\succsim_P^z$ from $z$, using the definition of $\succ$ in terms of $\succsim$ we have, for all $z_Q$, that

$$x_P \succ_P^z y_P \text{ if and only if } (x_P, z_Q) \succ (y_P, z_Q).$$

It follows that $F$ increases with $u$, and similarly with $v$.

Finally, by (4.5), continuity of $U(x)$ implies that of $u(x_P)$, $v(x_Q)$, connectedness of $\mathscr{X}$ that of $\mathscr{X}_P$, $\mathscr{X}_Q$. Hence, for any fixed $z$ in $\mathscr{X}$, the ranges of the functions $U(x)$, $u(x_P)$, $v(x_Q)$, $U(x_P, z_Q)$, $U(z_P, x_Q)$ for all $x_P$ in $\mathscr{X}_P$, $x_Q$ in $\mathscr{X}_Q$ are intervals, nondegenerate unless $u(x_P)$ and/or $v(x_Q)$ is constant. But then $F(u, v(z_Q))$ and $F(u(z_P), v)$ are, for any fixed $z$ in $\mathscr{X}$, increasing functions of $u$ and $v$, respectively, defined on one interval and taking on all the values in another. This is possible only if $F(u, v)$ is continuous in $u$ for each $v$, and in $v$ for each $u$. Since $F(u, v)$ increases in both $u$, $v$, it follows that $F(u, v)$ is continuous in $u$ and $v$ jointly.

## 5. Additively Separable Representation in the Case of Three Independent Components of Consumption

Three independent components of consumption suffice to show the essential traits of the case with $n$ such components, where $n \geqq 3$. We shall therefore in this section consider a preference ordering $\succsim$ on a product

$$\mathscr{X} = \mathscr{X}_P \times \mathscr{X}_Q \times \mathscr{X}_R \tag{5.1}$$

of three spaces. To make sure that this is really three for the purpose of our reasoning, we shall need a concept of sensitivity of $\succsim$ in a factor space. We shall say that $\succsim$ is *sensitive* in $\mathscr{X}_P$ if there exist $x_P$, $y_P$, $z_Q$, $z_R$ such that

$$(x_P, z_Q, z_R) \succ (y_P, z_Q, z_R). \tag{5.2}$$

This will ensure that the induced ordering $\succsim_P^z$ will not declare all vectors $x_P$ equivalent.

Given a reference vector $z = (z_P, z_Q, z_R)$, $\succsim$ now induces six orderings, $\succsim_P^z$, $\succsim_Q^z$, $\succsim_R^z$, $\succsim_{P,Q}^z$, $\succsim_{Q,R}^z$, $\succsim_{P,R}^z$ on various factor spaces, defined along the following lines:

$$\begin{cases} x_P \succsim_P^z y_P \text{ means } (x_P, z_Q, z_R) \succsim (y_P, z_Q, z_R) \\ (x_P, x_Q) \succsim_{P,Q}^z (y_P, y_Q) \text{ means } (x_P, x_Q, z_R) \succsim (y_P, y_Q, z_R), \text{ etc.} \end{cases} \tag{5.3}$$

PROPOSITION 2 (DEBREU (1960), 3 components only, modified). *Let* $\succsim$ *be a continuous preference ordering of all consumption vectors* $x=(x_P, x_Q, x_R)$ *such that* $x_P, x_Q, x_R$ *belong to spaces* $\mathscr{X}_P, \mathscr{X}_Q, \mathscr{X}_R$, *which are connected subsets of Euclidean spaces of* $n_P, n_Q, n_R$ *dimensions, respectively. Let* $\succsim$ *be sensitive in each of P, Q, R, and let* $\succsim_P^z, \succsim_Q^z, \succsim_R^z, \succsim_{P,Q}^z, \succsim_{Q,R}^z$ (as defined above) *be independent of z. Then there exist functions* $u^*(x_P)$, $v^*(x_Q)$, $w^*(x_R)$, *defined and continuous on* $\mathscr{X}_P, \mathscr{X}_Q, \mathscr{X}_R$, *respectively, such that* $\mathscr{X}$ *is represented by*

$$U^*(x) = u^*(x_P)+v^*(x_Q)+w^*(x_R). \tag{5.4}$$

*This representation is unique up to a linear transformation*

$$u'(x_P) = \beta_P+\gamma u^*(x_P), \qquad v'(x_Q) = \beta_Q+\gamma v^*(x_Q), \tag{5.5}$$

$$w'(x_R) = \beta_R+\gamma w^*(x_R), \qquad \gamma>0.$$

In principle, the representation (5.4) is still ordinal. That is, any function $U'(x)$ obtained from $U^*(x)$ by (3.3) is likewise a continuous representation of $\succsim$. However, unless $\varphi$ happens to be linear as in (5.5), the representation $U'(x)$ cannot be written simply as a sum of functions each depending on one of the vectors $x_P$, $x_Q$, $x_R$ only, as $U^*(x)$ is written in (5.4). It is only in this limited sense that the representation by $U^*(x)$ can be called cardinal.

In the proof of Proposition 2 given in Subsection 5* we shall follow the general ideas of Debreu's beautiful geometrical proof, and of the work of BLASCHKE and BOL (1938) on which it builds forth. We modify his reasoning in one respect in order to avoid making the assumption that the sixth induced ordering, $\succsim_{P,R}^z$, is also independent[10] of $z$.

5*. *Proof of Proposition 2.* Since the Cartesian product

$$\mathscr{X} \equiv \mathscr{X}_P \times \mathscr{X}_Q \times \mathscr{X}_R$$

is a connected subset of a Euclidean space of $n=n_P+n_Q+n_R$ dimensions,

[10] The redundancy of that assumption, as well as the importance of that redundancy for the analysis of utility over time, were perceived and demonstrated by GORMAN (1965, 1968a) for the case of differentiable utility functions. In a recent paper, GORMAN (1968b) has given a complete discussion of the structure of representations with regard to separability and additive separability, without differentiability assumptions. His results imply that, in Proposition 2, the premises that $\succsim_P^z, \succsim_Q^z, \succsim_R^z$ are independent of $z$ are also implied in those made about $\succsim_{P,Q}^z$ and $\succsim_{Q,R}^z$. This further strengthening, important in itself, turns out to be less crucial to the particular application of Proposition 2 made in Chapter 4 than the dropping of the assumption that $\succsim_{P,R}^z$ does not depend on $z$.

the premises of Proposition 1 are satisfied. Hence $\succsim$ is represented by a continuous function

$$U(x) \equiv U(x_P, x_Q, x_R) \tag{5.6}$$

defined on $\mathscr{X}$. Since an additive constant does not affect the representation, we shall anchor $U(x)$ by requiring that, for some specific reference vector $z$,

$$U(z) = 0. \tag{5.7}$$

The five induced orderings $\succsim_P, \succsim_Q, \succsim_R, \succsim_{P,Q}, \succsim_{Q,R}$ (superscripts $z$ have been dropped because these are now independent of $z$) are therefore represented by the continuous functions

$$\begin{cases} u(x_P) \equiv U(x_P, z_Q, z_R), \quad v(x_Q) \equiv U(z_P, x_Q, z_R), \\ \qquad\qquad\qquad\qquad\qquad\qquad w(x_R) \equiv U(z_P, z_Q, x_R), \\ W(x_P, x_Q) \equiv U(x_P, x_Q, z_R), \quad \overline{U}(x_Q, x_R) \equiv U(z_P, x_Q, x_R), \end{cases} \tag{5.8}$$

respectively. Since the domains of all these functions are connected, the range of each is an interval. For three of the ranges we introduce the notations

$$\mathscr{U} = u(\mathscr{X}_P), \quad \mathscr{V} = v(\mathscr{X}_Q), \quad \mathscr{W} = w(\mathscr{X}_R). \tag{5.9}$$

Since $\succsim$ is sensitive in each of $P$, $Q$, $R$, none of the five intervals collapses to a point, and, by suitable choice of $z$, one can ensure that the point

$$u(z_P) = v(z_Q) = w(z_R) = W(z_P, z_R) = \overline{U}(z_Q, z_R) = 0 \tag{5.10}$$

is interior to all five ranges.

We now apply Result A twice to $U(x)$, once with the partitioning $x = (x_P, (x_Q, x_R))$, and once with $x = ((x_P, x_Q), x_R)$. With reference to the proof of Result A, this gives us the existence of increasing functions $F(W, w)$ and $G(u, \overline{U})$, such that, for all $x$ in $\mathscr{X}$,

$$U(x) = F(W(x_P, x_Q), w(x_R)) = G(u(x_P), \overline{U}(x_Q, x_R)). \tag{5.11}$$

The domains of the arguments $W$, $w$ of $F$ and $u$, $\overline{U}$ of $G$ are intervals over which the functions denoted by the same symbols range, respectively. Since these functions as well as $U(x)$ are continuous, $F$ and $G$ are continuous. To avoid repetition of similar reasoning, we announce in advance that the functions $F^{-1}$, $g$, $f$, $H$, $h$ yet to be introduced are likewise continuous and increasing on the nondegenerate intervals, or products thereof, over which their arguments range.

By inserting $x_R = z_R$ in (5.11), using (5.10) and (5.8), one has

$$F(W(x_P, x_Q), 0) = G(u(x_P), v(x_Q)),$$

and, if $F^{-1}$ is the inverse of $F(W, 0)$,

$$W(x_P, x_Q) = F^{-1}(G(u(x_P), v(x_Q)) \equiv g(u(x_P), v(x_Q)), \tag{5.12}$$

say, and symmetrically

$$\bar{U}(x_Q, x_R) = f(v(x_Q), w(x_R)). \tag{5.13}$$

We can now shed the variables $x_P$, $x_Q$, $x_R$. From (5.11), (5.12), and (5.13) we have

$$F(g(u, v), w) = G(u, f(v, w)) \equiv H(u, v, w) = H(t), \text{ say,} \tag{5.14}$$

where $t \equiv (u, v, w)$. Here $H(t)$ is defined on the three-dimensional cell $\mathscr{I} \equiv \mathscr{U} \times \mathscr{V} \times \mathscr{W}$, of which the origin $o = (0, 0, 0)$ is an interior point. The ordering $\succsim$ on $\mathscr{X}_P \times \mathscr{X}_Q \times \mathscr{X}_R$ represented by $U(x)$ induces an ordering on $\mathscr{I}$, which we likewise denote by $\succsim$, and which is represented by $H(t)$.

We shall study the level curves of $H(u, v, 0)$ and of $H(0, v, w)$. In the plane $w = 0$ we arbitrarily select (see Fig. 2) an indifference curve $\kappa$ not passing

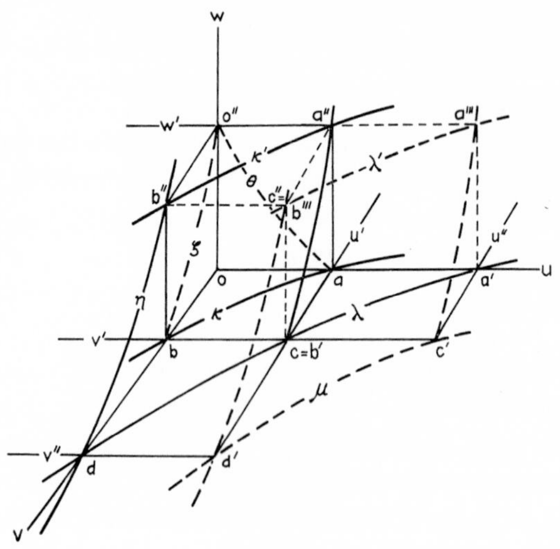


Fig. 2

through $o$, but close enough to $o$ for all the intersection points sought in the following construction to exist. If $\kappa$ intersects the $u$- and $v$-axes in $a=(u',0,0)$ and $b=(0,v',0)$, respectively, we have

$$a\sim b,\ \text{implying}\ g(u',0)=g(0,v') \tag{5.15}$$

by taking $w=0$ in the first member of (5.14). At most one intersection point exists in each case because $g(u,v)$ is increasing in each variable. Precisely one will exist if $\kappa$ passes close enough to $o$, because of the continuity of $g(u,v)$.

It will save words to refer to two points $s$, $t$ of $\mathscr{I}$ as *u-congruent* if they differ only in their $u$-coordinate,

$$s=(u^{(1)},v,w),\quad t=(u^{(2)},v,w).$$

Similarly we shall speak of $v$- and $w$-congruence.

We find $c\equiv(u',v',0)$, $v$-congruent to $a$, $u$-congruent to $b$, and draw through $c$ an indifference curve $\lambda$ in the plane $w=0$, which intersects the $u$-axis in $a'\equiv(u'',0,0)$, the $v$-axis in $d\equiv(0,v'',0)$. In particular,

$$c\sim a',\ \text{implying}\ g(u',v')=g(u'',0). \tag{5.16}$$

Finally we find $c'\equiv(u'',v',0)$, $v$-congruent to $a'$, $u$-congruent to $b$, and $d'\equiv(u',v'',0)$, $u$-congruent to $d$, $v$-congruent to $a$.

We now wish to prove that $d'\sim c'$. In Section 7 we shall show that Proposition 2 does not hold for a partitioning of $x$ into only two components.[11] Therefore, we shall need to go into the third dimension to prove that $d'\sim c'$.

On the indifference curve $\eta$ through $d$ in the plane $u=0$, we find $b''\equiv(0,v',w')$, $w$-congruent to $b$. Then

$$d\sim b'',\ \text{implying}\ f(v'',0)=f(v',w') \tag{5.17}$$

by the second member of (5.14). Finally we find $o''\equiv(0,0,w')$ on the $w$-axis, $v$-congruent to $b''$, and $a''\equiv(u',0,w')$, $u$-congruent to $o''$, $w$-congruent to $a$. Then, by taking $w=w'$ in the first member of (5.14), we see that (5.15) in its turn implies $a''\sim b''$. (In fact the indifference curves $\kappa$ and $\kappa'$ are point-by-point $w$-congruent.) Hence $c\sim d\sim b''\sim a''$, and therefore

$$c\sim a'',\ \text{implying}\ f(v',0)=f(0,w'). \tag{5.18}$$

The second round of the construction is similar to the first. It employs the points $a'''\equiv(u'',0,w')$, $u$- and $w$-congruent to $o''$ and $a'$, respectively, and

[11] See Section 7 below.

$c'' \equiv b''' \equiv (u', v', w')$, $u$-, $v$-, and $w$-congruent to $b''$, $a''$, and $c = b'$, respectively. We have

$$\left.\begin{array}{l}(5.17)\text{ implies } d' \sim b''' \\ (5.16)\text{ implies } c'' \sim a''' \\ (5.18)\text{ implies } a''' \sim c'\end{array}\right\}\text{ so } d' \sim c'.$$

Hence $d'$ and $c'$ are on the same indifference curve $\mu$ in the plane $w = 0$.

The rectangle $acc'a'$ has the following characteristics relative to the indifference curves $\kappa$, $\lambda$, $\mu$:

| incidence: | | | | | congruence type of | | | | |
|---|---|---|---|---|---|---|---|---|---|
| | $a$ | $c$ | $c'$ | $a'$ | | $a,a'$ | $c,c'$ | $a,c$ | $a',c'$ |
| is on | $\kappa$ | $\lambda$ | $\mu$ | $\lambda$ | is | $u$ | $u$ | $v$ | $v$ |

We shall call such a rectangle *inscribed in the curves* $\kappa$, $\lambda$, $\mu$. Since the origin could have been chosen anywhere in $\mathscr{I}$, we have found the following result, illustrated in Fig. 3.

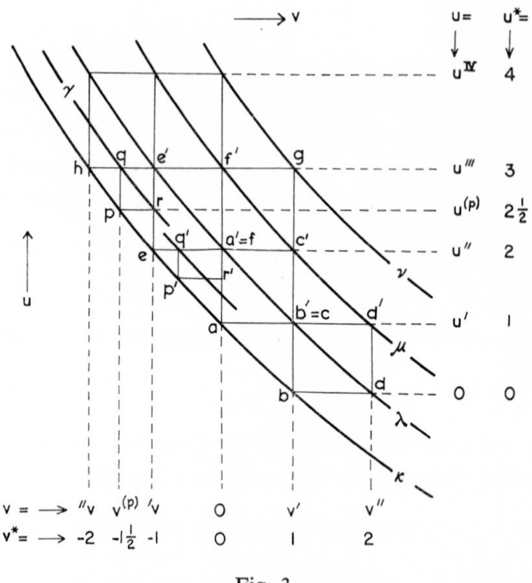


Fig. 3

**Result B.** *If three indifference curves* $\kappa$, $\lambda$, $\mu$ *possess an inscribed rectangle* $acc'a'$ *then* $\kappa$, $\lambda$, $\mu$ *possess adjoining inscribed rectangles* $bdd'b'$, $b' = c$, *and* *eff′e′, f=a′, provided only that the intersection points required by their construction exist.*

The remainder of the proof is based on the "geometry of webs" of BLASCHKE and BOL (1938). On any three indifference curves $\kappa$, $\lambda$, $\mu$ one can construct a sequence of such rectangles as indicated in Fig. 3, going as far in both directions as the intervals $\mathscr{U}$ and $\mathscr{V}$ permit. If there should be an infinite sequence of such rectangles inscribed in $\kappa$, $\lambda$, $\mu$, such a sequence cannot have a finite point of accumulation $t'$ in $\mathscr{I}$, because by the continuity of $\mathrm{H}(t)$ such a point would belong to each of $\kappa$, $\lambda$, $\mu$, which is a contradiction. Hence if $\mathscr{U}$ and $\mathscr{V}$ are bounded, an infinite sequence of inscribed rectangles can only have an accumulation point on the boundary of $\mathscr{I}$, and not belonging to $\mathscr{I}$.

A second sequence of rectangles can be inscribed in $\lambda$, $\mu$, $\nu$ if $\nu$ contains, for instance, the point $g$, $u$-congruent to $c'$ and $v$-congruent to $f'$. In this way the intersection of $\mathscr{I}$ with the plane $w=0$ is covered by rectangles inscribed in a sequence of indifference curves ..., $\kappa$, $\lambda$, $\mu$, $\nu$, ..., except possibly for uncovered margins near the endpoints (if finite) of $\mathscr{U}$, $\mathscr{V}$.

Furthermore, one can interpolate an indifference curve $\gamma$ "between" $\kappa$ and $\lambda$, say, by choosing $p$ on $eh$ (Fig. 3) so that $q \sim r$, and drawing $\gamma$ through $q$ and $r$. This construction can be extended over the full length of $\kappa$ and $\lambda$, repeated between $\lambda$ and $\mu$, etc. and possibly into any uncovered margins, and repeated again between $\kappa$ and $\gamma$, etc.

Let $\mathscr{U}'$ be the set of all $u$-coordinates $(0, u', u'', \ldots)$ of vertices of inscribed rectangles occurring in this construction repeated indefinitely, $\mathscr{V}'$ that of all $v$-coordinates. Then $\mathscr{U}'$ is dense in $\mathscr{U}$, $\mathscr{V}'$ in $\mathscr{V}$. We assign new coordinates $(u^*, v^*)$ to all points of $\mathscr{U}' \times \mathscr{V}$ in the manner indicated in the margins of Fig. 3. Then

$$u^* = \pi(u), \qquad v^* = \varphi(v), \tag{5.19}$$

are continuous and increasing functions on $\mathscr{U}'$ and $\mathscr{V}'$, respectively, for which

$$\pi(0) = \varphi(0) = 0. \tag{5.20}$$

These functions are extended to $\mathscr{U}$, $\mathscr{V}$, while retaining these properties by

$$\pi(u) \equiv \sup_{\substack{u' \leqq u \\ u' \in \mathscr{U}'}} \pi(u'), \qquad \varphi(v) \equiv \sup_{\substack{v' \leqq v \\ v' \in \mathscr{V}'}} \varphi(v').$$

It follows from the construction that for any two equivalent points $(u, v)$,

$(u', v')$ of $\mathscr{U}' \times \mathscr{V}'$ one has

$$u^* + v^* = \pi(u) + \varphi(v) = \pi(u') + \varphi(v') = u'^* + v'^* .$$

By continuity of $H(u, v, 0)$ this property extends to $\mathscr{U} \times \mathscr{V}$. Therefore, if we now define functions

$$u^*(x_P) = \pi(u(x_P)), \qquad v^*(x_Q) = \varphi(v(x_Q)),$$

the ordering $\succsim$, restricted to points of $\mathscr{X}$ for which $w(x_R) = 0$, is represented by the continuous function

$$u^*(x_P) + v^*(x_Q) . \tag{5.21}$$

By the independence of $\succsim_{P,Q}$, the same representation applies to any set of points of $\mathscr{X}$ on which $w(x_R)$ takes another constant value.

To extend this representation to all of $\mathscr{X}$, we return to Fig. 2 to note that (5.18) also implies $b \sim o''$. It follows that, had we carried out the preceding construction in the plane $u = 0$ instead of in $w = 0$, starting from $\zeta$ instead of from $\kappa$, we would have arrived at the same demarcation point $d$ by intersecting the $v$-axis with the indifference curve through $b''$ as we obtained by intersection with $\lambda$ through $b'$. Moving the origin successively to $b, d, \ldots$, we obtain that the same sequence of demarcation points $o, b, d, \ldots$ on the $v$-axis would have been obtained starting from $\zeta$ instead of from $\kappa$. But then the same must hold for the sequence of demarcation points $o, 'b, b, 'd, d, \ldots$ (not shown in the figures) obtained from $o, b, d, \ldots$ by interpolation, because the interpolated sequence could as well have been obtained without interpolation by starting with an indifference curve $'\kappa$ (not shown) defined by

$$w = 0, \qquad \pi(u) + \varphi(v) = \tfrac{1}{2} .$$

Since this reasoning extends to any number of interpolations, the construction starting from $\zeta$ would have led to the same function $v^*(x_Q)$, along with a similar function $w^*(x_R)$. It follows that $\succsim$ is continuously represented, on any set of points of $\mathscr{X}$ for which $u^*(x_P)$ takes a constant value, by

$$v^*(x_Q) + w^*(x_R) . \tag{5.22}$$

We shall finally show that $\succsim$ is represented on $\mathscr{X}$ by the continuous function[12]

$$U^*(x) = u^*(x_P) + v^*(x_Q) + w^*(x_R) . \tag{5.23}$$

[12] There is an affinity between the following reasoning and a study by ARROW (1952).

Consider two vectors $x = (x_P, x_Q, x_R)$, $x' = (x'_P, x'_Q, x'_R)$. By (5.11), (5.12), (5.13), (5.19) their order depends only on the corresponding utility vectors

$$(5.24) \qquad (u^*, v^*, w^*), \qquad (u'^*, v'^*, w'^*),$$

where $u^* = u^*(x_P)$, etc. Extending the usual notation $[m, m']$ for the interval $m \leqq u \leqq m'$ to

$$|[m, m']| \equiv \begin{cases} [m, m'] \text{ if } m \leqq m' \\ [m', m] \text{ if } m' < m, \end{cases}$$

we consider the set

$$\mathscr{S} \equiv |[u^*, u'^*]| \times |[v^*, v'^*]| \times |[w^*, w'^*]| .$$

This is a *block* (rectangular parallelepiped) of which each vertex has each coordinate in common with one or the other of the points (5.24), as shown in Fig. 4. On the points of each edge of $\mathscr{S}$ the ordering $\gtrsim$ is (strictly) monotonic as indicated by arrows, because of the monotonicity of $H$ in (5.14), and each such *edge ordering* is represented by the corresponding term in (5.23).

We must show that, for all possible dimensions of the block, the ordering $\gtrsim$ of each of the pairs $(a, h)$, $(b, e)$, $(c, f)$, $(d, g)$ is represented by (5.23). For $(a, h)$ this is already implied in the edge orderings $a \succ b \succ f \succ h$.

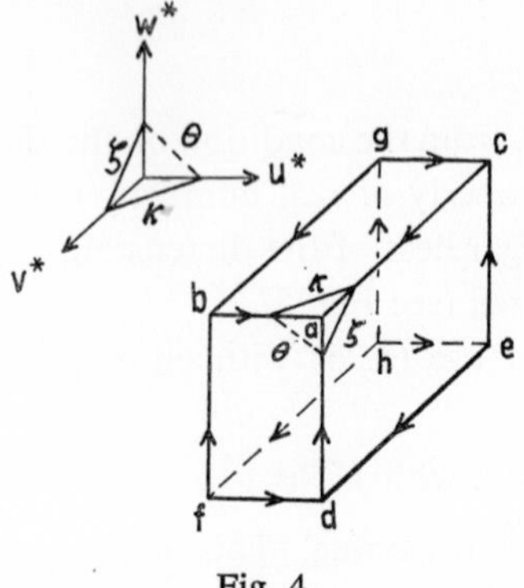

Fig. 4

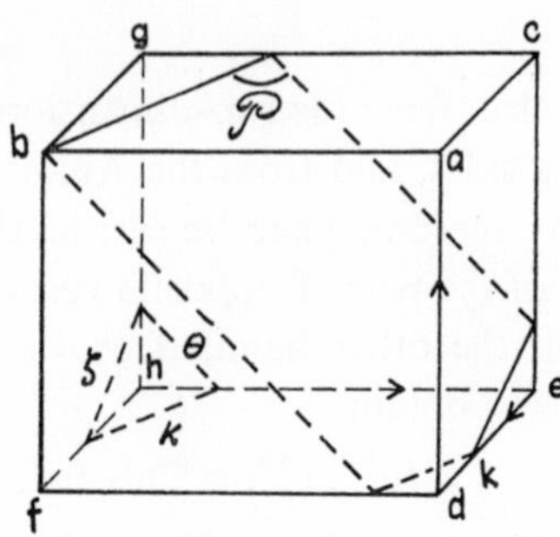

Fig. 5

Assume first that $v^* \neq v'^*$. Then if either $u^* = u'^*$ or $w^* = w'^*$, the remaining comparisons are settled by (5.22) or (5.21), respectively. Assume therefore that the block $\mathscr{S}$ is three-dimensional. We shall make use of the equivalences

$$(u^*, v^*, w^*) \sim (u^*+p, v^*-p, w^*) \sim (u^*+p, v^*-p+q, w^*-q) \sim \ldots,$$

implied in (5.21), (5.22) as long as we make sure that all points so compared are in $\mathscr{S}$. This means that all points of any line segment in $\mathscr{S}$ parallel to either $\kappa$ or $\zeta$ are equivalent, and these equivalences are represented by (5.23).

As an example, Fig. 5 shows the comparison of $b$ and $e$. We intersect $\mathscr{S}$ with a plane $\mathscr{P}$ through $b$ parallel to both $\kappa$ and $\zeta$. Since $a$, $h$ are on opposite sides of $\mathscr{P}$, the intersection is a two-dimensional convex polygon $\mathscr{Q}$ with edges parallel to $\kappa$, $\zeta$ or $\theta$. Now $\mathscr{P}$ and hence $\mathscr{Q}$ must intersect the broken line $h\ e\ d\ a$ in precisely one point $k$. Fig. 6, drawn in $\mathscr{P}$, shows how a broken line in $\mathscr{Q}$ with a finite number of segments parallel to $\kappa$ and $\zeta$ can be drawn to connect $b$ and $k$. This establishes the equivalence of $b$ and $k$, and its representation by (5.23). The comparison of $k$ and $e$ then is made through the edge orderings on $h\ e\ d\ a$, again represented by (5.23). In Fig. 5 $b \sim k \succ e$.

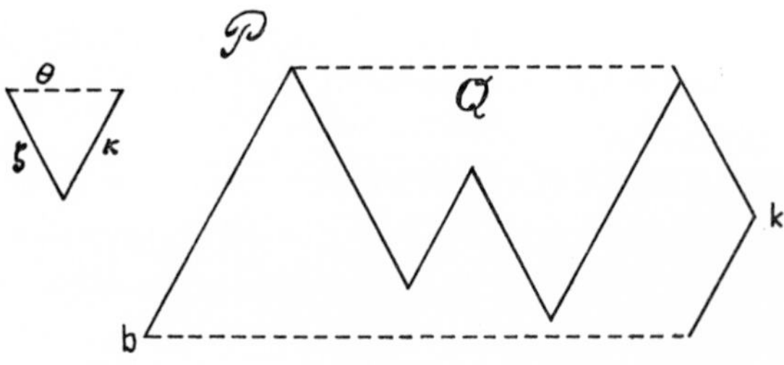


Fig. 6

It is clear from the two-dimensionality of $\mathscr{Q}$, from the condition on the slopes of its sides, and from the Archimedean property of real numbers, that the above reasoning can be carried through regardless of the dimensions of $\mathscr{S}$, and of the pair of opposite vertices compared (see Fig. 5).

On the other hand, if $v^* = v'^*$, we first use (5.25) with either $p \neq 0$ or $q \neq 0$ to obtain

$$(u''^*, v''^*, w''^*) \sim (u^*, v^*, w^*), \text{ say, with } v''^* \neq v^*,$$

and continue from there with the above reasoning. This procedure is unavailable with regard to *both* $(u^*, v^*, w^*)$ and $(u'^*, v'^*, w'^*)$ only if each is either $(\underline{u}, \underline{v}, \underline{w})$ or $(\bar{u}, \bar{v}, \bar{w})$, where $\underline{u}$, $\underline{v}$, $\underline{w}$, are finite lower endpoints of $\mathscr{U}^* \equiv u^*(x_P)$, $\mathscr{V}^*$, $\mathscr{W}^*$, included in $\mathscr{U}^*$, $\mathscr{V}^*$, $\mathscr{W}^*$, respectively, and $\bar{u}$, $\bar{v}$, $\bar{w}$ are similar upper endpoints. But then $v^* = v'^*$, $\bar{v} > \underline{v}$ forces $(u^*, v^*, w^*) = (u'^*, v'^*, w'^*)$, equality implying equivalence, represented by (5.23).

Finally, to discuss the uniqueness of (5.23), we note first from (5.10), (5.19), (5.20) that

$$u^*(z_P) = v^*(z_Q) = w^*(z_R) = 0.$$

Now assume that $\succsim$ is also represented by the continuous function

$$U'(x) = u'(x_P) + v'(x_Q) + w'(x_R).$$

We define

$$\beta_P \equiv u'(z_P), \text{ etc., } u''(x_P) \equiv u'(x_P) - \beta_P, \text{ etc.}$$

Then there exists $h(U^*)$ such that, for all $x$ in $\mathscr{X}$,

$$u''(x_P) + v''(x_Q) + w''(x_R) = h(u^*(x_P) + v^*(x_Q) + w^*(x_R)).$$

Inserting $x_R = z_R$, and thereafter $x_Q = z_Q$, or $x_P = z_P$, or both, we have, for all values of the omitted arguments $x_P$, $x_Q$, $x_R$,

$$u'' + v'' = h(u^* + v^*), \quad u'' = h(u^*), \quad v'' = h(v^*), \quad 0 = h(0),$$

hence

$$h(u^* + v^*) = h(u^*) + h(v^*), \quad h(0) = 0,$$

for all $(u^*, v^*)$ in $\mathscr{U}^* \times \mathscr{V}^*$.

This in turn implies

$$h(nu^*) = nh(u^*)$$

for all integer $n$ and all $u^*$ such that $u^*$ and $n\,u^*$ are in the interval $\mathscr{U}^*$. Among continuous functions $h(u^*)$, this property is possessed only by the linear functions

$$h(u^*) = \gamma u^*,$$

where $\gamma > 0$ because $h$ is increasing. This establishes the transformation (5.5). The proof of Proposition 2 is now complete.

## 6. Extensions to the Case of More than Three Independent Components of Consumption

Debreu has extended Proposition 2 to the case of $k > 3$ independent components of consumption. If we write

(6.1) $$\mathscr{X} = \mathscr{X}_1 \times \mathscr{X}_2 \times \ldots \times \mathscr{X}_k$$

for the factorization of the prospect space by independent components (with respect to each of which $\succsim$ is sensitive), he has assumed that the orderings induced by $\succsim$ on every product.

$$\mathscr{X}_{i_1} \times \mathscr{X}_{i_2} \times \ldots \times \mathscr{X}_{i_j}, \quad 1 \leqq j \leqq k-1, \tag{6.2}$$

of $j$ out of the $k$ spaces are independent of the reference vector.

We have already seen that for $k=3$ independent components only five out of the six such assumptions are needed. As mentioned in Footnote 10 above, GORMAN (1968b) has cut this down further to only two. In the same paper he has given minimal assumptions for the generalization of Proposition 2 to $k$ independent components. To avoid duplication, we mention here only one straightforward extension of Proposition 2 that helps prepare for Chapter 4.

RESULT C *Let the following orderings, induced on factor sets by a continuous ordering $\succsim$ on the product* (6.1) *of connected subsets of finite-dimensional Euclidean spaces be independent of the reference vector z,*

$$\begin{cases} \succsim_i \text{ on } \mathscr{X}_i, & i=1,2,\ldots,k, \quad k \geqq 3, \\ \succsim_{i,i+1} \text{ on } \mathscr{X}_i \times \mathscr{X}_{i+1}, & i=1,2,\ldots,k-1. \end{cases} \tag{6.2}$$

*Let $\succsim$ be sensitive in each $\mathscr{X}_i$. Then $\succsim$ is represented on $\mathscr{X}$ by a continuous function of the form*

$$U(x) = u_1(x_1) + u_2(x_2) + \ldots + u_k(x_k), \tag{6.3}$$

*unique up to an increasing linear transformation.*

6.* *Proof of Result C.* By Proposition 2, the statement is true for $k=3$. Suppose it is true if $k$ is replaced by $j-1$, where $4 \leqq j \leqq k$, and consider the ordering $\succsim^z_{1,\ldots,j}$ induced by $\succsim$ on the space

$$\mathscr{X}^{(j)} = \mathscr{X}_1 \times \mathscr{X}_2 \times \cdots \times \mathscr{X}_j,$$

using a reference vector $z$. Then Proposition 2 can be applied to the factorization

$$\mathscr{X}^{(j)} = \mathscr{X}^{(j-2)} \times \mathscr{X}_{j-1} \times \mathscr{X}_j$$

to give the existence of a continuous representation of the form

$$u^{(j-2)}(x_1, \ldots, x_{j-2}) + u^*_{j-1}(x_{j-1}) + u^*_j(x_j).$$

We compare the representation of $\succsim^z_{1,\ldots,j-1}$, obtained by holding $x_j$

constant in this expression, with

$$u_1(x_1)+ \dots +u_{j-1}(x_{j-1}),$$

given by the inductive hypothesis made. The reasoning used at the end of Section 5* to establish the essential uniqueness of additively separable representation then gives, with $\gamma>0$,

$$\begin{aligned} u_1(x_1)+ \dots +u_{j-2}(x_{j-2}) &= \gamma u^{(j-2)}(x_1, \dots, x_{j-2})+\delta \\ u_{j-1}(x_{j-1}) &= \gamma u^*_{j-1}(x_{j-1})+\delta^*, \end{aligned}$$

from which, by introducing $u_j(x_j)=\gamma u_j^*(x_j)$, one validates the inductive hypothesis for $\succsim^z_{1,\dots,j}$. By continued induction one obtains (6.3), unique up to an increasing linear transformation.

## 7. Reconsideration of the Case of Two Independent Components of Consumption

To show that the case of $k \geqq 3$ independent components of consumption leads to a more special class of representations than the case $k=2$, we must show that not every function of the separable form (4.4) can be transformed into the additively separable form

$$U^*(x) = u^*(x_P)+v^*(x_Q). \tag{7.1}$$

One readily verifies that any ordering representable by (7.1) must satisfy the condition that

$$\left.\begin{aligned} (x_P, x'_Q) &\sim (x'_P, x_Q) \\ (x_P, x''_Q) &\sim (x''_P, x_Q) \end{aligned}\right\} \text{ implies } (x'_P, x''_Q) \sim (x''_P, x'_Q). \tag{7.2}$$

Given any continuous representation of the separable form (4.4) of an ordering $\succsim$ on $\mathscr{X} = \mathscr{X}_P \times \mathscr{X}_Q$, the test (7.2) can be expressed in terms of the values

$$(u, u', u'') = (u(x_P), u(x'_P), u(x''_P)), \quad (v, v', v'') = (v(x_Q), v(x'_Q), v(x''_Q),$$

assumed by the functions $u(x_P)$, $v(x_Q)$ in the points $x$, $x'$, $x''$. The configuration of points and indifference curves expressing the test is shown in Fig. 7. It is more general than that of the corresponding points $a$, $b$, $d$, $d'$, $c'$, $a'$ in Fig. 3, but includes the latter as a special case. Since the latter configuration was already found, in the proof of Proposition 2, to be sufficient for the existence of the representation (7.1), either condition, (7.1) or (7.2), is both necessary and sufficient for such representability.

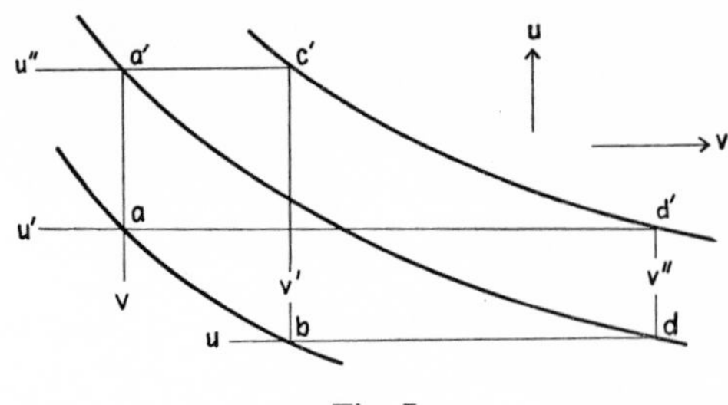


Fig. 7

The separable function

$$U(x) = (1+u)(1+u+v), \quad u = u(x_P) \geqq 0, \quad v = v(x_Q) \geqq 0,$$

fails to meet this test for a choice of points $x$, $x'$, $x''$ and functions $u$, $v$ such that

$$(u, u', u'') = (0, 1, 2), \qquad (v, v', v'') = (0, 3, 8).$$

Hence it cannot be transformed to the form (7.1).

*Note*: The references for Chapter 3 are included with those of Chapter 4.

CHAPTER 4

# REPRESENTATION OF PREFERENCE ORDERINGS OVER TIME[1]

TJALLING C. KOOPMANS



## 1. Preference over Time

In Section 1 of Chapter 3 we have argued the desirability of formalizing the idea of consumer's preference in terms of a *preference ordering* on a *prospect space*, before discussing the possibility of representing such an ordering by a *utility function*. The considerations there adduced have still greater force with regard to problems of evaluative comparison of growth paths for an indefinite future. If one interprets this as an infinite future, neither the concept of a utility function depending on infinitely many variables, nor that of a preference ordering on a space of infinitely many dimensions, has an obvious intuitive meaning. To start from the more basic one – the preference ordering – is therefore even more desirable in that case, in that it may help avoid implicit assumptions one is not aware of.

In the present chapter, therefore, the propositions of Chapter 3 are applied to the representation of preference orderings over time. Because of the close connections between the two chapters, the notations are almost identical, and a single list of references to the literature appears at the end of Chapter 4.

Before getting into details, a word is in order on the question whose preference is being studied. This question concerns the interpretation and relevance of the analysis, as distinct from the logical connections between

[1] This chapter reports on research under a grant from the National Science Foundation. It revises and extends Sections 5–9 of KOOPMANS (1966). I am indebted to Kenneth Arrow and Gerard Debreu for extremely valuable comments.

the properties of the ordering and the mathematical form of its representation. In regard to preference over time, the simplest interpretation of the orderings that have been studied most thus far is a normative one. One looks at various possible preference orderings that may be adopted, by whatever decision process, for the planning of an economy with a constant population size. New problems arise if population is expected to grow indefinitely or to keep changing in other ways.

Another possible interpretation is that one wishes to study descriptively the preference ordering of an individual with regard to his life-time consumption program, assuming that such an ordering is implicit in his decisions. For this interpretation the finite life span and the bequest motive need to be considered as well. For applications of such a preference ordering, see YAARI (1964).

Finally – the ultimate goal of a theory of preference over time for an economy with private wealth – one may wish to examine whether, or under what conditions, an aggregate preference ordering over time can be imputed, on an "as if" basis, to a society of individual decision-makers each guided by his own preference ordering over time.

In all these interpretations, normative or descriptive, the most intriguing problems arise from the fact that the future has a beginning but no discernible end. In contrast to this central problem, the question whether to use a discrete or a continuous time concept seems in the present state of knowledge primarily a matter of research tactics rather than of substance. So far the indications are that axiomatic analysis is somewhat simpler if one chooses discrete time. On the other hand, the maximization of a utility function of a given form under given technological constraints is often simpler with continuous time. We shall therefore here choose discrete time on the basis of expedience without further excuse or explanation.

## 2. Postulates Concerning a Preference Ordering over Time

We shall adopt a set of five postulates about a preference ordering $\gtrsim$ on a space ${}_1\mathscr{X}$ of *programs*, that is, of infinite sequences, denoted

$$(2.1) \qquad {}_1x \equiv (x_1, x_2, x_3, \ldots),$$

of vectors

$$(2.2) \qquad x_t \equiv (x_{t1}, x_{t2}, \ldots, x_{tn})$$

associated with successive time periods $t = 1, 2, 3, \ldots$. The *program space*

${}_1\mathscr{X}$ is the space of all such sequences, in which each vector $x_t$ is a point of the same (single period) *choice space* $\mathscr{X}$. Thus the components $x_{ti}$ of $x_t$ refer to a list of commodities, characteristics, or activities (as the case may be), which is the same for all $t$.

The postulates are modeled after those used in two earlier studies by Koopmans (1960) and by Koopmans, Diamond and Williamson (1964). The main difference is that the former studies presupposed the existence of a continuous representation. In the present study, the postulates refer to a continuous ordering, and the proximate aim of the study is to derive the existence of a continuous representation. Further differences will be noted in connection with the third and fifth postulates.

The problem of logical independence of the postulates is not investigated. The formulation and sequence of postulates is chosen primarily from the point of view of naturalness of interpretation. One case of recognized dependence between postulates is noted in Footnote 4.

It will be useful occasionally to employ short notations for finite or infinite segments of the program sequence, as follows,

$$ {}_1x \equiv (x_1, {}_2x) \equiv (x_1, \ldots, x_{t-1}, {}_tx) \equiv ({}_1x_{t-1}, {}_tx) . \tag{2.3}$$

In an infinite-dimensional space such as ${}_1\mathscr{X}$, the choice of the distance function is crucial for the meaning of the continuity concept implied in it. We shall adopt the function[2]

$$ D({}_1x, {}_1y) \equiv \sup_t d(x_t, y_t) \tag{2.4}$$

where $d(x_t, y_t)$ is the distance between the $t$-th period installments $x_t$, $y_t$ of the programs ${}_1x$, ${}_1y$, according to the definition

$$ d(x_t, y_t) \equiv \max_i |x_{ti} - y_{ti}| . \tag{2.5}$$

Postulate 1 (Continuity). *The program space ${}_1\mathscr{X}$ is the space of all programs ${}_1x$ such that, for all $t$, $x_t$ is in a choice space $\mathscr{X}$, which is a connected subset of $n$-dimensional Euclidean space. On the program space there exists a complete preference ordering $\succsim$, which is continuous with regard to the distance function* (2.4).

---

[2] The symbol $\sup_t d_t$ denotes the largest of the numbers $d_t$, $t = 1, 2, 3, \ldots$, if there is a largest, or the smallest number not exceeded by any $d_t$ if there is no largest. Such a number exists whenever $\mathscr{X}$ is bounded, that is, when the range of $d(x, y)$ for all $x$, $y$ in $\mathscr{X}$ is bounded. If $\mathscr{X}$ is unbounded we admit the possibility that $D({}_1x, {}_1y) = \infty$.

POSTULATE 2 (Sensitivity). *There exists a program* ${}_1x$ *in* ${}_1\mathscr{X}$ *and a vector* $y_1$ *in* $\mathscr{X}$ *such that*

$${}_1x = (x_1, x_2, x_3, \ldots) \succ (y_1, x_2, x_3, \ldots).$$

The first purpose of P2 is to exclude the trivial case where all programs in ${}_1\mathscr{X}$ are equivalent. However, P2 does more than that. It also excludes orderings in which the standing of any program ${}_1x$ relative to other programs is independent of any vector $x_t$ pertaining to any specific period $t$, but does depend on the asymptotic behavior of $x_t$ as $t$ tends to infinity.[3]

Next we introduce two independence postulates, P3′ and P3″, both of which will be maintained throughout Sections 2–6. In Section 7 we comment briefly on the case where P3″ is omitted. In these postulates we employ an arbitrary but fixed reference program,

$$\text{(2.6)} \qquad {}_1z = (z_1, {}_2z) = (z_1, z_2, {}_3z),$$

to define five orderings, induced by $\succsim$ on factor spaces of ${}_1\mathscr{X}$, and denoted $\succsim_1^z$, $\succsim_2^z$, ${}_1\succsim_2^z$, $\succsim_3^z$, $\succsim_2^z$, as follows:

$$\text{(2.7)} \qquad \begin{cases} x_1 \succsim_1^z y_1 & \text{means } (x_1, {}_2z) \succsim (y_1, {}_2z) \\ {}_2x \,{}_2\!\succsim^z {}_2y & \text{means } (z_1, {}_2x) \succsim (z_1, {}_2y) \\ (x_1, x_2) \,{}_1\!\succsim_2^z (y_1, y_2) & \text{means } (x_1, x_2, {}_3z) \succsim (y_1, y_2, {}_3z) \\ {}_3x \,{}_3\!\succsim^z {}_3y & \text{means } (z_1, z_2, {}_3x) \succsim (z_1, z_2, {}_3y) \\ x_2 \succsim_2^z y_2 & \text{means } (z_1, x_2, {}_3z) \succsim (z_1, y_2, {}_3z) \end{cases}$$

POSTULATE 3′ (Limited Independence). *The two orderings* $\succsim_1^z$, $\succsim_2^z$ *are independent of the reference program* ${}_1z$.

POSTULATE 3″ (Extended Independence). *The ordering* ${}_1\succsim_2^z$ *is independent of* ${}_1z$.

For convenient reference, we also introduce

POSTULATE 3 (Complete Independence). *Both* P3′ *and* P3″ *hold.*[4]

---

[3] A simple example of such an ordering $\succsim$ satisfying all postulates except P2 is that in which $\mathscr{X}$ is one-dimensional and $\succsim$ is represented by $\lim_{T\to\infty} \sup_{t\geqq T} x_t$. This ordering looks only at the highest consumption level that is, ultimately, and again and again thereafter, at least temporarily reached or arbitrarily closely approached. (Note the contrast between succinct mathematical notation and involved equivalent verbal statement$_1$.)

[4] By GORMAN (1968b) (see Footnote 10 of Chapter 3), the independence of ${}_1\succsim_2^z$ and ${}_2\succsim^z$ implies that of $\succsim_1^z$.

Whenever one or both of P3′, P3″ are assumed in what follows, the corresponding orderings will be denoted $\precsim_1, \precsim_2, {}_1\precsim_2$. Note that ${}_1\precsim_2$ would have been denoted $\precsim_{1,2}$ in Chapter 3.

In the earlier studies referred to above, the implications of P3′ were pursued at length, those of P3 only briefly mentioned. In this study, the emphasis is reversed.

Neither P3′ nor P3″ can be regarded as realistic. Taken together, they will be found to preclude all complementarity between the consumption of different periods. P3′ by itself will be seen to permit a limited complementarity among the utility levels to be associated with consumption in successive periods, but still no complementarity between individual commodities or activities in different periods. P3 or P3′ should therefore be looked upon as first approximations, made to facilitate exploration of the implications of the fourth postulate, the real objective of this study:

Postulate 4 (Stationarity). *There exists a first period vector $x_1^*$ in $\mathscr{X}$ with the property that the programs*

$$ {}_1x = (x_1^*, {}_2x) = (x_1^*, x_2, x_3, \ldots) $$

$$ {}_1y = (x_1^*, {}_2y) = (x_1^*, y_2, y_3, \ldots) $$

*are such that ${}_1x \precsim_1 {}_1y$ if and only if the programs*[5]

$$ {}_1v = (v_1, v_2, v_3, \ldots) = (x_2, x_3, x_4, \ldots) = {}_2x, $$

$$ {}_1w = (w_1, w_2, w_3, \ldots) = (y_2, y_3, y_4, \ldots) = {}_2y, $$

*defined by $v_t \equiv x_{t+1}$, $w_t \equiv y_{t+1}$, $t = 1, 2, \ldots$, are such that ${}_1v \precsim_1 {}_1w$.*

Before interpreting this postulate in less formal language, we note that, if one particular $x_1 = x_1^*$ in $\mathscr{X}$ has this property, then by P3′ every $x_1$ in $\mathscr{X}$ has this property. Using this, P4 says that if two programs ${}_1x$, ${}_1y$ have a common first-period vector $x_1 = y_1$, then the programs ${}_1v$, ${}_1w$ obtained by deleting $x_1$ from ${}_1x$ and from ${}_1y$, respectively, and advancing the timing of all subsequent vectors by one period, are ordered in the same way as ${}_1x$, ${}_1y$.

It is worth emphasizing that in this statement nothing is said or implied about the ordering of "then future" programs ${}_2x$, ${}_2y$ that may be applied

[5] In the notations ${}_2x$, ${}_2y$ as used here, there is no longer a necessary connection between the presubscript of ${}_2x$ and the timing of the first installment $x_2$ of that program. That is, $x_2$ simply means the vector that happened to represent second period consumption in the program ${}_1x$. In the program ${}_2x = {}_1v$, that same consumption occurs in the first period. With this point established, the notations ${}_1v$, ${}_1w$ will no longer be needed in what follows.

after the first period has elapsed. That is, no question of consistency or inconsistency of orderings adopted at different points in time is raised.[6] Only the ordering $\succsim$ applying "now" is under discussion. Applied repeatedly, P4 implies that the present ordering of two programs $(x_1, \ldots, x_{t-1}, {}_tx) \equiv ({}_1x_{t-1}, {}_tx)$ and $({}_1x_{t-1}, {}_ty)$ that start to differ in a designated way only from some point $t$ in time onward is independent both of what that point in time is, and of what the common values ${}_1x_{t-1}$ up to that point are.

The fifth and last postulate asserts, roughly, that the end result of an infinite sequence of improvements starting from some given program is itself an improvement over that program. If only a finite number of future periods is affected by all but a finite number of the improvements, such an assertion is already implied in P1, P3′, P4. For simplicity we will refer only to a sequence of improvements made to successive vectors in the program, taken one at a time. A similar postulate has been used by DIAMOND (1965). An alternative postulate in terms of improvements affecting several periods at a time is briefly considered in Subsection 6* below.

POSTULATE 5 (Monotonicity). *If* ${}_1x$, ${}_1y$ *are programs such that, for all* $t = 1, 2, \ldots, (x_1, x_2, \ldots, x_{t-1}, y_t, y_{t+1}, y_{t+2}, \ldots) \precsim (x_1, x_2, \ldots, x_{t-1}, x_t, y_{t+1}, y_{t+2}, \ldots)$ *then* ${}_1y \precsim {}_1x$.

It can be shown that, given all other postulates, P5 is implied in the following stronger postulate, used in a previous study (KOOPMANS (1960)).

POSTULATE 5′ (Extreme Programs). *There exist in* ${}_1\mathscr{X}$ *a best and a worst program.*

There is some interest in avoiding that stronger statement wherever possible, with a view to problems of optimal growth under continuing technical change.

On the basis of the postulates set out, we seek to construct a representation of $\succsim$ on the entire program space ${}_1\mathscr{X}$, or on as large a subspace of it as we can. Our strategy will be first to find such representations on suitably chosen subspaces of ${}_1\mathscr{X}$.

## 3. Representation of $\succsim$ on Any Subspace of Ultimately Identical Programs

Since the space ${}_1\mathscr{X}$ is infinite-dimensional, Proposition 1 cannot be directly applied to the ordering $\succsim$ given on it.[7] For this reason, we shall

---

[6] For a discussion of that question, see STROTZ (1957).

[7] While it is true that Proposition 1 can be extended to infinite-dimensional spaces having the topological property of "separability" (see DEBREU (1954, 1964)), the distance function (2.4) does not endow ${}_1\mathscr{X}$ with that property.

in the present section study $\succsim$ on the subspace ${}_1\mathscr{X}_T^z$ of all programs of the form

$$ {}_1x = ({}_1x_T\,,\, {}_{T+1}z)\,, \tag{3.1} $$

where ${}_1z$ is again an arbitrary but fixed reference program. Since programs in this subspace differ only in the segments ${}_1\mathscr{X}_T$, the ordering $\succsim$ on ${}_1\mathscr{X}$ restricted to the subspace ${}_1\mathscr{X}_T^z$ induces an ordering of sequences ${}_1x_T$ of length $T$ on the space ${}_1\mathscr{X}_T$. We shall denote this ordering by ${}_1\succsim_T$. In Subsection 3* we shall prove

RESULT D. *For all T, the ordering ${}_1\succsim_T$ is independent of ${}_1z$, and is represented by a function of the form*

$$ U_T({}_1x_T) = u(x_1) + \alpha u(x_2) + \cdots + \alpha^{T-1} u(x_T), \quad 0<\alpha<1\,. \tag{3.2} $$

*Here $u(x)$ is a continuous function defined on $\mathscr{X}$, and both $\alpha$ and $u(x)$ are independent of T.*

The proof proceeds through a succession of statements which we label (*Da*), (*Db*), ..., recording in each case the postulates and/or previous results used in the proof. The notations for induced orderings extend those of (2.7).

(*Da*; P3′, P4) The induced ordering ${}_t\succsim^z$ of sequences ${}_tx$, defined by restricting $\succsim$ to the set of programs $({}_1z_{t-1}\,,\, {}_tx)$ is independent of ${}_1z$ and of $t$.

(*Db*; P3′, P4) The induced ordering $\succsim_t^z$ of vectors $x_t$ is independent of ${}_1z$ and of $t$.

(*Dc*; P3, P4) The induced ordering ${}_{t-1}\succsim_t^z$ of vectors $(x_{t-1}\,,\, x_t)$ is independent of ${}_1z$ and of $t$.

(*Dd*; *C*, *Db*, *Dc*) The induced ordering ${}_1\succsim_T^z$ of sequences ${}_1x_T$ is independent of ${}_1z$, and is represented by a continuous function of the form

$$ U_T({}_1x_T) = u_1(x_1) + u_2(x_2) + \cdots + u_T(x_T)\,, \tag{3.3} $$

unique up to a linear transformation similar to (5.5) in Chapter 3.

(*De*; *Dd*, P4) One can choose the $u_i(x_i)$ in (3.3) in such a way that (3.2) holds with $\alpha>0$, where $\alpha$ is unique, and where $u(x)$ is unique up to a linear transformation

$$ u^*(x) = \beta + \gamma u(x), \qquad \gamma>0\,. \tag{3.4} $$

(*Df*; *De*, P5) $\alpha<1$.

3*. *Proof of Result D.* Clearly the continuity of $\succsim$ entails the continuity of all restricted orderings induced by it.

(*Da*). P3′ allows us to write

$$(3.5)\qquad \precsim_1^z = \precsim_1, \qquad {}_2\precsim^z = {}_2\precsim.$$

Using the symbol $\Leftrightarrow$ to denote logical equivalence, these statements are made explicit by

$$(3.6)\qquad \text{for all } {}_2x^*, x_1, y_1, \qquad (x_1, {}_2z) \succsim (y_1, {}_2z) \Leftrightarrow (x_1, {}_2x^*) \succsim (y_1, {}_2x^*),$$

$$(3.7)\qquad \text{for all } x_1^*, {}_2x, {}_2y, \qquad (z_1, {}_2x) \succsim (z_1, {}_2y) \Leftrightarrow (x_1^*, {}_2x) \succsim (x_1^*, {}_2y).$$

In particular, choosing for $x_1^*$ in (3.7) the $x_1^*$ occurring in P4, we have from P4

$$(3.8)\qquad \text{for all } {}_2x, {}_2y, \qquad (z_1, {}_2x) \succsim (z_1, {}_2y) \Leftrightarrow {}_2x \succsim {}_2y,$$

an implication which can be applied once more to give

$$(z_1, z_2, {}_3x) \succsim (z_1, z_2, {}_3y) \Leftrightarrow (z_2, {}_3x) \succsim (z_2, {}_3y) \Leftrightarrow {}_3x \succsim {}_3y, \text{ etc.}$$

These results are summarized in

$$(3.9)\qquad {}_t\succsim^z = {}_t\succsim = \cdots = {}_2\succsim = \succsim \qquad t = 2, 3, \ldots,$$

keeping in mind the notational practice explained in Footnote 5.

(*Db*). From (3.8) and (3.6), we have, for all ${}_1x^*$,

$$(z_1, x_2, {}_3z) \succsim (z_1, y_2, {}_3z) \Leftrightarrow (x_2, {}_3z) \succsim (y_2, {}_3z) \Leftrightarrow$$
$$\Leftrightarrow (x_2, {}_3x^*) \succsim (y_2, {}_3x^*) \Leftrightarrow (x_1^*, x_2, {}_3x^*) \succsim (x_1^*, y_2, {}_3x^*).$$

This reasoning and its repetition yield

$$(3.10)\qquad \succsim_t^z = \succsim_t = \cdots = \succsim_2 = \succsim_1, \quad t = 1, 2, 3, \ldots.$$

(*Dc*). We now bring in P3″, written as ${}_1\succsim_2^z = {}_1\succsim_2$. Together with (3.8) this implies that, for all ${}_1x^*$,

$$(z_1, x_2, x_3, {}_4z) \succsim (z_1, y_2, y_3, {}_4z) \Leftrightarrow (x_2, x_3, {}_4z) \succsim (y_2, y_3, {}_4z) \Leftrightarrow$$
$$\Leftrightarrow (x_2, x_3, {}_4x^*) \succsim (y_2, y_3, {}_4x^*) \Leftrightarrow (x_1^*, x_2, x_3, {}_4x^*) \succsim (x_1^*, y_2, y_3, {}_4x^*).$$

Since this can again be repeated, we have

$$(3.11)\qquad {}_{t-1}\succsim_t^z = {}_{t-1}\succsim_t = \cdots = {}_2\succsim_3 = {}_1\succsim_2, \quad t = 2, 3, \ldots.$$

(*Dd*). We consider ${}_1\succsim_T^z$, and note that $\succsim_t^z$, $t = 1, \ldots, T$ and ${}_{t-1}\succsim_t^z$, $t = 2, \ldots, T$, are all independent of ${}_1z$. By P2, $\succsim_1$ permits $x_1 \succ_1 y_1$, and by (3.10) a similar statement holds for $\succsim_t$, $t = 2, 3, \ldots$. The premises of Result C of Section 6 in Chapter 3 are therefore satisfied, and the representation

(3.3) follows. Hence ${}_1\succsim_T^z$ is independent of $z$, and we write ${}_1\succsim_T$ from here on.

(*De*). By (3.8) and (3.3), ${}_2\succsim_T$ is represented on ${}_2\mathscr{X}_T$ by either of the functions

$$u_2(x_2)+u_3(x_3)+\cdots+u_T(x_T),$$
$$u_1(x_2)+u_2(x_3)+\cdots+u_{T-1}(x_T).$$

It follows, along the lines of the uniqueness proof of Proposition 2, that, for all $x$ in $\mathscr{X}$ and all $T\geqq 3$,

$$u_{t+1}(x)=\beta_t+\alpha u_t(x),\quad t=1,\ldots,T-1,\quad \alpha>0.$$

Since we are free to choose each $u_t(x)$, $t=2,\ldots,T-1$, so as to have $\beta_t=0$ for all $t$, (3.2) results, with $u(x)=u_1(x)\equiv u^{(T)}(x)$, say, which might still depend on $T$. However, by comparing the representation (3.2) of ${}_1\succsim_T$ in terms of $u^{(T)}(x)$ with that in terms of $u^{(T+1)}(x)$ obtained from (3.2) with $T+1$ sustituted for $T$, one finds, again using the uniqueness argument, that the same $u^{(T)}(x)=u(x)$ can be used for all $T\geqq 3$, and hence, by holding ${}_3x$ constant, also for $T=1, 2$.

(*Df*). The proof of *Df* will be given in Section 4.

## 4. Representation of $\succsim$ on the Space of Ultimately Constant Programs

In this section we choose a favorable ground on which to face the infinite horizon by first restricting ourselves to the space ${}_{\text{con}}\mathscr{X}$ of *constant programs*

(4.1) $$ {}_{\text{con}}x\equiv(x,x,x,\ldots),$$

that is, of programs ${}_1x$ for which $x_t=x$ for all $t$.

The points of ${}_{\text{con}}\mathscr{X}$ are in a one-to-one correspondence

(4.2) $$ {}_{\text{con}}x\leftrightarrow x$$

to those of $\mathscr{X}$. Because for all $x$, $x'$ in $\mathscr{X}$,

(4.3) $$D({}_{\text{con}}x,{}_{\text{con}}x')=d(x,x'),$$

this correspondence preserves the distance function, and therewith the continuity concept. Moreover, if $x$, $y$ are vectors of $\mathscr{X}$ such that $y\precsim_1 x$, then, by *Db* and P5, if ${}_{\text{con}}x_T$ denotes the sequence $(x,x,\ldots,x)$ of $T$ identical vectors $x$,

(4.4) $$ {}_{\text{con}}y\precsim(x,{}_{\text{con}}y)\precsim\cdots\precsim({}_{\text{con}}x_T,{}_{\text{con}}y)\precsim\cdots\precsim{}_{\text{con}}x.$$

The continuous ordering $\succsim_1$ on $\mathscr{X}$ is therefore transformed by the correspondence (4.2) into the ordering $\succsim$ restricted to ${}_{\text{con}}\mathscr{X}$. In particular,

RESULT E. *Any continuous representation $u(x)$ of $\succsim_1$ on $\mathscr{X}$ is at the same time a continuous representation of $\succsim$ restricted to ${}_{\text{con}}\mathscr{X}$.*

Note that only limited independence (P3′) was used in the proof of Result E.

Next we consider the space $\mathscr{X}_{\text{con}}$ of *ultimately constant programs*, that is, of programs such that, for some $T \geqq 0$,

$$(4.5) \qquad {}_1x = ({}_1x_T, {}_{\text{con}}x) = (x_1, \ldots, x_T, x, x, \ldots)$$

(for $T=0$ the term ${}_1x_T$ is absent). One readily verifies that the reasoning that led to Result *De* also applies in any subspace $\mathscr{X}^{(T)}_{\text{con}}$ of $\mathscr{X}_{\text{con}}$ consisting of programs (4.5) *with a fixed T*. The only difference consists of an added term in (3.2). One now finds for all $T \geqq 2$ a continuous representation of $\succsim$, restricted to $\mathscr{X}^{(T)}_{\text{con}}$, by the function

$$(4.6) \qquad u(x_1) + \alpha u(x_2) + \ldots \alpha^{T-1} u(x_T) + f_T(u(x)), \quad 0 < \alpha,$$

where $f_T(u)$ is continuous and increasing. From this representation we can derive two representations of $\succsim$ restricted to $\mathscr{X}^{(T-1)}_{\text{con}}$, one (4.7a) by setting $x_1 = x_1^*$ and applying P4, the other (4.7b) by setting $x_T = x$, as follows,

$$(4.7a) \qquad U^{(a)}({}_1x) \equiv \alpha u(x_1) + \cdots + \alpha^{T-1} u(x_{T-1}) + f_T(u(x))$$

$$(4.7b) \qquad U^{(b)}({}_1x) \equiv u(x_1) + \cdots + \alpha^{T-2} u(x_{T-1}) + \alpha^{T-1} u(x) + f_T(u(x)).$$

By Result C these representations are, for all $T \geqq 3$, unique up to a linear transformation. Comparison of the first terms shows that

$$U^{(a)}({}_1x) = \alpha U^{(b)}({}_1x) + \beta,$$

which implies that

$$f_T(u) = \alpha^T u + \alpha f_T(u) + \beta.$$

Since $f_T(u)$ is increasing, we must have $\alpha < 1$, that is, *Df* above, thus completing the proof of Result D. Solving for $f_T(u)$ and dropping the constant term, we have

RESULT F. *On the space $\mathscr{X}_{\text{con}}$ of ultimately constant programs $\succsim$ is represented by the continuous function* (*with* $0 < \alpha < 1$)

$$(4.8) \quad U({}_1x) = U({}_1x_T, {}_{\text{con}}x) \equiv u(x_1) + \alpha u(x_2) + \cdots + \alpha^{T-1} u(x_T) + \frac{\alpha^T}{1-\alpha} u(x),$$

*unique up to a linear transformation.*

Note that in this function $T$ itself depends on the given ultimately constant program ${}_1x$. For definiteness one can specify that $T+1$ is the earliest time from which onward ${}_1x$ is constant. However, the same value of $U({}_1x)$ is obtained if one allows $T+1$ to be any time, earliest or not, beyond which ${}_1x$ is constant. It is for that reason that the function (4.8) represents $\succsim$ on the space $\mathscr{X}_{\text{con}}$ for *all* ultimately constant programs, regardless of the values of their "minimal" $T$.

## 5. Representation of $\succsim$ on the Space of Programs Bounded in Utility

It is now possible to indicate a large subspace of the program space on which the ordering $\succsim$ is represented by

$$U({}_1x) \equiv \sum_{t=1}^{\infty} \alpha^{t-1} u(x_t), \quad 0<\alpha<1. \tag{5.1}$$

We shall call a program ${}_1x$ *bounded in utility* if there exist vectors $\underline{x}$, $\bar{x}$ in $\mathscr{X}$ with $\underline{x} \prec_1 \bar{x}$ such that

$$\underline{x} \precsim_1 x_t \precsim_1 \bar{x} \text{ for all } t = 1, 2, \ldots. \tag{5.2}$$

We can then show

Proposition 3. *On the space ${}_1\mathscr{X}^*$ of all programs bounded in utility, the ordering $\succsim$ is represented by the continuous function* (5.1).

It is to be noted that for ultimately constant programs the function (5.1) is identical with that in (4.8). Hence Proposition 3 includes Result F.

5*. *Proof of Proposition 3.* We first note that if ${}_1x$ is bounded in utility, then,

$$u(\underline{x}) \leqq u(x_t) \leqq u(\bar{x}) \text{ for all } t,$$

and, since $0<\alpha<1$, the series in (5.1) is absolutely convergent, hence its sum exists and is continuous with respect to ${}_1x$.

Now let ${}_1x$ and ${}_1y$ be two programs bounded in utility, and define bounds applicable to both ${}_1x$ and ${}_1y$ by

$$\underline{z} \equiv \begin{cases} \underline{x} \text{ if } \underline{x} \precsim_1 \underline{y} \\ \underline{y} \text{ if } \underline{y} \prec_1 \underline{x} \end{cases}, \qquad \bar{z} \equiv \begin{cases} \bar{x} \text{ if } \bar{x} \succsim_1 \bar{y} \\ \bar{y} \text{ if } \bar{y} \succ_1 \bar{x} \end{cases},$$

$$\underline{u} \equiv u(\underline{z}), \qquad \bar{u} \equiv u(\bar{z}), \qquad \text{so } \underline{u} \leqq \bar{u}.$$

Assume first that $U({}_1x) > U({}_1y)$, and write

$$U({}_1x) - U({}_1y) \equiv 3\Delta > 0 .$$

For comparison purposes we consider two programs

$${}_1x^{(T)} = ({}_1x_T, {}_{\text{con}}\underline{z}), \qquad {}_1y^{(T)} = ({}_1y_T, {}_{\text{con}}\bar{z}),$$

where $T$ is chosen large enough to have

$$\left(\sum_{t=T+1}^{\infty} \alpha^{t-1}\right)(\bar{u} - \underline{u}) = \alpha^T \cdot \frac{\bar{u} - \underline{u}}{1 - \alpha} \leqq \Delta .$$

Because of $\underline{u} \leqq u(x_t) \leqq \bar{u}$ and similar inequalities for $y_t$ we then have

$$U({}_1x) - U({}_1x^{(T)}) = \sum_{t=T+1}^{\infty} \alpha^{t-1}(u(x_t) - \underline{u}) \leqq \Delta, \qquad U({}_1y^{(T)}) - U({}_1y) \leqq \Delta ,$$

and therefore

$$U({}_1x^{(T)}) - U({}_1y^{(T)}) \geqq \Delta > 0 .$$

Since ${}_1x^{(T)}$, ${}_1y^{(T)}$ are ultimately constant, this implies ${}_1x^{(T)} \succ {}_1y^{(T)}$ by Result F. But then, using P5, ${}_1x \succsim {}_1x^{(T)} \succ {}_1y^{(T)} \succsim {}_1y$, which yields

$$U({}_1x) > U({}_1y) \text{ implies } {}_1x \succ {}_1y , \tag{5.3}$$

confirming the representation (5.1) in this case.

Assume next that, for two programs ${}_1x$, ${}_1y$ bounded in utility,

$$U({}_1x) = U({}_1y) \text{ but } {}_1x \prec {}_1y . \tag{5.4}$$

Then there exists $t_0$ such that

$$x_{t_0} \prec_1 y_{t_0}, \text{ so } u(x_{t_0}) < u(y_{t_0}), \tag{5.5}$$

because "$x_t \succsim_1 y_t$ for all $t$" would contradict "${}_1x \prec {}_1y$" by P5.

Using the connectedness of $\mathscr{X}$, we draw an arc $\mathscr{A}$ in $\mathscr{X}$ connecting $x_{t_0}$ and $y_{t_0}$ (see Fig. 1). Then, by the continuity of $u(x)$, we can find a point $x$ on $\mathscr{A}$ such that

$$u(x) = u(x_{t_0}) \tag{5.6}$$

while, for each $\delta > 0$, there exists $x'$ on $\mathscr{A}$ such that

$$d(x, x') \leqq \delta , \tag{5.7a}$$

$$u(x') > u(x) . \tag{5.7b}$$

Using $P_1$ we can choose $\delta$ such that, if (5.7a) holds,

$$_1x \prec {_1x'} \equiv ({_1x_{t_0-1}}, x', {_{t_0+1}x}) \prec {_1y}.$$

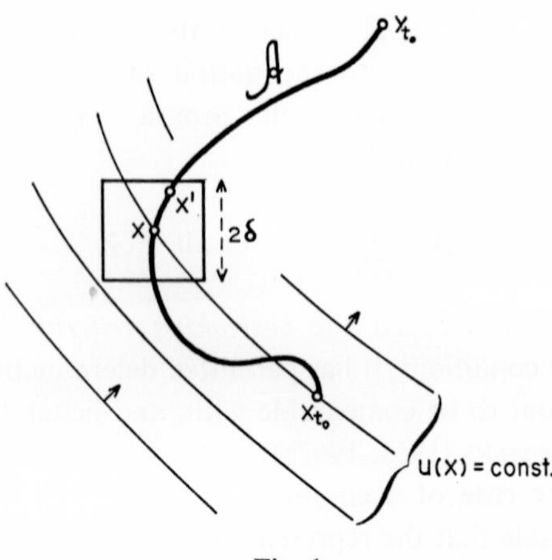


Fig. 1

But then, by (5.7b) and (5.1),

$$U({_1x'}) > U({_1x}) = U({_1y}) \text{ but } {_1x'} \prec {_1y},$$

a contradiction of (5.3). Hence (5.4) is false, and

$$U({_1x}) = U({_1y}) \text{ implies } {_1x} \sim {_1y},$$

confirming (5.1) in this case as well. Since the third case, $U({_1x}) < U({_1y})$, is symmetric to the first, the proof is now complete.

## 6. Concluding Remarks on the Representation of $\succsim$

The representations we have found show unexpectedly strong implications of the postulates used. It turns out that offsetting program changes in future periods can be determined on the basis of just two mathematical data,

(i) the function $u(x)$ which allows the comparison of "utility differences" within the same period, and

(ii) a constant discount factor $\alpha$ which extends that comparison to utility differences in different periods.

The representation may be called cardinal in the sense that only increasing linear transformations, applied simultaneously to $u(x)$ and to $U({}_1x)$, will preserve these simple properties.

Since $\alpha<1$ the present postulates do not permit expression of the ethical principle of treating all future generations' utilities on a par with present utilities. A way has been found to include that limiting case in models of optimal growth by retreating to the notion of a partial ordering. VON WEIZSÄCKER (1965) has proposed to call a program ${}_1x$ better than a program ${}_1y$ if there exists a $T \geqq 1$ such that

$$\sum_{t=1}^{T'} u(x_t) > \sum_{t=1}^{T'} u(y_t) \text{ for all } T' \geqq T.$$

This criterion has been called the *overtaking criterion* by GALE (1967). Under appropriate conditions, it has permitted determination of an optimal path which turns out to be comparable with, and better than, every other feasible path (KOOPMANS (1965, 1967a)).

Returning to the case of a complete ordering, with a discount factor $\alpha<1$, it is conceivable that the representation (5.1) can be extended on the basis of the present postulates to larger sets of programs not all bounded in utility. In Subsection 6* we allude to a reasoning from a strengthened monotonicity postulate that permits an extension to all programs for which the sum (5.1) exists.

It will be clear that, if $u(x)$ is unbounded on $\mathscr{X}$, then there exist programs for which the sum (5.1) diverges. In such cases the representation (3.2) restricted to a class of ultimately identical programs, all "divergent in utility," may still be valuable. It would permit formulating a partial optimality criterion in which a path is found to stand comparison with all other feasible paths differing from it in a finite number of future periods only. Other considerations would then have to be brought to bear on the choice of the class of ultimately identical programs.

6*. *An Alternative Monotonicity Postulate.* One might wish to strengthen P5 to

POSTULATE 5″ (Strong Monotonicity). *If* ${}_1x$, ${}_1y^{(i)}$, $i=1, 2, \ldots$, *are programs such that*

$$\left.\begin{aligned} &{}_1y^{(i)} \precsim {}_1y^{(i+1)}, \\ &{}_1y^{(i)}_{t_i} = {}_1x_{t_i}, \quad 0 \leqq t_i < t_{i+1}, \end{aligned}\right\} \quad \text{for all } i=1, 2, \ldots,$$

*then,* ${}_1y \precsim {}_1x$.

This postulate considers successive improvements each extending over an arbitrary number of periods, but where the set of periods affected by successive improvements becomes more and more remote in time. It allows one, for any program ${}_1x$ for which the sum (5.1) exists, to construct an equivalent constant program ${}_{\text{con}}x$ such that $U({}_1x) = U({}_{\text{con}}x)$, thus extending the representation (5.1) to all programs for which that sum exists. Conversely, for any program ${}_1x$ equivalent to a constant program, the sum (5.1) does exist.

## 7. Limited Independence, Time Perspective and Impatience

If instead of complete independence (P3) we postulate only limited independence (P3′), Proposition 2 is not available, and we must fall back on Result A. A study along these lines was made in two consecutive papers by KOOPMANS (1960) and by KOOPMANS, DIAMOND and WILLIAMSON (1964). The postulates of that study were the analogues of the present postulates of continuity (P1), sensitivity (P2), limited independence (P3′), stationarity (P4), and the existence of extreme programs (P5′), applied to a given utility function $U({}_1x)$ rather than to an ordering.[8]

A theorem by DIAMOND (1965, p. 173) now allows us to obtain all the results of the previous study from the present postulates P1′ (see Footnote 8), P2, P3′, P4, P5′ as applied to an ordering $\succsim$ on ${}_1\mathscr{X}$. The resulting representation $U({}_1x)$ of $\succsim$ is found to satisfy a *recursive relation*

$$U({}_1x) = V(u(x_1), U({}_2x)), \tag{7.1}$$

where $V(u, U)$ is a continuous function defined on the product of two nondegenerate intervals, which is increasing in each of its variables. This *aggregator function* indicates how the single-period utility $u(x_1)$ of the first installment $x_1$ of ${}_1x$ and the utility $U({}_2x)$ of the sequel ${}_2x$ (were that sequel to start immediately) are combined to form the utility of the entire program ${}_1x$. In particular, if P3 holds, $V(u, U) = u + \alpha U$.

The representation (7.1) is *ordinal* in the sense that any pair of continuous increasing functions $\Phi$, $\varphi$ with the appropriate domains will define an

[8] Apart from this difference, P1 was strengthened to make P1′, say, by adding two statements: (a) that the continuity on ${}_1\mathscr{X}$ of $U({}_1x)$ is uniform on each equivalence set, (b) that $\mathscr{X}$ is bounded and convex. The latter was used in the proof that the range $\mathscr{U}$ of $U({}_1x)$ is an interval. Alternatively, that result could have been obtained by adding to P5′ that among the extreme programs there are a best and worst constant program, or by deriving that statement in turn from a variant of P5 restricted to $\sim$.

alternative representation

$$(7.2)\qquad U^*({}_1x) \equiv \Phi(U({}_1x)) = \Phi(V(u(x_1), U({}_2x)) = V^*(u^*(x_1), U^*({}_2x)),$$

say, where

$$(7.3)\qquad u^*(x) \equiv \varphi(u(x)), \quad V^*(u^*, U^*) \equiv \Phi(V(\varphi^{-1}(u^*), \Phi^{-1}(U^*))).$$

This being so, the question arises what takes the place of the discount factor $\alpha$, the existence of which was derived in Section 3 from P3. In particular, what corresponds to the inequality $\alpha<1$ crucial to convergence of the representation (5.1)?

It is readily seen from (7.2) and (7.3) (KOOPMANS (1960, Section 14*)) that, in the case of a differentiable function $V(u, U)$, the discount factor associated with a constant program ${}_{\text{con}}x = (x, x, x, \ldots)$,

$$(7.4)\qquad \alpha(x) \equiv \left(\frac{\partial V(u, U)}{\partial U}\right)_{u=u(x),\, U=U({}_{\text{con}}x)}$$

satisfies $0 \leqq \alpha(x) \leqq 1$, and is invariant under differentiable increasing scale changes for $u$ and $U$. Moreover, as distinct from the representation (5.1), $\alpha(x)$ in (7.4) can vary with $x$. The limited independence postulate P3′ therefore allows scope for the idea already expressed by Irving FISHER (1930, Chapter IV, Sections 3 and 6) with regard to individual preferences: that the discount factor may depend on the level of present and prospective income.

As an illustration, let $\mathscr{X}$ be the closed unit interval $\mathscr{I} = (0, 1)$, let $u(x) = x$, and consider the aggregator function

$$(7.5)\qquad V(x, U) = U + (x - U)(a - bx + cU),$$

where we require that

$$(7.6)\qquad b,\ c,\ a-2b,\ a-b-c,\ 1-a-2c > 0.$$

Then, if we assign to $U$ the same range $\mathscr{I}$, $V(x, U)$ is increasing in both variables, and

$$(7.7)\qquad V(0, 0) = 0, \qquad V(1, 1) = 1.$$

Finally, since $U({}_{\text{con}}x) = x$ is the only root $U$ of $U = V(x, U)$ in the range $\mathscr{I}$,

$$(7.8)\qquad \alpha(x) = 1 - a + (b - c)x.$$

Hence the direction of change of $\alpha(x)$ with increasing income $x$ is given by the sign of $(b-c)$. Following FISHER (1930, Chapter IV, Section 6), many but not all economists I have consulted regard an increasing $\alpha(x)$ as the normal case. This implies that the ratio of the marginal utility of future consumption to that of present consumption increases as the level of the constant consumption flow ${}_{\text{con}}x$ is raised. Examples where the sign of $\mathrm{d}\alpha(x)/\mathrm{d}x$ depends on $x$ can also be constructed.

While $\alpha(x)$ is defined only for constant programs, there is a generalization[9] of the convergence condition $\alpha<1$ in (5.1) to the present case that applies in the entire range of $V(u, U)$. It is found that there exists a transformation function $\Phi$ (here one takes $\varphi(u)=u$) such that the function $V^*(u, U^*)$ in (7.3) satisfies (dropping asterisks)

$$V(u, U')-V(u, U) \leqq U'-U \text{ whenever } U'>U. \tag{7.9}$$

This inequality has been called the (*weak*) *time perspective* property of the utility scale resulting from the transformation $\Phi$. It says that the utility difference between two programs, measured in a suitable scale, does not increase (and generally diminishes) if both programs are postponed by one or more periods, while the same consumption or the same sequence of consumptions is inserted in the gaps so created. This inequality between utility differences is satisfied by a class of scales linked by transformations that include nonlinear as well as all linear transformations. For this reason, a representation $U({}_1x)$ satisfying (7.1) where $V(u, U)$ has the property (7.9) has been called *quasi-cardinal.*

There are indications that the weak inequality sign ($\leqq$) in (7.9) can be strengthened to strict inequality ($<$), referred to as *strong time perspective*, without strengthening the postulates. If so, it follows that the function $U({}_1x)$ can be reconstructed from a pair of functions $u(x)$, $V(u, U)$ implied in it. The example (7.5), (7.6) has the strong time perspective property as it stands, without requiring a prior scale change.

Precisely because it compares utility differences between pairs of programs, the time perspective inequality, strong or weak, does not by itself predict the choice within any one pair of programs. However, by elementary steps of reasoning, (7.9) implies a second family of ordinal inequalities, of which the simplest representative is

$$\begin{cases} \text{if} \quad u=u(x)<u'=u(x'), \quad U({}_{\text{con}}x) \leqq U \leqq U({}_{\text{con}}x'), \\ \text{then } V(u', V(u, U)) \underset{(=)}{>} V(u, V(u', U)). \end{cases} \tag{7.10}$$

[9] This generalization has been derived from statement (*a*) in Footnote 8. The proof uses a variant of the theory of Haar measure.

This inequality, weak or strong depending on whether the inequality (7.9) is weak or strong, has been called an *impatience* inequality. It indicates that if the single-period utility of a vector $x'$ exceeds that of a vector $x$, then any program $(x', x, {}_3x)$, in which ${}_3x$ is selected from a wide class of "continuations," is preferred (or equivalent) to the corresponding program $(x, x', {}_3x)$ in which the better item is moved from first to second place. The class of continuations ${}_3x$ permitted in (7.10) consists of all those which, if started immediately, would be ranked between ${}_{\text{con}}x$ and ${}_{\text{con}}x'$. This condition should be read in conjunction with Result E of Section 4, which holds also under the present assumptions.

The impatience inequality holds for a wider range of $U$-values than that indicated in (7.10), and can be generalized to the interchange of two disjoint segments ${}_tx_{t'}$, ${}_sx_{s'}$ of a program, that need not be of equal length or contiguous in time.

## 8. Nonstationary Orderings and Eventual Impatience

Diamond (1965) has studied the implications of postulates similar to those of this chapter, with the main difference that no explicit stationarity postulate corresponding to our P4 is present. However, a certain comparability over time is introduced by assuming, in one interpretation, that there is only a single consumption good ($\mathscr{X}$ is the closed unit interval $\mathscr{C}$), more of which is always better. In another interpretation leading to the same mathematical analysis, there is a given single-period utility function $u(x)$ mapping $\mathscr{X}$ onto $\mathscr{C}$, which is the same for all $t$. For simplicity, we shall adopt the notation of an ordering $\succsim$ of all programs ${}_1x$ on the denumerable product space $\mathscr{C} \times \mathscr{C} \times \ldots = {}_1\mathscr{C}$, say, that corresponds to the first interpretation. The nonstationarity then applies to the way in which the sequences ${}_1x$ of scalars $x_t$ enter into $\succsim$.

Diamond's postulates then can be shown[10] to be equivalent to specializations, to the case $\mathscr{X} = \mathscr{C}$, of our P1, P3, supplemented by a postulate P6 implying similar specializations of P2, P5, P5$'$.

Postulate 6 (General Monotonicity.) *If* $x_t \geqq y_t$ *for all* $t$, $x_t > y_t$ *for some* $t$, *then* ${}_1x \succ {}_1y$.

From these assumptions he derives the following property of *eventual impatience*: For any given program ${}_1x$ and any number $\varepsilon > 0$, there exists

[10] Using the results of Gorman (1968b) referred to in Footnote 10 of Chapter 3.

a $T$ such that

$$(8.1)\qquad {}_1x \succ (x_t, {}_2x_{t-1}, x_1, {}_{t+1}x) \text{ for all } t \geqq T \text{ with } x_1 \geqq x_t + \varepsilon .$$

In words, the interchange with $x_1$ of any $x_t$ which occurs sufficiently far into the future, and which falls short of $x_1$ by at least $\varepsilon$, diminishes the utility of the program ${}_1x$. This subtle result, which at first sight appears to miss its aim by a hair's breadth, is both vindicated and complemented by another theorem, attributed to Yaari, which hits the mark exactly (see DIAMOND (1965, p. 176)). It states that P6 and the present specialization of P1 taken together are incompatible with the statement

$$\text{for all } t \text{ and all } {}_1x \text{ in } {}_1\mathscr{X},\ {}_1x \sim (x_t, {}_2x_{t-1}, x_1, {}_{t+1}x),$$

that expresses "equal treatment of all generations."

Similar but somewhat stronger conclusions are obtained by Diamond by changing the distance function underlying P1 to

$$D^*({}_1x, {}_1y) = \sum_{t=1}^{\infty} (\tfrac{1}{2})^t d(x_t, y_t).$$

The results are stronger presumably because this modification explicitly reduces the weight attached, in the definition of continuity, to given consumption differences in a more distant future.

## 9. Concluding Remarks

The main results of the studies reported in this chapter appear to be two-fold.

In the first place the studies show a sequence of instances of increasing generality, in which a complete and continuous preference ordering of consumption programs for an infinite future necessarily gives a decreasing, or eventually decreasing, weight to consumption in a more distant future. Somewhat fancifully, one may say that the real numbers appear to be a sufficiently rich set of labels to accommodate in a continuous manner all infinite sequences of consumption vectors *only* if one gradually or eventually decreases the weight given to the more distant vectors in the preference ordering to be represented.

Secondly, the studies containing the stationarity postulate P4 have produced interesting special forms for the utility function $U({}_1x)$ in terms of simpler functions $u(x)$ and possibly $V(u, U)$, that facilitate the use of $U({}_1x)$ in models of optimal economic growth, and may perhaps suggest further parametrization or other specialization for econometric studies of individual consumption plans over time.

The use of substantive terms such as "consumption," "preference," "time" in what is essentially a formal mathematical analysis may hinder the perception of other possible applications in which one or more of these terms are inappropriate. The stationarity postulate, however, strongly suggests temporal or other consecutiveness in the vectors $x_t$, $t = 1, 2, \ldots$, as a condition for meaningful application. In DIAMOND's (1965) study, where stationarity in the aggregation of single-period utilities is dropped, consecutiveness is immaterial in spite of appearances to the contrary in the formulation of some of the postulates. What is interpreted as eventual impatience if $t$ stands for time is therefore also open to the wider interpretation that in *any* permutation of the vectors in the infinite sequence $x_t$, $t = 1, 2, \ldots$, the weight given to vectors further up in the sequence must eventually decrease.

## References

ARROW, K. J. (1952), "The Determination of Many-Commodity Preferences Scales by Two-Commodity Comparisons," *Metroeconomica*, *4*, 105–115.

ARROW, K. J. (1963), *Social Choice and Individual Values*, (2nd ed.), Wiley, New York.

AUMANN, R. (1964a), "Subjective Programming," Chapter 12 in SHELLY and BRYAN (eds.), *Human Judgments and Optimality*, Wiley, New York, pp. 217–242.

BLASCHKE, W. and G. BOL (1938), *Geometrie der Gewebe*, Springer, Berlin.

DEBREU, G. (1954), "Representation of a Preference Ordering by a Numerical Function," Chapter 11 in THRALL, COOMBS, and DAVIS (eds.), *Decision Processes*, Wiley, New York, pp. 159–165.

DEBREU, G. (1959), *Theory of Value*, Wiley, New York.

DEBREU, G. (1960), "Topological Methods in Cardinal Utility Theory," Chapter 2 in K. J. ARROW, S. KARLIN, and P. SUPPES (eds.), *Mathematical Methods in the Social Sciences*, Stanford University Press, Stanford, pp. 16-26.

DEBREU, G. (1964), "Continuity Properties of Paretian Utility," *International Economic Review*, *5*, 285–293.

DIAMOND, P. A. (1965), "The Evaluation of Infinite Utility Streams," *Econometrica*, *33*, 170–177.

EILENBERG, S. (1941), "Ordered Topological Spaces," *American Journal of Mathematics*, *63*, 39–45.

FISHER, I. (1930, original edition), *The Theory of Interest*, reprinted by Augustus Kelley, New York, 1961.

GALE, D. (1967), "On Optimal Development in a Multi-Sector Economy," *Review of Economic Studies*, *34*, 1–18.

GALE, D. (1968), "A Mathematical Theory of Optimal Economic Development," *Bulletin of the American Mathematical Society*, *74*, 207–223.

GOLDMAN, S. M. and H. UZAWA (1964), "A Note on Separability in Demand Analysis," *Econometrica*, *32*, 387–398.

GORMAN, W. M. (1959a), "Separable Utility and Aggregation," *Econometrica*, *27*, 469–481.

GORMAN, W. M. (1959b), "The Empirical Implications of a Utility Tree: A Further Comment," *Econometrica*, *27*, 489.

GORMAN, W. M. (1965), "Conditions for Additive Preferences," (unpublished),

GORMAN, W. M. (1968a), "Conditions for Additive Separability," *Econometrica*, *36*, 605–609.

GORMAN, W. M. (1968b), "The Structure of Utility Functions," *Review of Economic Studies*, *35*, 367-390.

KOOPMANS, T. C. (1960), "Stationary Ordinal Utility and Impatience," *Econometrica*, *28*, 287–309.

KOOPMANS, T. C. (1964), "On Flexibility of Future Preference," Chapter 13 in SHELLY and BRYAN (eds.), *Human Judgments and Optimality*, Wiley, New York, pp. 243–254.

KOOPMANS, T. C., P. A. DIAMOND, and R. E. WILLIAMSON (1964b), "Stationary Utility and Time Perspective," *Econometrica*, *32*, 82–100.

KOOPMANS, T. C. (1965), "On the Concept of Optimal Economic Growth," in *The Econometric Approach to Development Planning*, North Holland, Amsterdam, and Rand McNally, Chicago, (a reissue of *Pontificiae Academiae Scientiarvm Scripta Varia*, Vol. XXVIII, 1965), pp. 225–300.

KOOPMANS, T. C. (1966), "Structure of Preference over Time," Cowles Foundation Discussion Paper No. 206.

KOOPMANS, T. C. (1967a), "Objectives, Constraints and Outcomes in Optimal Growth Models," *Econometrica*, *35*, 1–15.

KOOPMANS, T. C. (1967b), "Intertemporal Distribution and 'Optimal' Aggregate Economic Growth," Chapter 5 in FELLNER *et al.*, *Ten Economic Studies in the Tradition of Irving Fisher*, Wiley, New York, pp. 95–126.

KOOPMANS, T. C., P. A. DIAMOND, and R. E. WILLIAMSON (1964), "Stationary Utility and Time Perspective, "*Econometrica*, *32*, 82-100.

LANCASTER, K. J. (1966a), "A New Approach to Consumer Theory," *Journal of Political Economy*, *74*, 132–157.

LANCASTER, K. J. (1966b), "Change and Innovation in the Technology of Consumption," *American Economic Review*, *56*, 14–23.

LEONTIEF, W. (1947a), "Introduction to a Theory of the Internal Structure of Functional Relationships," *Econometrica*, *15*, 361–373.

LEONTIEF, W. (1947b), "A Note on the Interrelation of Subsets of Independent Variables of a Continuous Function with Continuous First Derivatives," *Bulletin of the American Mathematical Society*, *53*, 343–350.

RADER, T. (1963), "The Existence of a Utility Function to Represent Preferences," *Review of Economic Studies*, *30*, 229–232.

SAMUELSON, P. A. (1947), "Some Special Aspects of the Theory of Consumer's Behavior," Chapter 7 in *Foundations of Economic Analysis*, Harvard University Press, Cambridge, pp. 172–202.

STROTZ, R. H. (1956), "Myopia and Inconsistency in Dynamic Utility Maximization," *Review of Economic Studies*, *23*, 165–180.

STROTZ, R. H. (1957), "The Empirical Implications of a Utility Tree," *Econometrica*, *25*, 269–280.

STROTZ, R. H. (1959), "The Utility Tree–A Correction and Further Appraisal," *Econometrica*, *27*, 482–488.

VON WEIZSÄCKER, C. C. (1965), "Existence of Optimal Programmes of Accumulation for an Infinite Time Horizon," *Review of Economic Studies*, *32*, 85–104.

WOLD, H. (1943), "A Synthesis of Pure Demand Analysis, Part II," *Skandinavisk* Aktuaritidskrift, pp. 220–263.

YAARI, M. E. (1964), "On the Consumer's Lifetime Allocation Process," *International Economic Review*, *5*, 304–317.

CHAPTER 5

# COMPARISONS OF INFORMATION STRUCTURES[1]

C. B. McGUIRE



## 1. Introduction

Can information be treated in some sense as one of the "commodities" of economic analysis? An underlying interest in that question motivates the investigations of this paper. Intuitively, the notions of more and less would seem to make as much sense when applied to the stuff, information, as to many other complex things that we are quite ready to treat as commodities. Upon more careful examination, however, we shall find it (perhaps to some, surprisingly) difficult to sort out in any precise and general fashion the components of information which give it economic value.

But of course we don't understand very well how to define such components in the case of more ordinary economic goods and services either. To what things in reality can (or ought) the "commodities" of abstract theory correspond? Every practical analysis confronts this problem immediately. Quite often – perhaps in part because those kinds of phenomena register most distinctly in the specialized vision of an economist – the question is, if not easily, at least directly resolved. The possible alternative candidates for "commodities" are obvious and the choices are made after rough guesses at the trade-off between aggregation and closeness of approximation. When

[1] My own interest in the questions treated in this paper was first stimulated by Jacob Marschak at the Cowles Foundation in 1958. The work there, supported by the Office of Naval Research under Contract Nonr-358(01), NRO47-066, resulted in Cowles Foundation Discussion Paper No. 72 with the same title as the present paper. The general aim of this investigation remains the same, but there the similarity ends. Completion of this paper was made possible through the generous support of the John Simon Guggenheim Memorial Foundation.

establishment of this mapping of real things into the "commodities" of theory is not so easy, theory has very little to say.[2]

The investigations of this paper may therefore have a bearing on the more general question of commodity definition. One of the advantages of choosing information as the context for study of this general question is that information is – as the reader will soon see – sufficiently complex in nature to raise a number of hard problems, and, at the same time, there is a simple and tentatively[3] widely agreed-upon formal structure, ready-to-hand, namely decision theory, which can serve as the abstract basis of the investigation. We would have a much more difficult time getting started with a similar investigation of, let us say, *education* for lack of such a formal structure.

## 2. Basic Model of the Decision Problem

Let $S=\{s_1, \ldots, s_{n_S}\}$ be a finite set of "states of the world," and $A=\{a_1, \ldots, a_{n_A}\}$ be a finite set of "acts." Both sets are to be regarded as mutually exclusive and exhaustive categorizations: one and only one state will occur, and one and only one act will be chosen. The result, or *payoff*, of choosing act $a$ when state $s$ occurs is specified by a real-valued function $U$ on $A \times S$ which we shall represent as an $n_A \times n_S$ matrix $[u_{as}]$.

The state $s$ will be regarded as a random variable distributed over $S$ according to an *a priori* distribution $p'=(p_1, \ldots, p_{n_S})$.

An information structure[4] $P=[p_{sy}]$ will be an $n_S \times n_Y$ Markov matrix which specifies, for each $s \in S$, a probability distribution over a finite set $Y=\{y_1, \ldots, y_{n_Y}\}$ of "signals." We may think of $P$ as an abstract description of a device employed by the decision maker to learn something about the prevailing (or true) value of $s$. Knowing $p$ and $P$, he learns the value of signal $y$. He then chooses an act $a$ which is in some sense good in the light of this often imperfect information about the true state $s$.

---

[2] One of the guises under which this problem occurs is the "quality" question (HOUTHAKKER (1951–52), HIRSHLEIFER (1955)).

[3] By "tentatively" is meant that while not all students of information accept the framework we use here for *all* of their own work, nearly all (statisticians for instance) information theorists know the framework and regard it as suitable for analysis of *some* questions.

[4] The term *information structure* is from J. MARSCHAK and RADNER (1971). BLACKWELL (1951, 1953) calls this same thing an *experiment*, and his usage has gained some popularity; to me his term too much connotes a particular real way of getting information. MORSE and SACKSTEDER (1966) use the term *statistical system*, and J. MARSCHAK and MIYASAWA (1968) say *information system*.

Throughout this paper we shall simply assume that the decision maker chooses an act which maximizes the conditional expectation of payoff given the signal. Let $D$ be an $n_Y \times n_A$ Markov matrix $[d_{ya}]$ describing the decision maker's (mixed) decision rule: $d_{ya} = Pr\{a|y\}$, i.e., the probability that act $a$ will be chosen when signal $y$ is received. The $n_S$ vector along the diagonal of the square matrix product $PDU$ we shall call a *payoff vector* $u$. The product[5] $u'p = \text{tr } PDU\hat{p}$ is the expected payoff when decision rule $D$ is employed with $P$. Our assumption about the decision maker then is that he chooses the Markov matrix $D$ so as to maximize tr $PDU\hat{p}$.

Notice that, since expected payoff is linear in $D$, nothing is lost by confining choice of $D$ to those representing extreme points of the set of $n_Y \times n_A$ Markov matrices, namely those Markov $D$ for which $d_{ya} = 1$ or $d_{ya} = 0$; these latter are the pure-strategy decision rules. Another fact, easily verified and useful for what follows, will be noted here:

$$\text{tr } U\hat{p}PD = \text{tr } DU\hat{p}P. \tag{2.1}$$

By $F(p|P, U)$ we shall mean the expected value of payoff under *optimal* choice of decision rule when the vector $p$ is the prior distribution on $S$, $P$ is the information structure, and $U$ is the payoff matrix. Thus[6]

$$F(p|P, U) \equiv \max_D \text{tr } PDU\hat{p} \tag{2.2}$$

with $D$ Markov. Use of this notation $F$ will always presume some specification of $n_S$, $n_Y$, and $n_A$.

The question to which we now turn is the central one of this paper: what comparative statements can be made about different information structures $P$ and $Q$? Is it possible to say, under certain circumstances, that $P$ conveys more or less "information" than $Q$? To begin to address this question we must first decide what it is that we want to study. If our object were to give to the vague notion of "information" a precision which accorded well with the intuitive content of the word in *all* its current uses, it could be argued that our present framework is too narrow. Information in personal communication and in music and art gives pleasure and means have been proposed for measuring information content in some of these cases.[7] But since the

---

[5] The carat over a vector $t$ will denote the diagonal matrix with

$$[\hat{t}]_{ij} = \begin{cases} t_i \text{ if } j = i \\ 0 \text{ otherwise.} \end{cases}$$

[6] Cf. (2.10) in Chapter 10.

[7] Cf. HERDAN (1956), DOLEZEL (1964), and COHEN (1962).

decision framework we are using here has no bearing (that we see) on these matters, the validity of *our* remarks on ways of comparing different information structures is limited to the little decision framework that we have specified.

In our investigations here we shall base all notions of more or less information on the function $F$ defined in (2). In taking this approach we follow BOHNENBLUST, SHAPLEY, and SHERMAN (1949); BLACKWELL (1951, 1953); J. MARSCHAK (1963); J. MARSCHAK and MIYASAWA (1968); MIYASAWA (1968); and J. MARSCHAK and RADNER (1971). On this basis, then, we shall be interested in examining the properties of information structures $P$ and $Q$ that makes $P$ "more informative" (i.e., more valuable) than $Q$ for all users, or for some users under some prior distributions, etc. More precisely: what are the properties of $P$ and $Q$ that make

$$F(t|P, U) \geq F(t|Q, U)$$

a) for all $t$ and all $U$?

b) for all $t$ and some $U$?

c) for some $t$ and some $U$?

To begin this study we shall first summarize some important results of Blackwell.

## 3. Blackwell's Theorem[8]

Let $u\,(P, U)$ be the set of attainable payoff vectors $v$ as the (mixed) decision rule $D$ varies over all $n_Y \times n_A$ Markov matrices; that is,

$$u(p, U) = \{v|v = \text{diagonal of } PDU \text{ for some Markov } D\}.$$

The set $u(P, U)$ is a closed, bounded, convex subset of $n_Y$-space. Now consider two information structures $P$ and $Q$ with a common state-of-the-world set $S$ and with signal sets $Y$ and $Z$, respectively. BOHNENBLUST, SHAPLEY, and SHERMAN (1949) propose that $P$ be regarded as *generally more informative* than $Q$ (written $P \supseteq Q$) if for all payoff matrices $U$ the set $u(Q, U)$ is contained in the set $u(P, U)$.

Blackwell's theorem is as follows:

---

[8] Here I follow, almost verbatim, the concise summary of Blackwell's theorem given by GRETTENBERG (1969). Blackwell's theorem is itself a summary of results of several writers. Martin Beckmann's independent proof of the equivalence of b) and c) – a problem put to him by J. Marschak – was never published.

THEOREM 1. *Let $P$ and $Q$ be information structures with a common (finite state-of-the-world set $S$ and finite signal sets $Y$ and $Z$ respectively. Each of the following conditions is equivalent:*

a) $P \supseteq Q$.

b) *There exists an $n_Y \times n_Z$ Markov matrix $M$ with $PM = Q$.*

c) *Define the numbers*

$$p_y^* \equiv \sum_s p_{sy}, \qquad q_z^* \equiv \sum_s q_{sz}$$

*and the vectors*

$$\alpha_y \equiv \left( \frac{p_{1y}}{p_y^*}, \frac{p_{2y}}{p_y^*}, \ldots, \frac{p_{nsy}}{p_y^*} \right)$$

*and*

$$\beta_z \equiv \left( \frac{q_{1z}}{q_z^*}, \frac{q_{2z}}{q_z^*}, \ldots, \frac{q_{nsz}}{q_z^*} \right)$$

*for $y = 1, \ldots, y_N$ and $z = 1, \ldots, n_Z$.*

*For any continuous convex function $\varphi$, defined for all $t = (t_1, \ldots, t_{ns})$ with $t_s \geq 0$, $\sum_s t_s = 1$, it is true that*

$$\sum_{y=1}^{nY} p_y^* \varphi(\alpha_y) \geq \sum_{z=1}^{nZ} q_z^* \varphi(\beta_z).$$

d) *With $\alpha_y$, $\beta_z$, $p_y^*$, $q_z^*$ as in c), there exists an $n_Z \times n_Y$ Markov matrix $R$ such that*

$$R \cdot \begin{bmatrix} \alpha_1 \\ \vdots \\ \alpha_{nY} \end{bmatrix} = \begin{bmatrix} \beta_1 \\ \vdots \\ \beta_{nZ} \end{bmatrix}$$

*and*

$$[p_1^*, \ldots, p_{nZ}^*] \cdot R = [q_1^*, \ldots, q_n^*].$$ [9]

[9] In what follows it will be convenient to define the "likelihood" matrices:

$$P^* = \begin{bmatrix} \alpha_1 \\ \vdots \\ \alpha_{n_Y} \end{bmatrix}' \text{ and } Q^* = \begin{bmatrix} \beta_1 \\ \vdots \\ \beta_{n_Z} \end{bmatrix}'$$

and the vectors

$$p^* \equiv (p^*, \ldots, p_{nY}^*) \text{ and } q^* \equiv (q^*, \ldots, q_{nZ}^*),$$

etc. Condition d) then becomes: There exists an $R$ such that $P^*R' = Q^*$ and $q^*R = p^*$.

For a proof of these equivalences, the reader is referred to BLACKWELL (1951) or GRETTENBERG (1964). The arithmetic connecting a) and d) will prove useful later. We have

$$Q = PM = P(\hat{p}^*)^{-1}\hat{p}^* M$$

and hence

$$Q(\hat{q}^*)^{-1} = [P(\hat{p}^*)^{-1}]\hat{p}^* M(\hat{q}^*)^{-1}$$

which is simply

$$Q^* = P^* R' .$$

We also have (letting $e$ stand for the unit vector)

$$R' q^* = p^*$$

because

$$R' q^* = \hat{p}^* M(\hat{q}^*)^{-1} q^* = \hat{p}^* Me = \hat{p}^* e = p^* .$$

To see that $R$ is Markov we calculate a column sum of $R'$:

$$\sum_y [R']_{yz} = \sum_y \frac{p_y^*}{q_z^*} m_{yz} = \frac{1}{q_z^*} \sum_y (\sum_s p_{sy}) m_{yz}$$

$$= \frac{1}{q_z^*} \sum_s (\sum_y p_{sy} m_{yz}) = \frac{1}{q_z^*} \sum_s q_{sz}$$

$$= \frac{q_z^*}{q_z^*} = 1 .$$

*Interpretation.* Proposition a) implies that the function $F(\cdot|P, \cdot)$ dominates the function $F(\cdot|Q, \cdot)$. For all payoff functions and all prior distributions on $S$, $P$ is at least as valuable as $Q$. Obviously such a strong relationship as $P \supseteq Q$ imposes a very incomplete ordering on the set of all information structures. It can be expected therefore to be of rather little direct usefulness in establishing whether $P$ is "better" than $Q$.

Proposition b) states that the signals $y$ from structure $P$ can (in Marschak's and Miyasawa's words) be "garbled" in such a way as to mimic exactly the probability characteristics of the signals $z$ received from structure $Q$. It is as though receipt of a signal $y$ is an instruction to operate "random device $y$" which generates signals in $Z$ with probabilities$(m_{y_1}, \ldots, m_{y_{n_Z}})$. That the possibility of such garbling implies that $P \supseteq Q$ is fairly obvious; that the reverse implication holds is surprising and difficult to prove. In MARSCHAK and MIYASAWA (1968) variations on the notion of garbling are explored in some detail. Notice that repeated application of a non-decomposable garbling matrix $M$ leads eventually to a "flat" information structure $PM^\infty$ in the same way that a Markov process whose transitions are described by $M$ goes eventually into states with equilibrium probabilities independent of starting states. By "flat" here is meant a structure whose matrix has rank 1: all rows are identical so that the posterior probability distribution over $S$ is independent of the signal received.

Notice also that Proposition b) takes care (if one wishes to handle it this way) of the purely notational problem of the indexing of signals. The structure $P$ represented by the matrix

$$\begin{bmatrix} .6 & .4 \\ \\ .3 & .7 \end{bmatrix}$$

is surely the same as the structure $Q$ whose matrix is

$$\begin{bmatrix} .4 & .6 \\ \\ .7 & .3 \end{bmatrix};$$

green lights might just as well mean "stop," and red lights "go." If, as usual, we choose to keep the columns of our matrices ordered, and if we associate one structure with one matrix, then we call upon Proposition b) to establish that indeed a) holds both ways, because of course

$$P = Q\left[\begin{smallmatrix} 0 & 1 \\ 1 & 0 \end{smallmatrix}\right] \text{ and } Q = P\left[\begin{smallmatrix} 0 & 1 \\ 1 & 0 \end{smallmatrix}\right].$$

When for some pair of structures $P$, $Q$ we have $PM = Q$ for some Markov $M$, we shall say that $Q$ is a *contraction* of $P$. Since $M$ can be regarded as a mapping of the set of information structures into itself we shall follow MORSE and SACKSTEDER (1966) in calling $M$ a *morphism*.

Proposition c) justifies the giving of the name "generally more informative" to the $P \supseteq Q$ condition because when the function $\varphi$ in c) is defined as

$$\varphi(t) = \max_d dU\hat{p}t,$$

where $d$ is a $1 \times n_A$ Markov matrix, we have

$$\begin{aligned}\sum_y p_y^* \varphi(\alpha_y) &= \sum_y p_y^* \max_d (dU\hat{p}\alpha_y) \\ &= \max_D \operatorname{tr} \hat{p}^* DU\hat{p}P^* \\ &= \max_D \operatorname{tr} DU\hat{p}P^*\hat{p}^* \\ &= \max_D \operatorname{tr} DU\hat{p}P \\ &= F(p|P, U).\end{aligned}$$

Proposition d) suggests a picture. Each "likelihood" vector $\alpha_y$ of a structure $P$ is a point in the $(n_S - 1)$ - simplex

$$T = \{(t_1, \ldots, t_{n_S}) | t_j \geq 0, \sum t_j = 1\}.$$

Connecting the points $\alpha_1, \ldots, \alpha_{n_Y}$ of $P$ we represent $P$ by a polyhedron in $T$. Proposition d) states that the $Q$ polyhedron is contained in the $P$ polyhedron. The second part of d) says that containment is not enough; that the weights on the points must also bear a certain relationship to each other.

Numerical examples are given in Section 5.

## 4. Lattices and Decompositions of Information Structures: Birkhoff's Theorem

The relation "generally more informative than" is only a partial ordering of the set of finite information structures on a given state-of-the-world set.[10] Blackwell's theorem, stating the equivalence of a) and d), makes this especially clear. Fig. 1 displays four information structures for the case $n_S = 3$ in terms of likelihood vectors as suggested in the last section. From the picture we see that both structures $P$ and $Q$ are contained in structure $T$ and, in turn, contain[11] structure $R$. We would need to check the second condition of d) to establish whether in fact $T \supseteq P \supseteq R$ and $T \supseteq Q \supseteq R$. But without any further checking we can state unambiguously that $P \supseteq Q$ is not true and $Q \supseteq P$ is not true, for neither triangle contains the other in Fig. 1.

[10] For brevity we shall hereafter omit the phrase "on a given-state-of-the-world set."

[11] The sign $\supseteq$ to relate information structures will be reserved throughout this paper for the Bohnenblust-Shapley-Sherman relationship. When our likelihood polyhedron is inside another we shall use the words "contained in."

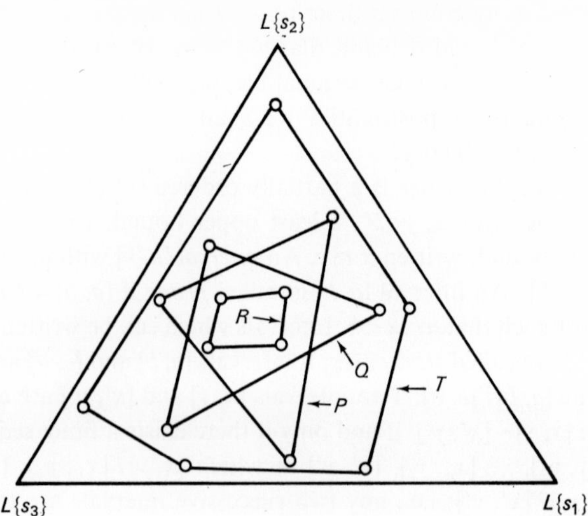


**Fig. 1.** Likelihood vectors for the signals of four information structures. (Notation: $L(s_k) = p_{s_k y}/p_y$ or $q_{s_k y}/q_y^*$, etc.)

Clearly then any search for a one-dimensional measure of "informativeness" is a vain one. That is to say, there exists no real-valued function $f$ on the set of information structures such that $f(P) \geq f(Q)$ if and only if $P \supseteq Q$. In particular the entropy, rate of transmission, and capacity functions of Shannon's information theory cannot, individually at least, serve as indicators of informativeness in the sense of Bohnenblust-Shapley-Sherman.[12]

But might there be $n$-dimensional measures of informativeness? In other words, can we find real-valued continuous functions $f_1, \ldots, f_n$ on the set of structures and a real-valued function $\varphi$ on the product of $R^n$ and the set of payoff functions such that

$$\varphi(f_1(P), \ldots, f_n(P); U) \geq \varphi(f_1(Q), \ldots, f_n(Q); U) \tag{4.1}$$

for all $U$ if and only if $P \supseteq Q$? Obviously, for $n > \max(n_S n_Y,\ n_S n_Z)$ such functions $f_i$ and $\varphi$ can be found. In that trivial case the components of the information structures are simply the parameters of the structure: thus $f_1(P) = p_{11},\ f_2(P) = p_{12}, \ldots, f_{n_S n_Y}(P) = p_{n_S, n_Y}$. But the real interest in searching for such functions $f_i$ is either a) to find components of information

[12] Comparisons of the "generally-more-informative-than" relationship and some of Shannon's functions are given in Marschak and Miyasawa (1968).

which represent more compact descriptions than the parameters themselves, in which case we should demand that $n<n_S \cdot n_Y$, or b) to find components which are more easily used, i.e., compatible, say, with a *linear* $\varphi$.

To investigate these possibilities we shall use some definitions and a theorem from lattice theory.

To begin with,[13] a *lattice* is a partially ordered set $(\mathscr{L}, \leq)$ which has, for every pair of elements $x, y \in \mathscr{L}$, a least upper bound, written $x \cup y$, and a greatest lower bound, written $x \cap y$. An *interval* $[a, b]$ with $a, b \in \mathscr{L}$ is the set $\{x \in \mathscr{L} | a \leq x \leq b\}$. An interval $[a, b]$ is called *prime* if $[a, b] = \{a, b\}$; that is, if there is no $x$ such that $a<x<b$. Intervals which can be written as $[x \cap y, x]$ and $[y, x \cup y]$ are called *transposes*; if intervals $[a, b]$ and $[c, d]$ are transposes we shall write $[a, b]T[c, d]$. Two intervals $[x, y]$ and $[x', y']$ are called *projective*, written $[x, y] \sim [x', y']$, if and only if there exists a finite sequence $[x, y]$, $[x_1, y_1]$, $[x_2, y_2]$, ..., $[x_n, y_n]$, $[x', y']$ in which $[x, y]T[x_1, y_1]$, $[x_1, y_1]T[x_2, y_2]$, ..., $[x_n, y_n]T[x', y']$; i.e., any two successive intervals are transposes. A *chain* is a sequence $x_1, x_2, x_3, \ldots$ of elements of $\mathscr{L}$ such that $x_k < x_{k+1}$ and $[x_k, x_{k+1}]$ is prime $(k = 1, 2, \ldots)$.

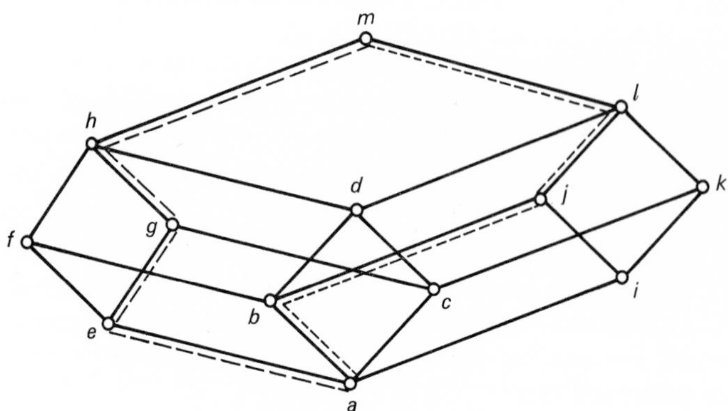


Fig. 2. An illustrative (modular) lattice.

In the familiar graphic representation of a lattice the elements of $\mathscr{L}$ are points and $x$ is joined to $y$ by an upward sloping line if and only if $x<y$ and $[x, y]$ is prime. The notions introduced above are illustrated in the lattice diagram of Fig. 2. There we see that $[e, h]T[a, d]$ since $[e, h] = [e, d \cup e]$ and

[13] This exposition of notions from lattice theory is based on BIRKHOFF (1948) and Chapter 14 of the *new* MACLANE and BIRKHOFF (1967). The latter is the easier presentation; nothing however is said there about valuations.

$[a, d] = [d \cap e, d]$; $[a, d]T[i, l]$ since $[a, d] = [d \cap i, d]$ and $[i, l] = [i, d \cup i]$. It follows that $[e, h] \sim [i, l]$.

We will be concerned here only with *modular* lattices: lattices in which $x \leq z$ implies $x \cup (y \cap z) = (x \cup y) \cap z$. An example of a non-modular lattice is given in Fig. 3; it can be shown, in fact, that every non-modular lattice has the lattice of Fig. 3 somewhere within it. The most interesting property of a modular lattice is given by the Jordan-Hölder-Dedekind theorem which we state as Theorem 2.

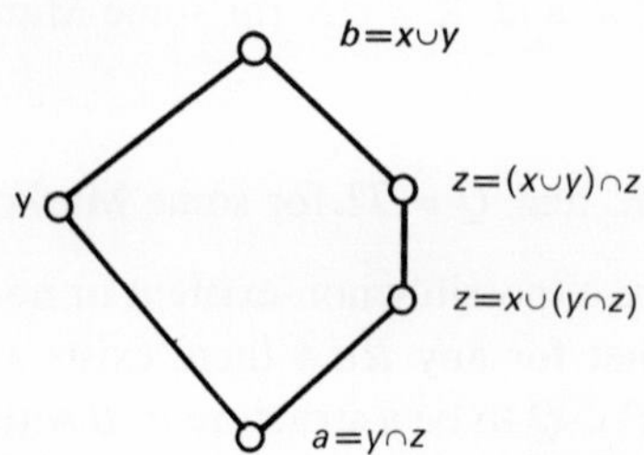


Fig. 3. Example of a non-modular lattice.

THEOREM 2. *Let $\alpha = (x, \ldots, y)$ and $\beta = (x, \ldots, y)$ be distinct chains connecting the same pair of elements x, y in a finite modular lattice. There is a 1–1 mapping $\varphi$ of the (prime) intervals of $\alpha$ to the (prime) intervals of $\beta$ such that $[c, d] \sim \varphi[c, d]$ for any interval $[c, d]$ in $\alpha$.*

For a proof the reader is referred to MACLANE and BIRKHOFF (1967). For an example consider the chains *a e g h m* and *a b j l m* in the lattice of Fig. 2. It is easily verified that for the $\varphi$ exhibited we have

$$\begin{aligned}
[a\ \ e] &\sim \varphi[a\ \ e] \equiv [l\ \ m] \\
[e\ \ g] &\sim \varphi[e\ \ g] \equiv [j\ \ l] \\
[g\ \ h] &\sim \varphi[g\ \ h] \equiv [a\ \ b] \\
[h\ \ m] &\sim \varphi[h\ \ m] \equiv [b\ \ j]
\end{aligned}$$

A real-valued function $v(x)$ defined on a lattice $\mathscr{L}$ which satisfies

$$v(x) + v(y) = v(x \cup y) + v(x \cap y) \tag{4.2}$$

is called a *modular* function or a *valuation*. A valuation is *isotone* if whenever $x \geq y$ then $v(x) \geq v(y)$.

The extension of Theorem 2 which is most useful for our purposes can now be stated. Here 0 denotes the *g.l.b.* of $\mathscr{L}$.

COROLLARY 2.1 (Birkhoff). *The different valuations on a modular lattice* $\mathscr{L}$ *of finite length correspond* $1-1$ *to the choices of* $v[0]$ *and values* $\lambda_t$ *assigned to the classes of projective prime intervals of* $\mathscr{L}$: $v(x)=v(0)+\Sigma_t\lambda_t t(x)$ *where* $t(x)$ *is the number of prime intervals projective to* $t$ *in any chain joining* $0$ *with* $x$.

Let us now attempt to define a lattice of information structures. Let $\mathscr{P}$ be the set of all information structures on $S\times Y$. Given two structures $P$ and $Q\in\mathscr{P}$, define $P\cap Q$ and $P\cup Q$ as follows. Let

$$A=\{R\in\mathscr{P}|R=PM \text{ and } R=QN \text{ for some Markov } M \text{ and } N\}$$

and

$$B=\{T\in\mathscr{P}|P=TK \text{ and } Q=TL \text{ for some Markov } K \text{ and } L\}.$$

Now define $P\cap Q$ to be a (possibly non-existent or non-unique) structure in $A$ with the property that for any $R\in A$ there exists a Markov $J$ such that $R=(P\cap Q)J$. Define $P\cup Q$ to be a structure in $B$ with the property that for any $T\in B$ there exists a Markov $H$ with $P\cup Q=TH$. If the "intersections" and "unions" so defined were unique then $(\mathscr{P},\subseteq)$ would be a proper lattice. $P\cap Q$ would be the generally most informative structure among those generally less informative than both $P$ and $Q$. $P\cup Q$ would be the generally least informative structure among those generally more informative than both $P$ and $Q$.

For the moment let us assume that these union and intersection operations do define a lattice.

On the lattice so defined we now wish to ask whether the expected gross payoff function $F(p|\cdot, U)$ regarded as a function with parameters $p$ and $U$ is a modular function. Is it true for all $p$, $U$ and $P$, $Q$ that

$$F(p|P,U)+F(p|Q,U)=F(p|P\cap Q,U)+F(p|P\cup Q,U)? \tag{4.3}$$

If (4.3) were true[14] then $F(p|\cdot, U)$ would be a valuation and, by Theorem 2, we could write

$$F(p|P,U)=\sum_t \lambda_t t(P)$$

where (interval) $t$ would represent a certain "prime" difference between information structures and $\lambda_t$ would be the payoff value of this difference. The numbers $\{t(p)\}$ would define the decomposition of information structure $P$ into prime components.

[14] And if "lattice" $\mathscr{P}$ can be somehow restricted so as to be finite and modular.

Instead, now, of examining these questions in the abstract, we are going to study some simple numerical examples.

## 5. Three Examples

We shall now examine three numerical examples. Example $A$ is a counter-example to the proposition that the expected payoff function $F$ is modular on what we have casually called the *lattice* $\mathscr{L}$ of information structures. The matter might end there but the other examples are suggestive of ways of pursuing the problem of finding a lattice of structures on which $F$ *is* modular. The examples $B$ and $C$ illustrate some of the difficulties in using Blackwell's notion of contraction to define a lattice and yet show that modularity holds true surprisingly frequently.

*Example A*

Let

$$P = \begin{bmatrix} 1 & 0 \\ \frac{1}{2} & \frac{1}{2} \end{bmatrix} \quad \text{and } Q = \begin{bmatrix} \frac{1}{2} & \frac{1}{2} \\ 0 & 1 \end{bmatrix}$$

so that

$$P^{*\prime} = \begin{bmatrix} \frac{2}{3} & 0 \\ \frac{1}{3} & 1 \end{bmatrix} \quad \text{and } Q^{*\prime} = \begin{bmatrix} 1 & \frac{1}{3} \\ 0 & \frac{2}{3} \end{bmatrix}.$$

From the likelihood diagram of Fig. 4, it is clear that

$$(P \cup Q)^* = \begin{bmatrix} 1 & 0 \\ 0 & 1 \end{bmatrix} \quad \text{and } (P \cap Q)^* = \begin{bmatrix} \frac{2}{3} & \frac{1}{3} \\ \frac{1}{3} & \frac{2}{3} \end{bmatrix}$$

so that

$$P \cup Q = \begin{bmatrix} 1 & 0 \\ 0 & 1 \end{bmatrix} \quad \text{and } P \cap Q = \begin{bmatrix} \frac{2}{3} & \frac{1}{3} \\ \frac{1}{3} & \frac{2}{3} \end{bmatrix}.$$

For the following four Markov matrices

$$M = \begin{bmatrix} \frac{2}{3} & \frac{1}{3} \\ 0 & 1 \end{bmatrix} \quad N = \begin{bmatrix} 1 & 0 \\ \frac{1}{3} & \frac{2}{3} \end{bmatrix}$$

$$K = \begin{bmatrix} 1 & 0 \\ \frac{1}{2} & \frac{1}{2} \end{bmatrix} \quad L = \begin{bmatrix} \frac{1}{2} & \frac{1}{2} \\ 0 & 1 \end{bmatrix}$$

we have $P \cap Q = PM = QN$ and $(P \cup Q) \cdot K = P$ and $(P \cap Q) \cdot L = Q$.

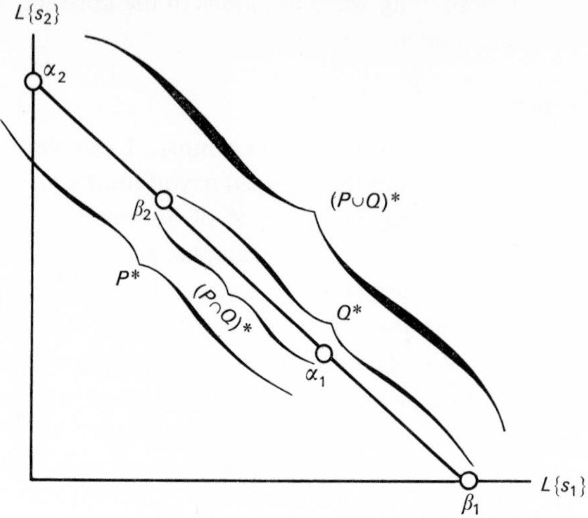


Fig. 4. Likelihood vectors for the signals of $P^*$ and $Q^*$ of Example A.

For $U = \left[\begin{smallmatrix}1 & 0\\ 0 & 1\end{smallmatrix}\right]$ the functions $F(\cdot|P, U)$, $F(\cdot|Q, U)$, $F(\cdot|P \cup Q, U)$ and $F(\cdot|P \cap Q, U)$ are plotted in Fig. 5. Obviously, for this particular payoff it is not true that $F(\cdot|P, U)+F(\cdot|Q, U) = F(\cdot|P \cup Q, U)+F(\cdot|P \cap Q, U)$. The function $F$ is therefore not modular.

*Example B*

Let

$$P = \begin{bmatrix} \frac{3}{4} & \frac{1}{4} \\ \\ \frac{1}{4} & \frac{3}{4} \end{bmatrix} \text{ and } Q = \begin{bmatrix} \frac{7}{31} & \frac{24}{31} \\ \\ \frac{1}{31} & \frac{30}{31} \end{bmatrix}$$

so that

$$P^* = \begin{bmatrix} \frac{3}{4} & \frac{1}{4} \\ \\ \frac{1}{4} & \frac{3}{4} \end{bmatrix} \text{ and } Q^* = \begin{bmatrix} \frac{7}{8} & \frac{4}{9} \\ \\ \frac{1}{8} & \frac{5}{9} \end{bmatrix}.$$

It is clear that we must have

$$(P \cup Q)^* = \begin{bmatrix} \frac{7}{8} & \frac{1}{4} \\ \\ \frac{1}{8} & \frac{3}{4} \end{bmatrix} \text{ and } (P \cap Q)^* = \begin{bmatrix} \frac{3}{4} & \frac{4}{9} \\ \\ \frac{1}{4} & \frac{5}{9} \end{bmatrix}$$

and consequently

$$P \cup Q = \begin{bmatrix} \frac{7}{10} & \frac{3}{10} \\ \frac{1}{10} & \frac{9}{10} \end{bmatrix} \text{ and } P \cap Q = \begin{bmatrix} \frac{3}{11} & \frac{8}{11} \\ \frac{1}{11} & \frac{10}{11} \end{bmatrix}.$$

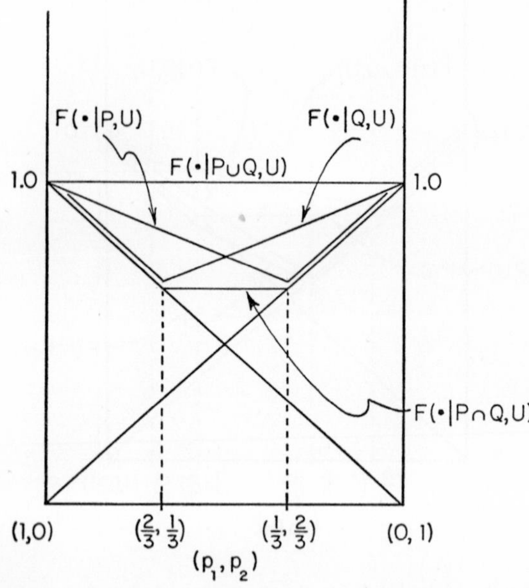


Fig. 5. Graphs of $F(\cdot|X, I)$ for $X = P$, $Q$, $P \cup Q$, $P \cap Q$, as in Example A.

Notice, in carrying out this computation, that it is not true that $R^{**} = R$ for an arbitrary Markov $R$. So the problem above is to find a Markov $P \cup Q$ such that $(P \cap Q)^*$ is as required. That the matrices given satisfy this condition is easily verified.

For the following four Markov matrices

$$M = \begin{bmatrix} \frac{4}{11} & \frac{7}{11} \\ 0 & 1 \end{bmatrix} \qquad N = \begin{bmatrix} 1 & 0 \\ \frac{2}{33} & \frac{31}{33} \end{bmatrix}$$

$$K = \begin{bmatrix} 1 & 0 \\ \frac{1}{6} & \frac{5}{6} \end{bmatrix} \qquad L = \begin{bmatrix} \frac{10}{31} & \frac{21}{31} \\ 0 & \frac{21}{31} \end{bmatrix}$$

we have $P \cap Q = PM = QN$ and $(P \cup Q) \cdot K = P$ and $(P \cup Q) \cdot L = Q$.

Using the payoff $U = I$ once again we plot the four $F$ functions in Fig. 6. The function $F$ is seen to be not modular.

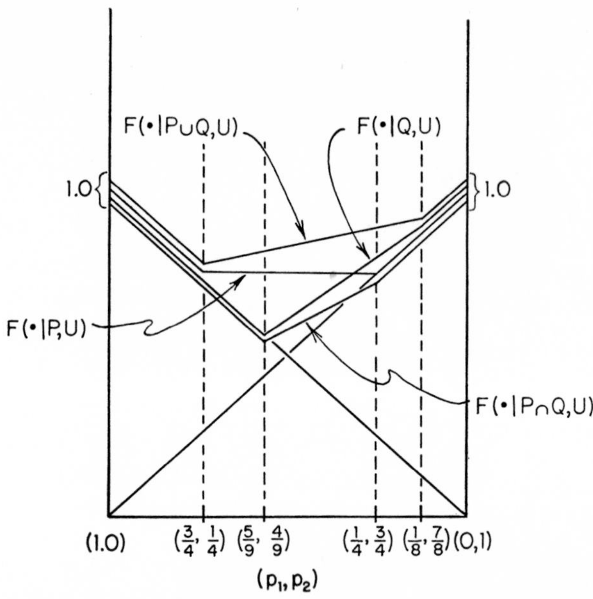


Fig. 6. Graphs of $F(\cdot|X, I)$ for $X = P$, $Q$, $P \cup Q$, $P \cap Q$ as in Example B.

*Example C*

Let

$$P = \begin{bmatrix} \frac{6}{15} & \frac{6}{15} & \frac{3}{15} \\ \frac{2}{15} & \frac{10}{15} & \frac{3}{15} \\ \frac{2}{15} & \frac{4}{15} & \frac{9}{15} \end{bmatrix} \text{ and } Q = \begin{bmatrix} \frac{6}{15} & \frac{3}{15} & \frac{6}{15} \\ \frac{2}{15} & \frac{9}{15} & \frac{4}{15} \\ \frac{2}{15} & \frac{3}{15} & \frac{10}{15} \end{bmatrix}$$

so that

$$P^* = \begin{bmatrix} .6 & .3 & .2 \\ .2 & .5 & .2 \\ .2 & .2 & .6 \end{bmatrix} \text{ and } Q^* = \begin{bmatrix} .6 & .2 & .3 \\ .2 & .6 & .2 \\ .2 & .2 & .5 \end{bmatrix}.$$

Plotting these likelihood (column) vectors of $P^*$ and $Q^*$ in a 2-simplex we get the triangles $\alpha_1, \alpha_2, \alpha_3$, and $\beta_1, \beta_2, \beta_3$ of Fig. 7.

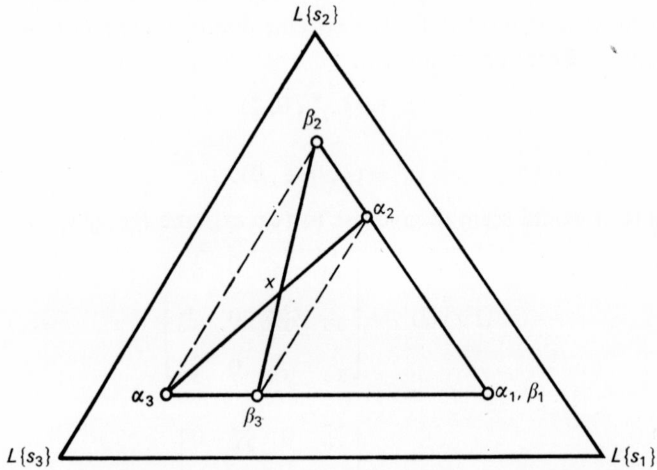


Fig. 7. Likelihood vectors for the signals of $P$ and $Q$ of Example A.

To contain both the $P^*$ and $Q^*$ triangles $(P \cup Q)^*$ must clearly be the triangle $\alpha_1, \beta_2, \alpha_3$, so

$$(P \cup Q)^* = \begin{bmatrix} .6 & .2 & .2 \\ .2 & .6 & .2 \\ .2 & .2 & .6 \end{bmatrix}$$

and consequently

$$P \cup Q = \begin{bmatrix} .6 & .2 & .2 \\ .2 & .6 & .2 \\ .2 & .2 & .6 \end{bmatrix}.$$

The quadrangle $\alpha_1, \alpha_2, x, \beta_3$ would seem to give us the likelihood vectors for a four-signal structure $(P \cap Q)^*$. Thus

$$(P \cap Q)^* = \begin{bmatrix} .6 & .3 & \frac{9}{35} & .3 \\ .2 & .5 & \frac{13}{35} & .2 \\ .2 & .2 & \frac{13}{35} & .5 \end{bmatrix}.$$

(The third column, representing point $x$, is found by observing that $\frac{3}{7}\beta_3 + \frac{4}{7}\beta_2 = \frac{3}{7}\alpha_2 + \frac{4}{7}\alpha_3 = x$.) To determine $P \cap Q$ we must find a non-negative 4-vector $t$ such that $(P \cap Q)^* t = (1, 1, 1)'$. Since this system is underdetermined, we ask, instead, for the extreme points of the set of $t$'s satisfying the equations. There are two such:

$$t^1 = (\tfrac{1}{3}, \tfrac{4}{3}, 0, \tfrac{4}{3})$$

and

$$t^2 = (\tfrac{2}{3}, 0, \tfrac{7}{3}, 0).$$

These in turn would seem to give rise to two extreme $P \cap Q$'s

$$(P \cap Q)^1 = \begin{bmatrix} \frac{6}{30} & \frac{12}{30} & 0 & \frac{12}{30} \\ \frac{2}{30} & \frac{20}{30} & 0 & \frac{8}{30} \\ \frac{2}{30} & \frac{8}{30} & 0 & \frac{20}{30} \end{bmatrix}$$

and

$$(P \cap Q)^2 = \begin{bmatrix} \frac{12}{30} & 0 & \frac{18}{30} & 0 \\ \frac{4}{30} & 0 & \frac{26}{30} & 0 \\ \frac{4}{30} & 0 & \frac{26}{30} & 0 \end{bmatrix}.$$

Each of these is a contraction both of $P$ and of $Q$. But neither is a contraction of the other, so neither satisfies the definition of $P \cap Q$. In fact, in this case, there exists no information structure satisfying this definition.

Curiously, though, for $(P \cap Q)^1$ we have

$$(5.1) \qquad F(\cdot|P, U) + F(\cdot|Q, U) = F(\cdot|P \cup Q, U) + F(\cdot|(P \cap Q)^1, U)$$

*for all* $U$. To verify this we need a lemma which will be useful later as well.

From (2.1) and (2.2) we have $F(p|P, U) = \max_D \operatorname{tr} DU\hat{p}P$. Now, for an arbitrary matrix $A$, define $\sigma(A) \equiv \Sigma_j \max_i a_{ij}$. Obviously $\sigma(A) = \max_D \operatorname{tr} DA$, so another useful formula for computing payoff is

$$(5.2) \qquad F(p|P, U) = \sigma(U\hat{p}P).$$

Next, let us define an operation $\oplus$ on pairs of matrices $B$ and $C$ with the same number of rows. $B \oplus C$ will be a matrix whose set of column vectors is the union of the sets of column vectors of $B$ and $C$ except that if any two columns in the union are proportional their vector sum is to replace the two. Thus, for example,

$$\begin{bmatrix} 4 & 3 & 5 \\ 2 & 7 & 1 \end{bmatrix} \oplus \begin{bmatrix} 6 & 10 & 1 \\ 3 & 2 & 2 \end{bmatrix} = \begin{bmatrix} 10 & 15 & 3 & 1 \\ 5 & 3 & 7 & 2 \end{bmatrix}.$$

LEMMA. *$\sigma(AB)+\sigma(AC)=\sigma(A(B\oplus C))$ and, in particular,*

$$F(p|P, U)+F(p|Q, U) = F(p|(P \oplus Q), U).$$

The proof is obvious. Application of the lemma to the pairs of matrices $P$ and $Q$, and $P \cup Q$ and $(P \cap Q)^1$ verifies (5.1) immediately, since $P\oplus Q = (P \cup Q)\oplus(P \cap Q)^1$.

It is *not* true that

$$F(\cdot|P, U)+F(\cdot|Q, U) = F(\cdot|\mathrm{P} \cup Q, U)+F(\cdot|(P \cap Q)^2, U),$$

as can be seen by computing $F$ for $U=I$ and $p=(\frac{1}{3}, \frac{1}{3}, \frac{1}{3})$.

Because, as often happens in cases like example $C$, the function $F$ so *nearly* exhibits the property of modularity, it would seem worth exploring this subject further.

## 6. Modularity by Construction

Let $\mathscr{G}$ be the set of $(n_Y+n_Z)$-vectors $g=(g_1, \ldots, g_{n_Y+n_Z})'$ with $0\leq g_i\leq 1$ such that $[P\vdots Q]g=e$ where $e$ is the unit vector $e=(1, 1, \ldots, 1)'$. For any $g\in\mathscr{G}$ the matrices $R_g\equiv[P\vdots Q]\hat{g}$ and $R_{e-g}\equiv[P\vdots Q](\widehat{e-g})$ are both Markov matrices and may be regarded as information structures. The set $\mathscr{G}$ is a convex polytope, symmetric around the point $\frac{1}{2}\, e\in\mathscr{G}$ in the sense that if for a vector $h$ it is true that $(\frac{1}{2}e+h)\in\mathscr{G}$ then $(\frac{1}{2}e-h)\in\mathscr{G}$ also.

THEOREM 3. *If $g\in\mathscr{G}$ then*

$$\sigma(WR_g)+\sigma(WR_{e-g}) = \sigma(WP)+\sigma(WQ)$$

*for all $W$.*

*Proof.* By the lemma, we have

$$\sigma(WR_g)+\sigma(WR_{e-g}) = \sigma(W(R_e \oplus R_{e-g}))$$

and

$$\sigma(WP)+\sigma(WQ) = \sigma(W(P \oplus Q)).$$

The two right-hand sides are equal because

$$R_e \oplus R_{e-g} = [P\vdots Q]\hat{e}+[P\vdots Q](\widehat{e-g}) = P \oplus Q.$$

The next question is this: can one always find a $g\in\mathscr{G}$ such that $R_g\supseteq P$ and $R_g\supseteq Q$ and $P\supseteq R_{e-g}$ and $Q\supseteq R_{e-g}$? If this can be done for every $P$, $Q$ pair then we would define $P \cup Q = R_g$ and $P \cap Q \equiv R_{e-g}$ for this $g$ and we would have a lattice of information structures on which $F(p|\cdot, U)$ is modular for all $p$ and $U$. Notice that the partial ordering of structures induced by these definitions would be in agreement with but less complete than "$\supseteq$."

The following example shows the kind of difficulty that can arise when one tries to construct a pair $R_g$ and $R_{e-g}$ with such properties.

*Example D*

Let

$$P = \begin{bmatrix} \frac{2}{3} & 0 & \frac{1}{3} \\ 0 & \frac{2}{3} & \frac{1}{3} \\ 0 & 0 & 0 \end{bmatrix} \text{ and } Q = \begin{bmatrix} 0 & .10 & .90 \\ .28 & 0 & .72 \\ .42 & .40 & .18 \end{bmatrix}$$

so that

$$P^* = \begin{bmatrix} 1 & 0 & .2 \\ 0 & 1 & .2 \\ 0 & 0 & .6 \end{bmatrix} \text{ and } Q^* = \begin{bmatrix} 0 & .2 & .5 \\ .4 & 0 & .4 \\ .6 & .8 & .1 \end{bmatrix}.$$

The columns of $P^*$ and $Q^*$ are plotted in "likelihood" space in Fig. 8.

If $R_{e-g}$ is to be a contraction of both $P$ and of $Q$ then every coordinate of the vector $(e-g)$ must be zero except those corresponding to $\alpha_3$ and $\beta_3$, because positive weight on any of the other points would cause $R_{e-g}$ to lie partly outside either the $P$ triangle or the $Q$ triangle. But no combination of weights on $\alpha_3$ and $\beta_3$ alone will make $[P\vdots Q](e-g)' = e$ because, as the diagram illustrates, the vectors $\alpha_3$ and $\beta_3$ do not span the vector $e$ (shown in the diagram by the point $(\frac{1}{3}, \frac{1}{3}, \frac{1}{3}) = \frac{1}{3}e$, where $e$ pierces the 2-simplex).

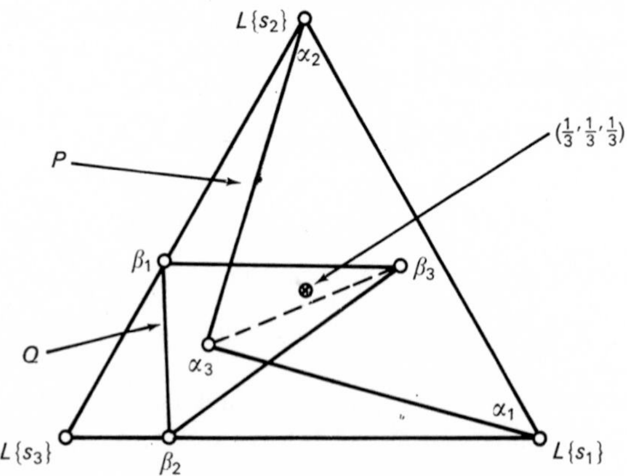


Fig. 8. Likelihood vectors for the signals of $P$ and $Q$ of Example D.

In this case, then, there exists no $g \in \mathcal{G}$ such that $R_g$ is more and $R_{e-g}$ less generally informative than both $P$ and $Q$.

In the theorem and corollary that follow we examine the conditions under which such an extreme $R_g$, $R_{e-g}$ pair does exist.

Of two information structures $P$ and $Q$, we shall say that $P$ *overlaps* $Q$ if the columns of both matrices can be reordered and partitioned each into two sets $[P_A \vdots P_B]$ and $[Q_A \vdots Q_B]$ and there exists a Markov matrix $M$ such that $Q_B = P_A M$.

THEOREM 4. *If P overlaps Q then*

a) *There exists a Markov matrix R such that* $Q_B^* = P_A^* R'$ *and* $R' Q^* B = P_A^*$; *and*

b) $$[P_A \vdots P_B \vdots Q_A \vdots Q_B] \cdot \begin{bmatrix} e & \vdots & 0 \\ 0 & \vdots & e \\ e & \vdots & 0 \\ 0 & \vdots & e \end{bmatrix} = [e \vdots e]$$

(*where the e's and* 0*'s stand, respectively, for unit and zero column vectors of suitable lengths*).

*Proof.* a) The construction of an $R$ satisfying a) is exactly the same as that given just after Theorem 1. The only difference between that situation and this is that $P_A$ and $Q_B$ are not Markov; but that property is not used in this proof.

b) $[Q_A \vdots Q_B]e = 1$ since $Q$ is Markov, so $[Q_A \vdots P_A M]e = 1$. Then $[Q_A \vdots P_A] \cdot \left[\frac{e}{M_e}\right] = 1$. But $M$ is Markov so $Me = e$. This establishes that

$$[P \vdots Q] \begin{bmatrix} e \\ 0 \\ e \\ 0 \end{bmatrix} = e.$$ Since $[P \vdots Q]e = 2e$ we have

$$[P \vdots Q] \cdot \left( \begin{bmatrix} e \\ e \\ e \\ e \end{bmatrix} - \begin{bmatrix} e \\ 0 \\ e \\ 0 \end{bmatrix} \right) = 2e - e$$

which completes the proof.

COROLLARY 4.1. *If P overlaps Q and, for the same partitions, Q overlaps P then there exists a vector* $g \in \mathcal{G}$ *such that* $R_g \supseteq P$, $R_g \supseteq Q$, $P \supseteq R_{e-g}$, *and* $Q \supseteq R_{e-g}$.

*Proof.* By hypothesis there exist Markov matrices $M$ and $N$ such that

$$[P_A \vdots Q_A] \begin{bmatrix} I & \vdots & 0 \\ \cdots & & \cdots \\ 0 & \vdots & N \end{bmatrix} = [P_A \vdots P_B], \tag{6.1}$$

$$[Q_A \vdots P_A] \begin{bmatrix} I & \vdots & 0 \\ \cdots & & \cdots \\ 0 & \vdots & M \end{bmatrix} = [Q_A \vdots Q_B], \tag{6.2}$$

$$[P_A \vdots P_B] \begin{bmatrix} M & \vdots & 0 \\ \cdots & & \cdots \\ 0 & \vdots & I \end{bmatrix} = [Q_B \vdots P_B], \tag{6.3}$$

and

$$[Q_A \vdots Q_B] \begin{bmatrix} N & \vdots & 0 \\ \cdots & & \cdots \\ 0 & \vdots & I \end{bmatrix} = [P_B \vdots Q_B]. \tag{6.4}$$

Theorem 4 tells us that the matrices on the extreme left of (6.1) and (6.2) and the matrices on the extreme right of (6.3) and (6.4) do indeed represent information structures; in fact, except for column ordering (which can be corrected by premultiplying the center matrix in each case by a permutation matrix) each of the first two represents $R_g$ and each of the last two represents $R_{e-g}$. The center matrices are obviously Markov. Application of Theorem 1 completes the proof.

We now give an example of a pair of structures $P$ and $Q$ satisfying the mutual-overlap condition of the corollary.

*Example E*

Let

$$P = [P_A \vdots P_B] = \frac{1}{80} \begin{bmatrix} 0 & 0 & 16 & \vdots & 38 & 26 \\ 24 & 16 & 0 & \vdots & 14 & 26 \\ 8 & 24 & 32 & \vdots & 12 & 4 \end{bmatrix}$$

and

$$Q = [Q_A \vdots Q_B] = \frac{1}{80} \begin{bmatrix} 8 & 24 & 32 & \vdots & 12 & 4 \\ 24 & 16 & 0 & \vdots & 14 & 26 \\ 0 & 0 & 16 & \vdots & 38 & 26 \end{bmatrix}$$

so that

$$P^* = [P_A^* \vdots P_B^*] = \begin{bmatrix} 0 & 0 & .33 & \vdots & .59 & .46 \\ .75 & .40 & 0 & \vdots & .22 & .46 \\ .25 & .60 & .67 & \vdots & .19 & .08 \end{bmatrix}$$

and

$$Q^* = [Q_A^* \vdots Q_B^*] = \begin{bmatrix} .25 & .60 & .67 & \vdots & .19 & .08 \\ .75 & .40 & 0 & \vdots & .22 & .46 \\ 0 & 0 & .33 & \vdots & .59 & .46 \end{bmatrix}.$$

For

$$M = \begin{bmatrix} .25 & .75 \\ .50 & .50 \\ .75 & .25 \end{bmatrix}$$

we have $Q_B = P_A M$ and $P_B = Q_A M$. In this highly symmetric case the $M$ and $N$ of the corollary are equal; this is not always true, of course.

In Fig. 9 the signals of the four structures $P$, $Q$, $R_g$, and $R_{e-g}$ are plotted in likelihood space. We have given the $g$-label to the "outside" structure and the $(e-g)$-label to the "inside" structure, but of course this assignment can be reversed. On the diagram $P$ and $Q$ are shown by solid lines and $R_g$ and $R_{e-g}$ by dotted lines.

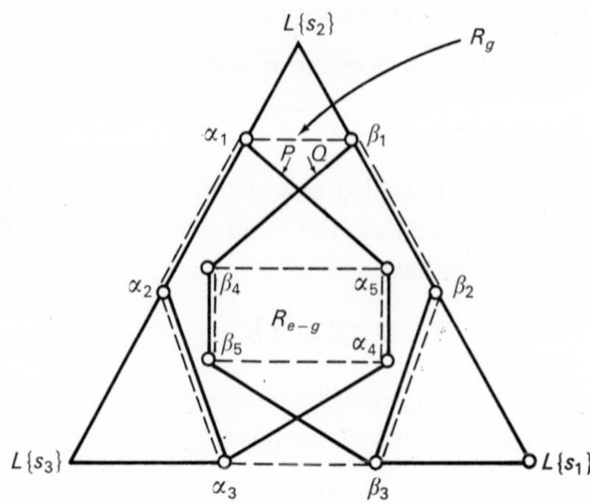


Fig. 9. Likelihood vectors for the signals of $P$, $Q$, $R_g$, and $R_{e-g}$ of Example E.

## 7. Partial Comparisons

Up to this point our comparisons of information structures have been based solely on dominance relationships: is $P$ *generally* more informative than $Q$? In the other literature the word "generally" is not used in describing the relation "$\supseteq$" between structures but, in those studies which treat payoff functions explicitly, either one finds comparisons based on dominance ($F(t|P, U) \geq F(t|Q, U)$ for *all* $t$ and *all* $U$) or else one finds a specific payoff function and a comparison tailored to that particular use.[15]

When it is not true that $P \supseteq Q$ (i.e., that $P$ is *generally* more informative than $Q$) nor that $Q \supseteq P$, we may ask for what payoff matrices $U$ and prior probability distributions $p$ is it true that $P$ is "more informative" than $Q$? Because $U$ and $p$ are not separately identifiable in the expected gross payoff function (2.2), let us write $W$ for the $n_A \times n_S$ matrix product $U\hat{p}$, and postpone statements about $U$ and $p$ separately until the analysis is complete. We shall call $W$ a "payoff function" for short.

Define the (row) *ravel*[16] of an $m \times n$ matrix $A$ to be the row vector obtained by concatenating the rows of $A$:

$$\vec{A} = [a_{11}, \dots, a_{1n}, a_{21}, \dots, a_{2n}, \dots, a_{m1}, \dots, a_{mn}].$$

Turn the arrow around to denote the column vector obtained by concatenating the columns of $A$:

$$\overleftarrow{A} = [a_{11}, \dots, a_{m1}, a_{12}, \dots, a_{m2}, \dots, a_{1n}, \dots, a_{mn}]'.$$

The relation between the two operations is given by

$$\overleftarrow{A} = \overrightarrow{(A')}'$$

which, of course, may be regarded as a definition of the column ravel. If a matrix product $AB$ is square then the inner product of the vectors $\vec{A}$ and $\overleftarrow{B}$ is well defined; in fact, we have

$$\operatorname{tr} AB = \vec{A}\overleftarrow{B}.$$

In (2.1) we wrote expected payoff as a function of the decision rule $D$ in the form tr $U\hat{p}PD$. Writing $W$ for $U\hat{p}$, we have, using the new notation,

$$\operatorname{tr} U\hat{p}PD = \vec{W}\overleftarrow{PD}. \tag{7.1}$$

For given $W$ and $P$ we will be interested in the values taken by this inner product as $D$ ranges over the set $\mathscr{D}$ of all $n_Y \times k$ Markov decision matrices. The size of $P$ determines the number $n_Y$; the number $k$ will be determined by the specification of the partial comparison to be made.

---

[15] Example: The mean-squared-error loss function of control theory.

[16] This useful operation and term, although not the notation, comes from IBM (1969), *APL/360 User's Manual*, p. 328.

Define the closed bounded convex set in $n_S k$-space

$$\overleftarrow{P\mathscr{D}} = \{v | v = \overleftarrow{PD} \text{ for some } D \in \mathscr{D}\}.$$

Now let us specify a set $\mathfrak{A}$ of payoff functions and ask under what conditions on information structures $P$ and $Q$ is it true that for all $W \in \mathfrak{A}$ $P$ is more informative than $Q$? To make the question a little easier we shall extend the set $\mathfrak{A}$ so that the set

$$\vec{\mathfrak{A}} \equiv \{\vec{W} | W \in \mathfrak{A}\}$$

is a *subspace* of $n_S k$-space where $k$ is equal to the highest $n_A$ for any $W \in \mathfrak{A}$ (we assume such a highest $n_A$ exists). Call this whole $n_S k$-space $\mathscr{U}$.

The innocent alteration contemplated involves adding $k - n_A$ dominated acts to any $W \in \mathfrak{A}$ for which $n_A < k$; the extension closes the set $\mathfrak{A}$ to the operation of linear combinations. In the rest of this discussion we shall assume that $\mathfrak{A}$ has been extended.

Let $\pi$ be the orthogonal projection of $\mathscr{U}$ onto $\vec{\mathfrak{A}}$ and let $\pi^{\perp}$ be the orthogonal projection of $\mathscr{U}$ onto the subspace $\vec{\mathfrak{A}}^{\perp}$, the orthogonal complement of $\vec{\mathfrak{A}}$. Payoff (7.1) can now be written

$$\begin{aligned} \vec{W}\overleftarrow{PD} &= [\pi(\vec{W}) + \pi^{\perp}(\vec{W})][\pi(\overleftarrow{PD}) + \pi^{\perp}(\overleftarrow{PD})] \\ &= \pi(\vec{W})\pi(\overleftarrow{PD}) + \pi^{\perp}(\vec{W})\pi^{\perp}(\overleftarrow{PD}). \end{aligned}$$

For $W \in \mathfrak{A}$ the right-hand term vanishes and $\pi(\vec{W}) = \vec{W}$ so we have

$$\vec{W}\overleftarrow{PD} = \vec{W}\pi(\overleftarrow{PD}) \text{ for } W \in \mathfrak{A}. \tag{7.3}$$

THEOREM 5. *Let $P$ and $Q$ be information structures with a common (finite) state-of-the-world set $S$ and finite signal sets $Y$ and $Z$, respectively. Let $\mathfrak{A}$ be an (extended) set of payoff functions with $k$ acts. Each of the following conditions is equivalent.*

*a)* $\pi(\overleftarrow{P\mathscr{D}})$ contains $\pi(\overleftarrow{Q\mathscr{E}})$
*where $\pi$ is the orthogonal projection of $\mathscr{U}$ onto $\vec{\mathfrak{A}}$, $\mathscr{D}$ is the set of all $n_Y \times k$ Markov matrices and $\mathscr{E}$ is the set of all $n_Z \times k$ Markov matrices;*

*b) $Q$ is a $\mathfrak{A}$-contraction of $P$, i.e., for every $E \in \mathscr{E}$ there exists a $D \in \mathscr{D}$ such that $\pi(\overleftarrow{PD}) = \pi(\overleftarrow{QE})$;*

*c)* $\max_{D \in \mathscr{D}} \vec{W}\overleftarrow{PD} \geq \max_{E \in \mathscr{E}} \vec{W}\overleftarrow{QE}$ *for all $W \in \mathfrak{A}$.*

*Proof.* a) and b) are just different ways of saying the same thing and since $\vec{W}v = \vec{W}\pi(v)$ for $\vec{W} \in \vec{\mathfrak{A}}$ it is equally obvious that b) implies c). We have only to argue that c) implies a). Each $W \in \mathfrak{A}$ defines a supporting hyperplane (in the subspace $\vec{\mathfrak{A}}$) of the set $\pi(\overleftarrow{P\mathscr{D}})$, namely,

$$\{v \in \vec{\mathfrak{A}} | \vec{W} v = \max_{D \in \mathscr{D}} \vec{W} \pi(\overleftarrow{PD})\}.$$

By c) we have, for $\vec{W} \in \vec{\mathfrak{A}}$,

$$\max_{D \in \mathscr{D}} \vec{W} \pi(\overleftarrow{PD}) \geq \max_{E \in \mathscr{E}} \vec{W} \pi(\overleftarrow{QE}).$$

So the set $\pi(\overleftarrow{Q\mathscr{E}})$ is on the same side of every supporting hyperplane of $\pi(\overleftarrow{P\mathscr{D}})$. This establishes a).

When condition c) of Theorem 5 holds for two structures $P$ and $Q$ and a set $\mathfrak{A}$ of payoff functions, we shall say that *$P$ is more informative than $Q$ with respect to $\mathfrak{A}$, $P \supseteq Q(\mathfrak{A})$*. If $\vec{\mathfrak{A}}$ equals the whole payoff space where the dimension of $\mathscr{U}$ is $kn_S$, then we say (following Blackwell[17]) that *$P$ is more informative than $Q$ for $k$-decision problems*. If this $k$-comparison property holds for all $k$, then, of course, $P$ is *generally* more informative than $Q$. Notice that when $\vec{\mathfrak{A}} = \mathscr{U}$ we have $\pi(v) = v$ for any $v \in \mathscr{U}$, so condition b) of Theorem 5 becomes:

*For every $E \in \mathscr{E}$ there exists a $D \in \mathscr{D}$ such that $\overleftarrow{PD} = \overleftarrow{QE}$ or equivalently that $PD = QE$.*[18]

In comparing this condition with condition b) of Theorem 1, we must remember that $D$ and $E$ have no more than $k$ columns here.

We turn now to a closer examination of the transformation of payoff functions and information structures which is brought about by the projection of $\mathscr{U}$ onto $\vec{\mathfrak{A}}$.

For given $kn_S$-dimensional $\mathscr{U}$ and, say, $h$-dimensional subspace $\vec{\mathfrak{A}}$, let $B$ be a matrix of size $kn_S \times kn_S$ whose columns constitute an orthogonal basis for $\mathscr{U}$ and a subset of whose columns comprise an orthonormal basis for $\vec{\mathfrak{A}}$. A payoff function $\vec{W} \in \mathscr{U}$ is transformed by the projection into $\vec{W}B$ and an information structure-decision function pair $\overleftarrow{PD}$ is transformed into $B'\overleftarrow{PD}$. In these terms, the equivalence of conditions b) and c) which is asserted by Theorem 5 may be interpreted as follows. If $P \supseteq Q(\mathfrak{A})$, then for every $E \in \mathscr{E}$ there is a $D \in \mathscr{D}$ that makes $B'\overleftarrow{QE}$ equal to $B'\overleftarrow{PD}$ *on the coordinates of* $\vec{\mathfrak{A}}$. Where an element of $B'\overleftarrow{QE}$ differs from an element of $B'\overleftarrow{PD}$ the corresponding element of $\vec{W}B$ for $W \in \vec{\mathfrak{A}}$ is equal to zero.

---

[17] BLACKWELL (1953), pp. 269–271.

[18] In this special case our condition b) of Theorem 5 becomes identical to Blackwell's condition (1) of his Theorem 9 concerning $k$-comparisons (1953), p. 270.

The test for the validity of $P \supseteq Q(\mathfrak{A})$ is most interesting when $\mathfrak{A}$ has the following very special property. Let $w_a$ stand for a row of the matrix $W$. We shall call $\mathfrak{A}$ *M-special* when

$$(7.4) \qquad \mathfrak{A} = \{W = \begin{bmatrix} w_1 \\ \vdots \\ w_k \end{bmatrix} | w_a \in M \text{ for } a = 1, \ldots, k\}$$

for some $n$-dimensional subspace $M$ of $n_S$-space. Next, let column vectors $v_1, \ldots, v_k$ be an orthonormal basis for $\mathscr{U}$ with $v_1, \ldots, v_n$ an orthonormal basis for $\vec{\mathfrak{A}}$, and define the matrices

$$V_1 \equiv [v_1, \ldots, v_n, 0, \ldots, 0],$$

$$V_2 \equiv [0, \ldots, 0, v_{n+1}, \ldots, v_k],$$

$$V \equiv V_1 + V_2 .$$

Now extend the carat notation to matrices so that, for instance, $\hat{P}$ stands for a $k$-block-diagonal matrix

$$\hat{P} = \begin{bmatrix} P & & 0 \\ & P & \\ 0 & & P \end{bmatrix}.$$

Next, let

$$B_1 \equiv \hat{V}_1$$

$$B_2 \equiv \hat{V}_2$$

$$B \equiv \hat{V}.$$

We can now state the following corollary to Theorem 5.

COROLLARY. *When $\mathfrak{A}$ is M-special then $P \supseteq Q(\mathfrak{A})$ if and only if for every $E \in \mathscr{E}$ there exists a $D \in \mathscr{D}$ such that $V_1 PD = V_1 QE$.*

*Proof.* The equivalence of b) and c) asserted by Theorem 5 tells us that $P \supseteq Q(\mathfrak{A})$ if and only if for every $E \in \mathscr{E}$ there exists a $D \in \mathscr{D}$ such that $\pi(\overleftarrow{PD}) = \pi(\overleftarrow{QE})$. Since $B_1'$ is the matrix representation of the linear transformation $\pi$ we can write this equality as

$$B_1' \overleftarrow{PD} = B_1' \overleftarrow{QE}$$

or

$$B_1' \hat{P} \overleftarrow{D} = B_1' \hat{Q} \overleftarrow{E}$$

or

$$\hat{V}_1' \hat{P} \overleftarrow{D} = \hat{V}_1' \hat{Q} \overleftarrow{E}$$

or

$$\widehat{V_1' P\overleftarrow{D}} = \widehat{V_1' Q\overleftarrow{E}} \tag{7.5}$$

or

$$V_1' PD = V_1' QE,$$

establishing the proof.

This matrix representation of $Q$ as a $\mathfrak{A}$-contraction of $P$ is the partial-comparison analog of the interesting property b) of Theorem 1 concerning the general comparison.

In terms that J. MARSCHAK (1963) has proposed, (7.5) states roughly that the information that $P$ and $Q$ convey is the same with respect to states of the world that are "payoff-relevant." What they say about non-"payoff-relevant" states is of no importance.

We end our investigations with a question. Consider the set $\varphi(Q|\mathfrak{A})$ of structures precisely equal in informativeness to $Q$ with respect to $\mathfrak{A}$, and the set $\varphi(P|\mathfrak{A}^{\perp})$ of structures precisely equal in informativeness to $P$ with respect to $\mathfrak{A}^{\perp}$ where

$$\mathfrak{A}^{\perp} \equiv \{W | \overrightarrow{W}\overleftarrow{V} = 0 \text{ for all } V \in \mathfrak{A}\}.$$

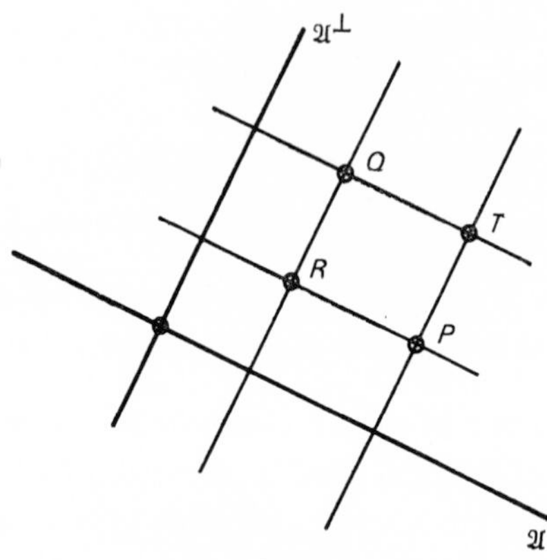


Fig. 10.

Let $R$ be a (the ?) structure in the intersection $\varphi(Q|\mathfrak{A}) \cap \varphi(P|\mathfrak{A}^{\perp})$. Similarly, let $T$ be a structure in the intersection $\varphi(P|\mathfrak{A}) \cap \varphi(Q|\mathfrak{A}^{\perp})$. If $P \supseteq Q(\mathfrak{A})$ and $Q \supseteq P(\mathfrak{A}^{\perp})$ then $T \supseteq P(\mathfrak{A}^{\perp})$, $T \supseteq Q(\mathfrak{A})$, $P \supseteq R(\mathfrak{A})$, and $Q \supseteq R(\mathfrak{A}^{\perp})$; Fig. 10 portrays these relationships.

Can any "generally more informative" relationships be derived in this situation? Is it true, for instance, that $P \supseteq R$? Under what conditions can one define a lattice by putting $P \cap Q = R$ and $P \cup Q = T$? And finally, is expected payoff a modular function here?

## References


BIRKHOFF, G. (1948), *Lattice Theory*, American Mathematical Society Colloquium Publication, Vol. XXV (revised edition).

BIRNBAUM, A. (1961), "On the Foundations of Statistical Inference: Binary Experiments," *Annals of Mathematical Statistics*, *32*, 414–435.

BLACKWELL, D. (1951), "Comparison of Experiments," in J. NEYMAN (ed.), *Proceedings of the Second Berkeley Symposium on Mathematical Statistics and Probability*, pp. 93–102.

BLACKWELL, D. (1953), "Equivalent Comparisons of Experiments," *Annals of Mathematical Statistics*, *24*, 265–272.

BOHNENBLUST, H. F., L. S. SHAPLEY, and S. SHERMAN (1949), "Reconnaissance in Game Theory," Research Memorandum RM-208, RAND Corporation, Santa Monica, California.

COHEN, J. E. (1962), "Information Theory and Music," *Behavioral Science*, *7*, 137–163.

DE GROOT, M. H. (1962), "Uncertainty, Information and Sequential Experiments," *Annals of Mathematical Statistics*, *33*, 404–419.

DE GROOT, M. H. (1966), "Optimal Allocation of Observations," *Annals of Institute Mathematics*, *18*, 13–28.

DOLEZEL, L. and R. W. BAILEY, *Statistics and Style*, American Elsevier Publishing Co., Inc., New York.

GRETTENBERG, T. L. (1964), "The Ordering of Finite Experiments," *Transactions of the Third Prague Conference on Information Theory, Statistical Decision Functions, Random Processes*, Czechoslovak Academy of Sciences, Prague, pp. 193–206.

HERDAN, G. (1956), *Language as Choice and Chance*, P. Noordhoff Groningen.

HIRSHLEIFER, J. (1955), "The Exchange between Quantity and Quality," *Quarterly Journal of Economics*, *69*, 596–606.

HOUTHAKKER, H. S. (1951–1952), "Compensated Changes in Quantities and Qualities Consumed," *Review of Economic Studies*, *19*, 155–164.

IBM (1969), *APL/360 User's Manual*,

LECAM, L. (1964), "Sufficiency and Approximate Sufficiency," *Annals of Mathematical Statistics*, *35*, 1419–1455.

LINDLEY, D. V. (1956), "On a Measure of the Information Provided by an Experiment," *Annals of Mathematical Statistics*, *27*, 986–1005.

MACLANE, SAUNDERS and G. BIRKHOFF (1967), *Algebra*, Macmillan, New York.

MARSCHAK, J. (1963), "The Payoff-Relevant Description of States and Acts," *Econometrica*, *31*, 719-725.

MARSCHAK, J. and K. MIYASAWA (1968), "Economic Comparability of Information Systems," *International Economic Review*, *9*, 137–174.

MARSCHAK, J. and R. RADNER (1971), *The Economic Theory of Teams*, Yale University Press, New Haven (forthcoming).

MIYASAWA, K. (1968), "Information Structures in Stochastic Programming Problems," *Management Science*, *14*, 275–291.

MORSE, N. and R. SACKSTEDER (1966), "Statistical Isomorphism," *Annals of Mathematical Statistics*, *37*, 203–214.

CHAPTER 6

# THE VALUE OF AND DEMAND FOR INFORMATION

KENNETH J. ARROW



## 1. A Model of Behavior under Uncertainty

In what follows it is assumed that the only actions available are bets on the occurrence of states of nature. This case may be more interesting than appears at first sight since, in the general competitive equilibrium of a pure exchange economy under uncertainty, only these bets need take place, all other random investments being expressible in terms of the basic bets; see ARROW (1953). Let $X_i$ be the odds on the occurrence of state of nature $i$; i.e., an individual who bets on state $i$ receives $X_i$ for each dollar bet if state $i$ occurs and nothing otherwise. The number of states of nature, $S$, is assumed to be finite.

The individual is supposed to have fixed total resources, to which we assign the value 1. Let $a_i$ be the amount bet by the individual on the occurrence of state $i$. For the most part we assume that all resources are invested

$$\sum_i a_i = 1\,. \tag{1.1}$$

The individual is assumed, as usual, to maximize the expected value of a utility function with diminishing marginal utility:

$$\sum_i p_i\, U(a_i X_i)\,, \tag{1.2}$$

where $p_i$ is the (subjective) probability of state $i$, and $U(y)$ is the utility of income $y$. From the usual Kuhn-Tucker conditions, the optimum $a_i$ is characterized by (1.1) and the relations

$$\begin{aligned} p_i X_i U'(a_i X_i) &= \lambda \text{ for } a_i > 0\,, \\ p_i X_i U'(0) \quad &\leqq \lambda \text{ for } a_i = 0\,, \end{aligned} \tag{1.3}$$

for some $\lambda$ (a Lagrange multiplier).

For later reference, consider the special case where $U$ is the (natural) logarithm. Since $U'(0) = +\infty$, the second line of (1.3) cannot hold. The expected utility, (1.2), becomes

$$\sum_i p_i \log a_i + \sum_i p_i \log X_i .$$

Since the second term is independent of $a_i$, maximization of (1.2) is equivalent to maximization of the first term, which does not involve the $X_i$ 's. In fact, for the logarithmic utility function, $a_i = p_i$. The optimal policy does not involve the odds, and the optimal value is

$$\sum_i p_i \log p_i + \sum p_i \log X_i . \tag{1.4}$$

As a slight digression, suppose for the moment that the individual is not required to invest all his wealth, so that (1.1) is replaced by

$$\sum_i a_i \leqq 1 . \tag{1.5}$$

The individual's wealth if state $i$ occurs is then

$$a_i X_i + 1 - \sum_i a_i .$$

The question may be asked, under what conditions is the constraint (1.5) binding; i.e., when will the individual bet all his money? *If* $U'(0) = +\infty$, *then the individual will invest all his money if and only if there exists a system of bets such that the individual cannot lose.* The last statement, symbolically, means the existence of $\bar{a}_i (i = 1, \ldots, S)$, such that

$$\bar{a}_i \geqq 0, \sum_i \bar{a}_i = 1, \bar{a}_i X_i \geqq 1 \text{ for all } i ,$$

which is equivalent to the condition

$$\sum_i (1/X_i) \leqq 1 . \tag{1.6}$$

*Proof.* Let

$$b = 1 - \sum_j a_j ;$$

then we seek to maximize

$$\sum_i p_i U(a_i X_i + b) ,$$

subject to the constraints,

$$\sum_i a_i + b = 1, \ a_i \geqq 0, \ b \geqq 0 .$$

Necessary conditions for an optimum are

$$p_i X_i U'(a_i X_i + b) \leqq \lambda, \tag{1.7}$$

$$p_i X_i U'(a_i X_i + b) = \lambda \text{ if } a_i > 0, \tag{1.8}$$

$$\sum_i p_i U'(a_i X_i + b) \leqq \lambda. \tag{1.9}$$

Suppose (1.7–1.9) hold with $b = 0$ (all resources invested). If, for some $i$, $a_i = 0$, then, since $U'(0) = +\infty$, (1.7) could not hold. Hence, $a_i > 0$, all $i$, and (1.8) holds for all $i$. If both sides of (1.8) are divided by $X_i$ and then summed over $i$, it follows from (1.9) that

$$\lambda \sum_i (1/X_i) \leqq \lambda,$$

and, since $\lambda > 0$ by (1.8), (1.6) holds.

For the converse, consider any system of bets, $a_i$, $b$ for which $b > 0$. Let $a_i' = a_i + b\,\bar{a}_i$, $b' = 0$. Then

$$a_i' X_i + b' = a_i X_i + b\bar{a}_i X_i \geqq a_i X_i + b,$$

and then, trivially,

$$\sum_i p_i U(a_i' X_i + b') \geqq \sum_i p_i U(a_i X_i + b),$$

while also

$$\sum_i a_i' + b' = \sum_i a_i + b \sum_i \bar{a}_i + \sum_i a_i + b = 1,\ a_i' \geqq 0,\ b' \geqq 0.$$

Hence, under the hypothesis, for any system of bets in which not all money is invested, there is another at least as good for which all money is invested.

*Note 1.* The existence of a sure system of bets is sufficient for an individual to invest all his money even if $U'(0) < +\infty$, but it is not necessary as can easily be seen if $U$ is linear, $p_j X_j > 1$, some $j$, in which case it is optimal to invest all in that $i$ for which $p_i X_i$ is a maximum even if there is no sure system.

*Note 2*, The optimal set of bets need not be a sure set, as the logarithmic case shows; as seen above, the optimal policy requires $a_i = p_i$, independent of the $X_i$ 's, so we certainly can have $p_i X_i < 1$ for some $i$, even if there exists a sure bet.

## 2. Amount and Value of Information

The *amount of information* about the state of the world is given, according to Shannon, by

$$H = -\sum_i p_i \log p_i . \tag{2.1}$$

The most interesting economic interpretation of this quantity is given by the proposition that a communications channel with capacity $H$ could convey a message giving the state of the world with arbitrarily small error. If we assume that the cost of a channel is proportional to its capacity, we find, as J. MARSCHAK (1959, p. 81) has pointed out, that the amount of information is a measure of the supply price, not of the demand.

An attempt to interpret $H$ as the *value* (in the demand sense) *of information* was begun by KELLY (1956) and completed by BELLMAN and KALABA (1957) and by J. MARSCHAK (1959, pp. 92–95). The value of a given channel is defined as the difference between the maximum utilities achievable with and without the channel. In the case of a logarithmic utility function, this does indeed lead to $H$, although of course the definition yields different results in general. If a channel of capacity $H$ is installed, then the individual knows the state of the world and bets everything on it; his return is $X_i$, which has a utility of $\log X_i$. Hence, his expected return is

$$\sum_i p_i \log X_i .$$

If we compare this with (1.4), the maximum utility achievable without information, we see indeed that the value of information is precisely $H$.

In this case, the value of information is independent of the rewards. It can be shown that this is the only such case; *if the value of information is independent of the rewards, then the utility function must be logarithmic.*

*Proof.* Choose $a$ to maximize (1.2) subject to (1.1); the maximum value of (1.2) is the utility received without information. If the channel is installed, the expected return, by the argument just applied to the logarithmic case, is

$$\sum_i p_i U(x_i) ,$$

and the value of information, $V$, is

$$V = -\sum_i p_i U(a_i X_i) + \sum_i p_i U(X_i) . \tag{2.2}$$

The hypothesis is that $V$ is independent of the $X_i$'s. Differentiate (2.2) partially with respect to $X_j$, and equate the derivative to 0.

(2.3) $$p_j a_j U'(a_j X_j) + \sum_i p_i X_i U'(a_i X_i)(\partial a_i/\partial X_j) = p_j U'(X_j).$$

From (1.1),

(2.4) $$\sum_i (\partial a_i/\partial X_j) = 0.$$

If the strict inequality holds in (1.3), then $a_i = 0$ and would remain 0 for small variations in $X_j$, so that $\partial a_i/\partial X_j = 0$ in that case. Hence, whether the equality or the inequality holds in (1.3), we have

$$p_i X_i U'(a_i X_i)(\partial a_i/\partial X_j) = \lambda(\partial a_i/\partial X_j).$$

Sum over $i$, use (2.4), substitute into (2.3), and divide through by $p_j$.

(2.5) $$a_j U'(a_j X_j) = U'(X_j).$$

If $U'(0)$ is finite, then, from (2.5), $a_j > 0$; if $U'(0)$ is infinite, then, from (1.3), $a_j > 0$; hence, $a_j > 0$ in any case, and the equality holds in (1.3). Then eliminate $U'(a_j X_j)$ from (1.3) and (2.5):

(2.6) $$\lambda a_j = p_j X_j U'(X_j).$$

Sum over $j$; from (1.1),

(2.7) $$\lambda = \sum_j p_j X_j U'(X_j).$$

Suppose now that the function $U(X)$ were such that, for some $X = X^0$, $\mathrm{d}[XU'(X)]/\mathrm{d}X \neq 0$. From (2.7), $\partial\lambda/\partial X_i \neq 0$ for $X_i = X^0$ and then, from (2.6),

(2.8) $$\partial a_j/\partial X_i \neq 0 \text{ for } i \neq j,\ X_i = X^0.$$

Multiply through in (2.5) by $X_j$, and let $j = 2$:

(2.9) $$a_2 X_2 U'(a_2 X_2) = X_2 U'(X_2).$$

Let $z = a_2 X_2$, $R$ the range of $z$ when $X_1$ is held fixed at $X^0$ and $X_2, \ldots, X_n$ vary freely. By assumption, the right-hand side is not identically constant; the left-hand side is thus also not constant, so $R$ must contain more than one point and is a non-degenerate, possibly infinite, interval. Differentiate (2.9) with respect to $X_1$:

(2.10) $$\left.\frac{\mathrm{d}[zU'(z)]}{\mathrm{d}z}\right|_{z = a_2 X_2} X_2(\partial a_2/\partial X_1) = 0.$$

From (2.8) and (2.10) we see that, for $X_2>0$, $\mathrm{d}[zU'(z)]/\mathrm{d}z=0$ for all $z$ in $R$, and therefore, for some $K$, $zU'(z)=K$ for all $z\in R$. But since $X_2$ can be chosen arbitrarily, (2.9) states that $XU'(X)=K$ for all $X>0$, so that $U(X)$ is indeed logarithmic.

So far, channels have been noiseless, and their choice has been an all-or-none proposition. Discrete choices are never convenient for economic analysis. A continuous version of channel choice makes use of Shannon's *rate of transmission*. Suppose the channel conveys a message $j=1, \ldots, M$, which has some joint distribution with the state of the world. Specifically, let $q_{ji}$ be the probability that message $j$ will be transmitted if the state of the world is in fact $i$, while $p_i$ is, as before, the probability of state $i$. Then $q_{ji}p_i$ is the joint probability that the world is in state $i$ and that the message transmitted is $j$. The receiver of the message is interested in a different set of probabilities, namely, the conditional probability, $p_{ij}$, that the state of the world is $i$ if the message transmitted is $j$, and $q_j$, the unconditional probability that the message transmitted is $j$. The two sets of probabilities are linked by the relations,

$$q_{ji}\, p_i = p_{ij}\, q_j\,.$$

When message $j$ arrives, the conditional information about the state of the world which has not yet been acquired is,

$$H(i/j) = -\sum_i p_{ij} \log p_{ij}\,,$$

which is the same as (2.1) for a given message $j$. Since the message is itself a random variable, the quantity of relevance to the user is the mathematical expectation of $H(i/j)$, where $j$ is the random variable, i.e.,

$$E_j[H(i/j)] = \sum_j H(i/j)\, q_j\,.$$

If $H(i)$ is the amount of information in a noiseless channel, then the rate of transmission $R(i,j)$ is defined as

$$H(i) - E_j[H(i/j)]\,. \tag{2.11}$$

$R(i,j)$ is symmetric in $i$ and $j$.

If a noisy channel with rate of transmission $R$ is installed and a message $j$ is received, the individual will optimize as in Section 1, but he will use he conditional probabilities of states. An easy calculation then shows that *the value of information in the channel* (the expected gain in maximum obtainable utility due to the messages) *is precisely the rate of transmission*, again independent of the odds, *when the utility function is logarithmic*.

### 3. The Demand for Information

J. MARSCHAK (1959, p. 80) refers to the value of information as the demand price. That is, a channel will be worth acquiring if the value exceeds the cost. This cannot be the case. Indeed, as we have just seen, if the utility function is logarithmic and there are constant costs in channel capacity, both the value of information and its cost are proportional to the amount of information; the individual will then either buy an infinite channel or no channel at all or be indifferent among all channel capacities. This hardly seems reasonable.

Marschak compares the utility of income with the cost. Obviously, there is a dimensional problem here; costs are measured in terms of dollars or resources, not in terms of utilities. In effect, if $Y$ is income and $C$ costs, Marschak is maximizing a function of the general form, $U(Y) - C$, or, more precisely, the expected value of such a function. From the viewpoint of the individual, it is net income, $Y - C$, that he winds up with, and to which utility should be attached. The same difficulty appears in attempts, such as those of SAVAGE (1954, p. 214) and of RAIFFA and SCHLAIFER (1961, Chapter 4), to provide a rigorous basis for sampling theory[1]; it also appears in ECKSTEIN's treatment of the economics of flood control (1961, pp. 471–474, especially Eq. (5.5)). A fully correct formulation is given by LA VALLE (1968).

Let, then, $c$ be the cost of channel capacity per unit. Then the individual must choose a channel with messages $j$ and a policy $a_i(j)$ stating the allocation as a function of the message so as to maximize

$$\sum_j q_j \sum_i c_{ij} U\left[a_i(j) X_i - cR\right],$$

where $R$ is the rate of transmission of the channel.

Consider again the special case where $U$ is logarithmic. First, optimize on the policy. It can easily be seen that

$$a_i(j) = p_{ij}\left[1 - cR \sum_k (1/X_k)\right] + (cR/X_i),$$

[1] RAIFFA and SCHLAIFER recognize the special assumptions made and seek to justify them (1961, pp. 79–81).

so that the maximum value of utility becomes, after substituting the definition of $R$,

$$\sum_i p_i \log p_i + \sum_i p_i \log X_i + R + \log[1 - cR \sum_k (1/X_k)],$$

which then has to be optimized with respect to $R$, yielding

$$R = -1 + [1/c \sum_k (1/X_k)].$$

There is an alternative approach which yields the same solution, properly interpreted. Suppose the cost of the channel is subtracted from the initial resources rather than from the final outcome. Then the maximand is

$$\sum_j q_j \sum_i p_{ij} \log [a_i(j) X_i],$$

with the constraint

$$\sum_i a_i(j) = 1 - cR.$$

The optimum policy then is obviously

$$a_i(j) = p_{ij}(1 - cR),$$

and the maximum value of utility is

$$\sum_i p_i \log p_i + \sum_i p_i \log X_i + R + \log(1 - cR).$$

The optimum value of $R$ is then

$$R = -1 + (1/c).$$

The apparent discrepancy is the same as the problem discussed at the beginning of the paper. There are really two unconnected kinds of money, initial and final; only if the resource constraint takes the form (1.5) is there a possibility of arbitraging between them. If

$$\sum_k (1/X_k) = 1,$$

there is a system of bets which will exactly break even for certain. This condition, used in ARROW (1953, Equation (5)), insures the identity of the two solutions in this case. It could be thought of as a simple numéraire condition.

The simplicity of the solution in the logarithmic case will not generalize. For one thing, the increased value due to the channel will not depend solely on its transmission rate. Two channels with the same rate may nevertheless yield different increments in utility.

## References

Arrow, K. J. (1953), "Le rôle des valeurs boursières pour la répartition la meilleure des risques," in *Econométrie*, Colloques Internationaux du Centre National de la Recherche Scientifique, *11*, 41–47, Imprimerie Nationale, Paris; English translation (1964), "The Role of Securities in the Optimal Allocation of Risk-Bearing," *Review of Economic Studies*, *31*, 91–96.

Bellman, R. E. and R. Kalaba (1957), "Dynamic Programming and Statistical Communication Theory," *Proceedings of the National Academy of Sciences*, *43*, 749–751.

Eckstein, O. (1960), "A Survey of the Theory of Public Expenditures Criteria," *Public Finances: Needs, Sources, and Utilization*, Princeton University Press, Princeton, pp. 439–494.

Kelly, J. L., Jr. (1956), "A New Interpretation of Information Rate," *Bell System Technical Journal*, *35*, 917–926.

La Valle, I. (1968), "On Cash Equivalents and Information Evaluation under Uncertainty, Part I: Basic Theory," *Journal of the American Statistical Association*, *63*, 252–276.

Marschak, J. (1959), "Remarks on the Economics of Information," *Contributions to Scientific Research in Management*, Western Data Processing Center, University of California, Los Angeles, pp. 79–98.

Raiffa, H. and R. Schlaifer (1961), *Applied Statistical Decision Theory*, Harvard Business School, Boston.

Savage, L. J. (1954), *The Foundations of Statistics*, Wiley, New York.

CHAPTER 7

# DECISIONS OVER TIME

MARTIN J. BECKMANN



Time affects decisions in at least four ways:

(1) the time structure of preferences, e.g., the higher valuation of current over future consumption;

(2) the time structure of production possibilities, e.g., the greater productivity of round-about time consuming production processes;

(3) the time structure of macro-economic development, in particular accumulation of productive capital and of technical knowledge over time, and finally;

(4) the time structure of decision processes, in particular the acquisition of specific information as decisions unfold in time.

The first aspect is treated in Chapter 4 by T.C. KOOPMANS; the second has been the subject of the Austrian theory of capital, and the third of the theory of optimal economic growth, one of the major research areas in contemporary mathematical economics. The fourth aspect is perhaps that which is most germane to the theory of decisions and the present essay will be focussed on it.

## 1. Introduction

For purposes of analysis and computation, in order to see a complex decision program through it is often convenient to break it down into simpler steps to be analyzed in sequence. While these sequences may form complicated networks, possibly with "feedback" (NEMHAUSER (1966)), many problems are of a type where a single (linear) sequence is involved.

Such a sequence is generated as follows. Consider a single decision, a "step." The outcome of an action in a state of the world is:

i) an immediate payoff,

ii) another state of the world.

The new state (which may be identical with the previous one) gives rise to a new decision.

The sequence may, in principle, go on forever or may be terminated by a termination rule. For instance, a termination rule may specify:

the number of decisions to be made: the horizon of the problem, or

the set of states in which the sequence terminates, or a combination of both.

Termination may also be a random event, whose probability is some function of the number of decisions made or of the state or of both.

For certain decisions both absolute time and the length of time between steps may be important, but in this essay the emphasis will be on the sequential aspect. Decisions will be thought of as interspersed with periods of unit length. Usually future costs and returns will be discounted with an appropriate discount factor $\rho$, $0<\rho<1$. This discount factor may express both:

i) the terms of exchange of future against present utility, and
ii) the chance of termination of the decision sequence.

In principle the discount factor may be a function of absolute time as well as of the time interval under consideration. For simplicity we shall assume that the same discount factor $\rho$ applies to all unit periods. The number of states and the number of actions will be assumed finite, but the horizon may be infinite. We take for granted that in all situations involving risk and uncertainty the expected value of utility is the relevant objective function. The object of the decision process is now the maximization of the expected sum of payoffs properly discounted. In other words we assume that payoffs are in utility terms, and that total utility is the sum of (discounted) utilities in the various periods (cf. Chapter 4).

Randomness, i.e., risk has been introduced already with respect to the termination of the decision sequence. More importantly, risk may also be present in the decisions themselves. Thus, the following elements may not be known with certainty to the decision-maker:

1) the horizon – as mentioned earlier;
2) the payoff;
3) the state resulting from the action and the known present state;
4) the present state (when some initial state or initial state probabilities and all past actions are known);
5) the transition probabilities.

The decision maker is assumed always to know his past and present actions. As usual we denote by risk the situation where probabilities are known, by uncertainty the situation where (subjective) *a priori* probabilities are revised in the light of experience. Thus, a Bayesian approach is taken to uncertainty.

Cases 1 and 2 are similar to the case of certainty since what matters is the expected payoff. In case 3 payoff and transition depend on the current state, which is known, and on the action. If a decision rule were given that selects for each state an action as a function of that state, or a probability distribution of actions conditional on the state, then transition probabilities would be conditional on the current state only. The behavior of the system could be described by a Markov chain. In the present situation, transition and payoff also depend on the decision maker's action. It will be shown that the problem is still a Markov decision problem.

In case 4, as the result of a known initial state (or initial distribution of states) and of all subsequent actions, a probability distribution for the present state is given. Since this distribution is conditional on the initial state and on all past actions, the concept of a state variable must be broadened to include initial state and past actions. The number of different states, while finite, is dependent on the number of past decisions. Formally we have still the same model as in case 3, while computationally the problem is so much harder as to be unmanageable in all but the simplest cases.

In case 5 it is usually assumed that after the decision is made, the resulting new state can be observed so that a statistical analysis can be performed *ex post*. Using a Bayesian procedure it is possible to generate probability estimates for the next transition, conditional on all past states, the present state, all past decisions, and the next decision. Again the "state" turns into an inclusive catalogue of past states and actions. So far only those cases have yielded to an analysis where the effect of past states and actions can be summarized in terms of one or two sufficient statistics: the number of past observations, and their sum (or mean), say.

The importance of the Markov case lies not only in the fact that the more complicated situations 4 and 5 may be reduced to it, in principle, but in the decisive advance which it achieves over the decision situation under certainty. Under certainty sequential analysis is just a convenient method of computation; under risk, however, it is the only way of introducing strategies, i.e. decisions conditional on states into the analysis. The alternative would be to fix all decisions in advance, regardless of later information about the states of the world. Only in a sequential model can strategies, that is decision rules for all states, be subjected to analysis. It is well known that this applies also to games. As a theoretical tool, sequential analysis has been used in two-person-zero-sum games of perfect information, in particular to prove that a well defined value of the game exists at each state of the play, and that decisions need not be randomized. A general analysis of two-person-zero-sum-games in extensive form is handicapped by the difficulties created by information sets. However, this will not be pursued here (VON NEUMANN, MORGENSTERN (1953)).

## 2. Certainty

*2.1 Identification of actions with states.* We assume that payoffs are functions of the current and the next state and that they are independent of the number of decisions taken previously or subsequently. This rules out terminal payoffs in the case where termination depends on the horizon.

Suppose now that there are several actions leading from one state to another state but with different payoffs. Then, we can exclude as inefficient all actions with a smaller than the maximum payoff and retain only one with a maximal payoff. In this way a one-to-one correspondence is set up *in each state* between actions and the states they are leading to.

A geometric interpretation can now be given to the sequential decision problem. Let the states of the world be represented as vertices of a network. The possible actions, i.e., transitions designate links of the network. The lengths of the links are the payoffs – provided we admit, when necessary, negative measures of length. We assume that (after suitable transformations) all payoffs have the same sign.

This network interpretation of decision sequences suggests two basic types of problems:

i) find the path of maximal length from a given point to a terminal set of points, traversing no link more than once;
ii) find the path of maximal length from a given starting point traversing $n$ links without restriction as to the number of times any particular link is traversed.

Problem i) is the prototype of the decision problem without repetition of states; it is similar to that of finding shortest routes in a network.

Problem ii) includes that of determining a cycle which yields the highest average return per edge. It is the prototype of the decision problem with repetition of states. Under our restrictions to finite sets of states, all problems with infinite horizon must involve repetition of states.

The longest route problem and that of determining the cycles of maximal length per link may both be solved as Linear Programs. We remark in passing that the dual variables of this Linear Program correspond to the value function to be discussed below, and that the efficiency conditions are equivalent to the "principle of optimality" (BECKMANN (1968)).

*2.2 Recursive optimization.* The principal tool in investigating sequential decision problems is recursive analysis, better known as dynamic programming. Consider a decision problem of finite horizon $n$. (For problems with terminal states the same considerations apply *mutatis mutandis.*) We separate the composite decision problem into the first decision, and the remaining ones.

Let $i = i_0$ be the current state,
$i_1, i_2 \dots i_n$ be the subsequent states traversed by an optimal decision sequence.

Denote the payoffs of a transition from $i$ to $j$ by $a_{ij}$, the total payoff by $v$. Total payoff is a function of the initial state $i$ and the horizon $n$, $v_n(i)$. When termination is in a given set of states, $v$ depends only on $i$. Now, in the case $\rho = 1$, we have

$$v_n(i_0) = \max_{i_1, i_2, \dots i_n} (a_{i_0 i_1} + a_{i_1 i_2} + a_{i_2 i_3} + \dots + a_{i_{n-1} i_n}) \tag{2.1}$$

where the transitions $i_k\ i_{k+1}$ must be feasible. Feasibility may be described in terms of neighborhood sets $S_i$, i.e., the sets of points connected by a link to $i$. We have then

$$v_n(i_0) = \max_{i_1 \in S_{i_0}} \Bigl(a_{i_0 i_1} + \max_{\substack{i_2, i_3, \dots, i_n \\ i_{k+1} \in S_{i_k} \\ k = 1, 2, \dots, n-1}} [a_{i_1 i_2} + a_{i_2 i_3} +, \dots, a_{i_{n-1} i_n}]\Bigr).$$

By definition the second maximum term is $v_{n-1}(i_1)$.
Hence,

$$v_n(i_0) = \max_{i_1 \in S_{i_0}} [a_{i_0 i_1} + v_{n-1}(i_1)]$$

or simply

$$v_n(i) = \max_{j \in S_i} [a_{ij} + v_{n-1}(j)]. \tag{2.2}$$

If we specify, e.g.

$$v_0(i) = 0 \tag{2.3}$$

then (2.2) and (2.3) determine all $v_n(i)$ for finite $i$, $n$ by induction. Equation (2.2) is known as the "Principle of Optimality" (BELLMAN (1957)). It introduces a value function or "state evaluation function" (RADNER (1963)) as a principal device for the recursive determination of solutions. One of its first uses, independent of Bellman's discovery, has been in optimal inventory control (ARROW, HARRIS, MARSCHAK (1951)).

The solution is a sequence of decisions, which are to be made in the various states and for the various horizons. Thus, the solution may be given in terms of a *decision rule*

$$j = d(i, n)$$

where $i$ refers to the state in which the decision is made and $n$ to the number of decisions yet to be made.

Of course, value functions may be constructed for any decision rule including a nonoptimal one. In fact, such value functions are essential to a method of solution known as policy iteration (see below). Let $\delta = \{d(i, n)\}$ be a decision rule and $v_n(i, \delta)$ be the associated value function. Thus,

$$v_n(i, \delta) = a_{id(i,n)} + v_{n-1}(d(i, n), \delta)\,. \tag{2.4}$$

A special case is that in which decisions depend only on the state and not on the horizon – a *stationary* decision rule $d(i, n) = d(i)$.

*2.3 Infinite horizon.* Given a stationary decision rule or assuming an optimal decision rule it is easy to show that a unique value function exists even for infinite horizons provided future payoffs are discounted. Moreover, this value function determines an optimal decision rule. The value function is a unique solution of the equation stating the principle of optimality without horizon:

$$v(i) = \max_{j \in S_i} \left[a_{ij} + \rho v(j)\right]. \tag{2.5}$$

Moreover, the principle of optimality generates all optimal decision rules.

The proofs of these propositions are analogous to those for the stochastic decision problems under risk in the next section.

*2.4 Nature of the solutions.* Given these results about the value function, the optimal decision rule $j = d(i)$ determined as a maximizer of (5) is seen to depend only on the current state $i$. In view of the finiteness of the set of states the following possibilities arise:

i) the initial state recurs after a finite number of transitions and the problem is repeated: the optimal policy consists of repeated cycles, or
ii) after traversing an initial sequence of nonrecurrent states the decision process enters into a cycle which repeats itself indefinitely.

How does this solution depend on the horizon and on the discount rate?

THEOREM 1. *Let $i$ be a state with a unique optimal initial decision $j$ in the infinite horizon problem. There exists an $N$ such that for fixed $\rho$, $0<\rho<1$, the optimal initial decision in state $i$ is identical for all $n>N$.*

*Proof.* Let $j_n$ denote the optimal initial decision in a problem with horizon $n+1$, so that

$$a_{ij_n}+v_n(j_n) \geq a_{ij}+v_n(j)$$

and

$$a_{ij_\infty}+v(j_\infty) > a_{ij}+v(j) \qquad \text{for } j \neq j_\infty .$$

Define

$$\varepsilon = \min_{j \neq j_\infty} \left[a_{ij_\infty}+\rho v(j_\infty)-a_{ij}-\rho v(j)\right].$$

Since $j_\infty$ is, by assumption, unique $\varepsilon$ as defined is always positive. Since, for $\rho<1$, $v_n(i)$ converges for all $i$ there exists an $N$ such that

$$|v_n(i)-v(i)| < \frac{\varepsilon}{3} \qquad \text{for } n>N .$$

Now suppose, contrary to the assertion of the theorem, that for every $N$ there exists an $n>N$ with $j_n \neq j_\infty$. In the present case we have, for $n>N$,

$$a_{ij_\infty}+v_n(j_\infty)>a_{ij_\infty}+v(j_\infty) - \frac{\varepsilon}{3} = v(i) - \frac{\varepsilon}{3}$$

$$>a_{ij_n}+v(j_n)+\varepsilon - \frac{\varepsilon}{3} > a_{ij_n}+v_n(j_n) - \frac{\varepsilon}{3} + \varepsilon - \frac{\varepsilon}{3}$$

or

$$a_{ij_\infty}+v_n(j_\infty)>a_{ij_n}+v_n(j_n)$$

contradicting the optimality of $j_n$ in the $n+1$ horizon problem. For $n>N$, therefore, $j_n=j_\infty$.

When $\rho=1$, Theorem 1 need not be true. It can happen that the first decision always depends on $n$. Example:

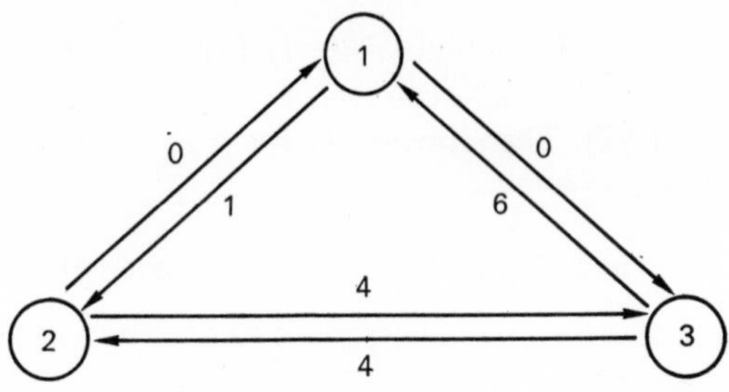


Fig. 1

One verifies that

$$\begin{array}{ll} d_1(1,\ 1) = 2 & v_1(1) = 1 \\ d_2(1,\ 2) = 3 & v_2(1) = 6 \\ d_3(1,\ 3) = 2 & v_3(1) = 11 \\ d_4(1,\ 4) = 3 & v_4(1) = 14 \\ d_5(1,\ 5) = 2 & v_5(1) = 19 \end{array}$$

$$d_n(1, n) = \begin{cases} 3 & n \text{ even} \\ 2 & n \text{ odd} \end{cases} \qquad v_n(1) = \begin{cases} 4(n-2)+6 & n \text{ even} \\ 4(n-2)+7 & n \text{ odd} \end{cases}$$

THEOREM 2. *Suppose $\hat{\jmath}$ is the optimal act for given horizon n, current state i, and discount rate $\hat{\rho}$. Then $\hat{\jmath}$ is nearly optimal in the neighborhood of $\hat{\rho}$; that is to say, for arbitrarily small $\varepsilon > 0$ there exists a $\delta > 0$ such that*

$$a_{i\hat{\jmath}} + v_n(\hat{\jmath}) > v_n(i) - \varepsilon \qquad \text{for } |\rho - \hat{\rho}| < \delta .$$

*Moreover, if $\hat{\jmath}$ is uniquely optimal at $\hat{\rho}$, then it is optimal in the neighborhood of $\hat{\rho}$.*

*Proof.* Since $v_n(i)$ is a continuous function of $\rho$, it is true that $a_{ij} + \rho v_{n-1}(j)$ is a continuous function of $\rho$. Denote this function by $f_j(\rho)$ for fixed $n$ and $i$. For an arbitrary $\varepsilon > 0$ let $\delta_j(\varepsilon) > 0$ be that number for which

$$|f_j(\rho) - f_j(\hat{\rho})| < \varepsilon \text{ if } |\rho - \hat{\rho}| < \delta_j(\varepsilon)$$

and define $\delta_j(0) = 0 (j = 1,2, \ldots)$.

Now let $\delta = \min_j \delta_j(\varepsilon/2)$ for arbitrary $\varepsilon > 0$. The first part of the theorem follows from the observation that for $\rho$ in the open interval $(\hat{\rho} - \delta,\ \hat{\rho} + \delta)$ we have

$$f_{\hat{\jmath}}(\rho) > f_{\hat{\jmath}}(\hat{\rho}) - \varepsilon/2 \geq f_j(\hat{\rho}) - \varepsilon/2 > f_j(\rho) - \varepsilon .$$

For the second part of the theorem let

$$\theta = \min_{j \neq \hat{\jmath}} [f_{\hat{\jmath}}(\hat{\rho}) - f_j(\hat{\rho})]$$

and let $\gamma = \min_j \delta_j(\theta/2)$. Then obviously for $\rho$ in the open interval $(\hat{\rho} - \gamma,$ $\hat{\rho} + \gamma)$ it is true that

$$f_{\hat{\jmath}}(\rho) \geq f_{\hat{\jmath}}(\hat{\rho}) - \theta/2 \geq f_j(\hat{\rho}) + \theta/2 \geq f_j(\rho)$$

for all $j \neq \hat{\jmath}$.

## 3. Risk

*3.1 Generalities.* Let the outcome of an action $k$ in a state $i$ be a transition to another state $j$ with a known probability $p_{ij}^k$ and a payoff $a_{ij}^k$. Of course,

$$p_{ij}^k \geqq 0 \quad \text{and} \quad \sum_j p_{ij}^k = 1 .$$

The expected payoff in one period depends on the state and the action taken,

$$\sum_j p_{ij}^k a_{ij}^k = a_i^k , \text{ say.}$$

Let the terminal payoffs be zero. The optimal decision in the one-period problem is determined by $\max_k a_i^k = a_i^{\hat{k}}$, say, where $\hat{k} = d_1(i)$ is the first decision rule.

A value function is then defined by

$$v_1(i) = a_i^{\hat{k}} = \max_k a_i^k .$$

If a sequence of $n$ decisions is to be made, the maximal expected discounted payoff is

$$v_n(i) = \max_{k_1} \left[a_i^{k_1} + \rho \sum_{i_1} p_{ii_1}^{k_1} \max_{k_2} \left[a_{i_1}^{k_2} + \rho \sum_{i_2} p_{i_1 i_2}^{k_2} \max_{k_3} [\ldots]\right]\right]$$

or

$$v_n(i) = \max_k \left[a_i^k + \rho \sum_j p_{ij}^k v_{n-1}(j)\right] \tag{3.1}$$

observing the definition of $v_{n-1}(j)$.

*3.2 Infinite horizon.* We now show that for positive $a_i^k$ and $\rho < 1$ the sequence $v_n(i)$ is monotone increasing and bounded with respect to $n$.

To show monotonicity by induction, observe that

$$v_1(i) = a_i^{\hat{k}} > 0 = v_0(i)$$

and suppose that $v_n(i) > v_{n-1}(i)$ for all $i$, for $n = 1, \ldots, N$.

Consider

$$\begin{aligned} v_{N+1}(i) &= \max_k \left[a_i^k + \rho \sum_j p_{ij}^k v_N(j)\right] \\ &\geqq a_i^k + \rho \sum_j p_{ij}^k v_N(j) \qquad (3.2) \\ &> a_i^k + \rho \sum_j p_{ij}^k v_{N-1}(j) , \end{aligned}$$

by the induction assumption. This inequality applies also for that $k$ which maximizes the right-hand side of (3.2).

$$v_{N+1}(i) > \max_k \, [a_i^k + \rho \sum_k p_{ij}^k v_{N-1}(j)] = v_N(i).$$

Therefore, $v_n(i)$ is monotone increasing with respect to $n$ for all $n$, $i$.

If $a_i^k < M$ all $i, k$ it is easy to show by induction that $v_n(i) < \dfrac{M}{1-\rho}$ (the proof being left to the reader). Therefore, for every fixed $i$ the bounded monotone sequence $v_n(i)$ has a limit $v(i)$. The associated decision rule is the maximizer of

$$a_i^k + \rho \sum_j p_{ij}^k v(j).$$

Convergence of the value function $v_n(i)$ therefore induces convergence of the decision rule $d_n(i)$ according to Theorem 1, provided the decision rule is unique for each state.

Now by virtue of convergence of $v_n(i)$, $v(i)$ differs by arbitrarily little from the result of $n$ successive maximizing actions and therefore $v(i)$ is the maximum expected discounted payoff for the decision problem with unlimited horizon. Thus,

THEOREM 3. *For the infinite horizon problem with* $a_i^k > 0$ *for all* $i$, $k$, *and* $\rho < 1$ *there exists an optimal decision rule* $\hat{k} = \hat{d}(i)$ *which is the limit of the decision rules for finite horizons. A value function for the infinite horizon problem exists. It is the limit of value functions for finite horizons and satisfies the equation*

$$v(i) = \max_k \, [a_i^k + \rho \sum_j p_{ij}^k v(j)]. \tag{3.3}$$

*The optimal decision rule* $\hat{k} = \hat{d}(i)$ *is the maximizer of the right-hand side of* (3.3) *so that*

$$a_i^{\hat{k}} + \rho \sum_j p_{ij}^{\hat{k}} v(j) = \max_k \, [a_i^k + \rho \sum_j p_{ij}^k v(j)].$$

As a corollary we have:

LEMMA 1. *Equation* (3.3) *has a solution.*

We now prove:

LEMMA 2. *The solution* $v(i)$ *of equation* (3.3) *is unique for all* $i$ *with positive state probabilities.*

*Proof.* Let $u(i)$ and $v(i)$ be two solutions.
Then,

$$v(i)-u(i)=\rho\sum_j p_{ij}[v(j)-u(j)].$$

Let $i_0$ be a component for which $|v(i)-u(i)|$ is maximal. Then,

$$\begin{aligned}|v(i_0)-u(i_0)| &= \rho\,|\sum_j p_{i_0 j}(v(j)-u(j))|\\ &\leqq \rho\sum_j p_{i_0 j}|v(j)-u(i)|\\ &\leqq \rho\,|v(i_0)-u(i_0)|.\end{aligned}$$

Since $0<\rho<1$ this implies $|v(i_0)-u(i_0)|=0$. This concludes the proof of Lemma 2.

THEOREM[1] 4. *The principle of optimality* (3.3) *generates all optimal decision rules.*

*Proof.* Let $d(i, m)$ be an optimal decision rule and suppose it depends not only on the current state $i$ but also on some parameter $m$, e.g., the number of previous decisions or the initial state. Let $m_1, m_2, \ldots, m_n$ denote the sequence of $m$. Consider an arbitrary sequence of decision rules $k_1(j)$, $k_2(j)$ ..., $k_n(j)$. By definition of an optimal policy, for every initial state $i$

$$a_i^{k_1}+\rho\sum_j p_{ij}^{k_1}\,[a_j^{k_2}+\rho\sum_l p_{jl}^{k_2}\,[\ldots\;]]\leqq a_i^{d(i,m_1)}+\rho\sum_j p_{ij}^{d(i,m_1)}\,[a_j^{d(j,m_2)}+\;\ldots\;].$$

The inequality holds in particular if for $n=2, 3, \ldots$ the $k$ sequence is chosen to be

$$k_n(j)=d(j,m_n).$$

The identical expressions in large brackets are convergent. Denote them by $v(j,m)$. Then,

$$a_i^{k_1}+\rho\sum_j p_{ij}^{k_1}\,v(j,m)\leqq a_i^{d(i,m_1)}+\rho\sum p_{ij}^{d(i,m_1)}\,v(j,m).$$

[1] Since this was written, Blackwell's more general treatment of discounted Dynamic Programming has appeared (BLACKWELL (1965)), and this includes Theorem 4.

By definition the right-hand side is $v(i, m)$. Since the equality sign is taken on for $k_1 = d(i, m_1)$ we have

(3.4) $$v(i, m) = \max_k \left[a_i^k + \rho \sum_j p_{ij}^k v(j, m)\right]$$

as a value function generating this optimal decision rule.

Observe that (3.4) is identical with equation (3) which was shown to have the unique solution $v(i)$ independent of $m$. Therefore, neither the value function nor the optimal decision rule involve any further parameters $m$. In particular, it follows that for an unlimited horizon decision problem the optimal decision rule is independent of the initial state and of the number of previous decisions. Now suppose that an arbitrary stationary decision rule $k = d(i)$ is given. An associated value function is obtained by solving

$$v(i, \delta) = a_i^{d(i)} + \rho \sum_j p_{ij}^{d(i)} v(j, \delta).$$

A unique solution always exists for $0 < \rho < 1$ since $1/\rho$ is not a characteristic root of $(p_{ij}^{d(i)})$ the largest real characteristic root being 1. Now if

$$v(i, \delta) \geqq a_i^k + \rho \sum_j p_{ij}^k v(j, \delta)$$

for all $i$, $k$ then by Theorem 3, $\delta$ is an optimal decision rule. If $\delta$ is nonoptimal there must therefore exist an $i$ and a $k$ for which

(3.5) $$v(i, \delta) < a_i^k + \rho \sum_j p_{ij}^k v(j, \delta).$$

We will now show that an improved decision rule can be found to which is associated a value function $\geqq v(i, \delta)$ and "$>$" for the $i$ in (3.5). This is the method of policy iteration (HOWARD (1960)).

*3.3 Policy iteration.* For an arbitrary value function $v$ define a decision rule $\hat{\delta}(v)$ by

(3.6) $$\hat{d}(i) = \hat{k} \text{ where}$$

$$a_i^{\hat{k}} + \rho \sum_j p_{ij}^{\hat{k}} v(j) = \max_k \left[a_i^k + \rho \sum_j p_{ij}^k v(j)\right] \text{ for all } i.$$

Now for a value function $v(\cdot, \delta)$ associated with a given decision rule $\delta$ we have

(3.7) $$v(i, \delta) = a_i^{d(i)} + \rho \sum_j p_{ij}^{d(i)} v(j, \delta).$$

For decision rule $\hat{\delta}(v(\cdot, \delta))$ it is true that

$$v(i, \delta) \leq a_i^{\hat{d}(i)} + \rho \sum_j p_{ij}^{\hat{d}(i)} v(j, \delta). \tag{3.8}$$

If $\delta$ is non-optimal, strict inequality holds for some $i$.

A new value function $v(i, \hat{\delta})$ is defined by

$$v(i, \hat{\delta}) = a_i^{\hat{d}(i)} + \rho \sum_j p_{ij}^{\hat{d}(i)} v(j, \hat{\delta}). \tag{3.9}$$

Taking differences of (3.9) and (3.8):

$$v(i, \hat{\delta}) - v(i, \delta) \geqq \rho \sum_j p_{ij}^{\hat{d}(i)} [v(j, \hat{\delta}) - v(j, \delta)] \tag{3.10}$$

with strict inequality holding for some $i$.

Consider the smallest $v(i, \hat{\delta}) - v(i, \delta)$. Suppose the minimum is taken on for $i = i_0$. Now

$$\begin{aligned} v(i_0, \hat{\delta}) - v(i_0, \delta) &\geqq \rho \sum_j p_{ij}^{\hat{d}(i)} [v(j, \hat{\delta}) - v(j, \delta)] \\ &\geqq \rho \sum_j p_{ij}^{\hat{d}(i)} [v(i_0, \hat{\delta}) - v(i_0, \delta)] \\ &= \rho [v(i_0, \hat{\delta}) - v(i_0, \delta)]. \end{aligned}$$

Thus

$$[v(i_0, \hat{\delta}) - v(i_0, \delta)](1 - \rho) \geqq 0.$$

Therefore,

(3.11) $v(i, \hat{\delta}) \geqq v(i, \delta)$ for all $i$ (for some $i$, "$>$" holds in view of (3.10)).

One "policy iteration" has now been completed. It may be repeated to obtain still another $\delta$ and $v$.

Only a finite number of different decision rules $d(i)$ and hence of equation systems (3.4) exist. Because of (3.11) no equation system may be repeated. But the algorithm can be continued as long as (3.10) applies to any $i$. Therefore eventually

$$a_i^k + \rho \sum_j p_{ij}^k v(j, \delta) \leqq v(i, \delta) \qquad \text{for all } i.$$

The equality sign is taken on by choosing $k = d(i)$, where $d(i)$ is the last and optimal decision rule.

*3.4 An inventory problem.* As an illustration consider the inventory problem with demands in period $t$ depending on the demands in period $t-1$ but not any earlier demands. Let $s$ be the stock level, let $i$ be the previous demand, let $b$ be a proportional ordering cost and let $f_j$ be the expected shortage and storage cost when the terminal stock level is $s_j$. Let $v(s, i)$ denote the minimum discounted expected cost under an optimal policy. The principle of optimality now says

$$(3.12) \qquad v(s,i) = \min_{k \geq s} \left[ b(k-s) + \sum_j p_{ij} f_{k-j} + \rho \sum_j p_{ij}\, v(k-j, j) \right].$$

Because of the proportional ordering cost, the value function permits the decomposition

$$v(s,i) = -bs + u(i)$$

which transforms the principle of optimality (3.12) to

$$(3.13) \qquad u(i) = \min_k \left[ bk + \sum_j p_{ij} f_{k-j} - \rho \sum_j p_{ij}\, b(k-j) + \rho \sum_j p_{ij}\, u(j) \right]$$

$$= \rho \sum_j p_{ij} \left[ u(j) + bj \right] + \min_k \left[ kb(1 - \rho \sum_j p_{ij}) + \sum_j p_{ij} f_{k-j} \right]$$

and the problem is thereby reduced to the one-period problem of minimizing for every $i$

$$\min_k \left[ kb(1-\rho) + \sum_j p_{ij} f_{k-j} \right],$$

that is, of finding for each previous demand level the best new starting stock.

*3.5 Remarks on the Markov decision model.* For an analysis of sequential decisions under risk, this model is of sufficient flexibility to cover all cases where decisions depend on information that may be represented in terms of a finite number of sufficient statistics, to be designated as "states." Its main drawback is that of Dynamic Programming generally: only in exceptional cases is it possible to predict the structure of the solution – its qualitative character as opposed to its numerical values.

The model includes some cases of special interest to decision theory:

1) No state variable. This means that prior to taking an observation, there is no relevant information in the past. The most important application seems to be to stopping rules. If one has not stopped in the past, then the decision to stop will depend only on the observation to be made and on the horizon (the number of times we may postpone the decision). In a less efficient formulation of the problem, the observation would be the state variable.
2) The transition probabilities can be reduced to a distribution, e.g.,

$$p_{ij}^k = p_{j-i}^k.$$

3) The decision $k$ fixes an intermediate state $k$, and the stochastic element is in the transition from that state:

$$p_{ij}^k = p_{kj} \,.$$

In that case it is possible to state the principle of optimality in terms of the state $k$ which prevails after a decision

$$v_n(k) = \sum_j p_{kj} \left[\max_h a_j^h + v_{n-1}(h)\right].$$

The advantage of this formulation is that the set of controlled states $k$ is never larger and often much smaller than that of all states $i$ so that computations are easier.

4) A combination of 2) and 3) is

$$p_{ij}^k = p_{k-j} \,.$$

This occurs in the inventory problem, and in the related problems of maintenance and repair.

The special cases discussed so far permit simplification. The following case creates a complication:

5) Information can be purchased at a cost by a special action, $k=1$. This makes the transition probabilities in subsequent periods dependent on an action in this period. Therefore past decisions $k=1$, and associated information must be included in the definition of the present state. Provided memory is finite, the problem can still be formulated as a Markov decision problem, albeit a complicated one.

## 4. Uncertainty

By definition this is the situation when probabilities $p_i^k$ are not known while the current state $i$, and the decision $k$ are always known. In addition, we require some *a priori* information about the probabilities, for instance, that they belong to a certain family. This is essentially the same problem as in sequential statistical decision theory, the main difference being that in the latter the set of actions is typically restricted to three: accept, reject, continue (ARROW, BLACKWELL, and GIRSHICK (1949)).

In order not to burden the discussion with technical problems assume the simplest possible case: let the transition probabilities have the special form $p_{ij}^k = p_{k-j}$ as in the inventory problem. Some prior information must be assumed about these probabilities (SCARF (1959), BELLMAN (1961), J. MARSCHAK (1963)). For instance, let $p_r$ be geometric

$$p_r = \begin{cases} (1-q)\,q^r & r \geqq 0 \\ 0 & \text{otherwise} \end{cases} \tag{4.1}$$

where $q$ is unknown. Assume that the decision maker believes that $q$ may have any value between 0 and 1 with equal probability. Then to him the prior distribution of demand is

$$\text{prob}(r) = \int_0^1 (1-q)\,q^r\,dq = \frac{1}{(r+1)(r+2)}$$

so that

$$p_{k-j} = \frac{1}{(k+1-j)(k+2-j)}.$$

Now suppose that demands $r_1, r_2, \ldots, r_m$ have been observed in the first $m$ periods. (We are now in period $m+1$.) By Bayes' formula the distribution of $q$ is then

$$\text{prob}(q|r_1, r_2, \ldots, r_m) = \frac{(1-q)^m\,q^{r_1+r_2+\ldots+r_m}}{\int_0^1 (1-q)^m\,q^{r_1+r_2+\ldots+r_m}\,dq}$$

and the revised prior distribution of demand is

$$\text{prob}(r|r_1, \ldots, r_m) = \frac{\int_0^1 (1-q)^{m+1}\,q^{R+r}\,dq}{\int_0^1 (1-q)^m\,q^R\,dq}$$

where we have written $R = r_1 + r_2 + \ldots + r_m$.
Letting

$$B(i, j) = \frac{\Gamma(i)\,\Gamma(j)}{\Gamma(i+j)}$$

denote the Beta function, we may write

$$\text{prob}(r|r_1, \ldots, r_m) = \frac{B(m+2, R+r+1)}{B(m+1, R+1)}. \tag{4.2}$$

This distribution depends only on the number of past periods $m$ and on the accumulated demand $R$,

$$\text{prob}(r|r_1, \ldots, r_m) = \text{prob}(r|R, m).$$

Now the same would be true of all members of the binomial and negative binomial families of distributions. It follows that the optimal policy and value function for these distributions should also depend only on $m$ and $R$ in addition to the state variable $i$ and to the horizon $n$.

$$\begin{aligned}(4.3)\qquad v_{m,n}(i, R) &= \max_k \{\sum_j a_{ij}^k \, p_{k-j}(R, m) + \\ &\qquad + \rho \sum_j p_{k-j}(R, m) \, v_{m+1,n-1}(j, R+k-j)\} \\ &= \max_k \{a_i^k(m, R) + \rho \sum p_r(m, R) \, v_{m+1,n-1}(k-r, R+r)\}.\end{aligned}$$

Even under these favorable conditions the optimal decision depends on at least four variables – in the case of an infinite horizon on three variables. Calculation of the value function and of the optimal decision rule raises, therefore, formidable problems of computation. Only in special cases has anything approaching a rigorous analysis been possible. Consider, for instance, the case where the cost structure is such that the decisions become independent from period to period. This is, for instance true for the inventory problem without ordering cost (SCARF (1959)). Let there be no fixed cost and assume that proportional ordering costs are absorbed as a rental charge to be part of the carrying cost of inventory. The principle of optimality then has the form

$$(4.4)\quad v_{m,n}(i, R) = \min_k \{\sum_r p_r(R, m) \, a_{k-r} + \sum_r p_r v_{m+1,n-1}(k-r, R+r)\}$$

where $k$ is the desired stock level (which can be achieved at zero cost) and $k-r$ is the stock level at the end of the period, which determines expected storage and shortage costs $a_{k-r}$.

Observe that the right-hand side is independent of $i$, the inventory level, so therefore $v_{m,n} = v_{m,n}(R)$. By induction this can be shown to be true also for $v_{m+1,n-1}$. Equation (4.4) assumes the form

$$\begin{aligned}(4.5)\qquad v_{m,n}(R) &= \min_k \sum_r p_r(m, R) \left[a_{k-r} + \rho v_{m+1,n-1}(R+r)\right] \\ &= \rho \sum_r p_r v_{m+1,n-1}(R+r) + \min_k \sum_r p_r(R, m) \, a_{k-r}.\end{aligned}$$

In effect, therefore, the problem is now a single period problem which does not require a recursive analysis other than that involved in calculating demand probabilities. Define the one-period loss function

(4.6)
$$a_i = \begin{cases} hi & i \geqq 0 \\ -gi & i < 0. \end{cases}$$

Now

$$\min_k \sum_r p_r a_{k-r} = \min_k h \sum_{r=0}^{k-1} (k-r)\, p_r + g \sum_{r=k}^{\infty} (r-k)\, p_r$$

is taken on when

(4.7)
$$P_{k-1} = \frac{g}{h+g}$$

where $P_k$ is the cumulative distribution of demand. (4.7) is also known as the newsboy formula.

In the special case of the geometric demand distribution,

$$P_r = 1 - q^{r+1}$$

it is more convenient to write

(4.8)
$$q^k = \frac{h}{h+g}$$

$$\frac{h}{h+g} = \int_0^1 q^k \operatorname{prob}(q|R, m)\, dq$$

$$= B(R+k+1, m+1)/B(R+1, m+1)$$

$$= \frac{(R+k)!\, m!/(R+k+m+1)!}{R!\, m!/(R+m+1)!}$$

$$= \frac{(R+1)(R+2) \dots (R+k)}{(m+R+2) \dots (m+R+k+1)}.$$

For large *n*, *R*, applying Stirling's formula

$$\frac{h}{h+g} \doteq \frac{(R+k)^{R+k+\frac{1}{2}}(R+m+1)^{R+m+\frac{3}{2}}}{R^{R+\frac{1}{2}}(R+k+m+1)^{R+k+m+\frac{3}{2}}}$$

(4.9)
$$\frac{h}{h+g} \doteq \frac{1}{\left(1 + \dfrac{m+1}{R+k}\right)^k}$$

which for

$$\frac{R}{M} = \mu = \frac{q}{1-q} \tag{4.10}$$

becomes the ordinary newsboy formula

$$\frac{h}{h+g} = \frac{1}{\left(1+\frac{1}{\mu}\right)^k} = \frac{1}{\left(1+\frac{1-q}{q}\right)^k} = q^k. \tag{4.11}$$

## References


Arrow, K. J., D. Blackwell, and M. A. Girshick (1949), "Bayes and Minimax Solutions of Sequential Decision Problems," *Econometrica*, *17*, 213–244.

Arrow, K. J., T. Harris, and J. Marschak (1951), "Optimal Inventory Policy," *Econometrica*, *19*, 250–272.

Beckmann, M. J. (1968), *Dynamic Programming of Economic Decisions*, Springer-Verlag, Heidelberg.

Bellman, R. E. (1957), *Dynamic Programming*, Princeton University Press, Princeton.

Bellman, R. E. (1961), *Adaptive Control Processes: A Guided Tour*, Princeton University Press, Princeton.

Blackwell, D. (1965), "Discounted Dynamic Programming," *Annals of Mathematical Statistics*, *36*, 226–235.

Howard, R. (1960), *Dynamic Programming and Markov Processes*, M.I.T. Press, Cambridge.

Marschak, J. (1963), "On Adaptive Programming," *Management Science*, *9*, 517–526.

Nemhauser, G. L. (1966), *Introduction to Dynamic Programming*, Wiley, New York.

Radner, R. (1963), *Notes on the Theory of Economic Planning*, Center of Economic Research, Athens.

Scarf, H. (1959), "Bayes Solutions of the Statistical Inventory Problem," *Annals of Mathematical Statistics*, *30*, 490–508.

von Neumann, J. and O. Morgenstern (1953), *Theory of Games and Economic Behavior*, Princeton University Press, Princeton.

CHAPTER 8

# THEORIES OF BOUNDED RATIONALITY

HERBERT A. SIMON



## 1. Introduction

Rationality denotes a style of behavior that is appropriate to the achievement of given goals, within the limits imposed by given conditions and constraints. Theories of rational behavior may be normative or descriptive – that is, they may prescribe how people or organizations should behave in order to achieve certain goals under certain conditions, or they may purport to describe how people or organizations do, in fact, behave. This essay will be concerned with the structure of theories of rational behavior, whether they are intended prescriptively or descriptively.

*Individual and organizational rationality.* A theory of rational behavior may be concerned with the rationality of individuals or the rationality of organizations. In fact, the two bodies of theory are not wholly distinct.[1] One plausible distinction between them is that a theory of organizational rationality must treat the phenomena of goal conflict, while a theory of individual rationality need not. This is only partly correct, for goal conflict may be important in individual as in group behavior – it is a major theme of so-called "dissonance theory" in psychology. (See N. P. CHAPANIS and J. A. CHAPANIS (1964).) A theory of individual behavior microscopic enough to concern itself with the internal organization (neurological or functional) of the central nervous system will have a significant organizational component. A theory of organizational behavior macroscopic enough to treat the organization as a monolith will be a theory of an "individual." Although this chapter will be aimed primarily at understanding individual rationality, I shall not hesitate to use the theory of the firm – classically, the theory of a

[1] This point was made by J. MARSCHAK (1955) in his first paper on teams, "Elements for a Theory of Teams." I shall follow his good precedent.

monolithic entrepreneur – as a convenient and enlightening illustrative example.

From the standpoint of this chapter, then, the distinction between individual and organization will not be very important. A more significant taxonomy of theories of rational behavior, for our purposes, differentiates them by the assumptions they make about the "givens" – the given goals and given conditions. Particularly important is the distinction between those theories that locate all the conditions and constraints in the environment, outside the skin of the rational actor, and those theories that postulate important constraints arising from the limitations of the actor himself as an information processor. Theories that incorporate constraints on the information-processing capacities of the actor may be called *theories of bounded rationality.*

*Rationality in the classical theory of the firm.* The classical theory of the firm in its simplest form provides a useful standard for comparing and differentiating theories of rationality. In the theory of the firm, the given objective is to maximize profits, where profit is defined as the difference between gross receipts from sales and cost of production. The given conditions are two in number:

(I) *the demand function*: the quantity demanded is a function of price:

$$q_d = D(p), \text{ or } p = D^{-1}(q_d). \tag{1}$$

Since gross receipts equal price times quantity, the demand function determines gross receipts:

$$R = pq_d. \tag{2}$$

(II) *the cost function*: the cost of production is a function of the quantity produced:

$$C = C(q_s). \tag{3}$$

If the quantity produced equals the quantity demanded,

$$q_s = q_d, \tag{4}$$

then the profit, to be maximized, is simply the difference between gross receipts and the cost of production:

$$\text{Profit} = R - C = pq - C(q), \tag{5}$$

and, under appropriate assumptions regarding differentiability, we will have for the maximum profit:

$$\text{(6)} \qquad \mathrm{d}(R-C)/\mathrm{d}q = p + q\,\mathrm{d}(D^{-1}(q))/\mathrm{d}q - \mathrm{d}C(q)/\mathrm{d}q = 0\,.$$

The constraints in this theory, the demand and cost functions, $D$ and $C$, are both located in the actor's environment. He is assumed to find the solution of equation (6). To do this, he must have perfect knowledge of these constraints, and must be able to perform the necessary calculations – to set the derivative of profit with respect to quantity equal to zero and to solve the resulting algebraic equation.

*The limits of rationality.* Theories of bounded rationality can be constructed by modifying these assumptions in a variety of ways. *Risk and uncertainty* can be introduced into the demand function, the cost function, or both. For example, certain parameters of one or both of these functions can be assumed to be random variables with known distributions. Then the assumption of the actor's perfect knowledge of these functions has been replaced by the assumption that he has perfect knowledge of their distributions. This change in assumptions may, in turn, make it easier or more difficult to carry out the calculations for finding the optimum – usually it becomes much more difficult than in the corresponding case of certainty.

Another way in which rationality can be bounded is by assuming that the actor has only *incomplete information about alternatives.* Fewer models have been constructed to deal with this situation than with the situation in which he has incomplete information about consequences. However, in certain search models it is assumed that the actor knows the probability distribution of profits in a population of possible alternative actions. Specific actions become available to him – say, by random sampling from this population – as a function of the amount of resources he devotes to search. His task is to find the alternative that maximizes his expected profit net of the search cost. In this class of models, selecting the best alternative from among those already discovered is assumed to be a trivial problem; the decision question has been switched to the question of how much of the actor's resources should be allocated to search.[2]

[2] For an example, see STIGLER (1961). Theories of the allocation of resources to search can also be constructed to deal with incomplete information about consequences. Sequential sampling theory falls into this category, for it answers the question: shall I make a decision now, or wait until I have gathered additional information? The question is answered by comparing the incremental cost of enlarging the sample with the expected gain through the resulting average improvement in the decision.

Finally, rationality can be bounded by assuming *complexity* in the cost function or other environmental constraints so great as to prevent the actor from calculating the best course of action. Limits on rationality stemming from this source have not been prominent in classical theories of rational behavior. However, in numerical analysis, the theory of approximation provides analogues, for it is concerned with the rate at which an approximation can be expected to improve as a function of amount of computational effort. By introducing explicitly into that theory the cost of computational effort, it can be transformed into a theory of optimal approximation.

*Alternatives to the classical goals.* The classical theory can be modified not only by altering the nature of the conditions and constraints, but also by altering the nature of the given goals. Some modern theories of the firm depart from the classical theory, not along any of the dimensions mentioned above, but by postulating different goals from the classical goal of profit maximization.

BAUMOL (1959, pp. 45–53), for example, has developed a model in which the firm maximizes sales subject to the constraint that profit should not be less than a specified "satisfactory" level. According to this theory of Baumol, equation (6) in the classical model should be replaced by:

$$\mathrm{d}R/\mathrm{d}q = p + q\,\mathrm{d}(D^{-1}(q))/\mathrm{d}q = 0\,, \tag{6'}$$

subject to the constraint that

$$P = R - C \geq P^*\,. \tag{7}$$

It may be observed that the informational and computational requirements for applying Baumol's theory to concrete situations are not very different from the requirements of the classical model.

This essay will not be concerned with variants of the theory of rationality that assume goals different from profit or utility maximization, except to the extent that there is significant interaction between the assumptions about goals and the assumptions about conditions and constraints. We shall see, however, that this is a very important exception. In actual fact, most of the variants of the theory that make significant modifications in the assumptions about conditions and constraints also call for assumptions about goals that are different from the classical assumptions of profit or utility maximization. The reasons for this interaction will appear as we proceed.

## 2. Approaches to Rational Choice in Chess

A number of the persons who have engaged in research on rational decision-making have taken the game of chess as a microcosm that mirrors interesting properties of decision-making situations in the real world. The research on rational choice in chess provides some useful illustrations of alternative approaches to rationality.

The problem confronting a chess player whose turn it is to move can be interpreted in either of two ways. First, it can be interpreted as a problem of finding a good (or the best) strategy – where "strategy" means a conditional sequence of moves, defining what move will be made at each successive stage after each possible response of the opponent.

Second, the problem can be interpreted as one of finding a set of accurate evaluations for the alternative moves immediately before the player.

From a classical standpoint, these two problems are not distinguishable. If the player has unlimited computational power, it does not matter whether he selects a complete strategy for his future behavior in the game, or selects each of his moves, one at a time, when it is his turn to play. For the way in which he goes about evaluating the next move is by constructing alternative complete strategies for the entire future play of the game, and selecting the one that promises the best return (i.e., the best return under the assumption that the opponent will also do *his* best to win). This is the approach taken in the von Neumann-Morgenstern theory of games (VON NEUMANN and MORGENSTERN (1953)).

*The game-theoretical definition of rationality in chess.* As von Neumann and Morgenstern observed, chess is a trivial game. "... if the theory of Chess (i.e., the complete tree of possible games) were really fully known there would be nothing left to play" (*ibid.*, p. 125). Each terminus of the tree of possible games represents a win, loss, or draw for White. Moving backward one branch on the tree, the player whose move it is at that branch can examine the termini to which it could lead by his choice of move, and can choose the move having the preferred terminus. The value of that terminus becomes, then, the value of the branch that leads to it. Working backward in this way, a value – win, lose, or draw for White – can be assigned to each position, and ultimately to each of the initial legal moves for White. Now each player can specify an optimal strategy – a strategy that will guarantee him at least as good an outcome as any other – by specifying which move he would select at each branch point in the tree whenever it is his move.

Unfortunately, as von Neumann and Morgenstern also observed, the triviality of chess offers no practical help to a player in actually choosing a move. "But our proof, which guarantees the validity of one (and only one) of these three alternatives [that the game must have the value of win lose or draw for White], gives no practically usable method to determine the true one. This relative, human difficulty necessitates the use of those incomplete, heuristic methods of playing, which constitute 'good' Chess; and without it there would be no element of 'struggle' and 'surprise' in that game" (*ibid.*).

What "impracticality" means becomes more vivid when we calculate how much search would be involved in finding the game-theoretically correct strategy in chess. On the average, at any given position in a game of chess, there are about 30 legal moves – in round numbers, for a move and its replies, an average of about $10^3$ continuations. Forty moves would be a not unreasonable estimate of the average length of a game. Then there would be perhaps $10^{120}$ possible games of chess. Obviously the exact number does not matter: a number like $10^{40}$ would be less spectacular, but quite large enough to support the conclusions of the present argument.

Studies of the decision-making of chess players indicate strongly that strong players seldom look at as many as one hundred possibilities – that is one hundred continuations from the given position – in selecting a move or strategy. One hundred is a reasonably large number, by some standards, but somewhat smaller than $10^{120}$! Chess players do not consider all possible strategies and pick the best, but generate and examine a rather small number, making a choice as soon as they discover one that they regard as satisfactory (see DE GROOT (1965)).

Before we consider in detail how they do it, let us return to the classical model and ask whether there is any way in which we could make it relevant to the practical choice problem, taking account of the size of the problem space, in a game like chess. One possible way would be to replace the actual problem space with a very much smaller space that approximates the actual one in some appropriate sense, and then apply the classical theory to the smaller approximate space.

This approach was taken in some of the early computer programs for playing chess and checkers. In the Los Alamos program, for example, the computer generated all legal moves, all legal replies to each, and so on, two moves deep. Each of the terminal positions thus generated (about a million in a two-move analysis) was evaluated, and the minimax procedure applied, working backwards, to find the best first move. Thus, a space of about

$10^6$ elements was substituted for the space of $10^{120}$ elements that represents the "real" world of chess.

The scheme was approximate, because the actual chess values of the million terminal positions were not known, and could not be known accurately without returning to the space of $10^{120}$ elements – that is, returning to the game-theoretical analysis of the full game. In place of these unknown true values, approximate values were computed, using rules of thumb that are commonly employed by chess players – conventional numerical values for the pieces, and measures of mobility. Thus, the approximate scheme was not guaranteed to select the objectively best move, but only the move leading to the positions that appeared best, in terms of these heuristic criteria, after an analysis two moves deep. Experience indicates that it is not possible to make such approximate evaluations accurately enough to enable the program to play good chess. The optimal decision in the approximated world is not necessarily even a good decision in the real world.

*Satisficing processes in chess thinking.* Chess programs now exist that take the alternative course, trying to emulate the human chess player in looking at only a very few continuations. The effectiveness of such a scheme depends critically on three components: the *move generators*, processes that select the continuations to be explored; the *evaluators*, processes that determine how good each continuation is; and the *stop rules*, criteria that determine when the search should be terminated and a move selected.

By scanning a chess position, features of the position can be detected that suggest appropriate moves. To take an extreme case, suppose a chess player discovers, when it is his move, that one of his Pawns attacks the opponent's Queen. Obviously, the capture of the Queen by the Pawn is one move that deserves consideration. It may turn out to be a poor move – another piece will checkmate him, say, if he captures the Queen – but its superficial merits are obvious, and its deficiencies can only be detected by considering it and evaluating it dynamically. A simple process that would generate this move, and others like it, would consist in determining which of the opponent's pieces were attacked by a piece of lesser value, or were undefended and attacked by any piece. Thus, a suitable set of move-generating processes might identify for further analysis all or most of the moves deserving serious consideration. If the generators were ordered appropriately, they might usually identify first the most promising moves, then the ones slightly less promising, and so on.

Possible moves, produced by the move generators, can be evaluated by a combination of static and dynamic criteria. Static criteria are features of the position, or differences between successive positions. Thus, one of the important static evaluators used by all chess players is the piece count: each piece is assigned a conventional value (say, Pawn = 1, Knight and Bishop = 3, Rook = 5, Queen = 9), and the sums of the values for the two players are compared. In general, if the piece count of one player exceeds that of the other by more than one point (or even, in many cases, by a single point), the player with the higher count can find a winning continuation *unless* the balance is very quickly redressed by a sequence of forceful moves. (Thus, it does not matter being 5 points down if you can capture the opponent's Queen on the next move without further reprisals.)

The short-run tactical considerations are handled by carrying out dynamic analysis of plausible continuations until a position is reached that is sufficiently quiet or "dead" that it can safely be evaluated by means of the static evaluators. These static evaluators are then propagated backwards to the move under consideration by the familiar minimax procedure.

Two kinds of stop rules are needed in a program having this structure: rules to stop exploration at dead positions that can be evaluated statically, and rules to stop the entire process and select a move when a satisfactory one has been found. The former class of stop rules has already been discussed; the latter needs to be examined more closely. If the alternatives in a choice situation are not given, but have to be discovered or invented, and if the number of possible alternatives is very large, then a choice has to be made before all or most of them have been looked at. It was precisely this difficulty in the classical requirement of comparing all alternatives that led to the approach described here. But if all alternatives are not to be examined, some criterion must be used to determine that an adequate, or satisfactory, one has been found. In the psychological literature, criteria that perform this function in decision processes are called *aspiration levels*. The Scottish word "satisficing" (= satisfying) has been revived to denote problem solving and decision making that sets an aspiration level, searches until an alternative is found that is satisfactory by the aspiration level criterion, and selects that alternative (SIMON (1957), Part IV).

In satisficing procedures, the existence of a satisfactory alternative is made likely by dynamic mechanisms that adjust the aspiration levels to reality on the basis of information about the environment. Thus, in a chess-playing program, the initial aspiration level can be set (preferably with a little upward bias) on the basis of a static evaluation of the position. As alternative moves are considered and evaluated by dynamic and static analysis, the evaluation of the position can gradually be reduced until the best move discovered so far reaches or exceeds in value the aspiration level.

*The limits of rationality in chess.* In the introductory section of this paper, three limits on perfect rationality were listed: uncertainty about the consequences that would follow from each alternative, incomplete information about the set of alternatives, and complexity preventing the necessary computations from being carried out. Chess illustrates how, in real world problem-solving situations, these three categories tend to merge.

If we describe the chess player as choosing a *strategy*, then his difficulty in behaving rationally – and the impossibility of his behaving as game theory says he should – resides in the fact that he has incomplete information as to what alternatives (strategies) are open to him. He has time to discover only a minute fraction of these strategies, and to specify the ones he discovers only incompletely.

Alternatively, if we describe the chess player as choosing a *move*, his difficulty in behaving rationally lies in the fact that he has only rough information about the consequences of adopting each of the alternatives (moves) that is open to him. It would not be impossible for him to generate the whole set of his legal moves, for they seldom number more than about thirty. However, he can evaluate them, even approximately, only by carrying out further analysis through the immense, branching, move tree. Since only a limited amount of processing time is available for the evaluation, he must allocate the time among the alternative moves. The practical facts of the matter are that it is usually better to generate only a few of the entire set of legal moves, evaluating these rather thoroughly, than it is to generate all of them, evaluating them superficially. Hence the good chess player does not examine all the moves open to him, but only a small fraction of them. (Data presented by DE GROOT (1965) suggest that typically a half dozen to a dozen of a set of thirty legal moves may be generated and explored by the chess player.)

From still a third standpoint, the chess player's difficulty in behaving rationally has nothing to do with uncertainty – whether of consequences or alternatives – but is a matter of complexity. For there is no risk or uncertainty, in the sense in which those terms are used in economics or statistical decision theory, in the game of chess. As von Neumann and Morgenstern observe, it is a game of perfect information. No probabilities of future events need enter the calculations, and no contingencies, in a statistical sense, arise.

From a game-theoretical standpoint, the presence of the opponent does not introduce contingencies. The opponent can always be counted on to do his worst. The point becomes clear if we replace the task of playing chess with the task of proving theorems. In the latter task, there is no opponent. Nor are there contingencies: the true and the derivable theorems reside eternally in Plato's heaven. Rationality in theorem proving is a problem only because the maze of possible proof paths is vast and complex.

What we refer to as "uncertainty" in chess or theorem proving, therefore, is uncertainty introduced into a perfectly certain environment by inability – computational inability – to ascertain the structure of that environment. But the result of the uncertainty, whatever its source, is the same: approximation must replace exactness in reaching a decision. In particular, when the uncertainty takes the form of an unwieldy problem space to be explored, the problem-solving process must incorporate mechanisms for determining when the search or evaluation will stop and an alternative will be chosen.

*Satisficing and optimizing*. The terms satisficing and optimizing, which we have already introduced, are labels for two broad approaches to rational behavior in situations where complexity and uncertainty make global rationality impossible. In these situations, optimization becomes approximate optimization – the description of the real-world situation is radically simplified until reduced to a degree of complication that the decision maker can handle. Satisficing approaches seek this simplification in a somewhat different direction, retaining more of the detail of the real-world situation, but settling for a satisfactory, rather than an approximate-best, decision. One cannot predict in general which approach will lead to the better decisions as measured by their real-world consequences. In chess at least, good players have clearly found satisficing more useful than approximating-and-optimizing.

A satisficing decision procedure can often be turned into a procedure for optimizing by introducing a rule for optimal amount of search, or, what amounts to the same thing, a rule for fixing the aspiration level optimally. Thus, the aspiration level in chess might be adjusted, dynamically, to such a level that the expected improvement in the move chosen, per minute of additional search, would just balance the incremental cost of the search.

Although such a translation is formally possible, to carry it out in practice requires additional information and assumptions beyond those needed for satisficing. First, the values of alternatives must be measured in units comparable with the units for measuring search cost, in order to permit comparison at the margins. Second, the marginal productivity of search – the expected increase in the value per unit of search time – must be estimated on some basis or other. If one were designing a chess-playing program, it is doubtful whether effort spent in attempting to imbed the program in such a dynamic optimizing framework would be nearly as worthwhile as equivalent effort spent in improving the selectivity of the program's move-generating and move-evaluating heuristics.

Another quite different translation between optimizing and satisficing schemes has also been suggested from time to time. A chess program of the "classical" type, which makes optimal decisions in an approximated world, can be regarded as a particular kind of satisficing program, in which "satisfactory" is defined by the approximating procedure that is used. Hence, it is difficult to draw a formal distinction between optimizing and satisficing procedures that is so iron-clad as to prevent either from being reinterpreted in the frame of the other. The practical difference, however – the difference in emphasis that results from adopting one viewpoint or the other – is often very great.

In research on optimizing procedures, considerable attention has been paid to the formal properties of the evaluation functions, to the existence and efficiency of procedures for computing the optimum, and to procedures for reducing uncertainty (e.g., forecasting methods). The nature of the approximations that are necessary to cast real-world problems into forms suitable for optimization, and the means for choosing among alternative approximations, have been less fully and less systematically studied. Much effort, for example, has gone into the discovery of efficient algorithms for solving linear programming problems. Finding an appropriate way of formulating a concrete real-world decision problem as a linear-programming problem remains largely an art.[3]

Research on satisficing procedures has focussed primarily on the efficiency of search – on the nature of the heuristic methods that enable the rare solutions in enormous spaces of possibilities to be sought and found with moderate amounts of search effort. Since moderate changes in heuristics often make order-of-magnitude changes in search effectiveness, highly accurate means for assessing the quality of solutions or the effort required to find them may be relatively unimportant. It probably does not require delicate evaluation functions or stop rules to change a duffer's chess play to a reasonably effective move-choosing program.

---

[3] The work of A. Charnes and W. W. Cooper (1961) is full of sophisticated examples of this art. See, for instances, Appendix B and Chapter 11 of Volume I.

## 3. Bounded Rationality in Design

The engineering activities usually called "design" have not been much discussed under the heading of rational decision-making. The reason for this should be clear from the foregoing discussion: classical decision theory has been concerned with choice among *given* alternatives; design is concerned with the discovery and elaboration of alternatives. Our exploration of the microcosm of chess has indicated, however, how the theory of design can be assimilated to a satisficing theory of rational choice. Let me spell the point out a little more fully.

Consider that interpretation of chess which views the task as one of choosing a strategy, and not just a single move. Specifically, consider a situation where a player is searching for a combination (a strategy) that will definitely checkmate his opponent, even though it may require sacrifices of pieces along the way. A chess player will ordinarily not enter into such a course of action unless he can see it through to the end – unless he can *design*, that is, a water-tight mating combination.

As we have seen already, the evaluations and comparisons that take place during this design process are not, in general, comparisons among complete designs. Evaluations take place, first of all, to guide the search – the elaboration of the design itself. They provide the basis for decisions that the design should be elaborated in one direction rather than another. Complete designs (in this case, mating combinations), when they are finally arrived at, are not generally evaluated by comparing them with alternative designs, but by comparing them with standards defined by aspiration levels. In the chess situation, as soon as the player discovers a strategy that guarantees a checkmate, he adopts it. He does not look for all possible checkmating strategies and adopt the best (H. A. SIMON and P. A. SIMON (1962)).

In the design of complex objects – a bridge, say, or an airplane – the process has an even more involved search structure. Here, the early stages of search take place in highly simplified spaces that abstract most of the detail from the real-world problem, leaving only its most important elements in summarized form. When a plan, a schematized and aggregated design, has been elaborated in the planning space, the detail of the problem can be reintroduced, and the plan used as a guide in the search for a complete design.

More than two spaces may be used, of course; there may be a whole hierarchy of planning spaces, leading from a highly abstract and global design to successive specification of detail. At each of these levels of abstraction, the design process, too, may be differently structured. Since the more abstract spaces tend to be "smoother," it is often possible to use optimization models for planning purposes, reverting to satisficing search models to fill in the detail of the design. Thus, linear programming or dynamic programming may be used for general planning of factory operations, while more heuristic techniques are used for scheduling of individual jobs. In other situations, the overall design process may employ satisficing search procedures, while optimizing techniques may be used to set parameters once the general design has been fixed.[4]

## 4. Bounded Rationality in Management Science

Most of the formal techniques that constitute the technical backbone of management science and operations research are procedures for finding the best of a set of alternatives in terms of some criterion – that is, they fall in our category of "classical" procedures. Linear and dynamic programming are among the most powerful of these techniques. The dominant approach to problems in this sphere has been to simplify the real-world problems to the point where the formal optimizing models can be used as approximations.

Some industrial problems of a combinatorial sort have not yielded easily to this approach. Typically, the recalcitrant problems involve integer solutions, or, what usually amounts to the same thing, the consideration of possible permutations and combinations of a substantial number of elements. Warehouse location is a problem of this kind. The task is to "determine the geographical pattern of warehouse locations which will be most profitable to the company by equating the marginal cost of warehouse operation with the transportation cost savings and incremental profits resulting from more rapid delivery" (KUEHN and HAMBURGER (1963), p. 643).

A heuristic program devised by KUEHN and HAMBURGER (1963) for locating warehouses has two parts: "(1) the main program, which locates warehouses one at a time until no additional warehouses can be added to the distribution network without increasing total costs, and (2) the bump and shift routine, ..., which attempts to modify solutions ... by evaluating the profit implications of dropping individual warehouses or of shifting them from one location to another" (*ibid.*, p. 645).

---

[4] Some modern semi-automated procedures for the design of chemical processing plants proceed from heuristic techniques for selecting the unit operations and their flow, then employ linear programming to determine the parameters of the system so specified.

This program fits our earlier characterization of design procedures. A possible plan is gradually built up, step by step, through a search procedure, and then possible local modifications are investigated before the final plan is settled upon. In building up the initial plan, locations are tried that are near concentrations of demand, adding at each step the warehouse that produces the greatest cost savings for the entire system. Only a fraction of the possible warehouse sites, which preliminary screening selects as "promising," are evaluated in detail at each stage. Finally, a so-called "bump-shift" routine modifies the programs tentatively arrived at by (1) eliminating warehouses no longer economical because new warehouses have been introduced at later steps of the program, (2) considering shifting warehouses to alternative sites within their territories. The flow diagram of the warehouse location programs, which will serve to illustrate the typical structure of heuristic programs when they are formalized, is shown in Fig. 1.

Kuehn and Hamburger have carried out some detailed comparisons of the heuristic program with optimizing techniques. They conclude that "in theory, a linear programming approach ... could be used to solve the problem. In practice, however, the size and nonlinearities involved in many problems are such that application is not currently feasible" (*ibid.*, p. 658). They attribute the superior performance of the heuristic program to two main causes: "(1) computational simplicity, which results in substantial reductions in solution times and permits the treatment of large-scale problems, and (2) flexibility with respect to the underlying cost functions, eliminating the need for restrictive assumptions" (*ibid.*, p. 656).

Perhaps the technique most widely used in management science to deal with situations too complex for the application of known optimization methods is simulation. The amount of detail incorporated in the simulation of a large system is limited only by computational feasibility. On the other hand, simulation, unaided by other formal tools of analysis, provides no direct means for discovering and evaluating alternative plans of action. In simulation, the trial and error is supplied by the human investigators rather than by the technique of analysis itself (see FORRESTER (1961)).

## 5. Conclusion

The theory of rational decision has undergone extremely rapid development in the past thirty years. A considerable part of the impetus for this development came, during and since World War II, from the attempt to use formal decision procedures in actual real-world situations of considerable

## A HEURISTIC PROGRAM FOR LOCATING WAREHOUSES

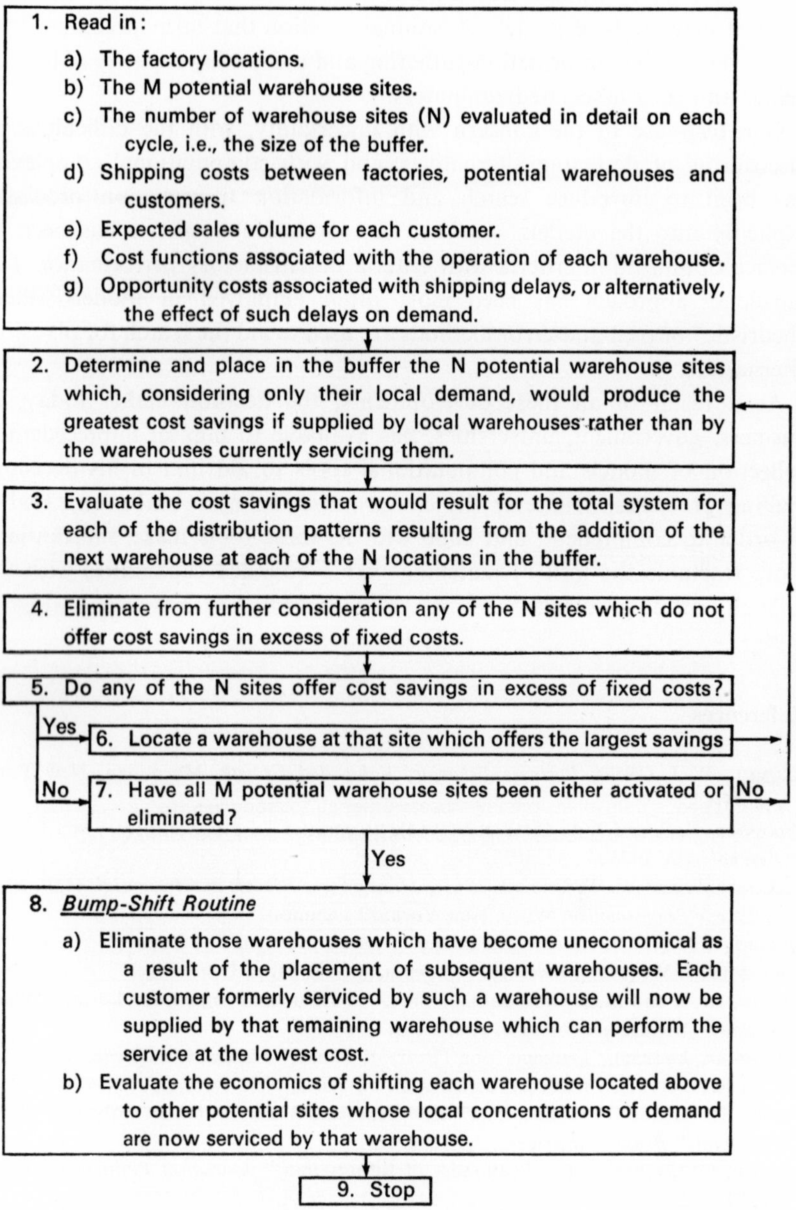

1. Read in:
   a) The factory locations.
   b) The M potential warehouse sites.
   c) The number of warehouse sites (N) evaluated in detail on each cycle, i.e., the size of the buffer.
   d) Shipping costs between factories, potential warehouses and customers.
   e) Expected sales volume for each customer.
   f) Cost functions associated with the operation of each warehouse.
   g) Opportunity costs associated with shipping delays, or alternatively, the effect of such delays on demand.

2. Determine and place in the buffer the N potential warehouse sites which, considering only their local demand, would produce the greatest cost savings if supplied by local warehouses rather than by the warehouses currently servicing them.

3. Evaluate the cost savings that would result for the total system for each of the distribution patterns resulting from the addition of the next warehouse at each of the N locations in the buffer.

4. Eliminate from further consideration any of the N sites which do not offer cost savings in excess of fixed costs.

5. Do any of the N sites offer cost savings in excess of fixed costs?

Yes → 6. Locate a warehouse at that site which offers the largest savings → (return to 2)

No → 7. Have all M potential warehouse sites been either activated or eliminated? No → (return to 2)

Yes ↓

8. *Bump-Shift Routine*
   a) Eliminate those warehouses which have become uneconomical as a result of the placement of subsequent warehouses. Each customer formerly serviced by such a warehouse will now be supplied by that remaining warehouse which can perform the service at the lowest cost.
   b) Evaluate the economics of shifting each warehouse located above to other potential sites whose local concentrations of demand are now serviced by that warehouse.

9. Stop

Fig. 1. Flow diagram

complexity. To deal with this complexity the formal models have grown in power and sophistication. But complexity has also stimulated the development of new kinds of models of rational decision that take special account of the very limited information-gathering and computing capacity of human beings and their associated computers.

One response to the concern with uncertainty, with the difficulties of discovering or designing alternatives, and with computational complexity has been to introduce search and information transmission processes explicitly into the models. Another (not exclusive) response has been to replace optimization criteria with criteria of satisfactory performance. The satisficing approach has been most often employed in models where "heuristic" or trial-and-error methods are used to aid the search for plausible alternatives.

As a result of all these developments, the decision maker today, in business, government, universities, has available to him an unprecedented collection of models and computational tools to aid him in his decision-making processes. Whatever the compromises he must make with reality in order to comprehend and cope with it, these tools make substantially more tractable the task of matching man's bounded capabilities with the difficulty of his problems.

## References

BAUMOL, W. J. (1959), *Business Behavior, Value and Growth*, Macmillan, New York, pp. 45–53.

CHAPANIS, N. P. and J. A. CHAPANIS (1964), "Cognitive Dissonance: Five Years Later," *Psychological Bulletin*, *61*, 1023.

CHARNES, A. and W. W. COOPER (1961), *Management Models and Industrial Applications of Linear Programming*, Wiley, New York, (2 volumes).

DE GROOT, A. (1965), *Thought and Choice in Chess*, Mouton, The Hague.

FORRESTER, J. W. (1961), *Industrial Dynamics*, M.I.T. Press, Cambridge.

KUEHN, A. A. and M. J. HAMBURGER (1963), "A Heuristic Program for Locating Warehouses," *Management Science*, *9*, 643-666.

MARSCHAK, J. (1955), "Elements for a Theory of Teams," *Management Science*, *1*, 127–137

SIMON, H. A. (1957), Part IV in *Models of Man*, Wiley, New York, pp. 196–279.

SIMON, H. A. and P. A. SIMON (1962), "Trial and Error Search in Solving Difficult Problems," *Behavioral Science*, *7*, 425–429.

STIGLER, G. J. (1961), "The Economics of Information," *Journal of Political Economy*, *69*, 213–225.

VON NEUMANN, J. and O. MORGENSTERN (1953), *Theory of Games and Economic Behavior*, (3rd ed.), Princeton University Press, Princeton, pp. 125.

CHAPTER 9

# NORMATIVE THEORIES OF ORGANIZATION: AN INTRODUCTION

ROY RADNER

1. New elements in the several-person decision problem. – 2. Formal structure of the several-person decision problem. – 3. Optimality, equilibrium, viability. – 4. An example: pure exchange. – 5. Organizing.

## 1. New Elements in the Several-Person Decision Problem

We shall look at the problem of optimal organization as a several-person decision problem. As compared with the single-person decision problem, a number of new elements appear:

(a) Individual members of the organization may differ with respect to possibilities of action, with respect to their information, and with respect to their preferences. Within the expected utility framework, we may distinguish – with regard to preferences – differences in beliefs about events from differences in preferences among (sure) consequences.

(b) The multi-person character introduces the possibility of uncertainty about other members' actions as well as about the state of nature.

(c) Differences among individuals with respect to preferences lead to a new problem of definition of optimality, both for the organization as a whole, and for members of the organization.

It will be seen that there is no generally accepted criterion of optimality, and likewise no generally accepted way to characterize mutual uncertainty about individual behavior. These two points are clearly related. The concept of optimality will be replaced by a concept of "viability," but it appears that in order to make such a concept quite precise in any given several-person decision problem, it is necessary to have information about the particular possibilities of communication among the decision makers during the process of organizing, and about their anticipations regarding each others' behavior.

## 2. Formal Structure of the Several-Person Decision Problem

As in the case of the single-person decision problem, let

$S$ = the set of alternative *states of nature*,

$C$ = the set of alternative *consequences*,

$A$ = the set of alternative *acts* available to the organization; every act is a function from $S$ to $C$.

Acts are generated by individual *strategies*. Let $\beta_i$ be a strategy of individual $i$ ($i = 1, \ldots, m$), and let $\beta \equiv (\beta_1, \ldots, \beta_m)$ be a joint strategy for the organization. In a way to be described below, every joint strategy determines an act for the organization; i.e., if $\mathscr{B}$ is the set of available joint organization strategies, then there is a function ,say $\mathbf{F}$ from $\mathscr{B}$ into $A$.

Every member $i$ is assumed to have a preference pre-ordering, say $\succsim_i$, on the set $A$ of available organization acts. It should be emphasized that the consequences refer to the organization as a whole, so that an individual might be interested only in some aspect of a given consequence (e.g., his own consumption, as a components of an $m$-tuple of consumptions).

The generation of acts by strategies is assumed to take place by means of a system of observation, communication, computation, and action. Imagine that there is a sequence of elementary dates $t = 1, \ldots, T$ at which these activities take place, and let

$B_{ijt}$ = the set of alternative messages from $i$ to $j$ at date $t$;

$B_{0jt}$ = the set of alternative observations of Nature by $j$ at date $t$ ("messages from Nature to $j$");

$\beta_{jt}$ = a function from $\underset{i=0}{\overset{m}{\times}} B_{i,j,t-1}$ to $\underset{k=0}{\overset{m}{\times}} B_{jkt}$;

$\beta_j \equiv (\beta_{j1}, \ldots, \beta_{jT})$;

$\beta \equiv (\beta_1, \ldots, \beta_m)$, a joint strategy for the organization, constrained to be in $\mathscr{B}$.

A message sent at date $t$ is to be thought of as being received at date $(t+1)$. Messages that take more than one elementary time unit from sending to receipt may be thought of as passing through a sequence of "dummy" organization members (stations on a communication link). A message sent by an individual to himself is interpreted as "remembering."

For a given joint strategy, $\beta$, every state of nature $s$ determines an array $((b_{i0t}))$ of decisions – called a joint decision. Every joint decision, together with a state of nature, has a consequence. Thus every $\beta$ determines, indirectly, an act. Denote this mapping of strategies into acts by $\boldsymbol{F}$.

The *normal form* of the *m*-person decision problem is a specification of

$$\mathscr{B}, A;$$
$$\boldsymbol{F}: \mathscr{B} \to A;$$
$$(\succsim_1, \dots, \succsim_m).$$

The *extensive form* includes, in addition to the above, the specification of $S$, $C$, the sets $B_{ijt}$, and the function that transforms (state-of-nature, joint-decision) pairs into consequences.

If all of the preference pre-orderings, $\succsim_i$, are identical, then we have the special case of a *team* (J. MARSCHAK (1955), and Chapter 10). In this case there is no ambiguity about the appropriate concept of optimatility. Nevertheless, the relation between strategies and acts is in general more complicated than in the single-person case, and we have to deal with phenomena of interaction, coordination, communication, etc.

The general situation is usually called a *game*.

## 3. Optimality, Equilibrium, Viability

If the $m$ preference orderings, $\succsim_i$, are not identical, then one cannot order acts from the point of view of the organization in a way that does not contradict at least one of the individual orderings. Further, one cannot expect to find an act that is maximal for all individual orderings simultaneously.

From the point of view of any given (nonempty) subset $I$ of the set $M$ of members of the organization, one can at least define a *partial* ordering of acts, say $\succsim_I$, that does not conflict with the preferences of any individual in $I$, as follows[1]:

$$\alpha' \succsim_I \alpha \text{ means that for every } i \text{ in } I,\ \alpha' \succsim_i \alpha.$$

(In particular, $\succsim_{(i)}$ is identical to the complete pre-ordering $\succsim_i$.) We shall also have occasion to use the following notation:

$$\alpha' \sim_I \alpha \text{ means that for every } i \text{ in } I,\ \alpha' \sim_i \alpha;$$
$$\alpha' \succ_I \alpha \text{ means that } \alpha' \succsim_I \alpha \text{ but not } \alpha' \sim_I \alpha.$$

[1] Although this notation is not strictly unambiguous, it will always be clear from the context whether $\succsim_x$ refers to an individual $x$ or a group $x$.

Since every joint strategy in $\mathscr{B}$ determines an act, the several preference pre-orderings of acts induce corresponding orderings of strategies, which we shall indicate by the same symbols, $\gtrsim_i$, $\gtrsim_I$, etc.[2]

Special interest attaches to $\gtrsim_M$. If an act is maximal with respect to $\gtrsim_M$, then no other act is strictly better from the point of view of some individual, without at the same time being strictly worse from the point of view of another individual (in other words, "$\alpha$ is maximal with respect to $\gtrsim_M$" means that there is no $\alpha'$ such that $\alpha' \succ_M \alpha$). Such a maximal act is often called *Pareto-optimal.* There will, of course, typically be many Pareto-optimal acts – if there are any at all – and two such acts will typically not be equivalent from the point of view of any one individual.

In view of the difficulty of defining "optimality" for the organization as a whole in terms of a single ordering of acts, attempts have been made to substitute some concept of "equilibrium" or "viability." Roughly speaking, an act is an equilibrium if no one of some specified class of groups of individuals would have both the incentive and the ability to change the act by means of a change in their own joint choice of strategies.

When contemplating a change in its joint strategy, a group of individuals might want to consider whether or not such a change would induce further changes by others. Two different concepts of equilibrium or viability have been studied, differing according to whether such further changes are or are not taken account of.

By a *coalition* is meant a nonempty set of individuals (a nonempty subset of $M$). We shall say that a joint strategy $\beta$ in $\mathscr{B}$ can be *upset* by a coalition $I$ if, roughly speaking, the coalition can change $\beta$ into a joint strategy that it prefers, by changing only strategies of its own members. Formally, for any (joint) strategy $\beta$ in $\mathscr{B}$ define $\mathscr{B}^I(\beta)$ to be the set of joint strategies that can be obtained by changing the individual strategies of members of the coalition $I$, i.e., $\mathscr{B}^I(\beta)$ is the set of all $\beta'$ in $\mathscr{B}$ such that

$$\beta_j' = \beta_j \text{ for } j \text{ not in } I .$$

A strategy $\beta$ can be *upset* by a coalition $I$ if there is a strategy $\beta'$ in $\mathscr{B}^I(\beta)$ such that

$$\beta' \succ_I \beta . \tag{9.1}$$

[2] Indeed, the *normal form* is sometimes understood to consist of a specification of the set $\mathscr{B}$ of available joint strategies, together with the $m$ pre-orderings on $\mathscr{B}$.

In particular, to say that $\beta$ cannot be upset by $M$ is equivalent to saying that $\beta$ is Pareto-optimal. On the other hand, a joint strategy that cannot be upset by any one-member coalition is called a *Nash-equilibrium.*

The definition of upsetting suggests, if only implicitly, the possibility of some kind of agreement among the members of the coalition; otherwise, the achievement of a preferred coalition strategy would appear to be left to chance. This in turn would seem to require the existence of some means of communication among individuals, which means are to be used in the process of choosing a joint strategy, but are not explicitly described already in the specification of the message sets $B_{ijt}$.

Suppose that during this (hypothetical) process of choosing a joint strategy, a particular strategy, say $\beta$, is under consideration, and that $\beta$ can be upset by a coalition $I'$, by a change to a strategy $\beta'$. It may be that $\beta'$ itself can be upset by a coalition $I''$, by a change to a third strategy, say $\beta''$, such that

$$\beta \succ_i \beta''$$

for one or more members $i$ of $I'$. In this case the process of "upsetting" could lead to an actual worsening of the positions of one or more members of the coalition $I'$ that started the process. Hence, if such further "upsetting" is anticipated, the members of any coalition would be well advised to adopt a more conservative attitude towards a proposed change of joint strategy.

One such conservative attitude is expressed by the concept of "blocking." We shall say that an act $\alpha$ can be *blocked* by a coalition $I$ if there is a joint strategy for the coalition such that, whatever the strategies adopted by the other members of the organization, the resulting act will be preferred to $\alpha$ by the coalition $I$. Formally, $\alpha$ can be blocked by $I$ if there are individual strategies $\hat{\beta}_i$, $i$ in $I$, such that any strategy $\beta$ in $\mathscr{B}$ for which

$$\beta_i = \hat{\beta}_i,\ i \text{ in } I,$$

has the property,

$$F(\beta) \succ_I \alpha. \tag{9.2}$$

Let $\mathscr{I}$ be any collection of coalitions $I$. An act $\alpha$ will be called *viable with respect to* $\mathscr{I}$ if there is no coalition in $\mathscr{I}$ that can block $\alpha$. Three special cases invite particular attention:

*Case 1.* $\mathscr{I}_1 \equiv \{M\}$. This is equivalent to the definition of Pareto-optimality.

*Case 2.* $\mathscr{I}_2 \equiv$ the collection of all one-member coalitions. This corresponds, in the case of blocking, to the Nash-equilibrium in the case of upsetting.

*Case 3.* $\mathscr{I}_3 \equiv$ the collection of all possible coalitions. In this case the set of all acts that are viable with respect to $\mathscr{I}_3$ is called the *core*.

From the point of view of overall organizational efficiency, Pareto-optimality is a minimal requirement. On the other hand, no member of the organization can be expected to accept an act that can be blocked by him alone; hence, viability with respect to $\mathscr{I}_2$ would also appear to be a minimal requirement.

An act in the core has the "strongest possible viability" against blocking, and, in particular, is Pareto-optimal. Hence, the core, if it is not empty, seems to offer a good solution to the problem of optimal organizational decision.

In the definitions of upsetting and blocking given above, it might be objected that not all members of $I$ necessarily have a positive incentive to adopt the "preferred" coalition strategy, since the definitions do not exclude the possibilities that, for some $i$ in $I$, in (9.1)

$$\beta' \sim_i \beta,$$

or, in (9.2)

$$\boldsymbol{F}(\beta) \sim_i \alpha.$$

Hence, we might wish to consider the stronger group preference relation:

$$\alpha' \gg_I \alpha \text{ means that for every } i \text{ in } I,\ \alpha' \succ_i \alpha$$

(to be read: $I$ strongly prefers $\alpha'$ to $\alpha$).

Correspondingly, we would define "strongly upset" and "strongly blocked" by replacing $\succ_I$ by $\gg_I$ in (9.1) and (9.2).

The definitions of upsetting and blocking implicitly express certain assumptions about anticipations on the part of one coalition concerning whether or not further changes of joint strategy are to be made by other organization members. It has also been pointed out that the concept of a coalition strategy implies the existence of some communication among prospective coalition members. One can easily imagine that quite complicated assumptions about anticipations and about the possibilities of coalition formation might be appropriate for a given organizational context. Pursuing this train of thought would lead us away from the search for a simple and universal characterization of "rationality" in organizational behavior, and towards a proliferation of special theories with a large element of descriptive detail. At the present stage of development of the formal theory of organization, we must perhaps be satisfied with such a direction of research.[3]

## 4. An Example: Pure Exchange

To illustrate the foregoing concepts, we shall consider the classical example of pure exchange. This will also serve to introduce some of the material in succeeding chapters. Let there be $m$ traders and $l$ commodities. In state of the environment $s$, trader $i$ has an initial (nonnegative) endowment of each commodity; the $l$-dimensional vector representing $i$'s initial endowment will be denoted by $\omega_i(s)$. As a result of the decisions of the traders (in a manner to be made precise below), each trader $i$ will end up with a consumption vector, denoted by $c_i$. The alternative *consequences* are defined to be the alternative $m$-tuples $c = (c_1, \ldots, c_m)$. We assume that the preferences of trader $i$ depend only on his own consumption.

### *4.1 The Give-Away Game*[4]

In order to complete the description of the game, we must specify the strategies available to each trader. Suppose each trader $i$ observes his own initial endowment, and then gives a vector $x_{ij}$ to trader $j$ ($j = 1, \ldots, m$), according to some decision rule, $\xi_{ij}$. We impose the natural constraints that the amounts given must be nonnegative, and must sum to the trader's initial endowment, i.e., for every state of the environment $s$,

$$\xi_{ij}[\omega_i(s)] \geqq 0, \qquad j = 1, \ldots, m, \tag{9.3}$$

$$\sum_{j=1}^{m} \xi_{ij}[\omega_i(s)] = \omega_i(s).$$

Notice that $x_{ii}$ is the vector given by trader $i$ to himself.

A *strategy* for trader $i$ is therefore determined by his $m$-tuple of rules $\xi_{ij}$, which must, of course, satisfy the constraints (9.3). For given strategies, an act $\alpha = (\alpha_1, \ldots, \alpha_m)$, relating consequences to states, is determined by

$$\alpha_j(s) = \sum_{i=1}^{m} \xi_{ij}[\omega_i(s)]. \tag{9.4}$$

[3] For discussion of various solution concepts for games see NASH (1951), SHAPLEY (1953), AUMANN and MASCHLER (1964), HARSANYI (1963, 1966), and AUMANN (1967). On the relationship between individual preference and group choice, see ARROW (1963).

[4] This example was suggested by H. Scarf. A similar example was used by SHAPLEY and SHUBIK (1969) to discuss the allocation of undesirable commodities.

The assumption that trader $i$'s preferences depend only on his own consumption means that his preferences among acts $\alpha$ depend only on his own component $\alpha_i$. For example, his preferences might be represented by expected utility

$$\sum_s u_i[\alpha_i(s)]\,\phi_i(s), \tag{9.5}$$

where $u_i$ is his utility function defined on sure consumption vectors, and $\phi_i$ is his subjective probability function on states of the environment (see Chapter 2).

The above game might be called the *Give-Away Game with Incomplete Information*, because each trader's decision is based only on information about his own initial endowment. A variant of this game, in which each trader bases his decisions on complete information about the endowments of all traders – i.e., in which $x_{ij}$ depends on $\omega_1(s), \ldots, \omega_m(s)$ – might be called the *Give-Away Game with Complete Information*.

We shall return presently to the information question, but for the time being let us consider a special case in which there is only one state of the environment, that is, in which the initial endowments $\omega_1, \ldots, \omega_m$, are constants and are known to all the traders. Suppose further that each trader's preferences, which depend only on his own consumption, are strictly monotone increasing in each commodity. Trader $i$'s strategy is now just an $m$-tuple $(x_{i1}, \ldots, x_{im})$, and an act is an $m$-tuple $c=(c_1, \ldots, c_m)$, given by

$$c_j = \sum_{i=1}^{m} x_{ij}, \qquad j = 1, \ldots, m. \tag{9.6}$$

First, consider the concept of Nash-equilibrium. Any joint strategy $x=(x_{ij})$ such that $x_{ij} \succ 0$ for some $i \neq j$ can be *upset* by trader $i$; he need only set

$$x_{ij} = \begin{cases} \omega_i, & \text{for } j = i, \\ 0, & \text{for } j \neq i. \end{cases} \tag{9.7}$$

Call the joint strategy defined by (9.7) for each $i$ the "no-trade strategy." From our assumption of the strict monotonicity of preferences, it follows that the no-trade strategy is the unique Nash equilibrium.

On the other hand, two or more traders can typically benefit from trade among themselves. In this situation, the no-trade strategy is not Pareto-optimal.

Any single trader can guarantee to himself a level of satisfaction at least equal to that provided by the no-trade strategy, by keeping all his initial endowment for himself (again we use the monotonicity assumption). Therefore, any single trader can *block* an act that is not at least as good from his point of view as the no-trade strategy. Thus, for example, if trader $i$'s initial endowment is not zero (in all coordinates), then the act that gives *all* resources to some *other* trader, say $j$, can be blocked by $i$. But this act is clearly Pareto-optimal. Thus, we have a case in which some Pareto-optimal act can be blocked by a single trader.

The *core* is the set of acts $(c_1, \ldots, c_m)$ that cannot be blocked by *any* coalition. We might ask whether, in this example, there are any such acts; the following argument shows indeed that, with some additional assumptions, the core is not empty.

*4.2 Competitive Equilibrium*

First, we must define a *competitive equilibrium*; this is a pair $(c, p)$, where $c = (c_1, \ldots, c_m)$ is an act, and $p$ is a nonnegative $l$-dimensional vector (interpreted as a vector of prices), such that, for each $i$, the consumption vector $c_i$ is a most preferred vector among all nonnegative consumption vectors $x$ satisfying the "budget constraint"

$$p \cdot x \leqq p \cdot \omega_i$$

($p{\cdot}z$ denotes the inner product of the vectors $p$ and $z$). If we make additional assumptions (e.g., that the utility functions $u_i$ in (9.5) are continuous and concave and that all endownments are positive), then it can be shown that there exists a competitive equilibrium (see, for example, DEBREU (1959)).[5]

Call an act $c$ *competitive* if for some $p$, the pair $(c, p)$ is a competitive equilibrium. In Chapter 13, it is shown that every competitive act is in the core (Theorem 1 – the assumptions are somewhat more general than those already stated for this example). Therefore, by the theorem on the existence of a competitive equilibrium, the core is not empty.

Theorem 1 of Chapter 13 shows that the core contains the set of competitive acts. Theorem 2 of that chapter shows that, roughly speaking, if the number of traders is large, then the core is approximately the same as the set of competitive acts. This proposition, due in its original form to Edgeworth, is one of the basic propositions of the welfare economics of perfect competition. Another basic proposition in this area is that, except for certain "boundary cases," every Pareto-optimal act is competitive. (This does not

[5] Note that the definition of an act in this example implies that demand equals supply, i.e., that total consumption of each commodity equals the total initial endowment.

depend on the number of traders being large.) An extension of this last proposition (together with the theorem on existence of competitive equilibrium) to much more general economic models, including production, can be found in DEBREU, (1959)).

*4.3 Uncertainty*

Let us now return to the question of information. Notice that in the definition of competitive equilibrium the behavior of each trader requires him to know only his own initial endowment (and his own preferences), *provided he also knows the price vector p*. Thus, in some sense, the price information is an adequate substitute for information about the initial endowments of other traders, at least if we are satisfied with the core (or Pareto-optimality) as a solution concept. The prices associated with competitive equilibria typically depend, of course, on the initial endowments of all of the traders. If we assume that, at least initially, the individual traders do not know the endowments of the other traders, then we are back in the situation of uncertainty described at the beginning of this section. Chapters 10, 11, 12, and 14, contain discussions, from various points of view, of the general problem of effective communication and computation, where the communication and/or computation moves the game from one of very incomplete information to one of less incomplete – or even complete – information, and where effectiveness is measured with respect to one of the concepts of viability (such as Pareto-optimality) discussed above. These discussions are, of course, not confined to the present example of a trading game. Nevertheless, it will be seen that much of the material has been influenced, directly or indirectly, by the consideration of prices and market mechanisms (see especially Chapters 11, 12, and 14).

## 5. Organizing

Many of the questions that interest economists and organization theorists may be interpreted as problems of how to devise "the rules of the game" so as to induce a desired performance by the organization. We may consider the message sets $B_{ijt}$ and the set $\mathscr{B}$ of feasible joint strategies as reflecting in part, technological constraints, and in part, constraints imposed by the "organizer." The organizer may be some individual, perhaps a member of the organization (e.g., the owner of a firm), or some group (e.g., the stockholders of a corporation, or the body politic), which may or may not overlap with the membership of the organization.

The problem of the organizer is perhaps not qualitatively different from the general decision problem, so that the same general principles can be expected to apply. In particular, the organizer will have beliefs concerning the behavior of the individual members (or prospective members) of the organization, and preferences among alternative acts by the organization. If the organizer is an individual, then his problem of organization can be analyzed within the context of the team decision problem, even though the individual members of the organization do not have identical preferences on the set of acts. In this case, the organizer can regard the behavior of the members of the organization as one aspect of the state of nature. On the other hand, if the organizer is a group, then we are thrown back into the general context of game theory, with all of its attendant unresolved difficulties.

The problem of organizing is often decomposed into two separate problems: (1) describe modes of individual member behavior that would lead to organizational behavior that is optimal from the point of view of the organizer; (2) devise "incentives" to induce individual members to conform to the desired behavior. For example, in his article on the guidance of production in a socialist state, F. M. Taylor outlined modes of behavior by enterprise managers and by the central planning board that, under certain conditions, would lead to an efficient allocation of resources. He did not attempt to solve the problems of how to induce managers to maximize accounting profits and introduce technological innovations, or of how to induce the central planning board to adjust prices in the proper direction. On the other hand, the U.S. antitrust laws are designed to induce firms to behave "competitively," under the assumption that "competitive" individual behavior will lead to efficient performance of the entire (economic) organization. As with most such decompositions, there is a danger that the approximation to an over-all optimum depends sensitively on a good solution to *both* problems (1) and (2). Thus, "bureaucratization" of a Taylor-type socialist economy could conceivably lead to worse results than those achieved by an oligopolistic capitalist economy; or enforcement of the antitrust laws in a sector in which the conditions for the efficiency of "perfect competition" were otherwise not fulfilled might make things worse instead of better.[6]

Although the problem of organizing can in a formal way be subsumed under the general decision problem, there are special features that are

---

[6] For a discussion of allocation of resources in a socialist economy, see WARD (1967), and the references cited there.

peculiar to it. Perhaps the one that has attracted the most attention is the question of so-called "optimal decentralization." We may think of decentralization as a special case of division of labor, where the "labor" in question is that of making decisions. The organizer can regard the members of the organization as "machines," receiving messages as inputs, and producing messages and actions as outputs, according to predictable (although possibly stochastic) modes of behavior. Beyond this, the organizer can utilize the members not only to produce messages and actions according to prescribed rules, but also *to produce strategies*, and even *modifications of the organization*. Indeed, most of what is popularly called "decision making" in an organization refers to strategy-choosing and organization-modification, rather than rule-following.

One might say that an organization is *information-decentralized* to the extent that different members have different information, and *authority-decentralized* to the extent that individual members are expected (by the organizer) to choose strategies and/or modify the rules of the game. With these concepts of decentralization, all but the simplest organizations are decentralized to some extent in both senses. This serves to emphasize that the crucial question usually is not "how much decentralization," but rather "how to decentralize."

## References


ARROW, K. J. (1963), *Social Choice and Individual Values*, (2nd ed.), Wiley, New York.

AUMANN, R. J. (1967), "A Survey of Cooperative Games without Side Payments," Chapter 1 in M. SHUBIK (ed.), *Essays in Mathematical Economics, in Honor of Oskar Morgenstern*, Princeton University Press, Princeton, pp. 3–27.

AUMANN, R. J. and M. MASCHLER (1964), "The Bargaining Set for Cooperative Games," in M. DRESHER, L. S. SHAPLEY, and A. W. TUCKER (eds.), *Advances in Game Theory*, Princeton University Press, Princeton, pp. 443–476.

DEBREU, G. (1959), *Theory of Value*, Wiley, New York.

HARSANYI, J. C. (1963), "A Simplified Bargaining Model for the N-person Cooperative Game," *International Economic Review*, *4*, 194–220.

HARSANYI, J. C. (1966), "A General Theory of Rational Behavior in Game Situations," *Econometrica*, *34*, 613–634.

NASH, J. F. (1951), "Non-Cooperative Games," *Annals of Mathematics*, *54*, 286–295.

SHAPLEY, L. S. (1953), "A Value for N-person Games," in H. W. KUHN and A. W. TUCKER (eds.), *Contributions to the Theory of Games*, Vol. II, Princeton University Press, Princeton.

SHAPLEY, L. S. and M. SHUBIK (1969), "On the Core of an Economic System with Externalities," *American Economic Review*, *59*, 678–684.

WARD, B. (1967), *The Socialist Economy*, Random House, New York.

CHAPTER 10

# TEAMS[1]

ROY RADNER



## 1. Introduction

In an organization, individuals typically differ in at least three important respects: (1) they control different action variables; (2) they base their decisions on different information; (3) they have different preferences, where, as in Chapter 2, *preference* is understood to comprise both tastes and beliefs. In Chapter 9 we presented the model of a *game* as a suitable mathematical framework for the normative analysis of organizations.

However, many interesting aspects of organizations are related to differences of types (1) and (2) only. Furthermore, in some cases the members of the organization may have nearly identical preferences; or, as in the case of the organizing of machines, it may be appropriate to consider only the preferences of the organizer. Finally, in its present state of development, the theory of games of more than two persons does not appear to provide many clues as to how to proceed in a general analysis of organizations.

All of this suggests the study of theoretical organizations in which differences of type (3) are absent, that is, in which there is a single payoff function reflecting the common goals of the members, or of the organizer. J. Marschak has called such an organization a *team* (see J. MARSCHAK (1955)). In the theory of teams, as in statistical decision problems in general, two basic questions are: (a) for a given structure of information, what is the optimal decision function? (b) what are the relative values of alternative structures of information?

[1] This chapter is based on research supported by the Office of Naval Research under contract ONR 222(77) with the University of California.

For example, in the pre-computer age, airline ticket agents were authorized to sell tickets on any particular flight with only partial (if any) information about what reservations had been booked on that flight by other agents. One can study the best rules for these agents to use under such circumstances, taking account of the joint probability distribution of demands for reservations at the several offices, the losses due to selling too many or too few reservation in total, and so forth. One can also study the additional value that would result from providing the agents with complete information about the other reservations already booked; such an additional value figure would place an upper limit on the expense that it would be worthwhile to incur in order to provide the agents with that information.[2]

Similar problems arise in many cases in which a number of agents sell or distribute a commodity provided by a common source of supply. For example, consider the day-to-day operation of the sales force in a typical wholesale bakery (leaving aside problems of advertising, of price policy, and of obtaining new customers).[3] Suppose that the sales force consists of truckdriver salesmen who daily visit each of their given customers (i.e., grocery stores) leaving, on consignment, amounts of bread to be decided by the salesmen. At the end of the day the salesman returns to the plant and submits an order for the next day. In the market facing a bread salesman price is constant (in the short run) and the quantity of fresh bread demanded at this price is one of the random variables characterizing the state of the environment. If the short-run marginal cost of production is not the same for all levels of output (e.g., because it is necessary to pay overtime wage rates to produce beyond "normal" capacity) then the marginal profit associated with an additional order by one salesman may depend upon the total orders placed by the other salesmen. In this case there is an advantage to be gained by "centralizing" the decision about the quantities to be supplied to each salesman. However, this advantage may be offset by the costs and/or difficulties of gathering and utilizing all the relevant information at a central decision unit. This information comes from different sources: (1) observations by salesmen in their respective markets; (2) historical records kept by the salesmen, the order clerks, the sales manager, etc.; (3) observations or forecasts of events in other departments of the company, or in other companies, such as changes in production conditions, product design, price,

[2] See BECKMANN (1958) for an analysis of airlines reservations problems along these lines.

[3] This example is taken from MCGUIRE (1961), where the reader will find an analysis of several models of sales organization from the point of view of the theory of teams.

or advertising, unusual weather, strikes, etc. In this example, the "organization" is characterized by the structure of observation and communication, and by the way in which decisions about orders are made.

In this chapter we develop the basic analytical framework for a theory of optimal decision functions and information structures in a team. We also illustrate the theory with a number of theorems characterizing optimal team decision functions for a given information structure. In Chapter 11 we illustrate the comparison of information structures with an extended example of the allocation of scarce resources under uncertainty.

In Section 2 the concepts of information structure and decision function are reviewed in the context of a team. Sections 1–3 are devoted to characterizations of best decision functions for a given information structure. A necessary condition for optimality – the so-called person-by-person satisfactoriness condition – is shown to be sufficient if the team payoff function is concave and differentiable in the team decision variables. This condition is the specialization to the case of a team of the concept of Nash equilibrium, which was introduced in Chapter 9.

In Section 4 there is an extended discussion of the case in which the team payoff function is quadratic in the decision variables. In this case the person-by-person-satisfactoriness condition can be applied to derive a system of equations that characterize the optimal decision functions. These equations have a particularly simple form – amenable to calculation – in two cases. First, if the set of states of the environment is finite, then there are finitely many decisions to be determined and the optimal values of these decisions are determined by a system of linear equations. Second, if there is a continuum of states of the environment and if all of the information variables have a joint (multivariate) normal distribution, then the optimal team decision functions are linear in the information variables, and the coefficients in these linear functions can be determined by a system of linear equations. (For this last result we also need to assume that in the payoff function the coefficients of the second degree terms are independent of the state of the environment.)

If the team payoff function is concave polyhedral (i.e., "piecewise linear" and concave) then the person-by-person-satisfactoriness condition is not in general sufficient to determine an optimum. However, in this case the determination of optimal team decision rules for a given information structure can be reduced to a linear programming problem; this reduction is illustrated with two examples in Section 5.

In Section 6 we suggest how the formal concept of information structure can be used to clarify the discussion of centralization and decentralization, and how different specific structures of information are generated by different processes of observation, communication, and computation.

Finally, in Section 7, we sketch an extension of the theory of teams to the case of a dynamic environment. In particular we point out that a single person in a dynamic decision problem can typically be viewed as a team, since decisions at different dates are typically based upon different information. We illustrate this by applying the theorems of Section 4 to give a simple, general proof of the Simon-Theil certainty equivalence theorem.

## 2. Information Structure and Decision Functions

In Chapter 9, an *act* of an organization was described as being generated by a process of observation, communication, computation, and action. In most of this chapter, we consider a somewhat less general formulation, in which acts are generated by what will be called *information structures* and *decision functions*. This formulation has already been discussed in Chapter 5, in the context of the single-person decision problem, and it is a simple matter to extend the formulation to the team.

As before, let

$S =$ the set of alternative states of the environment (Nature),
$C =$ the set of alternative consequences, and
$A =$ the set of alternative acts available to the team; every act $a$ in $A$ is a function from $S$ to $C$.

For every member $i$ of the team ($i = 1, \ldots, m$) let $Y_i$ be a set, to be interpreted as the set of alternative *signals* that $i$ can receive as information. An *information function* for member $i$ is a function, say $\eta_i$, from $S$ to $Y_i$; the interpretation is that

$$y_i = \eta_i(s) \tag{2.1}$$

is the signal that $i$ receives if state $s$ obtains.

Also, for every member $i$, let $D_i$ be the set of alternative decisions that $i$ can take. A *decision function* for $i$ is a function, say $\delta_i$, from $Y_i$ to $D_i$; the interpretation is that

$$d_i = \delta_i(y_i) \tag{2.2}$$

is the decision that $i$ takes if he receives the information signal $y_i$. Thus, given the information function $\eta_i$ and the decision function $\delta_i$, if state $s$

obtains, then $i$ will take the decision

$$d_i = \delta_i[\eta_i(s)]. \tag{2.3}$$

We shall denote by $\eta = (\eta_1, \ldots, n_m)$ an *information structure* for the team, and by $\delta = (\delta_1, \ldots, \delta_m)$ a *team decision function.*[4]

Consequences to the team are assumed to be determined jointly by the state $s$ and the team decision $d = (d_1, \ldots, d_m)$, according to an *outcome function*, say, $\rho$:

$$c = \rho(s, d). \tag{2.4}$$

The outcome function for the team is to be given, whereas the information structure and the decision function may be subject to choice. Given the outcome function, $\rho$, an *act* is determined by an information structure $\eta$ and a team decision function $\delta$ according to

$$a(s) = \rho(s, \delta[\eta(s)]). \tag{2.5}$$

The set $A$ of available acts is determined by (2.5) and by the sets of available ¡nformation structures and decision functions, say $\mathscr{Y}$ and $\mathscr{D}$, respectively, i.e.,

$$\eta \in \mathscr{Y}, \qquad \delta \in \mathscr{D}. \tag{2.6}$$

We shall assume that the team's preferences among acts can be represented in terms of expected utility.[5] Thus there is a (utility) function $u$ defined on the set $C$ of consequences, and a probability function $\phi$ defined on the set $S$ of states[6] such that for the team, act $a$ is at least as preferred as act $a'$ if and only if

$$\sum_s \phi(s) u[a(s)] \geq \sum_s \phi(s) u[a'(s)]. \tag{2.7}$$

It will be convenient in this chapter to combine the outcome and utility functions into a single function, to be called the *payoff function:*

$$\omega(s, d) = u[\rho(s, d)]. \tag{2.8}$$

[4] In the case of a single-person team, the concepts of information function (for a team member) and information structure (for a team) coincide, of course; compare with Chapter 5. In that chapter, we considered so-called *noisy* information, in which, for each state of the environment, the signal could be uncertain. However, by a suitable extension of the description of the environment all noisy information can be formally treated as noiseless (just include the state of the signal-producing mechanism or channel in the state of the environment). For an extended treatment of noisy information and its relation to the general concept of information see MARSCHAK and RADNER (1971).

[5] See Chapter 2.

[6] For this exposition, we assume $S$ to be finite.

From the point of view of the team, a given pair $(\eta, \delta)$ – information structure and decision function – is to be judged by its expected payoff:

$$\Omega(\eta, \delta; \omega, \phi) = \sum_s \phi(s)\, \omega(s, \delta[\eta(s)])\,. \tag{2.9}$$

In this chapter we restrict our attention to the case in which each member's decision variable, $d_i$, is numerical (scalar). However, almost all of the results of this chapter can also be directly interpreted in terms of vector-valued decision variables.[7]

The above formulation can also be generalized to express constraints on the joint decisions of the team. These constraints may even depend on the state of the environment; problems of this type are considered in Sections 4 and 5.

Since the very specification of a decision function requires the specification of an information structure, it is meaningful to compare two decision functions given the same information structure.

The situation is different, however, with respect to comparisons among information structures. Given the payoff function $\omega$ and the probability function $\phi$, it is natural to compare two information structures in terms of the maximum expected payoffs achievable with each one.[8] Thus, we shall say that $\eta_1$ is as valuable as $\eta_2$, given $\omega$ and $\phi$, if

$$\max_\delta \Omega(\eta_1, \delta; \omega, \phi) \geq \max_\delta \Omega(\eta_2, \delta; \omega, \phi)\,. \tag{2.10}$$

It is tempting to try to compare information structures without reference to the payoff and/or probability functions. This can be done in terms of the partition induced by the information structure, but this gives rise only to a partial ordering.

To simplify the exposition, let us consider for the moment the case of a one-person team; in this case an information structure is characterized by a single information function, $\eta$, from $S$ to a signal set $Y$. For any signal $y$ in $Y$ let $\eta^{-1}(y)$ denote the set of states $s$ in $S$ such that $\eta(s) = y$. As $y$ ranges over all of $Y$, the various sets $\eta^{-1}(y)$ form a *partition* of $S$; two states $s$ and $s'$ are in the same set of this partition if they give rise to the same signal, i.e., $\eta(s) = \eta(s')$. Denote this partition by $\mathscr{P}_\eta$.

If two information structures give rise to the same partition, then they essentially provide the same information. This is so because they make available to the decision maker the same set of alternative acts.

---

[7] Of course, in a more general setting, decision variables could be discrete as well as continuous, or nonnumerical (e.g., "shoot" or "don't shoot").

[8] See Chapter 5, Section 2, Equation (2).

## 3. Best Decision Functions

In this section we characterize team decision functions that are optimal – i.e., maximize expected payoff – for a given information structure. We first consider a necessary condition for optimality, that the team decision function cannot be improved by changing the decision function of any single member, and show that this condition is also sufficient for optimality if the payoff function is concave and differentiable in the decision variables for every fixed state of the world. In the next two sections we consider two special classes of payoff function (considered as a function of the decision variables for each fixed state of the world): (1) quadratic, and (2) polyhedral (or piece-wise linear).

*Person-by-Person-Satisfactory Decision Functions.* Consider a team decision problem, as formulated in the previous section, with a fixed information structure, $\eta$, for the team, and a given set, $\mathscr{D}$, of available team decision variables.[9] We shall call a team decision function *person-by-person-satisfactory* (pbps) if it cannot be improved – i.e., its expected payoff cannot be increased – by changing any single member's decision function, $\delta_i$. It is clear that an optimal team decision function is necessarily person-by-person-satisfactory. However, the converse is not in general true, as the following example shows.

Consider a team of two members, whose payoff function is independent of $S$, with contour lines as in the accompanying figure; for example,

$$u(d_1, d_2) = \min \{-d_1^2-(d_2-1)^2, -(d_1-1)^2-d_2^2\}, \tag{3.1}$$

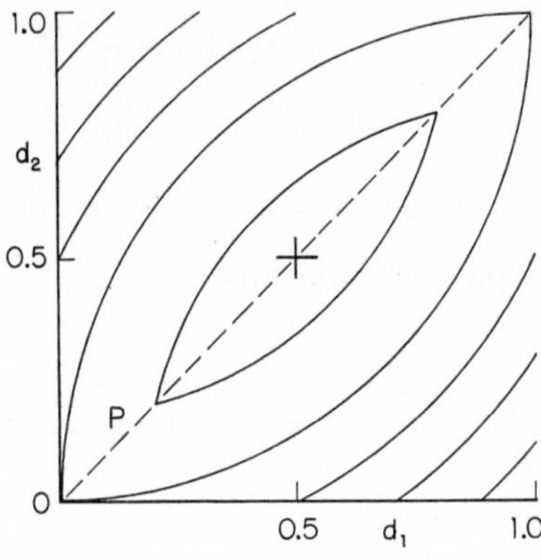


Fig. 1.

[9] Recall that each member's decision variable is assumed to be scalar.

where each decision variable $d_i$ is real. It is easily verified that any $d$ for which $d_1 = d_2$ is person-by-person-satisfactory (e.g., point $P$ in the figure) whereas the maximum value of $u$ (namely, $-0{,}5$) is attained only at $d_1 = d_2 = \frac{1}{2}$. Note that $u$ may be strictly concave in $d$, as is (3.1).

We shall show that a pbps team decision function is optimal if for each fixed state of the world the payoff function is concave and differentiable in the members' decision variables. First, we derive a condition equivalent to pbps-ness, in terms of maximizing conditional expectations. Let $\bar{\delta}$ be a given team decision function, and suppose that the decision functions of all but one, say, $i$, of the team members are fixed to be $\bar{\delta}_j (j \neq i)$. For any state $s$, and any decision $d_i$ of member $i$, the resulting payoff to the team is

$$(3.2a) \qquad \bar{\omega}_i(s, d_i; \bar{\delta}) \equiv \omega(s, \bar{\delta}_1[\eta_1(s)], \dots, d_i, \dots, \bar{\delta}_m[\eta_m(s)]).$$

Hence, for any decision function $\delta_i$ of member $i$, the expected payoff to the team is

$$\sum_s \phi(s)\, \bar{\omega}_i(s, \delta_i[\eta_i(s)]; \bar{\delta}).$$

Given the decision function $\bar{\delta}_j$ of the other team members, the problem that faces $i$ is therefore essentially a single-person decision problem, with payoff function

$$\bar{\omega}_i(s, d_i; \bar{\delta})$$

and with information structure $\eta_i$. Therefore, *for any signal $y_i$ with positive probability, the (or a) best decision for i is one that maximizes the conditional expected payoff*

$$(3.2b) \qquad E\{\bar{\omega}_i(s, d_i; \bar{\delta}) | \eta_i(s) = y_i\}.$$

To summarize, a team decision function $\bar{\delta}$ is pbps if and only if, for each $i$,

$$(3.3) \qquad \bar{\delta}_i(y_i) \text{ is a } d_i \text{ that maximizes } E\{\bar{\omega}_i(s, d_i; \bar{\delta}) | \eta_i(s) = y_i\}$$

for each signal $y_i$ with positive probability.

THEOREM 3.1. *If*

(1) *the team payoff function $\omega(s, d)$ is concave and differentiable in $d$ for every state $s$ in the finite set $S$;*

(2) *the set $\mathscr{D}$ of team decision functions is the set of all m-tuples $\delta = (\delta_1, \dots, \delta_m)$, such that $\delta_i$ is a real-valued function defined on $Y_i$;*

(3) *the team decision function $\hat{\delta}$ is person-by-person satisfactory;*

*then $\hat{\delta}$ is optimal.*

*Proof.* Let $\delta$ be any other team decision function in $\mathscr{D}$, and define for any $m$-vector $k=(k_1, \ldots, k_m)$:

$$\beta_i(s) \equiv \delta_i(s)-\hat{\delta}_i(s), \qquad i=1, \ldots, m;\ s \in S; \tag{3.4}$$

$$f(s, k) \equiv \omega\left[s, \hat{\delta}_1(s)+k_1 \beta_1(s), \ldots, \hat{\delta}_m(s)+k_m \beta_m(s)\right], \quad s \in S;$$

$$F(k) \equiv \sum_s \phi(s) f(s, k).$$

It is easy to verify that for each $s$ in $S$, $f(s, k)$ is concave and differentiable in $k$, and that $F$ is also concave and differentiable in $k$. Note that for every $k$, the $m$-tuple

$$(\hat{\delta}_1+k_1 \beta_1, \ldots, \hat{\delta}_m+k_m \beta_m) \tag{3.5}$$

is a team decision function in $\mathscr{D}$, and that $F(k)$ is the expected payoff for that decision function. Hence, to prove that $\hat{\delta}$ is optimal it suffices to prove that $F(k)$ is maximized at $k=0$.

Since $\hat{\delta}$ is pbps, it follows that for any $k$ that has all coordinates but one equal to zero,

$$F(k) \leqq F(0);$$

in other words, for each $i$, if $k_j=0$ for all $j \neq i$, then $F(k)$ reaches a maximum at $k_i=0$. Since $F$ is differentiable this implies that all the partial derivatives of $F$ are zero at $k=0$:

$$F_i(0)=0, \quad i=1, \ldots, m. \tag{3.6}$$

But $F$ is also concave, hence, (3.6) is sufficient to guarantee that $F$ attains a global maximum at $k=0$, which completes the proof of the theorem.

Notice that in the example of (3.1), the payoff function is not differentiable along the line $a_1=a_2$.

## 4. Teams with Quadratic Payoff Functions

In this section we shall explore the consequences of assuming that for every state of the world the payoff is a quadratic function of the team action variables. Particular attention will be given to the case in which (1) the coefficients of the second degree terms do not depend upon the state of the world, and (2) the relevant random variables are normally distributed. In this case the optimal decision variables will be shown to be linear functions of the information variables, and an explicit algorithm for their computation will be given.

A quadratic payoff function may be thought of as an approximation, for each state of the world, to an arbitrary smooth payoff function in the neighboorhood of the best team action, say, $\gamma(x)$, corresponding to the state of the world $x$.

In a quadratic formulation, the variances and correlations of the information variables have an especially important role (whatever the probability distribution). In fact, the theory of the quadratic team has interesting connections with the statistical theory of regression (see RADNER (1962)).

Suppose that each team member $i$ (1, ..., $m$) has a real-valued decision variable, $d_i$, and that the payoff function is

$$\omega(s, d) = \lambda(s) + 2 \sum_{i=1}^{m} \mu_i(s)\, d_i - \sum_{i,j=1}^{m} \nu_{ij}(s)\, d_i d_j, \tag{4.1}$$

where the $\lambda$, $\mu_i$, and $\nu_{ij}$ are all real-valued functions of the state of the world $s$. We confine our attention to situations in which there is a maximum payoff for every fixed $s$; for this reason we make the assumption that the matrix $((\nu_{ij}[s]))$ is positive definite for every $s$ (we also take it to be symmetric).

THEOREM 4.1. *If the payoff function is given by (4.1), and if* $y_i = \eta_i(s)$ $(i = 1, \ldots, m)$ *are the information functions for the team, and if the matrix* $((\nu_{ij}[s]))$ *is symmetric positive definite for every s, then the optimal decision functions* $\delta_1, \ldots, \delta_n$ *are determined (uniquely) by the following conditions:*

$$\delta_i(y_i)\, E(\nu_{ii}|y_i) + \sum_{j \neq i} E(\delta_j \nu_{ij}|y_i) = E(\mu_i|y_i), \quad i = 1, \ldots, m, \tag{4.2}$$

$$\text{all } y_i \in Y_i\,.$$

*Proof.* The theorem follows from Theorem 3.1 on the optimality of person-by-person-satisfactory decision functions, using the form (3.2*a*, *b*) of the condition of pbps-ness. For the quadratic case, (3.2*b*) takes the form

$$E\{-\nu_{ii} d_i^2 - 2 \sum_{j \neq i} \nu_{ij} d_i \delta_j + 2\mu_i d_i - \sum_{\substack{j \neq i \\ k \neq i}} \nu_{jk} \delta_j \delta_k + 2 \sum_{j \neq i} \mu_j \delta_j + \lambda | \eta_i(s) = y_i\}\,.$$

Differentiating this last with respect to $d_i$, and setting the derivative equal to zero, gives

$$E\{-2\nu_{ii} d_i - 2 \sum_{j \neq i} \nu_{ij} \delta_j + 2\mu_i | \eta_i(s) = y_i\} = 0\,.$$

Hence, for every $y_i$, $d_i = \delta_i(y_i)$ satisfies condition (4.2).

To prove the uniqueness of the solution of (4.2), suppose that $(\delta_1, \ldots, \delta_m)$ and $(\delta_1^*, \ldots, \delta_m^*)$ are two solutions of (4.2), and let

$$\gamma_i \equiv \delta_i - \delta_i^*, \qquad i = 1, \ldots, m.$$

We shall show that $\gamma_i$ is zero for every $i$. From condition (4.2), $\gamma_1, \ldots, \gamma_m$ satisfy

$$\gamma_i(y_i)\, E(v_{ii}|y_i) + \sum_{j \neq i} E(v_{ij}\gamma_j|y_i) = 0,$$

or

$$E\left(\sum_{j=1}^{m} v_{ij}\gamma_j|\eta_i(s) = y_i\right) = 0, \quad \text{all } i, \text{ all } y_i. \tag{4.3}$$

Multiplying (4.3) by $\gamma_i(y_i)$ and taking the expectation with respect to $y_i$ gives

$$E\left(\sum_{j=1}^{m} v_{ij}\gamma_i\gamma_j\right) = 0, \quad i = 1, \ldots, m. \tag{4.4}$$

Summing (4.4) over $i = 1, \ldots, m$ yields

$$E\left(\sum_{i,j} v_{ij}\gamma_i\gamma_j\right) = 0$$

or, in more detail,

$$\sum_s \phi(s) \sum_{i,j} v_{ij}(s)\, \gamma_i[\eta_i(s)]\, \gamma_j[\eta_j(s)] = 0. \tag{4.5}$$

Now, for every $s$, since the matrix $((v_{ij}[s]))$ is positive definite

$$\sum_{i,j} v_{ij}(s)\, \gamma_i[\eta_i(s)]\, \gamma_j[\eta_j(s)] \geqq 0, \tag{4.6}$$

with equality if and only if

$$\gamma_i[\eta_i(s)] = 0, \qquad i = 1, \ldots, m. \tag{4.7}$$

But, (4.5) and (4.6) are compatible only if for every $s$ such that $\phi(s)>0$ equality *does* hold in (4.6); hence (4.7) is satisfied for every such $s$. In other words, for every two solutions $(\delta_i)$ and $(\delta_i^*)$ of (4.2),

$$\delta_i(y_i) = \delta_i^*(y_i)$$

for every $y_i$ with positive probability. This completes the proof of Theorem 4.1.

If, as we have been assuming, the state of nature, $s$, can take on only a finite number of values, then (4.2) represents a system of linear equations as follows.

Suppose that

(1) the possible values of $s$ are $s^1, \ldots, s^N$;
(2) the possible values of the information variable $y_i$ are $y_i^1, \ldots, y_i^{N_i}$;
(3) the conditional probability that $y_j = y_j^n$, given that $y_i = y_i^h$, is $p_{ij}^{hn}$;
(4) the decision $\delta_i(y_i^h)$ is denoted by $d_i^h$.

Then, according to (4.2) the optimal values of the decisions $d_i^h$ are to be determined by the $(N_1 + N_2 +, \ldots, N_m)$ linear equations:

$$E(v_{ii}|y_i^h)\, d_i^h + \sum_{j \neq i} \sum_{n=1}^{N_j} p_{ij}^{hn}\, E(v_{ij}|y_i^h, y_j^n)\, d_j^n = E(\mu_i|y_i^h), \qquad i = 1, \ldots, m, \quad h = 1, \ldots, N_i. \tag{4.8}$$

More generally, (4.2) represents a system of integral equations. That system may have no solution, but if it does, it will be unique. The mathematical questions associated with the case of an infinite set of states of nature are discussed in RADNER (1962).

One specific case of an infinite $S$, viz., normal distributions, is noteworthy, however, for the linearity of the optimal decision functions.

THEOREM 4.2. *If*

(1) *the functions* $v_{ij}$ *in (4.1) are constants,* $v_{ij}(s) = q_{ij}$;
(2) *the information functions* $\eta_i$ *are vector-valued, with*

$$\eta_i(s) = (y_{i1}, \ldots, y_{iM_i}) \equiv y_i; \tag{4.9}$$

(3) *the functions* $\mu_i$ *and* $\eta_i$ *are jointly normal distributed, with*

$$\begin{aligned} &E y_{ij} = 0, \\ &\text{Var } y_{ij} = 1, \\ &\text{Correlation } (y_{ij}, y_{hk}) \equiv r_{jk}^{ih}, \; r_{jk}^{ii} = 0, \quad \text{for } j \neq k, \\ &E\mu_i \equiv m_i, \\ &\text{Covariance } (\mu_i, y_{ij}) \equiv f_{ij}; \end{aligned} \tag{4.10}$$

*then the optimal decision functions* $\delta_1, \ldots, \delta_m$ *are linear.*

$$\delta_i(y_i) = \sum_{k=1}^{M_i} b_{ik}\, y_{ik} + c_i, \tag{4.11}$$

*where the coefficients* $b_{ik}$ *and* $c_i$ *are determined by the systems of linear equations:*

$$\sum_{j=1}^{m} q_{ij} \sum_{k=1}^{M_j} r_{kh}^{ji} b_{jk} = f_{ih}, \quad i = 1, \ldots, m, \quad h = 1, \ldots, M_i, \tag{4.12}$$

$$\sum_{j=1}^{n} q_{ij} c_j = m_i, \quad i = 1, \ldots, m. \tag{4.13}$$

*Remark.* There is no loss of generality in assuming the first two lines of (4.10), since the given function $\eta_i$ can always be transformed into a function that has these properties, without essentially changing the information structure.

For a proof of Theorem 4.2, the reader is referred to RADNER (1962).

Theorem 4.1 can easily be generalized in two directions: (1) by taking each team member's decision variable to be vector-valued, and (2) by allowing (random) linear constraints on the decision variable of each team member. We present such a generalization without proof.

THEOREM 4.3. *Suppose that the payoff for the team is*

$$\omega(s, d) = \lambda(s) + 2 \sum_{i=1}^{m} \mu_i'(s) d_i - \sum_{i,j=1}^{m} d_i' Q_{ij}(s) d_j, \tag{4.14}$$

*where, for each i,* $d_i$ *and* $\mu_i$ *are vector-valued, and for each s, the matrix made up of the blocks* $Q_{ij}(s)$ *is symmetric and positive definite*[10]*; suppose further that for each i and s the decision variable* $d_i$ *is subject to the constraint*

$$B_i(s) d_i = \gamma_i(s); \tag{4.15}$$

*and finally, let* $\eta_1, \ldots, \eta_m$ *be the information structure for the team and suppose that, for each i, the matrix* $B_i$ *and the vector* $\gamma_i$ *are contractions*[11] *of* $\eta_i$*; then, there exist vector-valued functions* $\pi_1, \ldots, \pi_m$ *on S such that the optimal team decision functions* $\delta_1, \ldots, \delta_m$ *are determined uniquely by (4.15) and the following conditions:*

$$\sum_{j=1}^{m} E(Q_{ij}\delta_j|\eta_i) = E(\mu_i|\eta_i) - \tfrac{1}{2} B_i' \pi_i, \quad i = 1, \ldots, m. \tag{4.16}$$

[10] "Transpose" is denoted by a "prime."

[11] That is, $B_i$ and $\gamma_i$ are functions of $s$ that can be expressed as functions of $\eta_i$; in other words, if member $i$ knows $\eta_i(s)$, then he also knows $B_i(s)$ and $\gamma_i(s)$. See Chapter 5.

*(Note that, for each i, the function $\pi_i$ is a contraction of the information function $\eta_i$. For each i and s, $\pi_i(s)$ is the "Lagrangean multiplier" corresponding to the corresponding constraint (4.15).)*

COROLLARY 1. *The maximum expected payoff* (*i.e.*, *the expected payoff using the optimal decision function,* $\hat{\delta}_i$) *can be expressed as*

$$E\omega(s, \hat{\delta}) = E \sum_{i=1}^{m} (\mu_i' \hat{\delta}_i + \tfrac{1}{2}\pi_i' \gamma_i) + E\lambda(s). \tag{4.17}$$

COROLLARY 2. *If the matrices* $Q_{ij}$ *and* $B_i$ *are all constant* (*the same for all s*), *then for all information structures* $\eta_1, \ldots, \eta_m$ *such that* $\gamma_i$ *is a contraction of* $\eta_i (i = 1, \ldots, m)$, *the expected values of the optimal decision functions* $\delta_i$ *and of the Langrangean multipliers* $\pi_i$ *are the same for all such information structures, and are determined by the equations:*

$$\sum_{j=1}^{m} Q_{ij} E(\hat{\delta}_j) = E(\mu_i) - \tfrac{1}{2} B_i' E(\pi_i), \tag{4.18}$$

$$B_i E(\hat{\delta}_i) = E(\gamma_i), \qquad i = 1, \ldots, m.$$

COROLLARY 3. *Under the hypotheses of Corollary 2, the expected payoff using the optimal decision functions,* $\hat{\delta}_i$, *can be expressed as*

$$E\omega(s, \hat{\delta}) = E \sum_i [(\mu_i - E\mu_i)' (\hat{\delta}_i - E\hat{\delta}_i) + \tfrac{1}{2}(\pi_i - E\pi_i)' (\gamma_i - E\gamma_i)] + E\omega(s, E\hat{\delta}). \tag{4.19}$$

$$E\omega(s, E\hat{\delta}) = \sum_i [(E\mu_i)' (E\hat{\delta}_i) + \tfrac{1}{2}(E\pi_i)' (E\gamma_i)]. \tag{4.20}$$

Note that the term $E\omega(s, E\hat{\delta})$ is independent of the information structure $(\eta_1, \ldots, \eta_m)$, and that the first term in (4.19) is a sum of *covariances.*

## 5. Teams with Concave Polyhedral Payoff Function: Linear Programming Under Uncertainty

A polyhedral function is a generalization to the case of several variables of a piecewise linear function of one variable. In this section we shall illustrate how the problem of finding a best team decision function for a given information structure can be transformed into a linear programming problem if the team payoff function is concave and polyhedral.

The introduction of the complications of uncertainty and team structure into a programming problem tend to result in a substantial increase in the size of the problem. On the other hand, joint constraints on the actions of team numbers with different information may result in very restrictive constraints on the decision functions available to the team, thus simplifying the problem.

For a systematic discussion of the general concave polyhedral case, as well as a class of special cases in which certain simplification is possible, the reader is referred to MARSCHAK and RADNER (1971). The reader will also find there a discussion of duality theory and shadow prices for a team with a concave polyhedral payoff function.

*Example 5.A. A Team with a Concave Polyhedral Payoff Function*

Suppose that a firm has $n$ salesmen, each of whom goes out at the beginning of the period to get orders. Assume that the $i$-th salesman faces an unlimited demand, at price $(1+s_i)$; and on the basis of knowledge of that price, but not of the prices faced by the other salesmen, he must decide on the quantity $d_i$ that he will accept in orders. The orders of all the salesmen are filled centrally and the unit cost depends upon the total quantity ordered. The unit cost is 1 if the total quantity ordered does not exceed a certain limit $c$; but for that amount that exceeds $c$, the unit cost is $(1+f)$, with $f \geqq 0$.

Thus, the action variable for the $i$-th salesman is a nonnegative real number $d_i$; the state of nature is specified by the $n$-tuple $s=(s_1, \ldots, s_n)$; and the payoff function is

$$\omega(s, a) = \begin{cases} \sum_{i=1}^{n} d_i s_i, & \text{if } \sum_{i=1}^{n} d_i \leqq c, \\ \sum_{i=1}^{n} d_i s_i - f\left(\sum_{i=1}^{n} d_i - c\right), & \text{if } \sum_{i=1}^{n} d_i \geqq c, \end{cases} \tag{5.1}$$

$$= \min\{\Sigma d_i s_i, \Sigma d_i(s_i - f) + fc\}.$$

Figure 5.2 shows contours of $\omega$ for fixed $s$ and $n=2$. The arrows indicate the directions in which the payoff is increasing.

The state of nature $s$ will be supposed to be subject to the probability frequency function $\phi$.

The information structure is

$$\eta_i(s) = s_i. \tag{5.2}$$

The team decision problem can therefore be formulated as follows:

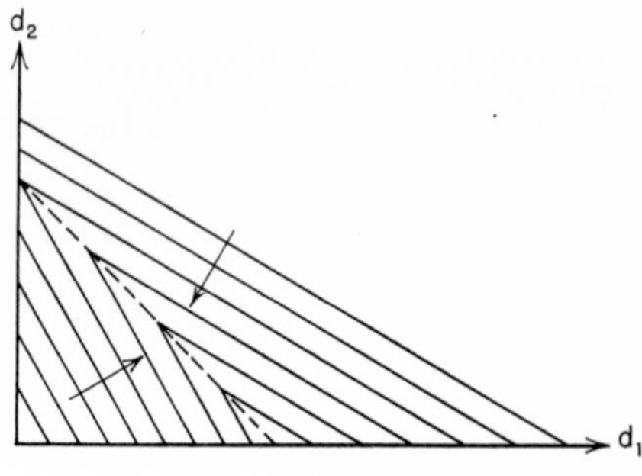


Fig. 2.

*Problem I.* Choose nonnegative functions $\delta_1, \ldots, \delta_n$ to maximize

$$E\omega(s, \delta[\eta(s)]) = \sum_s \omega(s, d_1[s_1], \ldots, \delta_n[s_n]) \phi(s).$$

We shall now show that the optimal team decision functions can be found by solving the following associated linear programming problem. (Recall that $s$ is assumed to be restricted to a finite set of possible values.)

*Problem II.* Choose nonnegative functions $\delta_1, \ldots, \delta_n$ and a nonnegative function $\varepsilon$ of $s$, to maximize

$$E\varepsilon(s) = \sum_s \varepsilon(s) \phi(s)$$

subject to the constraints

$$\varepsilon(s) \leqq \sum_i \delta_i(s_i) s_i, \qquad \text{for all } s, \tag{5.3}$$

$$\varepsilon(s) \leqq \sum_i \delta_i(s_i)(s_i - f) + fc, \qquad \text{for all } s.$$

(Note that, because $s$ is restricted to a finite set, the functions $\varepsilon, \delta_1, \ldots, \delta_n$ are each characterized by a finite sequence of numbers, so that Problem II is a finite-dimensional linear programming problem.)

For an optimal team decision function $\hat{\delta}$, consider the function

$$\hat{\varepsilon}(s) = \omega(s, \hat{\delta}[\eta(s)]). \tag{5.4}$$

By Equation (4.1) for every $s$, $\hat{\varepsilon}$ and $\hat{\delta}$ satisfy (5.3). On the other hand, if $\delta$ is any team decision function and $\varepsilon$ is any nonnegative function of $s$, with both satisfying (5.3), then

$$\varepsilon(s) \leqq \omega(s, \delta[\eta(s)]), \quad \text{for every } s, \tag{5.5}$$

and hence

$$E\varepsilon(s) \leqq E\omega(s, \delta[\eta(s)]) \leqq E\omega(s, \hat{\delta}[\eta(s)]) = E\hat{\varepsilon}(s). \tag{5.6}$$

In other words, of all nonnegative functions $\varepsilon$ for which there exists a team decision function $\delta$ such that $\varepsilon$ and $\delta$ satisfy (5.3), the function $\hat{\varepsilon}$ has the largest expected value.

On the other hand, if any such function $\varepsilon$ has an expected value as large as $E\hat{\varepsilon}$, then it follows from (5.5) and (5.4) that the corresponding team decision function $\delta$ is as good as $\hat{\delta}$.

Thus we have shown that $\delta$ is a solution of Problem I if and only if $(\delta, \varepsilon)$ is a solution of Problem II.

In the example just presented there were no constraints on the action variables other than that of nonnegativity. Other linear constraints can easily be handled by the above method, simply by adding them to both maximization problems (I and II). This is so even if the constraints have random parameters. For example, if the maximum total quantity that the hypothetical firm just described can supply, *at any cost*, is $c'$ (possibly a random variable), and if the firm insists on making *sure* that *all* orders are filled, then the constraint

$$\sum_i \delta_i(s_i) \leqq c', \qquad \text{for all } s \text{ (and possibly all } c') \tag{5.7}$$

is simply added to both Problems I and II above.

*Example 5.B. A Team with a Linear Payoff Function*

The simplest case of a polyhedral function is a linear function. In this case the original team decision problem is already in the linear programming form, and there is no need to go to the associated problem ("Problem II" above).

Consider Example 5.A above with the modification that supply is restricted absolutely to be no greater than $c$. Thus,

$$\omega(s, d) = \sum d_i s_i, \tag{5.8}$$

$$d_i \geqq 0, \quad \sum d_i \leqq c. \tag{5.9}$$

Here the team decision problem is:

Choose nonnegative functions $\delta_1, \ldots, \delta_n$ to maximize

$$E\omega(s, \delta[\eta(s)]) = \sum_s \sum_i \delta_i(s_i)\, s_i \pi(s_i) \tag{5.10}$$

subject to

$$\sum_i \delta_i(s_i) \leqq c, \qquad \text{for every } s. \tag{5.11}$$

Note that (5.10) and (5.11) are linear in the functions $\delta_1, \ldots, \delta_n$.

It may help the reader to see in more detail the special case in which $m=2$, and in which $s_1$ and $s_2$ can each take on one of two values, $s_{i1}$ and $s_{i2}$. Let the probability that $s_i = s_{in}$ be denoted by $p_{in}$, and let $\delta_i(s_{in})$ be denoted by $d_{in}$ $(i, n=1,2)$; then this team decision problem is:

Choose nonnegative numbers $d_{in}$ $(i,n=1,2)$ to maximize

$$\sum_i \sum_n d_{in} s_{in} p_{in} \tag{5.12}$$

subject to the constraints

$$\begin{aligned} d_{11} \quad + d_{21} \quad &\leqq c \\ d_{11} \quad\quad + d_{22} &\leqq c \\ d_{12} + d_{21} \quad &\leqq c \\ d_{12} \quad\quad + d_{22} &\leqq c. \end{aligned} \tag{5.13}$$

*Person-by-Person-Satisfactory Decision Functions.* A person-by-person-satisfactory decision function is not, in general, optimal if the payoff function is polyhedral. However, the fact that pbp satisfactoriness is a necessary condition for optimality is often helpful.

In Example 5.B the condition of pbp satisfactoriness leads almost immediately to an explicit solution if one further assumption is made.

For any fixed $i$, the conditional expectation of $\omega(s, \delta[\eta(s)])$, given $s_i$, is (see (5.8))

$$\delta_i(s_i)\, s_i + \sum_{j \neq i} E\left[\delta_j(s_j)\, s_j | s_i\right]. \tag{5.14}$$

Hence, for $\delta$ to be pbp optimal, $\delta_i(s_i)=0$ if $s_i > 0$; and if $s_i > 0$, then $\delta_i(s_i)$ must be equal to the largest value of $d_i$ for which

$$d_i + \sum_{j=i} \delta_j(s_j) \leq c \tag{5.15}$$

for every $s$ such that $s_i$ has the given value. *If it is assumed that the range of every variable $s_k$ is independent* of the values of the other variables, then in (5.15) all combinations of $s_j$'s are possible, so that $\delta_i(s_i)$ must equal some one number $\bar{d}_i$ for all $s_i > 0$. Hence, in order for $\delta$ to be pbp optimal it must be of the form

$$\delta_i(s_i) = \begin{cases} 0, & \text{if } s_i < 0 \\ \bar{d}_i, & \text{if } s_i > 0 \end{cases}, \qquad i = 1, \ldots, n, \tag{5.16}$$

where $\bar{d}_1, \ldots, \bar{d}_n$ are nonnegative numbers satisfying

$$\sum_i \bar{d}_i \leq c. \tag{5.17}$$

For such a team decision function, the expected payoff is

$$\sum_i \bar{d}_i E[s_i | s_i > 0]. \tag{5.18}$$

Hence, for the optimal team decision function $\delta$, $\bar{d}_i = c$ for some one $i$ for which $E(s_i | s_i > 0)$ is a maximum, and $\bar{d}_j = 0$ for all $j \neq i$. In other words, in the optimal team decision function, under the constraint that has been assumed, only one salesman ever accepts any orders (the others are "fired" !); he accepts an order equal to the full capacity of the firm whenever the price exceeds the unit cost, and otherwise accepts no orders at all.

*General Formulation.* A function $f$ of $m$ real variables will be called concave-polyhedral if there exist linear functions $f_1, \ldots, f_N$ such that

$$f = \min_{1 \leq n \leq N} f_n. \tag{5.19}$$

An example is given by Equation (4.1) in which $\omega$, for every fixed $s$, is a concave-polyhedral function of $d$ ($N = 2$). A concave-polyhedral function is a generalization of the case of several variables of a concave piecewise linear function of one variable.

In Chapter 5 of MARSCHAK and RADNER (1971) it is shown that if the team payoff function is concave polyhedral in the decision variables, for every state of the environment, then the problem of determining the optimal decision functions can be reduced to a linear programming problem. This programming problem is finite- or infinite-dimensional according as the set of states of the environment is finite or infinite.

The same reference also gives a detailed discussion of the corresponding duality theory, with an interpretation of the shadow prices, in the finite-dimensional case. An extension of the duality theory to the case of a countable set of states has been given by FISHER (1962).

## 6. Informational Decentralization, and Generation of Information Structures by Observation, Communication, and Computation

In Chapter 9, Section 5, we defined an organization to be *information-decentralized* to the extent that different members have different information on which to base their decisions. In the notation of the present chapter, a team is information-decentralized if not all of the information functions, $\eta_i$, are identical. As we noted before, all but the simplest organizations are information-decentralized to some extent. This results from the fact that the processes necessary to bring about a complete identity of information functions are costly; furthermore, individuals (and machines) have limited capacities for the handling and storage of information.

The several information structures of the members of a team can usually be viewed as being generated by processes of observation, communication, and computation. Suppose that team member $i$ observes a random variable $\zeta_i(s)$ and takes action $d_i$. If there is no communication among the persons, then person $i$'s information function is $\eta_i(s) = \zeta_i(s)$. On the other hand, if there is complete communication among the persons, then $\eta_i(s) = \zeta(s) \equiv [\zeta_1(s), \ldots, \zeta_n(s)]$. Alternatively, the latter information structure could be generated by all persons communicating their observations to a central agency, which computes the best actions, and communicates them to the corresponding persons. Still different information structures are generated if errors are introduced into the communications to or from the central agency or between team members.

Rarely does one encounter in a real organization the extremes of no communication or complete communication just described. Rather, one finds that numerous devices are used to bring about a partial exchange of information. For example, if each person $i$ disseminates some contraction of his own observation, say, $\tau_i[\zeta_i(s)]$, to all other persons in the team, then the resulting structure is

$$\eta_i = (\zeta_i, \tau), \qquad i = 1, \ldots, m, \tag{6.1}$$

where $\tau = (\tau_1, \ldots, \tau_m)$. A different type of decentralization is achieved by partitioning the persons into groups, with complete communication within groups, and no communication between groups.

A third type of decentralization is suggested by the phrase "management by exception." For example, suppose that the possible values of person $i$'s observation are partitioned into two subsets, $R_i$ and $\bar{R}_i$, labeled "exceptional" and "ordinary," respectively. Suppose further that whenever person

$i$'s observation is "ordinary" he bases his action upon that observation alone, whereas whenever his observation is "exceptional" he reports it to a central agency, or manager, who then decides the values of all action variables corresponding to exceptional observations, on the basis of all those exceptional observations. The information thus generated is, for each $i$,

$$\eta_i(s) = \begin{cases} \zeta_i(s), & \text{if } \zeta_i(s) \in \bar{R}_i, \\ \{\zeta_j(s)\}_{\zeta_j(s) \in R_j}, & \text{if } \zeta_i(s) \in R_i, \end{cases} \tag{6.2}$$

and might be called "reports of exceptions."[12]

The market provides a familiar example of this process of observation, communication, and computation (see Chapter 10). Actually, to speak of "the market" in this case is a gross oversimplification, since there are many different types of market, with considerable differences among the structures of information that they generate. Indeed, to date relatively little work has been done on characterizing the information structures generated by various market structures (see M. BECKMANN (1958), C. B. MCGUIRE (1961), and P. SCHMIDBAUER (1966)). Of course a market is not typically a team because the various economic agents do not have the same goals, although markets have sometimes been proposed as devices for allocating resources within a single organization in which the members do have a common goal. In the next chapter, we give an example of how a problem of allocation of resources can be formulated and analyzed as a team decision problem.

## 7. The Team in a Dynamic Environment

Thus far our treatment of the team decision problem has been "static," not in the sense that consideration of time has been excluded by our formulation of the decision problem, but rather in the sense that the special features of a decision problem associated with time have not been explicitly examined.

From a certain point of view, the introduction of time into a decision problem requires no change in the formulation of Section 2. Decisions about actions taken at different times are typically based on different information. To express this one may simply consider actions taken at different times as corresponding to "different" team members. Thus, if $d_i(t)$ denotes the action of person $i$ at time $t$ ($t = 1, \ldots, T$), and if $s(t)$ denotes

[12] For an analysis of several elementary information structures, see RADNER (1961) or MARSCHAK and RADNER (1971), Chapter 6.

the state of the world at time $t$, then the team action variable for the complete problem (with $mT$ "persons") is

(7.1) $$d = [d_1(1), \ldots, d_m(1), d_1(2), \ldots, d_m(T)],$$

and the state of the world for the complete problem is

(7.2) $$s = [s(1), \ldots, s(T)].$$

In particular, a "single-person sequential (dynamic) decision problem" looked at in this way can be interpreted as a team decision problem. The reason for singling out the time index for special treatment is that there is usually associated with the time element some special feature of the structure of information, of the statistical properties of the state of the world, or of the payoff function.

Perhaps the most common feature of the structure of information in time is generated by the presence of *memory*. A sequence $\{\eta(\cdot, t)\}$ of (one-period) information structures will be said to have *memory* if, for each $t$, $\eta(\cdot, t+1)$ is *as fine as* $\eta(\cdot, t)$ (see Chapter 5). However, memory is in general costly, and is therefore not a universal feature of dynamic decision problems. Indeed, the question of how much memory to provide for in any given situation (e.g., when to throw away files) is a special case of the general problem of choice of an information structure.

We shall not attempt here an extended discussion of the various special features of the team decision problem associated with the dynamic element.[13] Of particular interest is the effect of delay on the value of information. Typically, delays are introduced by the processes of communication and information processing by which the observations of the individual team members are transmitted to other team members. In such a situation, the team's information can be made more complete only by increasing the delay with which team members receive it, and one is interested in the optimal balance between timeliness and completeness of information.

To illustrate the point that a single-person dynamic decision problem can be looked at as a team decision problem we shall use Theorem 4.3 to prove the Simon-Theil theorem on certainty equivalence. This theorem states that the solution of a single-person dynamic decision problem, with a quadratic payoff function, can be obtained by solving instead a sequence of decision problems, one for each time $t$, in which at each time $t$ the random coefficients in the quadratic payoff function are replaced by the conditional expectations

---

[13] See MARSCHAK and RADNER (1971), Chapter 7.

of those coefficients given the information at time $t$. This theorem is valid under the condition that the information structure has memory, in the sense defined above. The Simon-Theil theorem does not appear to be generalizable to the case of a proper team, even with a quadratic payoff function , nor to the case of a single person with a nonquadratic payoff function[14].

Consider a "single person" who must take decisions sequentially with respect to a (finite) sequence of action vectors $d(1), \ldots, d(T)$, the payoff function being

$$(7.3) \qquad \omega(s, d) = 2 \sum_{t=1}^{T} \mu(s, t)' d(t) - \sum_{r,t=1}^{T} d(r)' Q(r, t) d(t),$$

where, for each $s$, $r$, and $t$, $\mu(s, t)$ is a vector and $Q(r, t)$ is a matrix. We assume that the square matrix made up of the blocks $Q(r, t)$ is positive definite and symmetric. Suppose further that at time $t$ the person's action $d(t)$ is to be based on the information $y(t) = \eta(s, t)$, according to some decision function $\delta(\cdot, t)$, i.e.,

$$(7.4) \qquad d(t) = \delta(y[t], t) = \delta(\eta[s, t], t).$$

For a fixed information structure $\eta = [\eta(\cdot, 1), \ldots, \eta(\cdot, T)]$ the person is to choose the best sequence $\delta(\cdot, 1), \ldots, \delta(\cdot, T)$ of decision functions, i.e., the decision functions that maximize the expected payoff.

As we noted above, this decision problem can, from a formal point of view, be regarded as a "team decision problem," with the person's decisions at different dates $t$ corresponding to different "members" of the "team."

It follows immediately from Theorem 4.3 of Section 4 that the optimal decision functions $\hat{\delta}(\cdot, t)$ are determined (uniquely) by the following conditions:

$$(7.5) \qquad \sum_{t=1}^{T} Q(r, t) E[\delta(\cdot, t) | \eta(\cdot, r)] = E[\mu(\cdot, r) | \eta(\cdot, r)], \quad r = 1, \ldots, T.$$

This is the form taken by the "person-by-person satisfactoriness" condition in this case.

Suppose that the decision maker's information structure $\eta$ has *memory* in the sense defined above, i.e., if $r \leqq t$, then $\eta(\cdot, t)$ is at least as fine as $\eta(\cdot, r)$.

---

[14] However, see MALINVAUD (1969) for a proof that the certainty equivalence theorem holds approximately for a single person with a differentiable payoff function, if the uncertainty about the state of the environment is sufficiently "small."

We shall show that there is a second decision problem associated with the original one such that:

(a) The payoff function is the same, except that in (7.3) each function $\mu(\cdot, t)$ is replaced by some function $\tilde{\mu}(\cdot, t)$ of the *initial information variable*, $y(1) = \eta(s, 1)$.

(b) The optimal decision function at time 1, say, $\tilde{\delta}(\cdot, 1)$, for the new problem is the same as that for the original problem.

The function $\tilde{\mu}(\cdot, t)$ that replaces $\mu(\cdot, t)$ in accordance with (a) is called the "*certainty-equivalent*" of $\mu(\cdot, t)$. *We shall show that the certainty equivalent of* $\mu(\cdot, t)$ *can be taken to be* $E[\mu(\cdot, t)|y(1)]$. This property of the quadratic payoff function was originally stated by SIMON (1956) and THEIL (1957).

It should be emphasized that the optimal decision functions $\tilde{\delta}(\cdot, t)$ in the second problem, for $t = 2, \ldots, T$, will typically not be the same as the optimal decision functions $\hat{\delta}(\cdot, t)$, for $t = 2, \ldots, T$ in the original problem. The former are sometimes called the "planned decisions." These plans must typically be revised when new information becomes available, as follows.

At time $t = 1$, the decision maker knows $y(1) = \eta(s, 1)$; he therefore knows $\tilde{\mu}[y(1), 1], \ldots, \tilde{\mu}[y(1), T]$ and can solve the second problem to obtain the decisions $\tilde{d}(t) \equiv \tilde{\delta}[y(1), t]$, $t = 1, \ldots, T$ (hence, the term "certainty-equivalent," since at time 1 he knows (is certain of) all the parameters of the second problem). Since (as we shall show), $\hat{\delta}(\cdot, 1) = \tilde{\delta}(\cdot, 1)$, the best decision at time 1 is $\tilde{d}(1)$.

Finally, we shall show that the "planned decisions" at time 1 are the mathematical expectations of the optimal decisions, given the information at time 1, i.e.,

$$\tilde{\delta}[y(1), t] = E\{\hat{\delta}[y(t), t]|y(1)\}, \quad t = 2, \ldots, T. \tag{7.6}$$

The importance of the certainty-equivalence theorem is that it enables the decision maker to substitute for the problem of determining $T$ decision *functions*, $\hat{\delta}(\cdot, 1), \ldots, \hat{\delta}(\cdot, T)$, the problem of determining $T$ decisions, $d(1), \ldots, d(T)$. Thus, it is not necessary to determine the best decision at a time $t$ for any value of the information signal $y(t)$ except the one actually observed. On the other hand, to obtain the best decision at time 1 requires solving a problem with $T$ variables $(\tilde{d}(1), \ldots, \tilde{d}(T))$; to obtain the best decision at time 2 requires solving a problem with $(T-1)$ variables, etc.

For example, if the decision maker observes at each time $t$ a variable that can take on one of $K$ values, and he remembers all past observations, then his information signal, $y(t)$, at time $t$ can in principle take on one of $K^t$ different values. Suppose that his action variable at each time $t$ is one-dimensional; then his decision function $\delta(\cdot, t)$ at time $t$ can effectively be represented by a vector with $K^t$ coordinates, and his sequence $[\delta(\cdot, 1), \ldots, \delta(\cdot, T)]$ of decision functions by a vector of

$$\sum_{t=1}^{T} K^t = \frac{K(K^{T-1} - 1)}{K-1} \tag{7.7}$$

coordinates. On the other hand, there are T variables $\tilde{d}(1), \ldots, \tilde{d}(\mathrm{T})$ in the certainty-equivalent problem at time 1, $(\mathrm{T}-1)$ variables in the certainty-equivalent problem at time 2, etc.; all in all there are

$$\sum_{t=1}^{T} (T - t + 1) = \frac{T(T+1)}{2} \tag{7.8}$$

variables in all the certainty-equivalent problems taken together. Note that, asymptotically, (7.7) increases like $K^{T-1}$, whereas (7.8) only increases like $T^2$.

Unfortunately, it does not appear that the certainty-equivalence theorem generalizes in any convenient way to the case of a proper team, nor to nonquadratic payoff functions.

To prove the certainty-equivalence theorem, take the conditional expectation of condition (7.5) (which determines the optimal decision functions) given $\eta(\cdot, 1)$. This gives

$$\begin{aligned} \sum_{t} Q(r, t)\, E\{E[\hat{\delta}(\cdot, t)|\eta(\cdot, r)]|\eta(\cdot, 1)\} \\ = E\{E[\mu(\cdot, r)|\eta(\cdot, r)]|\eta(\cdot, 1)\}, \qquad r = 1, \ldots, T. \end{aligned} \tag{7.9}$$

Since $\eta(\cdot, r)$ is as fine as $\eta(\cdot, 1)$, for each $r$, it follows from the theorem on iterated expectations[15] that for any function $f$ on $S$

$$E\{E[f|\eta(\cdot, r)]|\eta(\cdot, 1)\} = E[f|\eta(\cdot, 1)].$$

In particular,

$$E\{E[\hat{\delta}(\cdot, t)|\eta(\cdot, r)]|\eta(\cdot, 1)\} = E[\hat{\delta}(\cdot, t)|\eta(\cdot, 1)]$$

$$E\{E[\mu(\cdot, r)|\eta(\cdot, r)]|\eta(\cdot, 1)\} = E[\mu(\cdot, r)|\eta(\cdot, 1)].$$

---

[15] See, for example, FELLER (1968), p. 223.

Substituting these into (7.9) gives

$$(7.10) \qquad \sum_t Q(r, t)\, E[\hat{\delta}(\cdot, t)|\eta(\cdot, 1)] = E[\mu(\cdot, r)|\eta(\cdot, 1)], \quad r = 1, \ldots, T.$$

Define

$$(7.11) \qquad \tilde{\delta}(\cdot, t) \equiv E[\hat{\delta}(\cdot, t)|\eta(\cdot, 1)],$$

$$\tilde{\mu}(\cdot, t) \equiv E[\mu(\cdot, t)|\eta(\cdot, 1)];$$

then (7.10) becomes

$$(7.12) \qquad \sum_t Q(r, t)\, \tilde{\delta}(\cdot, t) = \tilde{\mu}(\cdot, r), \qquad r = 1, \ldots, T.$$

But this is the condition that determines the optimal decision function in a problem with payoff function

$$\tilde{\omega}(s, d) = 2 \sum_t \tilde{\mu}(s, t)'\, d(t) - \sum_{r,t} d(r)'\, Q(r, t)\, d(t),$$

and in which all decisions are based on complete information about $\tilde{\mu}(\cdot, 1), \ldots, \tilde{\mu}(\cdot, T)$. Note, however, that from (7.11)

$$\tilde{\delta}(\cdot, 1) = E[\hat{\delta}(\cdot, 1)|\eta(\cdot, 1] = \hat{\delta}(\cdot, 1),$$

so that $\tilde{\delta}(\cdot, 1)$ is the optimal decision function *at time 1* for the original problem.

Note that in the proof we only used the fact that $\eta(\cdot, t)$ is as fine as $\eta(\cdot, 1)$ for all $t$. However, to continue the process at time 2 we would need that $\eta(\cdot, t)$ is as fine as $\eta(\cdot, 2)$ for all $t > 2$, etc.

## References

BECKMANN, M. (1958), "Decision and Team Problems in Airline Reservations," *Econometrica*, *26*, 134–145.

FELLER, W. (1968), *An Introduction to Probability Theory and Its Applications*, Vol. I, (3rd ed.), Wiley, New York.

FISHER, C. (1962), "Linear Programming under Uncertainty in an $L_\infty$ Space," Technical Report No. 7, Center for Research in Management Science, University of California, Berkeley.

MALINVAUD, E. (1969), "First-Order Certainty Equivalence," *Econometrica*, *37*, 706–718.

MARSCHAK, J. (1955), "Elements for a Theory of Teams," *Management Science*, *1*, 127–137.

MARSCHAK, J. and R. RADNER (1971), *The Economic Theory of Teams*, Yale University Press, New Haven.

McGuire, C. B. (1961), "Some Team Models of a Sales Organization," *Management Science*, *7*, 101–130.

Radner, R. (1961), "The Evaluation of Information in Organizations," in *Proceedings of the Fourth Berkeley Symposium on Mathematical Statistics and Probability*, University of California, Berkeley, Vol. I, pp. 491–530.

Radner, R. (1962), "Team Decision Problems," *Annals of Mathematical Statistics*, *33*, 857–881.

Schmidbauer, P. (1966), "Information and Communications Requirements of the Wheat Market: an Example of a Competitive System," Technical Report No. 21, Center for Research in Management Science, University of California, Berkeley.

Simon, H. A. (1956), "Dynamic Programming under Uncertainty with a Quadratic Criterion Function," *Econometrica*, *24*, 74–81.

Theil, H. (1957), "A Note on Certainty Equivalence in Dynamic Planning," *Econometrica*, *25*, 346–349.

CHAPTER 11

# ALLOCATION OF A SCARCE RESOURCE UNDER UNCERTAINTY: AN EXAMPLE OF A TEAM[1]

ROY RADNER

1. Introduction. – 2. A formal model. – 3. A quadratic example. – 4. Information structure I. No communication. – 5. Information structure II. Complete communication. – 6. Information structure III. The one-stage Lange-Lerner market mechanism. – 7. Comparison of the information structures for the case of a large number of enterprises. – 8. Optimality of demand messages. – 9. A dynamic allocation process.

## 1. Introduction

In the previous chapter we outlined the general theory of teams, indicated how information structures could be compared, and showed how to calculate optimal team decision rules in certain cases. The present chapter is devoted to an extended example of a team, and illustrates how the theory can be used to analyze and compare alternative procedures for allocating a scarce resource among several enterprises, under conditions of uncertainty about the conditions of production and the supply of the scarce resource.

In addition to providing a tractable illustration of team theory, this chapter will try to throw new light on the informational role of "prices" and "demands" in the theory of allocation. T. A. Marschak (1959) and L. Hurwicz (1960) have emphasized the role of prices and demands as "messages" in a given allocation mechanism. (See also Chapters 12 and 14.) Now a message is not "informative" unless it tells the receiver something he didn't know before; hence the study of the value of an exchange of messages (e.g., between enterprise managers and resource managers) presupposes that (1) before the exchange the various agents had incomplete information about the relevant variables, and therefore could properly be said to be uncertain about them; and (2) different agents had, at least in part, information about different variables. In the application of the theory of teams to this situation we assume that this uncertainty can be expressed in terms

[1] This chapter is based on research supported in part by the National Science Foundation.

of probability distributions, and that the several agents have a common goal, namely, the maximization of (expected) output.

Furthermore, in the previous literature on allocation and price adjustment mechanisms it is usually assumed that the adjustment mechanism (an iterative procedure) is allowed to run until an equilibrium is reached, and, in most cases, the object of the analysis is to show that such an equilibrium is a solution of the problem of optimal allocation.[2] In the present example we emphasize the situation in which there is not sufficient time for equilibrium to be reached before decisions are made. In this case, even after some exchange of messages, the economic agents will have to take decisions on the basis of incomplete and different information, although this information will be more complete than it was before the exchange of messages.

The results of our example suggests that information in the form of "prices" and "demands" may be quite efficient even if the adjustment process is not allowed to reach equilibrium. The results also suggest that even though "demands" are calculated by the enterprise managers to maximize accounting profit using the "prices" transmitted to them by the resource managers, the same definition of profit cannot be used to calculate the optimal *decisions* of the enterprise managers based on the information provided by the "price" messages. However, these results are quite tentative and special, and much more work will be required before more definitive results along these lines can be obtained.[3]

## 2. A Formal Model

Suppose that there are $n$ enterprises, each with a single output, and that there is a single source of some scarce resource, which is an input for each of the enterprises. Let the output of enterprise $i$ be

$$f_i(L_i, K_i, \mu_i[s]), \quad i = 1, \ldots, n, \tag{2.1}$$

where $K_i$ is the quantity of the scarce resource allocated to enterprise $i$, $L_i$ is a decision to be taken by the manager of enterprise $i$, and $\mu_i(s)$ is a random variable depending on the state of nature, $s$, For example, $K_i$ might be the quantity of a raw material used in the production process,

[2] See, however, Chapter 12.

[3] GROVES (1969) has generalized the results of this chapter to the case of any number of scarce resources, and has provided approximation theorems for the nonquadratic case. The result in Section 8 is also due to him. Finally, he has proposed alternative definitions of profit that would give the enterprise managers the incentives to report the "correct" demand messages.

$L_i$ a parameter indicating the "choice of technique," and $\mu_i(s)$ a parameter of the production process about which there is some uncertainty. We shall further suppose that there is a "resource manager" $(i=n+1)$ whose task it is to allocate the total supply, $\kappa(s)$, of the resource to the enterprise managers, and that this total supply is also a quantity about which there may be some uncertainty.

The team members are thus the $n$ enterprise managers and the single resource manager; the decision variable of enterprise manager $i$ is $d_i = L_i$ (a real number), and the decision variable of the resource manager is $d_{n+1} = (K_1, \ldots, K_n)$, a vector whose components are subject to the constraint

$$(2.2) \qquad \sum_{j=1}^{n} K_j = \kappa(s), \qquad \text{each } s.$$

To specify the payoff functions, we assume that the payoff to the team is a linear index of output.

$$(2.3) \qquad \omega(s, d) = \sum_{j=1}^{n} w_j f_j(L_i, K_i, \mu_i[s]),$$

where $w_1, \ldots, w_n$ are positive numbers. The state of the environment can be adequately described[4] for this problem by the $(n+1)$-tuple

$$(2.4) \qquad s = [\mu_1(s), \ldots, \mu_n(s), \kappa(s)].$$

We shall consider some alternative information $\eta = (\eta_1, \ldots, \eta_{n+1})$ structures for this problem, all of which have the property that $\mu_i$ is a contraction[5] of $\eta_i$, for $i = 1, \ldots, n$, and $\kappa$ is a contraction of $\eta_{n+1}$. In other words, we assume that, whatever be the information structure, each enterprise manager observes the parameter, $\mu_i(s)$, of *his own* production function, and the resource manager observes the total supply, $\kappa(s)$, of the resource allocated.

First, let us apply Theorem (3.1) of Chapter 10 to derive a condition for optimal decision rules for any such information structure. Using Equations (3.2ab) of Chapter 10, we see that a team decision rule $\delta = (\delta_1, \ldots, \delta_{n+1})$ is person-by-person-satisfactory if:

(1) $L_i = \delta_i(y_i)$ maximizes the conditional expectation

$$(2.5) \qquad E\{f_i(L_i, K_i, \mu_i) | \eta_i(s) = y_i\}, \qquad \text{all } y_i \text{ in } Y_i, \text{ and } i = 1, \ldots, n,$$

---

[4] The actual environment may, of course, be more complicated, but this description is adequate to deal with the problem *as stated*, and more detail would be irrelevant. For a discussion of the choice of state and action descriptions see J. MARSCHAK (1963).

[5] See Footnote 11 of Chapter 10.

where, in (2.5), it is understood that[6]

$$K \equiv (K_1, \ldots, K_n) = \delta_{n+1}[\eta_{n+1}(s)]; \tag{2.6}$$

(2) for each $y_{n+1}$ in $Y_{n+1}$, $K = \delta_{n+1}(y_{n+1})$ maximizes the conditional expectation

$$E\left\{\sum_{j=1}^{n} w_j f_j(L_j, K_j, \mu_j) | \eta_{n+1}(s) = y_{n+1}\right\}, \tag{2.7}$$

subject to

$$\sum_{j=1}^{n} K_j = \kappa(s), \qquad \text{all } s, \tag{2.8}$$

where in the conditional expectation (2.7) it is understood that

$$L_j = \delta_j[\eta_j(s)], \quad j = 1, \ldots, n. \tag{2.9}$$

If the functions $f_j$ are each concave and differentiable in $L_j$ and $K_j$ for each value of $\mu_j(s)$, then by Theorem 3.1 of Chapter 10, a team decision function is optimal if and only if it is person-by-person-satisfactory.[7] Under this same hypothesis, (2.5) is maximized if and only if

$$E\{f'_{iL}(L_i, K_i, \mu_i) | \eta_i(s) = y_i\} = 0, \qquad \text{all } y_i \text{ in } Y_i, \tag{2.10}$$

where $f'_{iL}$ denotes the partial derivative[8] of $f_i$ with respect to $L_i$.

The conditional expectation (2.7) is maximized subject to (2.8) if and only if for each $y_{n+1}$ there is a number $\pi(y_{n+1})$ such that

$$w_j E\{f'_{jK}(L_j, K_j, \mu_j) | \eta_{n+1}(s) = y_{n+1}\} = \pi(y_{n+1}), \quad j = 1, \ldots, n, \tag{2.11}$$

where $f'_{jK}$ denotes the partial derivative of $f_j$ with respect to $K_j$.

(Since a negative allocation would presumably not make sense in this example, we have implicitly assumed that in the solution of (2.10) and (2.11) the allocations will turn out to be nonnegative.)

As usual, $\pi(y_{n+1})$ can be interpreted as a "shadow price." That is to say, (2.11) is the first order condition for maximizing the conditional expected

---

[6] In other words, $f_i(L_i, K_i, \mu_i)$ is to be regarded as a function on the set of states of the environment, taking the value $f_i[\delta_i(\eta_i[s]), \delta_{n+1,i}(\eta_{n+1}[s]), \mu_i(s)]$ for each $s$.

[7] Strictly speaking, Theorem 3.1 does not apply to our example because the variables $K_1, \ldots, K_n$ are subject to the constraint (2.8). However, the argument of the theorem can easily be extended to cover this case. Recall that the quadratic case with linear constraints was covered by Theorem 4.3 of Chapter 10.

[8] Interchanging the order of differentiation and expectation is legitimate here since the set of states is finite, and so the expectation is a finite sum.

"shadow profit,"

$$E\{w_j f_j(L_j, K_j, \mu_j) - \pi(y_{n+1}) K_j | \eta_{n+1}(s) = y_{n+1}\}, \tag{2.12}$$

where in (2.12) it is understood that

$$L_j = \delta_j[\eta_j(s)], \quad j = 1, \ldots, n. \tag{2.13}$$

But note that here the shadow price, $\pi(y_{n+1})$, figures in the decision of the resource manager, and not in the decisions of the enterprise managers. We shall return below to the role of shadow prices as information signals.

## 3. A Quadratic Example

As an example of the model of Section 2, suppose that every $w_j = 1$ and the "production functions" $f_j$ are quadratic in the variables $L_j$ and $K_j$, as follows:

$$f_j(L_j, K_j, \mu_j[s]) = 2\mu_{jL}[s] L_j + 2\mu_{jK}[s] K_j - L_j^2 - K_j^2 - 2qL_j K_j, \quad (|q| < 1). \tag{3.1}$$

(We have assumed that the coefficients of the quadratic terms are the same for all enterprises, and have chosen the units of measurement so that the coefficients of $L_j^2$ and $K_j^2$ are unity.) The coefficient $(-2q)$ measures, in a sense, the *complementarity* between $L_j$ and $K_j$ in the payoff function.

Corresponding to (2.10) and (2.11), the conditions that determine the optimal decision rules are

$$L_j + qE[K_j | \eta_j(s) = y_j] = E[\mu_{jL} | \eta_j(s) = y_j], \quad \text{every } j \text{ and } y_j; \tag{3.2a}$$

$$qE[L_j | \eta_{n+1}(s) = y_{n+1}] + K_j = E[\mu_{jK} | \eta_{n+1}(s) = y_{n+1}] - \frac{\pi(y_{n+1})}{2}, \quad \text{every } y_{n+1} \text{ and every } j; \tag{3.2b}$$

$$\sum_{j=1}^{n} K_j = \kappa(s), \qquad \text{every state } s. \tag{3.2c}$$

(We could also directly apply Theorem 4.3 of Chapter 10.)

If we write

$$\begin{aligned} L_j &= \lambda_j(s) \equiv \delta_j[\eta_j(s)], \\ K_j &= \kappa_j(s) \equiv \delta_{n+1,j}[\eta_{n+1}(s)], \end{aligned} \tag{3.3}$$

and recall that $\mu_j$ is a contraction of $\eta_j (j=1, \ldots, n)$, then (3.2) can be written more compactly as

(3.4a) $$\lambda_j + qE(\kappa_j|\eta_j) = \mu_{jL}, \qquad \text{every } j;$$

(3.4b) $$qE(\lambda_j|\eta_{n+1}) + \kappa_j = E(\mu_{jK}|\eta_{n+1}) - \frac{\pi}{2}, \qquad \text{every } j;$$

(3.4c) $$\sum_{j=1}^{n} \kappa_j = \kappa .$$

(Here, as elsewhere, we shall use the same symbol, $\pi$, to denote the function whose argument is $y_{n+1}$ and a function on the set of states of the environment whose value for state $s$ is $\pi[\eta_{n+1}(s)]$.) In accordance with standard practice, we shall often identify a random variable with the corresponding function on the basic probability space, which, in this case, is the set of states of the environment.

Notice that the best decision for enterprise $j$ depends upon the (conditional) expected allocation of the resource to it, and that the best allocations depend upon the (conditional) expected decisions of the enterprise managers. Thus the equations (3.4) represent an equilibrium of mutual expectations, taking account of the fact that these expectations are based upon (possibly) different information.

It will be useful in what follows to have an explicit expression for the shadow price $\pi(y_{n+1})$ in the quadratic case. Adding the equations (3.4b) for $j = 1, \ldots$, n, and dividing by $n$ we obtain

(3.5) $$qE(\bar{\lambda}|\eta_{n+1}) + \frac{\kappa}{n} = E(\bar{\mu}_K|\eta_{n+1}) - \frac{\pi}{2},$$

where

(3.6) $$\bar{\lambda} \equiv \frac{1}{n} \sum_{j=1}^{n} \lambda_j ,$$

$$\bar{\mu}_K \equiv \frac{1}{n} \sum_{j=1}^{n} \mu_{jK} .$$

Hence, we can solve (3.5) to get

(3.7) $$\frac{\pi}{2} = E(\bar{\mu}_K - q\bar{\lambda}|\eta_{n+1}) - \frac{\kappa}{n} .$$

Using this formula for the shadow price, we can derive a useful expression for the optimal allocations. Define

(3.8) $$\nu_i \equiv \mu_{iK} - q\mu_{iL}, \qquad i = 1, \ldots, n,$$
$$\bar{\nu} \equiv \bar{\mu}_K - q\bar{\mu}_L .$$

It is an easy exercise to show that

(3.9) $$\left(\kappa_i - \frac{\kappa}{n}\right) = E\{(\nu_i - \bar{\nu}) + q^2\left[E(\kappa_i|\eta_i) - \frac{1}{n}\sum_j E(\kappa_j|\eta_j)\right]|\eta_{n+1}\},$$
$$i = 1, \ldots, n.$$

[Use (3.4)–(3.8).]

*A Measurement Convention.* According to Theorem 4.3, Corollaries 2 and 3 of Chapter 10, in our present problem the expected values of the optimal decisions and of the shadow price do not depend upon the information structure; furthermore, the expected payoffs for all information structures have in common the term:

$$E\omega(s, E\hat{\delta}) = \sum_i [(E\mu_i)'(E\hat{\delta}_i) + (E\pi_i)'(E\gamma_i)],$$

which only depends on the expected values of the decisions, shadow prices, and random parameters. In our present problem the random parameters are the $\mu_{iL}$, the $\mu_{iK}$, and $\kappa$. There is no loss of generality in assuming

(3.10) $$E\mu_{iL} = E\mu_{iK} = E\kappa = 0, \quad i = 1, \ldots, n.$$

In other words, we adopt the convention of measuring the random parameters from their expected values. It follows from (3.10), and Corollary 1 of Theorem 4.3 of Chapter 10, that the optimal decisions and the shadow price have expected value zero:

(3.11) $$E\lambda_i = E\kappa_i = E\pi = 0, \quad i = 1, \ldots, n.$$

From Equation (4.19) of Chapter 10, then, the expected payoff for the optimal decision rules for any given information structure is

(3.12) $$E\omega(s, \hat{\delta}) = \sum_i [\mathrm{Cov}(\mu_{iL}, \hat{\lambda}_i) + \mathrm{Cov}(\mu_{iK}, \hat{\kappa}_i)] + \tfrac{1}{2}\mathrm{Cov}(\kappa, \pi)$$

(where $\mathrm{Cov}(X, Y)$ denotes the covariance between $X$ and $Y$).

*Assumptions About the Distribution of the Random Parameters.* We shall assume that the several random parameters, the $\mu_{iL}$, the $\mu_{iK}$, and $\kappa$, are statistically independent. We could carry out the analysis without this restrictive assumption, but the results would be much more complicated. The independence assumption is not unreasonable if we interpret the random parameters as reflecting "local variations" in technology, working conditions, and supply.

To express the assumption that the enterprises are "similar," we shall assume that $\mu_{1L}, \ldots, \mu_{nL}$ are identically distributed, and likewise that $\mu_{1K}, \ldots, \mu_{nK}$ are identically distributed. We shall use the notation

$$\begin{aligned} \text{Variance } (\mu_{iL}) &= \sigma_L^2, \\ \text{Variance } (\mu_{iK}) &= \sigma_K^2, \\ \text{Variance } (\kappa) &= \tau^2. \end{aligned} \tag{3.13}$$

## 4. Information Structure I. No Communication

Let us now consider several alternative information structures that might be generated by observation, communication, and computation (see Section 6 of Chapter 10), together with the corresponding optimal decision rules and expected payoffs.

Suppose that each enterprise manager $j$ observes $\mu_j(s)$, and that the resource manager observes the total supply, $\kappa(s)$, of the scarce resource. If no communication takes place among the managers, then the information structure for the team is

$$\begin{aligned} \eta_j(s) &= \mu_j(s), \qquad j = 1, \ldots, n; \\ \eta_{n+1}(s) &= \kappa(s). \end{aligned} \tag{4.1}$$

(Other information structures will be considered in subsequent sections.)

Since the resource manager has no information that would lead him to expect the parameters of one enterprise to be larger (or smaller) than those of any other enterprise, it is intuitively plausible that he should allocate the total supply equally among the enterprises, i.e., that

$$\kappa_i = \frac{\kappa}{n}, \qquad i = 1, \ldots, n. \tag{4.2}$$

As for the enterprise managers, their information is statistically independent of the supply of the resource, so that the conditional expectation of the allocation to any one resource manager, given his information, is equal to the unconditional expectation of $\kappa/n$, i.e.,

$$E(\kappa_i|\eta_i) = E\left(\frac{\kappa}{n}\right) = 0, \qquad i = 1, \ldots, n. \tag{4.3}$$

(Recall that we are measuring the supply of the resource from its expected value.) Hence, by applying the person-by-person-satisfactoriness condition (3.4a), we get the decision rule[9] for enterprise manager $i$,

$$\lambda_i = \mu_{iL}\,. \tag{4.4}$$

If (4.2) and (4.4) are the optimal decision rules, then, by (3.7), the shadow price of the resource must be

$$\pi = \frac{-2\kappa}{n}, \tag{4.5}$$

since $E(\bar{\mu}_K - q\bar{\lambda}|\eta_{n+1}) = E(\bar{\mu}_K - q\bar{\mu}_L|\kappa) = 0$.

It is easy to verify that (4.2), (4.4), (4.5) do indeed satisfy the optimality condition (3.4), and thus do represent the optimal decision rules and the shadow price. As one would expect, the larger the total supply, $\kappa(s)$, of the resource, the lower the shadow price, $\pi[\eta_{n+1}(s)]$; and the larger the coefficient, $\mu_{iL}(s)$, of $L_i$ in the payoff function, the larger the decision $\lambda_i(s)$. However, since the observation of $\mu_{iK}(s)$, the coefficient of $K_i$ in the payoff function, is never communicated to the resource manager, there is no way for him to make the allocation, $\kappa_i(s)$, depend on $\mu_{iK}(s)$.

To calculate the expected payoff for this information structure (with the optimal decision rules) we use formula (3.12). First, note that

$$\operatorname{Cov}(\mu_{iL}, \lambda_i) = \operatorname{Var}(\mu_{iL}) = \sigma_L^2,$$

$$\operatorname{Cov}(\mu_{iK}, \kappa_i) = \frac{1}{n}\operatorname{Cov}(\mu_{iK}, \kappa) = 0,$$

$$\operatorname{Cov}(\kappa, \pi) = -\frac{2}{n}\operatorname{Var}(\kappa) = -\frac{2\tau^2}{n}.$$

Hence, by (3.12), the maximum expected payoff is

$$\Omega_I = E\omega(s, \delta) = n\sigma_L^2 - \frac{\tau^2}{n}. \tag{4.6}$$

Recall that, because of our measurement convention (3.11), the expression (4.6) really represents the *difference* between the actual expected payoff and a constant term that does not depend on the information structure. Formula (4.6) indicates that, for fixed expected values of the random parameters, the

[9] To simplify the notation ,we omit the carets from the symbols when the context makes it clear that we are talking about optimal decision rules.

maximum expected payoff for the information structure "no communication" is higher, the larger the variance of $\mu_{iL}$, and is lower, the larger the variance of $\kappa$.

## 5. Information Structure II. Complete Communication

Complete communication among the decision makers would enable all of them to have complete information on the actual values taken on by all of the random parameters of the system. This would produce the information structure

$$\eta_i = (\mu_{1L}, \ldots, \mu_{nL}, \mu_{1K}, \ldots, \mu_{nK}, \kappa), \qquad i = 1, \ldots, n+1. \tag{5.1}$$

Alternatively, the same information structure could be produced by having the enterprise and resource managers report their observations to a "central planning board," which would then compute the enterprise decisions and the allocations, and transmit these to the managers.

If we apply the optimality conditions (3.4) to this information structure we must solve the following set of simultaneous equations (in the functions $\lambda_i$ and $\kappa_i$):

$$\begin{aligned} &\lambda_i + q\kappa_i = \mu_{iL} \\ &q\lambda_i + \kappa_i = \mu_{iK} - \frac{\pi}{2} \qquad i = 1, \ldots, n, \\ &\sum_{i=1}^{n} \kappa_i = \kappa . \end{aligned} \tag{5.1}$$

It is a routine exercise to show that the solution is

$$\lambda_i = \frac{\mu_{iL} - q\mu_{iK} + q(\pi/2)}{1-q^2}, \tag{5.2a}$$

$$\kappa_i = \frac{\nu_i - (\pi/2)}{1-q^2}, \tag{5.2b}$$

$$\frac{\pi}{2} = \bar{\nu} - (1-q^2)(\kappa/n), \tag{5.2c}$$

where, as before,

$$\nu_i \equiv \mu_{iK} - q\mu_{iL}, \qquad \bar{\nu} \equiv \frac{1}{n}\sum_{i=1}^{n} \nu_i .$$

In general, each optimal decision rule, and the shadow price, depends on all of the random parameters of the system. Note, however, that if there is no "complementarity" between $L_i$ and $K_i$ (i.e., $q=0$) then the optimal decision $\lambda_i(s)$ for manager $i$ does not depend upon the shadow price of the resource, and thus, not on the total supply of the resource.

Using (3.12) it is straightforward to calculate the maximum expected payoff:

$$\Omega_{\text{II}} \equiv \left[\frac{n}{1-q^2}\right]\left[\left(1-\frac{q^2}{n}\right)\sigma_L^2+\left(1-\frac{1}{n}\right)\sigma_K^2\right]-(1-q^2)\left(\frac{\tau^2}{n}\right). \tag{5.3}$$

Again, the expected payoff increases with $\sigma_L^2$ and decreases with $\tau^2$; in this case it also increases with $\sigma_K^2$.

It is of interest to examine the *increase* in expected payoff that complete communication provides, compared with no communication; we shall call this the *value* of full communication. From (4.6) and (5.3) we have

$$V_{\text{II}} \equiv \Omega_{\text{II}}-\Omega_{\text{I}} = \left(\frac{n-1}{1-q^2}\right)(q^2\sigma_L^2+\sigma_K^2)+\frac{q^2\tau^2}{n}. \tag{5.4}$$

As one would expect, this value is nonnegative, and is strictly positive if all the variances are positive, i.e., if there really is initial uncertainty about the random parameters of the system. However, it is noteworthy that in the case of zero complementarity between $L_i$ and $K_i$ ($q=0$), the value of communication depends only on the variance of the coefficients $\mu_{iK}$, and not on the variance of $\mu_{iL}$ or of the total supply $\kappa$ of the resource.

## 6. Information Structure III. The One-stage Lange-Lerner Market Mechanism

The various market mechanisms, or market-like mechanisms, that have been discussed in connection with the allocation of resources can be viewed as processes of communication by which information is exchanged among the decision makers of an economic system. Usually such processes are described in terms of an iterative procedure in which at each stage there is an exchange of information about "prices" and "demands" (or "supplies") between enterprise managers and resource managers and/or central planning boards. We consider here a one-stage process in which the resource manager announces a "price" and the enterprise managers respond with a set of "demands" for the scarce resource. On the basis of the resulting information structure the various managers then determine their decisions. We call this the "one-stage Lange-Lerner" information structure because the process is suggested by the discussion of market socialism by Lange and Lerner (see LERNER (1944) and WARD (1967)).

To make the information structure precise, we must define the "price" that the resource manager will communicate to the enterprise managers, and the rule by which the latter calculate their "demands."

Regarding the definition of "price," there are various alternatives. For example, one might consider the conditional expected shadow price, given the actual supply, $\kappa(s)$, of the scarce resource, i.e., (from (5.2c))

$$E(\pi|\kappa) = 2\left[E(\bar{v}|\kappa) - (1-q^2)\left(\frac{\kappa}{n}\right)\right] = -2(1-q^2)\left(\frac{\kappa}{n}\right). \tag{6.1}$$

Fortunately, in the one-stage communication it is not necessary to decide on a particular definition of price, since the price can (at most) depend upon $\kappa(s)$, which is the only information possessed by the resource manager that is not possessed by the enterprise managers at the time he sends out the price signal.

Regarding the specification of "demand," the literature suggests defining the demand for the scarce resource by enterprise $i$, given a "price" $\psi(s)$, to be that value $K_i^*$ such that $(L_i^*, K_i^*)$ maximizes the "profit"

$$f_i(L_i, K_i, \mu_i[s]) - \psi[s]K_i. \tag{6.2}$$

In the quadratic example we are considering, one easily calculates $K_i^*$ and $L_i^*$ to be

$$K_i^* = \frac{\mu_{iK}(s) - q\mu_{iL}(s) - \dfrac{\psi(s)}{2}}{1-q^2} = \frac{v_i(s) - \dfrac{\psi(s)}{2}}{1-q^2},$$

$$L_i^* = \frac{\mu_{iL}(s) - q\mu_{iK}(s) + \dfrac{q\psi(s)}{2}}{1-q^2}. \tag{6.3}$$

Notice that if $\psi(s)$ is the price communicated by the resource manager to the enterprise manager $i$, then the communication of the demand $K_i^*$ by the enterprise manager to the resource manager is equivalent to the communication of $v_i(s)$, since the resource manager already knows $\psi(s)$ and $q$. (If the resource manager did not know $q$, then we would have to treat $q$ as a random variable, i.e., a magnitude depending upon the state of the environment; see below for further remarks on this point.)

Therefore, in the light of the foregoing discussion, there is no loss of generality in supposing that the resource manager communicates the value of $\kappa(s)$ to each enterprise manager, and that each enterprise manager $i$ communicates $v_i(s)$ to the resource manager. The corresponding information structure implied by this is

$$\eta_i = (\mu_i, \kappa), \qquad i = 1, \ldots, n, \tag{6.4}$$

$$\eta_{n+1} = (\kappa, v_1, \ldots, v_n).$$

The reader should keep in mind, however, the "price" and "demand" interpretation of this information structure.

We shall show that the optimal allocation rule is

$$\kappa_i = \frac{\kappa}{n} + \frac{v_i - \bar{v}}{1 - q^2\left(\dfrac{n-1}{n}\right)}, \qquad i = 1, \ldots, n, \tag{6.5a}$$

the optimal enterprise decision functions are given by

$$\lambda_i = \mu_{iL} - q\left(\frac{\kappa}{n}\right) - \frac{qv_i}{\left(\dfrac{n}{n-1}\right) - q^2}, \tag{6.5b}$$

and the corresponding expected payoff is

$$\Omega_{\mathrm{III}} = \Omega_{\mathrm{I}} + V_{\mathrm{III}}, \tag{6.6}$$

$$V_{\mathrm{III}} = \frac{n(q^2\,{}^2_L + \sigma_K^2)}{\left(\dfrac{n}{n-1} - q^2\right)} + \frac{q^2\tau^2}{n}, \tag{6.7}$$

where $V_{\mathrm{III}}$ is the value of communication for this information structure.

Recall that the "demand," $K_i^*$ was defined (see (6.3)) as one component of the profit maximizing pair $(L_i^*, K_i^*)$. If the price communicated by the resource manager to the enterprise managers is defined by (6.1), i.e.,

$$\psi = E(\pi|\kappa) = -2(1-q^2)\left(\frac{\kappa}{n}\right), \tag{6.8a}$$

then the demand $K_i^*$ is given by

(6.8*b*)
$$K_i^* = \frac{\nu_i(s)}{1-q^2} + \frac{\kappa(s)}{n}.$$

Now this is not equal – except by accident – to the optimal allocation, $\kappa_i(s)$, as given by (6.4), nor is it equal to the expected allocation $E(\kappa_i|\eta_i)$. Hence, it is not surprising that $L_i^*$, the "profit" maximizing value of $L_i$ (see (6.3)), is not the same as the optimal decision $\lambda_i(s)$, as given by (6.5). Thus, although the enterprise managers use profit maximization to calculate the messages (demands) sent to the resource manager, *the optimal decisions by the enterprise managers are not those that maximize profits* (as profit has just been defined).

However, if $n$ is large, then $K_i^*$ and $E(\kappa_i|\eta_i)$ are approximately equal. This is seen from (6.8) and the easily verified equation,

(6.9)
$$E(\kappa_i|\eta_i) = \frac{\nu_i}{\left(\dfrac{n}{n-1}\right) - q^2} + \frac{\kappa}{n}.$$

It is not difficult to show that, for each enterprise $i$, the optimal decision $\delta_i(s)$ is "profit-maximizing" if in the formula (6.2) for profit the price announced by the resource manager is

$$\psi_i^*(s) = -2(1-q^2)\frac{\kappa(s)}{n} + \frac{2\nu_i(s)}{n-(n-1)q^2} = \psi(s) + \frac{2\nu_i(s)}{n-(n-1)q^2},$$

where $\psi(s)$ is given by (6.8a). Also, for this definition of price, the profit maximizing demand is equal to $E[\kappa_i|\eta_i(s)]$. But note that the prices $\psi_i^*(s)$ are (typically) different for different enterprises $i$, although if $n$ is large then each $\psi_i^*(s)$ is approximately equal to $\psi_i(s)$. Thus, $\psi_i^*(s)$ can be interpreted as an "adjustment" of $\psi(s)$ in the light of information available to $i$.

It should be pointed out that, *in this quadratic example*, a *second* price announcement by the resource manager would enable the team to take the decisions that are optimal for *complete* communication. This is clear from (5.2a)–(5.2c), since after the first exchange of messages the resource manager is able to compute the correct shadow price from the information now available to him.

To prove that (6.5ab) gives the optimal decision rules, it suffices to show that equations (3.4abc) are satisfied, with

$$\frac{\pi}{2} = \frac{\bar{\nu}}{1-\left(\frac{n-1}{n}\right)q^2} - (1-q^2)\frac{\kappa}{n}. \tag{6.10}$$

This is straightforward to verify, using (6.9) and

$$E(\mu_{jK} - q\lambda_j | \eta_{n+1}) = q^2\left(\frac{\kappa}{n}\right) + \frac{\nu_j}{1-\left(\frac{n-1}{n}\right)q^2} \tag{6.11}$$

## 7. Comparison of the Information Structures for the Case of a Large Number of Enterprises

We shall now show that the one-stage Lange-Lerner information structure gives almost as good results as does complete communication if the number of enterprises is large.

The difference between $V_{\mathrm{II}}$ and $V_{\mathrm{III}}$, obtained by subtracting (6.7) from (5.4), is

$$V_{\mathrm{II}} - V_{\mathrm{III}} = \frac{q^2}{(1-q^2)\left(\frac{n}{n-1} - q^2\right)}(q^2\sigma_L^2 + \sigma_K^2). \tag{7.1}$$

This difference is bounded above by a quantity that is independent of $n$, i.e.,

$$V_{\mathrm{II}} - V_{\mathrm{III}} \leqq \frac{q^2(q^2\sigma_L^2 + \sigma_K^2)}{(1-q^2)^2}. \tag{7.2}$$

On the other hand, (5.4) shows that $V_{\mathrm{II}}$ grows *at least as fast as n* (exactly how fast will depend upon what is assumed about the relationship between $n$ and $\tau^2$, i.e., between the number of enterprises and the variance of the total resource supply). Therefore,

$$\lim_{n\to\infty} \frac{V_{\mathrm{II}} - V_{\mathrm{III}}}{V_{\mathrm{II}}} = 0 \tag{7.3}$$

Thus, although $V_{\mathrm{III}} \leqq V_{\mathrm{II}}$ for all $n$, the *percentage* loss in using the one-stage Lange-Lerner structure rather than full communication tends to zero as the number of enterprises increases without limit.

Table 2 shows the value of communication for the two information structures, and also the asymptotic value of communication per enterprise under the assumption that $\tau^2 = n^2 \tau^2$.

## 8. Optimality of Demand Messages[10]

In the one-stage Lange-Lerner information structure, the demand messages from the enterprise managers to the resource manager are responses to the price message they have received from the resource manager. We shall

TABLE 1

SUMMARY OF INFORMATION STRUCTURES

| | Enterprise manager's information function | Resource manager's information function |
|---|---|---|
| I No communication | $\mu_i = (\mu_{iL}, \mu_{iK})$ | $\kappa$ |
| II Complete communication | $(\mu_1, \ldots, \mu_n, \kappa)$ | $(\mu_1, \ldots, \mu_n, \kappa)$ |
| III One-stage Lange-Lerner | $(\mu_i, \kappa)$ | $(\nu_1, \ldots, \nu_n, \kappa)$, where $\nu_i = \mu_{iK} - q\mu_{iL}$ |
| IV Complete exchange with the center | $(\mu_i, \kappa)$ | $(\mu_1, \ldots, \mu_n, \kappa)$ |

show that these are the best possible responses; in fact, the expected payoff to the team cannot be increased by having the enterprise managers send *complete information about their production functions to the resource manager.*

To demonstrate this point, we consider the information structure generated by a complete exchange of observed information between the resource manager and each enterprise manager (but without communication among enterprise managers). We shall call this "complete exchange with the center" (CEC); it is defined by:

(8.1)
$$\eta_i(s) = [\mu_i(s), \kappa(s)], \qquad i = 1, \ldots, n;$$
$$\eta_{n+1}(s) = [\kappa(s), \mu_1(s), \ldots, \mu_n(s)].$$

[10] This section is based on GROVES (1969).

TABLE 2

VALUE OF COMMUNICATION

| Information structure | Value of communication[1] | Asymptotic value[2] of communication |
|---|---|---|
| III One-stage Lange-Lerner | $n\left[\dfrac{q^2\sigma_L{}^2+\sigma_K{}^2}{\dfrac{n}{n-1}-q^2}\right]+\dfrac{q^2\tau^2}{n}$ | $n\left[\dfrac{q^2\sigma_L{}^2+\sigma_K{}^2}{1-q^2}+q^2\tau^2\right]$ |
| II Complete communication | $(n-1)\left[\dfrac{q^2\sigma_L{}^2+\sigma_K{}^2}{1-q^2}\right]+\dfrac{q^2\tau^2}{n}$ | ditto |

Notes: [1]See Equations (6.7) and (5.4).
$\sigma_L{}^2 \equiv \mathrm{Var}(\mu_{iL})$, $\sigma_K{}^2 \equiv \mathrm{Var}(\mu_{iK})$, $\tau^2 \equiv \mathrm{Var}(\kappa)$
[2]Asymptotic value is defined as $n \lim_{n\to\infty} V/n$. It is assumed here that $\tau^2 = n^2\tau_1^2$, where $\tau_1^2$ is the same for all $n$; this affects the second term only.

In the CEC information structure, the enterprise managers have the same information functions as they do under the one-stage Lange-Lerner (OSLL) structure; the information of the resource manager under OSLL is, however, a contraction of his information under CEC. Therefore, the value of OSLL cannot exceed the value of CEC. To show that OSLL is as valuable as CEC it is sufficient to show that the decision functions that are optimal for OSLL are also optimal for CEC. For this, it is sufficient to show that (6.5a), (6.5b), and (6.10) satisfy the optimality conditions (3.4), which, for the CEC information structure, take the form:

$$\begin{aligned} \lambda_j + qE(\kappa_j|\mu_j, \kappa) &= \mu_{jL}, \\ q\lambda_j + \kappa_j &= \mu_{jK} - \frac{\pi}{2}, \\ \sum_j \kappa_j &= \kappa . \end{aligned}$$

This is easily verified by use of the relation

$$E(\kappa_j|\mu_j, \kappa) = \frac{\kappa}{n} + \frac{v_i}{\dfrac{n}{n-1} - q^2} .$$

## 9. A Dynamic Allocation Process

Consider now a dynamic situation in which at each date $t = 0,1,2, \ldots$, etc., enterprise and resource managers face the team decision problem described in Sections 2 and 3. Thus, all of the random parameters and decisions will be dated, say: $\mu_i(s, t)$, $\kappa(s, t)$, $\lambda_i(s, t)$, $\kappa_i(s, t)$. Here the "environment," $s$, is to be thought of as a complete *history* of the relevant environmental variables (see Chapter 10, Section 7).

Suppose that one desires to maximize the total (possibly discounted) expected payoff over some (possibly infinite) period. Since we assume that the decisions at one date do not affect the random parameters at another date, and since the objective to be maximized is additive in the "single-date" payoffs, it is sufficient to choose the decision rules at any one date to maximize the expected payoff at that date.

Even so, our analysis of the previous sections will not completely carry over to the present "dynamic" situation if the information available to the managers at any one date $t$ depends on what has happened in the past. Of course, if the random variables $\mu_i(\cdot, t)$ and $\kappa(\cdot, t)$ at different dates are statistically independent, then the individual single-date decision problems can be solved independently. But if these random variables are dependent (in time) then the managers may be able to use information about the past to improve present decisions.

As an example, let us examine a dynamic analogue of the Lange-Lerner information structure of Section 6. Suppose that at each date $t$, the resource manager observes the total supply, $\kappa(s, t)$, and sends a price message, say, $\psi(s, t)$, to the enterprise managers. This price message arrives after a delay of one period. Similarly, at date $t$ each enterprise manager $i$ observes his coefficients $\mu_{iK}(s, t)$ and $\mu_{iL}(s, t)$, and transmits a demand message, say $K_i^*(s, t)$, to the resource manager.

We are not able to present an analysis of the optimal decision functions and value of communication for a problem of this type in the time dependent case. Nevertheless, it may be of interest to look at a full specification of such a problem, and get an idea of the difficulties in the way of a solution.

To complete the description of the information structure we must specify what information is memorized by the managers, and by what rules new messages are computed. For example, the enterprise managers may compute their demands solely as a function of the last received price, together with their current information on their production functions. Thus, let $[L_i^*(s, t)$,

$K_i^*(s, t)]$ maximize

$$f_i[L_i, K_i, \mu_i(s, t)] - \psi(s, t-1) K_i . \tag{9.1}$$

The resource manager may compute the new price as a function of the old price, $\psi(s, t-1)$, the new supply, $\kappa(s, t)$, and the total demand,

$$K^*(s, t) = \sum_{j=1}^{n} K_j^*(s, t) . \tag{9.2}$$

Notice that we have assumed no delay in the transmission of the messages $K_i^*(s, t)$. It is as if the price message $\psi(s, t-1)$ arrives at the enterprise during the night before day $t$, the demand message $K_i^*(s, t)$ arrives at the resource manager's office at the beginning of day $t$, and a new price message, $\psi(s, t)$, is calculated and transmitted to the enterprises during the night. Of course, one could consider a system with longer delays.

From (6.3) we have the formula for the "profit-maximizing" demand,

$$K_i^*(s, t) = \frac{v_i(s, t) - \frac{1}{2}\psi(s, t-1)}{1-q^2} . \tag{9.3}$$

If the resource manager uses a typical linear adjustment rule for the price (see, e.g., ARROW and HURWICZ (1962)), then

$$\psi(s, t) = \psi(s, t-1) + h[K^*(s, t) - \kappa(s, t)] . \tag{9.4}$$

If we use the symbol $\tilde{x}(t)$ to denote $[x(t), x(t-1), \ldots, x(0)]$, we can write the information structure in terms of the observations and price and demand messages as follows, assuming that each manager has a good memory:

$$\eta_i(s, t) = [\mu_i(s, t), \tilde{\psi}(s, t-1)] , \qquad i = 1, \ldots, n , \tag{9.5}$$
$$\eta_{n+1}(s, t) = [\tilde{\kappa}(s, t), \tilde{K}_1^*(s, t), \ldots, \tilde{K}_n^*(s, t), \psi(s, t-1)] .$$

Using (9.2)–(9.4) and the formula (5.2c) for the shadow price of the resource in the case of complete information, we can rewrite the information structure (9.5) in an equivalent form that brings out more clearly the random parameters involved. First, (9.2)–(9.4) can be solved to give the following difference equation in the price messages $\psi(s, t)$:

$$\psi(s, t) = (1-H)\psi(s, t-1) + H\pi(s, t) , \tag{9.6}$$

where

$$H \equiv \frac{hn}{2(1-q^2)} , \qquad \pi(s, t) \equiv 2[\bar{v}(s, t) - (1-q^2)\kappa(s, t)/n] . \tag{9.7}$$

Note that $\pi(s, t)$ is what the shadow price of the resource would be for the case of complete information.

The information structure (9.5) is equivalent to

$$(9.8) \qquad \eta_i(s, t) = [\tilde{\mu}_i(s, t), \tilde{\pi}(s, t-1)], \qquad i = 1, \ldots, n,$$

$$\eta_{n+1}(s, t) = [\tilde{\kappa}(s, t), \tilde{v}_1(s, t), \ldots, \tilde{v}_n(s, t)].$$

In principle, the optimal decision functions can be found by the methods of Chapter 10, Section 4. In particular, if the random parameters of the system have a joint normal distribution (i.e., form a multivariate Gaussian stochastic process), then the optimal decision functions of the managers will be linear functions of their observations and messages received up to that date (since $\pi(s, t)$ and $v_i(s, t)$ are linear in the random parameters, and hence, would also be normally distributed). However, we have not yet succeeded in providing a complete analysis of an interesting case of this model. It seems clear that the results of Sections 7 and 8 of this chapter would have to be modified in the present dynamic case, because (1) on the one hand, the price message $\psi(s, t-1)$, or $\pi(s, t-1)$, informs the enterprise managers about *past values* of the supply of the scarce resource (rather than about the "current" value, as in the static case), but (2) on the other hand, the price message can help each enterprise manager to predict the *current* average of $v_j(s, t)$ for the *other* enterprise managers, if the production parameters are serially dependent.

## References


Arrow, K. J., and L. Hurwicz (1960), "Decentralization and Computation in Resource Allocation," in R. Pfouts (ed.), *Essays in Economics and Econometrics*, University of North Carolina Press, Chapel Hill, pp. 34–104.

Groves, T. F. (1969), "The Allocation of Resources under Uncertainty: The Informational and Incentive Roles of Prices and Demands in a Team," NSF Technical Report No. 1, Center for Research in Management Science, University of California, Berkeley (mimeographed).

Hurwicz, L. (1960), "Optimality and Informational Efficiency in Resource Allocation Processes," Chapter 3 in K. J. Arrow, S. Karlin, and P. Suppes (eds.), *Mathematical Methods in the Social Sciences*, Stanford University Press, Stanford, pp. 27–46.

Lerner, A. (1944), *The Economics of Control*, Macmillan, New York.

Marschak, J. (1963), "The Payoff-Relevant Descriptions of States and Acts," *Econometrica*, *31*, 719–725.

Marschak, T. (1959), "Centralization and Decentralization in Economic Organization" *Econometrica*, *27*, 399–430.

Ward, B. (1967), *The Socialist Economy*, Random House, New York.

CHAPTER 12

# COMPUTATION IN ORGANIZATIONS: THE COMPARISON OF PRICE MECHANISMS AND OTHER ADJUSTMENT PROCESSES[1]

THOMAS A. MARSCHAK

1. Introduction. – 2. A special framework. – 3. The adjustment processes to be studied. – 4. The case of serially independent environments. – 5. The case of serially correlated environments. – 6. Concluding remarks.

## 1. Introduction

We shall be concerned in this paper with the good design of a team (MARSCHAK and RADNER (1971)) – the design of an organization whose members share certain preferences and are to respond in a desirable way to a changing environment. The discussion is partly motivated by economists' continuing interest in the formulation of decentralized "price" mechanisms to be used by planned economies, firms, and other organizations which it is helpful to view as teams. The current work on such mechanisms[2] seems aimed mainly at generating more of them so as to permit previously excluded conditions such as increasing returns and certain externalities. The very difficult question of choice between alternative decentralized mechanisms or between a decentralized mechanism and a centralized alternative – the question of what characterizes a "good" mechanism – has received little attention.

---

[1] This research was supported by National Science Foundation Grants GS–71 and GS–2078. An earlier version of the paper appeared in BORCH and MOSSIN (eds.), *Risk and Uncertainty* (Proceedings of an International Economic Association Conference), St. Martins Press, 1968.

[2] Recent efforts (all of which have some roots in the classic discussions of BARONE (1935), LANGE (1938), HAYEK (1945) and others) include: ARROW and HURWICZ (1962) on gradient methods; MALINVAUD (1967) on decentralization in national planning; MARGLIN (1963) on decentralized investment planning; MARGLIN (1967) and AOKI (1969) on decentralized allocation processes for certain kinds of increasing returns; DAVIS and WHINSTON (1966) on decentralization in the presence of externalities; DANTZIG and WOLFE (1961) on decomposed linear programming, with a national-planning interpretation by C. ALMON (1963); KORNAI and LIPTAK (1965), and WEITZMANN (1970) on other decomposed approaches to programming.

One may be able to formulate several extremely general problems of good design for a team. But if one wants to say something of interest about the comparative performance of alternative designs, especially designs that have something in common with price mechanisms, then in familiar fashion generality has to yield to tractability and arbitrary specializing assumptions have to be made.

Thus in a very general formulation one might consider a team composed of $n$ members. Each member repeatedly chooses an action and in addition sends and receives messages and stores and retrieves information. The team faces an environment which changes, say, according to a known stochastic process. A design for the team specifies precisely what happens within the team at each point of time for every possible realization of the stochastic process: what messages each member sends to every other, what action each member takes, what information each member stores or retrieves, what computations each member performs. At some points of time a member may be continuing his previous action but computing his next one, using the information he then has; at other moments he may be reading or writing a message or preparing (by performing certain computations) messages to be shortly written and sent; or he may be in the midst of reading or writing messages or storing and retrieving information. At certain moments his action will change.[3]

The sequence of communication, computing, and storage-retrieval tasks which a design implies for each succession of environments has to be carried out with certain equipment, which we may call "information-handling equipment." One version of the general problem of optimal design would require the equipment to have sufficient computing, communication, and storage capacity so that for each environment sequence each task is completed at the time assigned to it by the chosen design. The cost of alternative "sufficient" equipments, together with the sequence of actions generated by the design for each environment sequence determine the desirability of a given design. One might suppose in particular that the team's preferences as between designs are given by a payoff function defined on the set of all possible action-environment-equipment cost "histories": for a given environmental stochastic process one design is preferred to another if its expected payoff, using the best possible "sufficient" equipment, is higher.

Studying such a problem of optimal design in its full generality is unlikely

[3] In a still more general formulation, the distinction between "action-taking" and the other activities just mentioned (e.g., "message-writing") can be dropped.

to be worthwhile for at least two reasons. In the first place, the general formulation imposes no stability at all on the team's successive responses to its environment. Hence many suggestive properties of both real organizations and fictitious organizations studied by economists (organizations using price mechanisms) are not exploited; for in these cases the successive responses remain similar in important ways. In the second place, in such a general formulation the technology of communication, computation, and storage-retrieval, still so little understood and so difficult to characterize, must enter the problem in an extremely detailed and unwieldy fashion. For each design, all possible equipments meeting the design's requirements have to be considered and the best one found.

We shall accordingly consider here a problem of good design whose generality is greatly curtailed. It is relevant, however, to the comparative study of price mechanisms and alternative schemes. And it is a design problem in which the missing technological information is of a *relatively* modest sort, so that there may be some hope that specialists in information technology can eventually supply it.

The price mechanisms which have so far been proposed for teams have at least the following important properties in common:

(1) The team using the mechanism wants to achieve a high value of a many-valued payoff function (profit, planners' utility, national product) whose arguments are the actions taken by the members (e.g., production decisions, local plans) and the team's environment (market prices, resource availabilities, technical coefficients).[4]

(2) The members who participate in the operation of the mechanism (managers of production units, custodians of resources, local planners) observe part of the environment (the technology of a particular production unit, the prices in a particular market, the availability of a particular resource), but they are never required to transmit all of this specialized knowledge to anyone else. Instead, through a sequence of very limited information exchanges, each followed by an adjustment of "tentative" actions, they achieve final actions approximating those which a complete pooling of information could achieve.

(3) The information that is transmitted between members consists partly of signals which it is natural to think of as "prices."

(4) Formally the mechanism may be written as a difference-equation

---

[4] In important cases the action must also lie in a constraint set determined by the environment (e.g., resource requirements must not exceed resource availabilities).

system in which, at each iteration, each member's vector of tentative actions and of messages to be sent to others is given as a function of his information: his knowledge of the environment, his previous actions, and the messages previously sent to him by others. The number of the iteration may enter the function as well or it may not; if not one has the case of "temporally homogeneous" mechanisms. The system may be a first-order system or it may not. The main price mechanisms proposed appear to be, when appropriately formulated, both temporally homogeneous and first-order. In any case, the path of the system is well defined once initial values of all the variables are specified and it attains, in time, high values of the payoff function.[5]

The mechanisms are also frequently labeled "decentralized" and are proposed as alternatives to "centralized" schemes which are, indeed, sometimes held to be totally infeasible. The advantages of the decentralized mechanisms are presumed to lie in the small amount of information transmitted, in spreading of the computational burden among many members, possibly in desirable incentive properties, and – at least for temporally homogeneous schemes – in routineness of the tasks repeatedly performed.

For a thorough-going study of these advantages one must doubtless begin with a much more precise definition of the class of decentralized schemes than the rough sketch above. Some attempts in that direction were made in T. MARSCHAK (1959). In addition, L. HURWICZ (1966) has studied decentralization in a different but related context – that of an economy whose members successively adjust their trades by means of a temporally homogeneous difference-equation system that achieves Pareto-optimality at equilibrium. He has developed a complete and satisfying definition of a decentralized class of such schemes.

We shall consider (below) only one, rather arbitrary, definition of decentralization and will loosely use the term "centralized" to apply to certain schemes in need of convenient labeling. This will suffice for the main purpose, which is simply to illustrate some issues that arise in the limited choices of schemes open to the team we consider. The same issues must also be faced in any attempt to compare price mechanisms or to compare decentralized and centralized classes of schemes when these terms are given a more complete definition.

---

[5] For some schemes it may also be the case that computation is *decomposed* in a manner that is particularly efficient from a purely computational point of view. If all data *were* gathered in one central place, in other words, there might still be a good computational reason for using the scheme within that central place. For the Dantzig-Wolfe decomposition scheme this has been conjectured to be the case (see Footnote 31 below).

## 2. A Special Framework

It is a very helpful simplification to suppose that the team's environment changes only at discrete points of time, that it is instantly observed at those points of time, and that the environment does not change while the scheme is in operation. When the scheme has come to a halt, it has generated a set of actions that are a response to the environment. These actions are put into effect and they remain in force at least until the next environment occurs. (They may remain in force somewhat *beyond* that time, for they may remain in force while the next actions – a response to the next environment – are being generated.) Only once during its operation – when it terminates – does the scheme generate a new set of actions actually taken by the organization in response to the new environment; the scheme generates a whole sequence of *tentative actions*, but only the terminal one is put into effect.

One scheme is better than another if, very roughly speaking, it reaches appropriate new actions more quickly, even when the information-handling capacity at the disposal of the participants is well chosen in each of the two schemes. Speed is generally desirable because until actions that are a good response to the new environment have been generated, the actions in force are inferior (for example, they may be a response to the preceding environment, which may be only very weakly correlated with the current one). In some tasks – e.g., once-and-for-all long-range planning – one could argue that speed is desirable even though the relevant environment never changes, simply because of the opportunities that have to be foregone until the plan is ready. But changes in the environment seem to be an implicit part of most discussions, and we shall assume that they occur.

We proceed now to restrict the schemes considered and to formulate more precisely the problem of choice between schemes. We consider an organization of $n$ members which chooses actions $a=(a_1, \ldots, a_n)$ out of some unchanging set of actions and faces environments $\mu=(\mu_1, \ldots, \mu_n)$; $a_i$ and $\mu_i$ are real vectors, $i=1, \ldots, n$. The vector $\mu_i$, $i=1, \ldots, n$, is a random variable; each of its components has a finite mean. The $n$-tuple $\mu=(\mu_1, \ldots, \mu_n)$ always lies in a set $M$; its successive values are generated by a stochastic process known to the organization.

At an instant of time during which $\mu$ obtains and $a$ is in force, *payoff* per time unit is given by $W(a, \mu)$. Of two pairs $(a, \mu)$ prevailing at some instant of time the one with the higher value of $W$ is preferred, and of two alternative actions to be taken, at some instant of time, in the face of an unknown $\mu$, the one with the higher value of $EW(a, \mu)$ is preferred.[6] We assume in addition that alternative sequences of action-environment pairs are ranked according to the discounted sum of the payoffs accumulated during periods of unit length.

To be precise, let $\xi = [(a^0, \mu^0), (a^1, \mu^1), (a^2, \mu^2), \ldots]$ be a sequence of action-environment pairs, with $(a^r, \mu^r)$ prevailing for $v^r$ time units. Then $\xi$ and $[v^0, v^1, v^2, \ldots]$ define a time path followed by the action-environment pairs. Now divide this time path into time intervals of *unit* length and assume that during each such interval there are a finite number of distinct pairs. The typical interval, say the *qth*, contains the distinct pairs $(a^{q1}, \mu^{q1}), \ldots, (a^{qe_q}, \mu^{qe_q})$ with time durations $\delta^{q1}, \ldots, \delta^{qe_q}$, where $\sum_{i=1}^{e_q} \delta^{qi} = 1$. We can associate with $\xi$ a *total discounted payoff* $F(\xi)$ defined by

$$F(\xi) = \sum_{q=0}^{\infty} \rho^q \left[ \sum_{i=1}^{e_q} \delta^{qi} W(a^{qi}, \mu^{qi}) \right],$$

where $\rho$ is a discount factor and $0 < \rho < 1$. Then the organization prefers the sequence $\xi$ to a sequence $\xi'$ if and only if $F(\xi) > F(\xi')$.[7]

Moreover, given two gambles whose outcomes are action-environment sequences the organization prefers the first to the second if and only if the expected value of $F$ is higher.

Note that perhaps the most drastic implication of our assumptions so far is that current actions have no influence on the desirability of alternative future actions.[8] One way to allow for such influence would be to retain the environment $\mu$, which is totally beyond the control of the team, but to add a *state vector s* whose value depends on the *previous* action. Payoff would be a function of the triple $(a, \mu, s)$ and would enter discounted total payoff in the manner just shown. In principle we could then evaluate schemes for generating team actions using the framework to be presented below. For the present purposes, however, adding such a state vector would be false gene-

[6] To insure that all expected values in which we shall be interested are finite, it suffices to assume that $W(a, \mu)$ is, for every a, a measurable function of $\mu$ such that $EW(a, \mu)$ is finite. We make this assumption without referring to it again.

[7] Clearly a sufficiently small choice of time unit allows $F(\zeta)$ to approximate as closely as desired the quantity $\int_0^\infty e^{-\rho t} W(a^{r(t)}, \mu^{r(t)})\, dt$, which is the more usual discounted total payoff, where $\sum_{r=0}^{r(t)} v^r \leqq t \leqq \sum_{r=0}^{r(t)+1} v^r$

[8] In the case of choice among schemes for running a planned economy, for example, the simplification means that no investment decisions are made, only current operating decisions.

rality, since we shall not consider any cases in which current actions influence the desirability of alternative future actions.

The successive environments occur, and are instantly observed, at discrete points of time. We assume these points to be evenly spaced, *one time unit*, also occasionally called *one period*, occurring between them. In response to a new $\mu$ the organization starts to carry out a scheme, or, as we shall call it, an *adjustment process*, defined by the first-order difference equation system

$$a_i(t) = f^i[t, \mu, a(t-1)], \qquad i = 1, \ldots, n, \quad t = 1, 2, 3, \ldots$$

or, more compactly

$$a(t) = f[t, \mu, a(t-1)], \qquad t = 1, 2, 3, \ldots \tag{1}$$

The index $t$ denotes *iteration number*, not "clock" time. For an *initial value* of $a$, say $a(0) = a_0 = (a_{0_1}, \ldots, a_{0_n})$, the path followed by $a$ as the iterations proceed – the solution of the difference-equation system – is denoted $a(t, \mu, a_0) = [a_1(t, \mu, a_0), \ldots, a_n(t, \mu, a_0)]$. The vector $a_i(t, \mu, a_0)$, $i = 1, \ldots, n$, has the same dimension as $a_i$. We shall sometimes call $a(t, \mu, a_0)$ the organization's *tentative action* at iteration $t$.

We now specify that member $i$ observes $\mu_i$; is responsible for adjusting the tentative action $a_i(t)$ at each iteration $t$; and is also responsible for seeing that the action $a_i$ has at any instant of time the value the organization wants it to have at that instant. Then specifying $f$ also specifies precisely the information that each member must have at iteration $t$ about the parts of the environment observed by other members and about the previous tentative actions of other members. The messages that must be exchanged following an iteration $t$ in order for the adjustment process to function are therefore also implied.

There are a number of appealing properties that one could require an adjustment process to display given a payoff function $W$. One could require that $W[a(t, \mu, a_0), \mu]$ be, for each $\mu$, a strictly increasing function of $t$ – that for any fixed environment operating the process longer yields a better action. If $W$ is maximized at a unique value of $a$ for each $\mu$, one could require that the process be at equilibrium only at this value. One could require that for each $\mu$ the process converge – in a sense that has to be made precise – to its equilibrium value.

Though at least one of these properties characterizes each of the proposed price mechanisms, exactly why these properties should be valuable has not been made very clear. It is certainly possible, for example, that a process which does not converge to the maximizing action but eventually oscillates around, or converges to, some other "good" action performs better than one displaying the last two of the above properties, according to some reasonable measure of performance. In much of what follows we shall nevertheless adopt the traditional bias in favor of convergence to maximizing actions. The study of processes displaying this property, and the property's precise definition, will be given priority and a possible reason for the superiority of such processes, as well as a disadvantage of the convergence requirement will emerge.

Now consider the interval between two successive environments $\mu$ and $\mu^*$. At some *terminal iteration* $T$, but not later than the occurrence of $\mu^*$, the process will be halted and the action vector actually in force will at that instant be given the value $a(T, \mu, a_0)$. Between the observation of $\mu$ and the achievement of the $T$th iteration the organization has in force some *interim action* $\tilde{a}$.[9] Let us assume now that $f$ does not contain $t$ as an argument – so that the computational operations performed by each participant $i$ between any iterations $t-1$ and $t$ remain the same for all $t$, as do the dimensions of the messages sent by $i$. The adjustment process is temporally homogeneous. It is then reasonable to assume that given the organization's information-handling equipment it requires a time $C$, $C>0$, to complete each iteration (to pass from $a(t-1, \mu, a_0)$ to $a(t, \mu, a_0)$).[10] We shall call $C$ the *iteration time*. Following an iteration a member requires time to send information to those who need it to adjust their tentative actions, to read the messages which he receives, to perform the computations needed for his adjustment and to store and retrieve needed information. The iteration time is the time needed for *all* members to finish these tasks. Since the interval between successive environments is one time unit, our condition that the operation of the process must be stopped before the environment changes can be stated as

---

[9] In cases where the action vector has to lie in a constraint set (a set determined by $\mu$) we assume that (1) the interim action and (2) the action $a = a(T, \mu, a_0)$ are both feasible for $\mu$. If, for a given adjustment process, (2) is not true for all $T$, $\mu$, it becomes true for an appropriately modified version of the process.

[10] The assumption that it is the dimension of a message that determines the time required to send it over a given transmission line is valid only under certain further assumptions about the transmission technology, a point we later consider very briefly. Moreover, in assuming that the *first* iteration takes $C$ time units, as well as later ones, we implicitly assume that the time required for initial exchange and storage of information about the new environment $\mu$ (a task which never needs to be repeated for that $\mu$) equals the time required in subsequent iterations to retrieve this stored information.

*Assumption 1.* The terminal iteration $T$ chosen by the organization must satisfy $0 \leqq T \leqq 1/C$, where $C$ is the iteration time.

Between the two successive environments $\mu$ and $\mu^*$, the organization's total payoff is then given by

$$W(\tilde{a}, \mu)\, CT + W[a(T, \mu, a_0), \mu](1 - CT).$$

For a given probability distribution over the possible sequences of environments, and a given rule for choosing (after each new environment) the terminal iteration $T$, the interim action $\tilde{a}$, and the inital value $a_0$, the expected stream of payoffs that the organization enjoys depends only on $C$. If we know precisely the relation expressing this dependence for two adjustment processes $f$ and $f^*$, we can then make what we shall call a "technology-free" statement about which process is better. The organization wants to take into account the stream of the total *costs* (appropriately measured) incurred by repeated use of the equipment that is needed in order to achieve an iteration time of $C$. A technology-free statement says that *if* the costs of alternative information-handling capacities are such that the best choice of $C$ for adjustment process $f$ yields a larger expected stream of *net* payoffs (when appropriately discounted and summed) than the best choice of $C$ for adjustment process $f^*$, then $f$ is better than $f^*$. (Net payoff at an instant of time is a function of the action in force, the environment prevailing, *and* the flow of information processing costs at that instant.) Such an "if" statement is technology-free in the sense that it is a correct statement about two processes, no matter what properties the technology of information processing empirically displays.

Note that for two adjustment processes $f$ and $f^*$, different rules for choosing terminal iteration, interim action, and initial value – different *arrangements*, as we shall call them – lead to different technology-free statements about $f$ and $f^*$.

## 3. The Adjustment Processes to be Studied

To illustrate these matters more concretely, we shall consider still further restricted classes of payoff functions and adjustment processes.

First, however, it will be useful to make more precise the term *decentralized* as applied to the adjustment processes (1), since the term will frequently be used.

*Definition.* A *standard team* has $n$ members and a payoff function $W(a, \mu)$; the ith member observes $\mu_i$, is in charge of the action $a_i$, and adjusts the tentative action $a_i(t)$. An adjustment process defined by the first-order temporally homogeneous difference-equation system $a(t) = f[a(t-1), \mu]$ will be called a *decentralized process for a standard team* if the following is true for at least $n-1$ of the team's members $i$:

(i) the action $a_i$, in the charge of member $i$, effectively enters[11] the payoff function $W$,

(ii) the adjustments which the process requires for member $i$ are given by

$$a_i(t) = f^i[a(t-1), \mu_i].$$

This definition is one way (perhaps a rather drastic one) of capturing the main classical property of decentralized schemes – the privacy accorded each participant with respect to his knowledge of the environment – while still solving the rather delicate problem that any definition of decentralization must solve: how to rule out schemes which formally are decentralized according to the definition but which seem clearly centralized in the popular sense. If one did not rule out temporal nonhomogeneity, systems of more than first order, or extra "dummy" action variables not effectively entering the payoff function, one could disguise as "decentralized" schemes (in which member $i$ needs to know no other environment component than $\mu_i$) schemes in which all the $\mu_i$ are in fact made known to one or more persons.[12] Allowing conditions (i) and (ii) to be violated for one of the $n$ members permits one member to be a legitimate "price-setter" in a decentralized price mechanism: a member whose action (and tentative action) is a price vector that does not effectively enter the payoff function.

We shall assume now, for most of what follows, that each component $a_i$ of $a$ and $\mu_i$ of $\mu$ is a scalar, that for each $\mu$ in $M$, $W(a, \mu)$ is strictly concave and differentiable with respect to all coordinates of $a$, and that for each $\mu$, $W$ is maximized at a unique value, $\hat{a}(\mu)$, of the action vector $a$. We consider the *gradient-method* adjustment process wherein each coordinate of $a$ is adjusted at a rate proportional to the partial derivative of $W$ with respect to that coordinate. The process is the difference-equation system

$$a_i(t) - a_i(t-1) = hW_i[a(t-1), \mu], \qquad i = 1, \ldots, n, \tag{2}$$

where $W_i$ denotes $\partial W / \partial a_i$ and $h$ is a positive constant; it attains equilibrium, i.e., $a(t) = a(t-1)$, if and only if $a(t-1) = \hat{a}(\mu)$.

---

[11] That is, there exists a vector $(\mu^0, a_1^0, \ldots, a_{i-1}^0, a_{i+1}^0, \ldots, a_n^0)$, where $\mu^0 \in M$, such that if $\mu = \mu^0$, $a_1 = a_1^0, \ldots, a_{i-1} = a_{i-1}^0, a_{i+1}, = a_{i+1}^0, \ldots, a_n = a_n^0$ then for at least two values of $a_i$, $W$ takes different values.

[12] For an example, see 4.7 below.

If $W$ has the form

$$W(a, \mu) = \sum_{i=1}^{n} \mu_i a_i + S(a), \tag{3}$$

where $S(a)$ is strictly concave, then the process (2) has the form

$$a_i(t) - a_i(t-1) = h\{\mu_i + S_i[a(t-1)]\}, \qquad i = 1, \ldots, n, \tag{4}$$

and so has the principal property of decentralized schemes: no participant $i$ is required to communicate $\mu_i$, his knowledge of the environment, to anyone else. Each participant may be required, however, to know the preceding tentative actions of all other participants. If $W$ does not have the form (3) the adjustment process (2) may still have purely computational advantages, stemming partly from the fact that (as compared with direct calculation of $\hat{a}(\mu)$) it "decomposes" the problem of finding a good value of $a$ into a sequence of $n$ simultaneously computed "small" problems.

We shall be particularly interested in a special payoff function having the form (3). The function, studied in a related context by R. RADNER (1961), is quadratic:

$$W(a, \mu) = \mu' a - a' Qa$$

where $Q = (q_{ij})$ is a positive definite symmetric matrix and vectors without primes are to be interpreted as column vectors. The matrix $Q$ is, in fact, a matrix of "interactions"[13] in the sense that $q_{ij}$ is equal to the second partial derivative $\partial^2 W / \partial a_i \, \partial a_j$. For every $\mu$ the action maximizing $W$ is, $\hat{a}(\mu) = \frac{1}{2} Q^{-1} \mu$. The adjustment process (2) becomes

$$a_i(t) - a_i(t-1) = h\mu_i - 2h \sum_{j=1}^{n} q_{ij} a_j(t-1)$$

or, in matrix and vector notation,

$$a(t) = h\mu + (I - 2hQ)\, a(t-1). \tag{5}$$

It may appear at first sight that the general adjustment process (1) and the special decentralized adjustment processes (2) and (4) are quite remote from the decentralized price mechanisms which have been discussed and hence their study can shed little light on the virtues of these mechanisms.

---

[13] A payoff function of this form would characterize, for example, a firm with branch plants, each producing the same output (sold for a local price which is a random variable) and each using the same input; the total input required is bought by the firm as a whole in the face of an unchanging rising linear supply curve. The interaction $q_{ij}$ is the effect on the $i$th branch's marginal cost of an incremental increase in the $j$th branch's output.

For in the first place the aim of all mechanisms proposed is to achieve a high payoff subject to *constraints* on the actions; a distinctive property of the mechanisms is that either they continuously maintain feasibility of the tentative actions or they reverse departures from feasibility. In the second place, the participants in a number of the schemes, unlike the participants in (1), (2), and (4), never need to announce their tentative actions to anyone else.

With respect to the first point, we remark that if the original payoff function in a price mechanism is replaced by one that preserves the ranking of feasible pairs $(a, \mu)$, while assigning an extremely low payoff to infeasible pairs, it might well be possible to approximate the new payoff function by a strictly concave function, perhaps the quadratic one. If the payoff assigned to infeasible pairs is sufficiently small, the gradient-method adjustment process corresponding to such an approximating function would yield a feasible action at any terminal iteration.

With respect to the second point we remark that in at least one of the important "price" mechanisms (the Dantzig-Wolfe scheme for decomposing linear programming problems) the tentative actions *are* communicated. Moreover, in all the price mechanisms certain information other than knowledge of the environment is communicated – namely, prices and, in some cases, each participant's tentative demand for one or more commodities. It is by no means clear why such information is any easier to transmit than the tentative actions that have to be transmitted in the processes (1), (2), and (4).[14]

On the other hand, if the processes (2), (4), and (5) are to provide, like the price mechanisms, an appealing alternative to complete centralization of information and computation, then it may seem reasonable to require that the *number* of actions communicated at each iteration should at least be less than the dimension of the vector $\mu$ (which could be centrally collected and the action $\hat{a}(\mu)$ then computed directly). Reasonable as the requirement seems it yet rests on arbitrary assumptions about the technology of information handling, a point we return to in Section 4.7 below. If one accepts these assumptions then it is worth observing that in the quadratic case there

[14] It is true, of course, that the processes (5) and (9) require transmission of each participant's tentative actions to all the other participants and not just to a central agency. But it would change nothing in our study of the processes (5) and (9) to cut down the number of transmission lines by adding a central agency – an $(n+1)$th participant, analogous to the price-setting agency of the price mechanisms – who receives the tentative actions of each participant and relays it to all others.

are certain suggestive forms of the matrix $Q$ for which the number of "costly" action transmissions *is*, under a suitable interpretation, less than the dimension of $\mu$.

Consider, for example, a matrix $Q = Q^* = (q^*_{ij})$ of order $mv$ by $mv$. The $mv$ components of the action vector $a$ are divided up among $m$ "blocks" of members, and so are the $mv$ components of the environment vector $\mu$. Any two members of a block, say members $i$ and $j$ interact with each other in the sense that the second partial derivative $\partial^2 W/\partial a_i\, \partial a_j = q^*_{ij}$ has a nonzero value, say $q$, for $i \neq j$ and equals 1 for $i = j$. But between every member of a block except the $v$th member and every member of any other block there is no interaction (the relevant second partial derivative is zero). Between the *vth* members of every two blocks there is interaction: the relevant second partial derivative is equal to $r \neq 0$.

To summarize: for $k$, $\bar{k} = 0, \ldots, m-1$, $k \neq \bar{k}$, $q^*_{kv+v,\, \bar{k}v+v} = r$ and for $i, j = kv+1, \ldots, kv+v-1$, $q^*_{ij} = q$ when $i \neq j$ and 1 when $i = j$. For the case of 3 blocks of 3 members each, $Q^*$ is

$$\begin{pmatrix} 1 & q & q & 0 & 0 & 0 & 0 & 0 & 0 \\ q & 1 & q & 0 & 0 & 0 & 0 & 0 & 0 \\ q & q & 1 & 0 & 0 & r & 0 & 0 & r \\ 0 & 0 & 0 & 1 & q & q & 0 & 0 & 0 \\ 0 & 0 & 0 & q & 1 & q & 0 & 0 & 0 \\ 0 & 0 & r & q & q & 1 & 0 & 0 & r \\ 0 & 0 & 0 & 0 & 0 & 0 & 1 & q & q \\ 0 & 0 & 0 & 0 & 0 & 0 & q & 1 & q \\ 0 & 0 & r & 0 & 0 & r & q & q & 1 \end{pmatrix}$$

Assume $q$ and $r$ to be such that $Q^*$ is positive definite. To carry out the process (5) at an iteration $t$, each member of a block needs to know the actions of every other member of the block at $t-1$, but only the $v$th member needs to know the previous actions of members outside the block (namely the action of the $v$th member of every other block). A reasonable assumption is that the gathering of the actions in a block is much less costly, in an appropriate sense, than transmission of actions from one block (one "branch") to all the others. A centralized process, with direct computation of $\hat{a}(\mu) = \frac{1}{2}\, Q^{*-1}\, \mu$ in a central place, would require the transmission of all $mv$ components of $\mu$;[15] there is no simple and reasonable technological

[15] The inverse $Q^{*-1}$ is *not* in general such that $Q^{*-1}\, \mu$ can be computed knowing only a linear combination of each block's $\mu_i$'s. (If it were, then using such linear combinations

assumption under which it dominates the process (5), since the number of costly (intra-block) action transmissions in (5) is less than the dimension of $\mu$.

The principal reason for considering the processes (2), (4), and (5) is, of course, that while they are far easier to study than the price mechanisms that have been formulated,[16] all the comparison difficulties which we shall examine must also be faced for the price mechanisms.

What are the convergence properties of the difference-equation system (2)? In the first place one does not generally have strict global convergence; it is not true for all $W(a, \mu)$ strictly concave in $a$ that there exists an $h$ such that for all $a_0$ and all $\mu$

$$\lim_{t\to\infty} a(t, \mu, a_0) = \hat{a}(\mu). \tag{6}$$

As we shall see it is true, however, in the quadratic case – i.e., in the process (5). Nor is it generally true that for each $\mu$ and each individual value $a_0$ there exists a number $h(\mu, a_0)$ such that (6) holds for $h = h(\mu, a_0)$. The difficulty is that one cannot rule out (no matter how small $h$ is) (1) the possibility of *overshooting*, i.e., the possibility that at some iteration $t = t^*$, and for some $i$, the difference $a_i(t) - \hat{a}_i(\mu)$, which has so far been of constant sign, now changes sign; and (2) when this happens, the possibility that at some iteration $t_0$ after $t^*$ the variable in question may start fluctuating about its equilibrium value without converging to it.

A limited convergence property – that the neighborhood in which such fluctuation occurs can be made arbitrarily small – was studied by UZAWA (1958). The argument that such convergence holds was given for the case of a gradient-method difference equation system which converges, not to the unconstrained maximum of $W$ with respect to $a$, but to its maximum subject

---

the number of block-to-center transmissions in the centralized case would equal the number of actions that have to be sent between blocks in the process (5).) That such linear combinations do not exist is seen, for example, in the case $m = v = 2$, where

$$Q^{*-1} = \frac{1}{q^4 - r^2 - 1}\begin{pmatrix} I - q^2 & q^3 - q & qr & -r \\ q^3 - q & l - q^2 - r^2 & q^2 r & qr \\ qr & q^2 r & l - q^2 - r^2 & q^3 - q \\ -r & qr & q^3 - q & l - q^2 \end{pmatrix}$$

[16] The price mechanisms are difficult to study since it is very difficult to characterize the paths of variables in difference-equation systems that constrain the variables to satisfy inequalities. To make the comparisons of processes which we wish to make much must be known about the paths of the action variables and this is considerably easier if they are not constrained.

to the constraints $a \geqq 0$, $g_j(a) \geqq 0$, $g_j$ concave, $j = 1, \ldots, m$. Removing the constraints leaves the relevant parts of the argument intact (after suitable reinterpretation), but does not appear to strengthen the conclusion with respect to convergence. The convergence property shown by the argument is (for any fixed $\mu$) as follows:

For any $a_0$ and any $\varepsilon > 0$, there exists a number $\bar{h}(\mu, a_0, \varepsilon) > 0$ such that for $0 < h < \bar{h}(\mu, a_0, \varepsilon)$ there is an integer $t_0 > 0$ with the property

$$(7) \qquad D[a(t+1)] \leqq D[a(t)] \quad \text{for } 0 \leqq t \leqq t_0 \text{ and}$$
$$D[a(t)] \leqq \varepsilon \quad \text{for } t \geqq t_0,$$

where $D[a(t)]$ is the distance from $a(t)$ to the equilibrium value $\hat{a}(\mu)$, i.e.,

$$D[a(t)] = \sqrt{\sum_{i=1}^{n} [a_i(t) - \hat{a}_i(\mu)]^2}\,.$$

By the strict concavity of $W$, (6) also implies that

$$(8) \qquad W[a(t+1), \mu] \geqq W[a(t), \mu] \text{ for } 0 < t < t_0\,.$$

For a given $\mu$ and $a_0$ there are in general, then, two iterations at which the path followed by $a(t)$ displays an important change: the iteration $t^*$ at which overshooting first occurs, and the iteration $t_0 \geqq t^*$ at which $a(t)$ begins to fluctuate about $\hat{a}(\mu)$ without getting closer to $\hat{a}(\mu)$. It seems reasonable to suppose that the organization, knowing the above convergence property, prefers not to iterate beyond $t_0$. A difficulty is, however, that the $t_0$ and the $\bar{h}(\mu, a_0, \varepsilon)$ which the argument in UZAWA (1958) displays are functions of the equilibrium point $\hat{a}(\mu)$. Thus there appears to be no known way at present for the organization to choose an $\bar{h}(\mu, a_0, \varepsilon)$ and a terminal iteration prior to which fluctuation about $\hat{a}(\mu)$ does not occur, without sacrificing both the decentralized property of the adjustment process (when $W$ has the form (3)) and the computational justification for using the process in the first place. (For if $\hat{a}(\mu)$ is known, there is no reason to operate the process.)

The determination of $t^*$, however, presents no such difficulty, for strict concavity implies that

(9) For two values of $a$, say $a^*$ and $a^{**}$, the sign of $a_i^* - \hat{a}_i(\mu)$ is the same as the sign of $a_i^{**} - \hat{a}_i(\mu)$ for all $i$, if and only if sign of $W_i(a^*, \mu) =$ sign of $W_i(a^{**}, \mu)$ for all $i$.

Thus $t^*$ can be detected to have occurred as soon as some one member of the team, say the member in charge of $a_i$, observes that $W_i[a(t), \mu]$ has changed sign. If $W$ is of the form (3), $t^*$ can therefore be detected while preserving decentralization. (The action $a(t^*-1)$ can then be taken as the action to be put into force if it is desired to carry the process until the last possible iteration prior to overshooting.) Moreover, by taking $h$ sufficiently small, one can, for a given $\mu$ and $a_0$, either eliminate overshooting altogether or, if this is not possible, make $t^*$ as large as desired. Finally, if the organization is constrained to choose the terminal iteration $T$ from the interval $0 \leqq T < \min(t^*, 1/C)$, when overshooting occurs, and $0 \leqq T \leqq 1/C$ otherwise, then, as we shall see, (9) implies some results about the uniqueness of the best terminal iteration.

The choice of $h$ is certainly one of the important choices facing the organization. A small $h$ has the advantage of postponing overshooting, as well as shrinking the size of the region about $\hat{a}(\mu)$ in which fluctuation occurs. A small $h$ has the disadvantage that it increases the number of iterations required to reach a given value of $W$. While we shall concentrate here on varying the arrangement – the rules for choosing interim action, terminal iteration, and initial value – some changes in $h$ will also be discussed.

## 4. The Case of Serially Independent Environments

We shall now concentrate on the processes just presented for the case in which the successive environment vectors facing the organization are distributed independently of each other. The vector $\mu$ is always a drawing from the same set $M$, according to the same probability measure. We shall also assume, except as indicated, that each component $\mu_i$ of $\mu$ has mean zero and variance 1 and is uncorrelated with any other component. The latter conditions comprise

*Assumption 2.* $E\mu_i = 0$, $E\mu_i^2 = 1$, $E\mu_i\mu_j = 0$, $i \neq j$, $i, j = 1, \ldots, n$.

The assumption of no serial correlation is a strong one but seems an essential starting place; moreover, it renders Assumption 1 quite innocuous, for it is easy to see that with serial independence there can be no advantage in continuing to operate a process when the environment which initiated the current operation of the process no longer prevails.

We consider a number, but by no means all, of the possible arrangements – the possible choices of interim action, terminal iteration, and initial value – that the organization can make. Each arrangement seems worth examining, for, as we shall see, there may be sound reasons why the organization is constrained to choose it. For the arrangements considered the discussion deals partly with any adjustment process $a(t)=f[a(t-1), \mu]$, partly with any decentralized process, and partly with the specific processes (2), (4), and (5).

Throughout this section we shall assume that for a given process the iteration time $C$ is held at the same level for all arrangements considered. In comparing different arrangements, then, the cost of the information-handling equipment used plays no role.

### 4.1. Arrangement A: Constant Interim Action, Constant Initial Value, Terminal Iteration

*4.1.1. General Remarks about Arrangement A for the Processes Considered.* A highly routine response to a new environment is always to switch instantly to the same interim action $\tilde{a}$, and always to generate a new action by operating the chosen adjustment process for precisely $T$ iterations, starting always at the same initial value $a_0 = (a_{0_1}, \ldots, a_{0_n})$, all of whose components are known to all members. If routineness is sufficiently important to the organization, this may be the preferred arrangement and we shall examine it at some length. The organization's expected total payoff between two successive environments is then, for $0 \leqq T \leqq 1/C$,

$$\pi_1(C, T) \equiv E\{W(\tilde{a}, \mu)\, CT + W[a(T, \mu, a_0), \mu](1-CT)\}.$$

Since the environments are serially independent, the expected value of the discounted sum of future total payoffs is greater for one process than for another if and only if $\pi_1$ is greater. We can therefore ignore the discount factor altogether and may take $\pi_1$ as the measure of the process's performance.

If W is strictly concave in $a$ then the first term of the expression in braces is strictly concave in $\tilde{a}$. Moreover, the second term, $W[a(T, \mu, a_0), \mu](1-CT)$, does not depend on $\tilde{a}$. It follows that $\pi_1(C, T)$ is strictly concave in $\tilde{a}$ and that *there exists a unique best constant interim action $\tilde{a}$, independent of $T$ and $a_0$*. This best interim action is the action maximizing $EW(a, \mu)$; in the quadratic case this is $\hat{a}(E\mu) = 0$.

We shall not investigate the existence and uniqueness of a best initial value $a_0$, for fixed $T$ and $\tilde{a}$, except in the quadratic case for the process (5). Here the best $a_0$ is readily seen [17] to be independent of $T$ and $\tilde{a}$; it is always zero.

We turn now to the question of a best constant terminal iteration $T$, given

[17] From the solution to (5) , which is given below.

an $a_0$ and an $\tilde{a}$. This is a considerably more difficult matter, especially as $T$ must be an integer, constrained by Assumption 1 and perhaps by additional assumptions, to fall in a certain interval. Suppose the interval is $0 \leqq T \leqq T^*$, where $T^* \leqq 1/C$ and let $W_t$ denote $W[a(t, \mu, a_0), \mu]$. Let $\Delta W_t$ denote the first difference $W_t - W_{t-1}$ (defined for $t \geqq 1$), and $\Delta^2 W_t$ the seond difference $\Delta W_t - \Delta W_{t-1}$ (defined for $t \geqq 2$). It is easily seen that if

(10) $$\Delta W_t > 0 \text{ and } \Delta^2 W_t < 0 \text{ for all integers } t, \quad 2 \leqq t \leqq T^*,$$

then there is a unique integer $T$ in this interval maximizing $\pi_1(C, T)$ on the interval $0 \leqq T \leqq T^*$. For if (10) holds we have

$$W_t - 2W_{t-1} + W_{t-2} < 0, \qquad 2 \leqq t \leqq T^*.$$

Multiplying by the number $1 - Ct + C$, which is positive for $2 \leqq t \leqq T^*$, rearranging, and using $\Delta W_t > 0$, we obtain

$$W_t(1 - Ct) - W_{t-1}[1 - C(t-1)] < W_{t-1}[1 - C(t-1)] - W_{t-2}[1 - C(t-2)],$$
$$2 \leqq t \leqq T^*.$$

Hence $W(\tilde{a}, \mu)CT + W[a(T, \mu, a_0), \mu](1 - CT)$ has a negative second difference with respect to $T$ for $2 \leqq T \leqq T^*$. It follows that $\pi_1(C, T)$ has a negative second difference with respect to $T$ for all $T$, $2 \leqq T \leqq T^*$, so that a unique[18] integer $T$ maximizes $\pi_1(C, T)$ subject to $0 \leqq T \leqq T^*$.

These arguments make no use of the strict concavity of $W$. We summarize in the following proposition about any process $a(t) = f[a(t-1), \mu]$:

PROPOSITION 1. *If successive environments are independent, if the organization always uses the same interim action* $\tilde{a}$ *and the same initial value* $a_0$, *if the terminal iteration* $T$ *must lie in the interval* $0 \leqq T \leqq T^*$, *where* $T^* \leqq 1/C$, *and if* $\Delta W_t > 0$ *and* $\Delta^2 W_t < 0$ *for integers* $t$ *in this interval, then* $\Delta^2 \pi_1(C, T) < 0$ *over this interval and there is a unique best terminal iteration.*

The main practical interest of the proposition is that in many cases it permits the organization to approximate the best terminal iteration by treating the function $\pi_1(C, T)$ as continuous and differentiable in $T$, using the fact that $d^2\pi_1/dT^2 < 0$ to find $\hat{T}$, the value of $T$ maximizing $\pi_1$ on the

---

[18] Strictly speaking, there might be exactly *two* successive integers $T_1$, $T_2$ at which $\pi_t(C, T)$ is constant and is a maximum on the given interval. We let the word "unique" include this pathological case.

given interval, and taking the best terminal iteration to be the nearest integer to $T^*$.

Now if $W$ is strictly concave we have from (9) that prior to overshooting all partial derivatives $W_i$ keep the same sign. It follows immediately from equation (2) that prior to overshooting $\Delta W_t > 0$. It is also a consequence of the equation (2) and of strict concavity (i.e., of the negative definiteness of the matrix of second partial derivatives of $W(a, \mu)$ at any point $a$) that prior to overshooting

$$D[a(t)] - D[a(t-1)] > D[a(t+1)] - D[a(t)], \qquad t \geqq 1.$$

Strict concavity further implies for three values of $a$, say $a^*$, $a^{**}$, $a^{***}$ such that $W(a^*, \mu) < W(a^{**}, \mu) < W(a^{***}, \mu)$ and $D(a^{**}) - D(a^*) > D(a^{***}) - D(a^{**}) > 0$,

$$W(a^{***}, \mu) - W(a^{**}, \mu) < W(a^{**}, \mu) - W(a^*, \mu).$$

Hence it is also the case that $\Delta^2 W_t < 0$ prior to overshooting. By Proposition 1 we have that if $W$ is strictly concave and $h$ is chosen small enough (given the initial value $a_0$) so that overshooting does not occur prior to $T^* \leqq 1/C$, then on the interval $0 \leqq T \leqq T^*$ there is a *unique best constant terminal iteration for the organization that uses the process* (2).

It is now seen why the avoidance of overshooting is helpful for the uniqueness of the best $T$: for iterations $t$ *subsequent* to the first overshooting it may be that $W_t$ *temporarily drops*, so that $\Delta W_t > 0$, $\Delta^2 W_t < 0$ no longer holds.

We next investigate the possibility of overshooting in the quadratic case. The solution of (5) is, for an initial value $a_0$,

$$\text{(11)} \qquad \begin{aligned} a(t, \mu, a_0) &= [I-(I-2hQ)^t](2hQ)^{-1} h\mu + (I-2hQ)^t a_0 \\ &= \tfrac{1}{2}[I-(I-2hQ)^t]\, Q^{-1} \mu + (I-2hQ)^t a_0 . \end{aligned}$$

Let $\hat{W}$ denote the maximum of $W$; i.e., $\hat{W} = W[\hat{a}(\mu), \mu] = \frac{1}{4}\mu' Q^{-1} \mu$. After suitably rearranging we can write the path followed by the payoff $W$ in the form

$$\text{(12)} \qquad W[a(t, \mu, a_0), \mu] = \hat{W} - \tfrac{1}{4}\mu' H_t \mu + R_t ,$$

where $H_t = Q^{-1}(I-2hQ)^t Q(I-2hQ)^t Q^{-1}$ and $R_t = a_0'(I-2hQ)^t\, Q(I-2hQ)^t (Q^{-1}\mu - a_0)$. If $a_0 = 0$, $R_t = 0$. Because of the symmetry of $Q$, we can diagonalize; i.e., we can write $Q = BDB'$, where $D$ is the diagonal matrix of characteristic roots of $Q$ and $B$ is a matrix of characteristic vectors forming an orthonormal basis. Then $(I-2hQ)^t$ can be written $B(I-2hD)^t B'$

and $W[a(t, \mu, a_0), \mu]$ can be written

$$(13)\quad W[a(t, \mu, a_0), \mu] = \hat{W} - \tfrac{1}{4}\mu' BD^{-1}(I-2hD)^t D(I-2hD)^t D^{-1} B'\mu + R_t$$
$$= \hat{W} - \tfrac{1}{4}\mu' B(I-2hD)^{2t} D^{-1} B'\mu + R_t .$$

Now $\lim_{t\to\infty} a(t, \mu, a_0) = \hat{a}(\mu)$ if and only if the characteristic roots of $I-2hQ$ are less than 1 in absolute value. Since the roots of $Q$ are all positive, this means that for convergence we must have

$$(14)\qquad 0<h<1/\lambda ,$$

where $\lambda$ is the largest characteristic root of $Q$. If (14) is satisfied, overshooting is still possible for some $a_0$ and $\mu$. As far as the uniqueness of the best terminal iteration is concerned, however, overshooting is of no consequence in the quadratic case as long as (14) is satisfied. To show this we investigate the second difference $\Delta^2 W_t$, after observing first that (14) implies that the diagonal elements of $I-2hD$ are positive and hence, since $D$ has positive diagonal elements,

(15) the diagonal elements of $I-hD$ are $>0$.

For the case $a_0 = 0$ we have

$$\Delta W_t = \tfrac{1}{4}\mu' B(I-2hD)^{2(t-1)} D^{-1} B'\mu - \tfrac{1}{4}\mu' B(I-2hD)^{2t} D^{-1} B'\mu$$
$$= \tfrac{1}{4}\mu' B(I-2hD)^{2t-2}[I-(I-2hD)^2] D^{-1} B'\mu .$$

The term in brackets can be written $V \equiv 4hD(I-hD)$, which, by (15), is a diagonal matrix with positive diagonal elements. Therefore $\Delta W_t > 0$ for $t \geqq 1$. Moreover,

$$\Delta^2 W_t = \tfrac{1}{4}\mu' B(I-2hD)^{2t-2} VD^{-1} B'\mu - \tfrac{1}{4}\mu' B(I-2hD)^{2(t-1)-2} VD^{-1} B'\mu$$
$$= \tfrac{1}{4}\mu' B(I-2hD)^{2t-4}[(I-2hD)^2 - I]\, VD^{-1} B'\mu .$$

This time the term in brackets has negative diagonal elements so that $\Delta^2 W_t < 0$ for $t \geqq 2$. The extension of this result to the case $a_0 \neq 0$ is straightforward.

Thus if the organization picks $h$ once and for all so as to satisfy (14), there is, for any $a_0$, strict convergence to $\hat{a}(\mu)$ and no fluctuation in $W_t$. There is also, for any $a_0$ and any interim action $\tilde{a}$, a unique best constant terminal iteration $T$ in the interval $0 \leqq T \leqq 1/C$. One advantage of the convergence property – that it may make determination of best terminal iteration much easier – is well illustrated. The best constant $T$ depends on the choice of $\tilde{a}$

and $a_0$. Since, as we saw above, the best choice of $\tilde{a}$ and of $a_0$ is zero for the quadratic case, we can now state.

PROPOSITION 2. *The best T in the quadratic case is, under Assumptions 1 and 2, the T maximizing the function*

$$\pi_1(C, T) = EW[a(T, \mu, 0)](1-CT) = \tfrac{1}{4}(1-CT)\textstyle\sum_{i=1}^{n}(\bar{q}_{ii} - h_{T_{ii}}).$$

*on the interval* $0 \leqq T \leqq 1/C$, *where* $\bar{q}_{ii}$ *and* $h_{T_{ii}}$ *are the ith diagonal elements of* $Q^{-1}$ *and* $H_T$, *respectively.*

We make three further observations about Arrangement A. First, consider any adjustment process $a(t) = f[a(t-1), \mu]$ such that for all $(\mu, a_0)$, $\Delta W_t > 0$, $1 \leqq t \leqq 1/C$. If, for any value of $C$ there is a unique best terminal iteration in the interval $0 \leqq T \leqq 1/C$ does it become earlier or later as one decreases $C$? Proposition 1 and the argument leading to it provide an answer for the case of any process satisfying $\Delta W_t > 0$, $1 \leqq t \leqq 1/C$, and $\Delta^2 W_t < 0$, $2 \leqq t \leqq 1/C$. For such a process $\Delta^2 \pi_1(C, T) < 0$, $2 \leqq T \leqq 1/C$. Hence, the first integer $T$ in the interval $0 \leqq T \leqq 1/C$ for which one can assert "$\pi_1(C, T+1) < \pi_1(C, T)$ and $T+1 \leqq 1/C$" is the optimal $T$ when it exists; if no such $T$ exists then the largest integer in the interval is optimal. But, letting $\tilde{W} \equiv EW(\tilde{a}, \mu)$ and $\overline{W}_t \equiv EW_t$,

$$\pi_1(C, T) - \pi_1(C, T+1) = \overline{W}_T - \overline{W}_{T+1} + C\left[T(\overline{W}_{T+1} - \overline{W}_T) + (\overline{W}_{T+1} - \tilde{W})\right].$$

If $T$ is optimal for a given $C$ and $T > 0$, $T < 1/C$, then $\overline{W}_{T+1} > \tilde{W}$ (otherwise, iterating not at all would be superior to $T$) and the expression multiplying $C$ in the above equality is positive. It follows that no iteration later than T can be optimal if $C$ is replaced by any $C' > C$: either going from $T$ to $T+1$ now implies a larger drop in $\pi_1$ than before or else $T+1$ exceeds $1/C'$. If $C'$ is sufficiently larger than $C$ the new optimal iteration must be an earlier one. Similarly, if $C'$ is sufficiently *smaller* than $C$ and if $T+1$ is optimal for $C$ then $T$ becomes superior to $T+1$ for $C'$. For the extreme cases in which $T = 0$ or $T = 1/C$ are optimal for $C$ the same two assertions hold, modified to allow for the fact that no iterations earlier than $T = 0$ or later than $T = 1/C$ or $T = 1/C'$, respectively, are possible.

Note, however, that the effect of changing $C$ on the *product* of $C$ and the optimal iteration number – on the optimal interval, measured in "clock" time, during which computation occurs – is indeterminate. Roughly speaking, increasing the time required per iteration makes any previously unjustified iteration number unjustified *a fortiori*, but it may make the previously optimal total computing interval (in clock time) either too short (because too low an iteration number is now attained) or too long (because the "productivity" of each second of computing time is now lower and the previous interval is now not worth its "cost" in terms of deferred action).

In summary, we have:

PROPOSITION 3. *Under arrangement A if, on the interval* $0 \leqq t \leqq 1/C'$, $\Delta W_t > 0$ *and* $\Delta^2 W_t < 0$, *then replacing C by C′, where* $C' < C$, *cannot make the unique best terminal iteration earlier and will make it later if C′ is sufficiently smaller than C. Replacing C′ by C cannot make the best terminal iteration later and will make it earlier (provided it is not already zero) if C′ is sufficiently smaller than C. The effect of replacing C by C′ on the best total (clock) time spent in computation is indeterminate.*

Next we assert

PROPOSITION 4. *As long as* $EW(\tilde{a}, \mu) < EW[a(T, \mu, a_0), \mu]$, *a decline in C increases* $\pi_1(C, T)$ *for a fixed T, and does so at a constant rate; i.e.,* $\partial\pi_1(C, T)/\partial C$ *is a positive constant. If, however (under the same condition), T is always taken to be an optimal T,* $O \leqq T \leqq 1/C$, *for each C then the rate of the increase in expected total payoff as C decreases is generally not a constant, i.e.,* $d\pi_2/dC$ *is not a constant, where*

$$\pi_2(C) \equiv \max_{0 \leqq T \leqq 1/C} \pi_1(C, T).$$

An organization which uses an arbitrary constant terminal iteration, in other words, benefits from increases in its information-handling capacity in a manner quite different from that of an organization using the same adjustment process but using the best terminal iteration for each $C$. The condition $EW(\tilde{a}, \mu) < EW(a[T, \mu, a_0), \mu]$ is met, for example, for the process (2) ($W$ strictly concave) when $a_0$ is taken to equal $\tilde{a}$. It is certainly a reasonable condition to demand of any decision process and any $\tilde{a}$, $a_0$.

*4.1.2. Arrangement A in the Quadratic Gradient-Method Case with Identical Interactions.* Our final observation about Arrangement $A$ is a lengthy one. We shall consider the quadratic case for a particular matrix $Q$, namely the "identical-interaction" matrix for which $q_{ij} = q$, $i \neq j$, and $q_{ij} = 1$, $i, j = 1, \ldots, n$, where, to preserve positive definiteness, $-1/(n-1) < q < 1$.[19] In this case the process (5) displays, from one point of view, a very degenerate sort of decentralization. Since the initial actions $a_{0i}$ are known to all, it is possible

[19] This case of "identical interactions" was also given special attention by RADNER in (1961).

for each member to use the information he receives at iteration 1 to compute the $\mu_i$'s of all other members and thereupon to compute his optimal action. This is true of every $Q$ matrix with all nonzero elements but is not true, for example, of the "block" matrix $Q^*$ considered above, for in that case most members do not receive the tentative actions of members outside their blocks (since they do not need them for their computations) and hence they cannot reproduce the full vector $\mu$. When the $Q$ matrix has all nonzero elements, it is hard (though not impossible) to visualize an information technology for which it would be more costly to achieve the optimal action in a given time interval by individual computation of the vector $\mu$ than it would be to complete two iterations of the process (5). But the issues which we wish to examine are much more easily studied for the equal-interaction matrix than for any other; it is therefore an appropriate starting place.

Stimulated by the general question of how the "advantages" of decentralization change as one varies the "externalities" or "interactions" exhibited by the payoff function, we now investigate the performance of process (5) under Arrangement $A$ (with $a_0 = \tilde{a} = 0$) *as one varies the interactions* $q$ *while preserving the convergence of the process*. We are to preserve, that is to say, the property $\lim_{t\to\infty} a(t) = \hat{a}(\mu)$, which we saw to imply $\Delta W_t > 0$, $\Delta^2 W_t < 0$ and hence to be valuable in the determination of a best terminal iteration. For simplicity of exposition we consider mainly the case $n = 2$; the generalization of the results to any $n$ is tedious but straightforward.

Our principal motivation for studying this particular version of the externalities-decentralization question is as follows: We imagine the organization designer to confine himself, for fixed $q$, to choices of the pair $(h, T)$ such that $T$ can conveniently be shown to be best for $h$, that is, to choices for which the conditions $\Delta W_t > 0$, $\Delta^2 W_t < 0$ hold on the interval $0 \leqq T \leqq 1/C$. In the quadratic gradient-process case that is equivalent to confining his attention to all pairs $(h, T)$, where $0 \leqq T \leqq 1/C$ and $h$ is such that convergence holds. Given a value of $T$, say $T^*$ (with $0 \leqq T^* \leqq 1/C$), and given two values of $h$ such that convergence holds, the higher value of $h$ yields a higher value of $EW_T{}^*$, and hence of $\pi_1(C, T^*)$.

The motivation perhaps seems a trifle twisted. It would be more satisfying but much more ambitious to explore the effect of varying the interaction $q$ when for each $q$ the values of *both* $h$ and $T$ are best. Such values exist, since the set of integers satisfying $0 \leqq T \leqq 1/C$ is finite, and since, as one can show, there is for each fixed $T$ a unique best $h$, that is, an $h$ which maximizes $EW_T$ *without* being required to satisfy the convergence constraint (in fact, such a best $h$ may violate convergence). Although this is a much more difficult version of the question to study there is no reason *a priori* to expect the basic result we obtain below to vanish: increasing the interaction may still decrease the penalty due to decentralization.

Proceeding, then, with our specific version of the question, we note that the characteristic roots of the given matrix $Q$ are the root $1+(n-1)q$ and the root $1-q$, which has multiplicity $n-1$. An orthonormal matrix of characteristic vectors is $B=(b_{ij})$, where $b_{i1}=1/\sqrt{n}$, $i=1, \ldots, n$; $b_{ij}=1/\sqrt{(n-j+2)(n-j+1)}$, $i=1, \ldots, n-j+1$, $j=2, \ldots, n$; $b_{n-j+2,j}=\sqrt{(n-j+1)/(n-j+2)}$, $j=2, \ldots, n$; and $b_{ij}=0$, $i=n-j+2, \ldots, n, j=2, \ldots, n$.

The matrix $B$ appears as Table 1.

TABLE 1

| $\frac{1}{\sqrt{n}}$ | $\frac{1}{\sqrt{(n-1)(n-2)}}$ | $\frac{1}{\sqrt{(n-2)(n-3)}}$ | $\frac{1}{\sqrt{(n-3)(n-4)}}$ | $\frac{1}{\sqrt{(n-4)(n-5)}}$ | $\cdots$ | $\frac{1}{\sqrt{2}}$ |
|---|---|---|---|---|---|---|
| $\vdots$ | $\vdots$ | $\vdots$ | $\vdots$ | $\vdots$ | | $-\frac{1}{\sqrt{2}}$ |
| $\vdots$ | $\vdots$ | $\vdots$ | $\vdots$ | $\frac{1}{\sqrt{(n-4)(n-5)}}$ | | $\vdots$ |
| $\vdots$ | $\vdots$ | $\vdots$ | $\frac{1}{\sqrt{(n-3)(n-4)}}$ | $-\sqrt{\frac{n-4}{n-5}}$ | | $\vdots$ |
| $\vdots$ | $\vdots$ | $\frac{1}{\sqrt{(n-2)(n-3)}}$ | $-\sqrt{\frac{n-3}{n-4}}$ | 0 | $\cdots$ | 0 |
| $\frac{1}{\sqrt{n}}$ | $\frac{1}{\sqrt{(n-1)(n-2)}}$ | $-\sqrt{\frac{n-2}{n-3}}$ | 0 | 0 | $\cdots$ | 0 |
| $\frac{1}{\sqrt{n}}$ | $-\sqrt{\frac{n-1}{n-2}}$ | 0 | 0 | 0 | $\cdots$ | 0 |

Let the matrix $(h_{t_{ij}})=H_t$ (defined above), and let $(\bar{q}_{ij})=Q^{-1}$. Since $H_t=\frac{1}{4}\,\mu'\,B(I-2hD)^{2t}\,D^{-1}\,B'\mu$, one obtains after some calculation that under Assumption 2

$$\pi_1(C, T)=\tfrac{1}{4}(1-CT)\sum_{i=1}^{n}(\bar{q}_{ii}-h_{T_{ii}})=\tfrac{1}{4}(1-CT)\left[\sum_{i=1}^{n}\bar{q}_{ii}-\theta(n, q, h, T)\right]$$

where

$$\theta(n, q, h, T) = \sum_{i=1}^{n} h_{T_{ii}} = [1/(1-q)]\{1-[1-2h(1-q)]^{2T}\}$$
$$+\{1/[1+(n-1)q]\}\{1-[1-2h+(n-1)q]^{2T}\}$$
$$\cdot \sum_{k=2}^{n} [1+(n-k+1)^2]/[(n-k+2)(n-k+1)].$$

Note that $\frac{1}{4}\sum_{i=1}^{n} \bar{q}_{ii} = E\hat{W}$ and hence that $\theta(n, q, h, T)$ is the expected value of the "distance left to go" after $T$ iterations, i.e., $\theta = E\{\hat{W} - W[a(T, \mu, 0), \mu]\}$.

In order to compare the performance of process (5) with that of a centralized scheme for different values of $q$, it suffices to study the behavior of $\theta$, the expected distance left to go, as $q$ changes for a fixed $T$, $1 \leqq T \leqq 1/C$. For as we shall see $\theta$ determines the expected "penalty" suffered in the period between successive environments due to the imperfect information of the decentralized process (5). More precisely, this is the penalty due to computing for $T$ iterations and then taking the nonoptimal action $a(T, \mu, 0)$ for the rest of the period rather than operating a centralized process for just the iterations required to collect all $\mu_i$'s and to compute and disseminate the optimal action $\hat{a}(\mu)$ which is thereupon in force for the rest of the period.

Now for each $q$ in the interval $-1/(n-1) < q < 1$, there is a different upper bound for the values of $h$ which yield convergence. Since $1+(n-1)q$ is the largest root of $Q$ the convergence requirement (14) becomes[20]

$$0 < h < 1/[1+(n-1)q]. \tag{16}$$

One can easily verify

PROPOSITION 5. *For each $q$, the higher the value of $h$ satisfying* (16) *the higher the value of the payoff $W[a(T, \mu, 0), \mu]$ achieved at the terminal iteration $T$.*

We shall therefore examine the variation with respect to $q$ of the expected distance left to go when for each $q$, $h$ is chosen to be arbitrarily close to the upper bound which must not be exceeded if convergence is to be preserved. We examine the expected distance left to go, that is to say, for $h = 1/[1+(n-1)q] - \varepsilon(q)$, where $\varepsilon(q)$ is arbitrarily small.

---

[20] It may be noted that one could consider varying $n$ (the size of the organization) under the assumption that increasing $n$ by one increases the dimension of $\mu$ by one and increases by one the order of $Q$. Then the larger the organization the smaller must be $h$, if convergence is to be preserved, and hence the smaller the value of W attained at any iteration $T$.

Suppose, however, that we establish that over the $q$'s lying in some closed interval the function $\theta(n, q, 1/[1+(n-1)\,q], T)$ has a derivative of a certain sign with respect to $q$. Then the continuity with respect to $q$ and $h$ of $\theta$ and its partial derivatives also imply that there exists an $\varepsilon^*>0$ such that for each positive $\varepsilon<\varepsilon^*$, the partial derivative of $\theta(n, q, 1/[1+(n-1)\,q]-\varepsilon, T)$ with respect to $q$ has the same sign over the same interval. Accordingly it suffices for our purposes to investigate the derivative of $\bar{\theta}(n, q, T)\equiv\theta(n, q, 1/[1+(n-1)\,q], T)$ with respect to $q$ on the interval $-1/(n-1)\leqq q<1$.

In particular,

$$\bar{\theta}(2, q, T)=\frac{(3q-1)/(1+q)^{2T}}{1-q}+1/(1+q).$$

Its derivative with respect to $q$ can be written

$$\frac{1}{(1+q)^2}\left\{\left(\frac{3q-1}{1+q}\right)^{2T-1}\frac{1}{(1-q)^2}\,[8T(1-q)+(3q-1)(1+q)]-1\right\}. \tag{17}$$

This increases without limit as $q$ goes to one but is negative for $-1/3\leqq q\leqq 1/3$. Moreover,

$$\frac{\partial^2\theta(2, q, T)}{\partial q^2}=\frac{1}{(1+q)^2}\left[\frac{\mathrm{d}\varphi}{\mathrm{d}q}-\frac{2\varphi(q)}{1+q}\right],$$

where $\varphi(q)$ denotes the term in braces in (17) and

$$\frac{\mathrm{d}\varphi}{\mathrm{d}q}-\frac{2\varphi(q)}{1+q}=\left(\frac{3q-1}{1+q}\right)^{2T-1}\left[\frac{6q+2}{(1-q)^2}+\frac{2(1+q)(3q-1)}{(1-q)^3}+\frac{8T}{(1-q)^2}\right]$$
$$+\left(\frac{3q-1}{1+q}\right)^{2T-2}\left[\frac{8T(1-q)+(3q-1)(1+q)}{(1-q)^2(1+q)^2}\right](8T-6q-2)+\frac{2}{1+q},$$

which is positive for $1/3\leqq q<1$. It follows that there is some value of $q$, say $q_T$, which depends on $T$ $(T\geqq 1)$ and satisfies $1/3<q_T<1$, such that

$$\frac{\partial\bar{\theta}(2, q, T)}{\partial q}\begin{Bmatrix}<\\=\\>\end{Bmatrix}0 \text{ for } q\begin{Bmatrix}<\\=\\>\end{Bmatrix}q_T.$$

We can, moreover, say something about the relation between $q_T$ and $T$. To do so, let $T$ take, for the moment, all positive real values (not merely integers) in the interval $1\leqq T\leqq 1/C$. Observe that $\partial\bar{\theta}(2, q, T)/\partial q=0$ when

$\varphi(2, q, T)=0$ and that

$$\frac{\partial \varphi}{\partial T}=\frac{1}{(1+q)^2}\left\{8\left(\frac{3q-1}{1+q}\right)^{2T-1}(1-q)\right.$$

$$\left.+2[8T(1-q)+(3q-1)(1+q)]\left[\log\left(\frac{3q-1}{1+q}\right)\right]\left(\frac{3q-1}{1+q}\right)^{2T-1}\right\}$$

$$+2\left(\frac{3q-1}{1+q}\right)^{2T-1}\left\{4(1-q)+[8T(1-q)+(3q-1)(1+q)]\log\left(\frac{3q-1}{1+q}\right)\right\},$$

which is negative for $q>1/3$. Thus $\varphi(2, q, T)$ rises for $\frac{1}{3}\leqq q<1$ and $T$ fixed, is zero for $q_T$, and shifts down when the fixed value $T$ is replaced by the fixed value $T+\delta$, $\delta>0$. It follows that $q_{T+\delta}>q_T$, since $\varphi(2, q_{T+\delta}, T)>\varphi(2, q_{T+\delta}, T+\delta)=0$.

Let us summarize, extending the results to the case of any $n$. We have

PROPOSITION 6. *Let $Q$ be the identical-interaction matrix and let the decentralized process (5) be operated for $T\geqq 1$ iterations while $h$ is kept within ε of the upper bound which must not be exceeded if the process is to converge. Then for ε sufficiently small, the expected distance left to go bears the following relation to the strength, $q$, of the interaction between members of the team: as $q$ rises above $-1(/n-1)$ the expected distance left to go goes down but starts to rise at $q_T$, a value of $q$ lying between $-1/(n-1)$ and one; as $q$ approaches one the expected distance left to go increases without limit. The value $q_T$ is an increasing funciion of $T$.*

What happens in the interval $-1/(n-1)\leqq q<q_T$ might quite possibly be intuitively surprising. For one might intuitively feel that as $|q|$ increases the value of complete information must rise: since, roughly speaking, the impact of each member's action on the desirability of others' actions rises, the importance of knowing $\mu_i$'s other than one's own rises and the expected distance by which the decentralized payoff $W[a(T, \mu, 0), \mu]$ falls short of the full-information payoff $W[\hat{a}(\mu)]$ ought to rise. This is in fact the case at $T=0$, for then the expected distance left to go is $EW-EW[\hat{a}(\mu)]=\frac{1}{4}\sum_{i=1}^{n}\bar{q}_{ii}=[n+qn(n-2)]/4[1-(n-1)q^2+(n-2)q]$, which increases without limit as $q$ approaches one. (The case $T=0$ corresponds to a degenerate kind of decentralization in which no iterations are performed but only the best constant action, namely $a_0=0$, remains perpetually in force.) But in fact it is easily seen that for $T\geqq 1$ the expected "distance traveled," i.e., $EW[a(T, \mu, C), \mu]$, also increases without limit as $q$ approaches one: the

distance traveled depends on the steepness of the slopes $\partial W[a(t, \mu, 0), \mu]/\partial a_i$ at the iterations $t \leqq T$. For the interval $-1/(n-1) < q < q_T$, increasing $q$ increases the expected distance traveled by more than it increases $E\hat{W}$; for the interval $q_T < q < 1$ the reverse is true.

Translation of the above results about expected distance left to go into results about the performance of the process (5) as compared to a centralized process are not quite so straightforward as might be expected. Suppose that the information-handling equipment used to operate the centralized process is such that the process attains the optimal action $\hat{a}(\mu)$ in $\bar{C}$ time units, $\bar{C} < 1$. Let Arrangement $A$ be used in the centralized process, so that the interim action – in force until $\hat{a}(\mu)$ has been computed and its respective components made known to the appropriate members – is the best constant interim action, namely $\tilde{a} = 0$. Then, if the cost of the given equipment is ignored, the centralized process is preferred to the decentralized process if $E[(1-\bar{C})\, W] > E\{(1-CT)\, \hat{W}[a(T, \mu, 0), \mu]\}$. Now the translation of the previous result, which involves the derivative of $E\{\hat{W} - W[a(T, \mu, 0), \mu]\}$ with respect to $q$, can be stated as

PROPOSITION 7. *As $q$ rises in the interval $-1/(n-1) < q < q_T$, the superiority of the centralized process, i.e., the difference $E[(1-\bar{C})\, \hat{W}] - E\{(1-CT)\, W[a(T, \mu, 0), \mu]\}$, rises if $C > CT$; otherwise it may fall. In the interval $q_T < q < 1$ the superiority of the centralized process falls if $\bar{C} > CT$; otherwise it may rise.*

If the cost of the information-handling equipment is to be taken into account, then the relation of the centralization-decentralization comparison to the original result about expected distance left to go is even more remote-though it is less so if cost can simply be substracted from the "gross" payoffs $(1-CT)W[a(T, \mu, 0), \mu]$ and $(1-\bar{C})W$ to obtain the relevant "net" payoffs.[21]

In any case, the example has shown the extreme caution with which one has to view intuitively appealing statements such as "the stronger are interactions (externalities), the stronger the case for centralization."

Similar caution is warranted in viewing another appealing statement which can again be tested with respect to the process (5) under Arrangement $A$. This is the statement that if we drop the part of Assumption 2 which states $E\mu_i\mu_j = 0$, $i \neq j$, then the stronger is the correlation between any two environment components the less the advantage of centralization or full information, since (roughly speaking) the more member $i$'s own environment

---

[21] As discussed in 4.7 below.

component tells him about member $j$'s the less the penalty due to not knowing $j$'s component. To test this conjecture in the present context we assume that $\mu_i$ have constant variance-covariance matrix with ones on the diagonal and all off-diagonal elements equal to $\sigma$, where $-1/(n-1)<\sigma<1$, to insure positive definiteness.

For the case $n=2$, with the same identical-interaction matrix $Q$ as before, we find that the expected distance left to go for fixed $h$ is

$$E\hat{W}-EW[a(T,\mu,0),\mu]=\tfrac{1}{4}E\mu' H_T\mu$$
$$=\frac{(1+\sigma)[1-2h(1+q)]^{2T}}{1+q}+\frac{(1-\sigma)[1-2h(1-q)]^{2T}}{1-q}.$$

Proceeding as before, we set $h=1/1+q$ and the preceding expression becomes

$$\frac{1+\sigma}{1+q}+\frac{(1-\sigma)[(3q-1)/(1+q)]^{2T}}{1-q}.$$

The derivative of this expression with respect to $\sigma$ at positive values of $\sigma$ is constant; for $T\geqq 1$ it vanishes for $q=0$ and is positive for $q_T^*\leqq q<1$, where $q_T^*$ depends on $T$. In the interval $-1<q<q_T^*$ the derivative may change signs a number of times. For $T=0$, on the other hand, the expected distance left to go decreases as $\sigma$ increases above zero for all $q$ in the interval $-1<q<1$. So again the intuitive conjecture is correct if no iterations are carried out and one has instead the degenerate decentralization of a perpetually unchanged action; it is not correct when one or more iterations are performed. Summarizing for any $n$, we have

PROPOSITION 8. *If the correlation between any pair of environment components is the same, $h$ is chosen as in Proposition 6, and $T\geqq 1$, then in the identical-interaction case increasing the correlation above zero increases the expected distance left to go if $q_T^*\leqq q<1$; $q_T^*$ satisfies $-1/(n-1)<q^*<1$ and depends on $T$.*

## 4.2. ARRANGEMENT B: CONSTANT INTERIM ACTION, CONSTANT INITIAL VALUE, BEST CURRENT TERMINAL ITERATION

Suppose next that the organization uses a less routine arrangement: following each new environment it carries out the adjustment process (starting from a constant initial value) for a number of iterations that is some function of $\mu$, maintaining a constant interim action $\tilde{a}$ in the meantime. Of particular interest is the function of $\mu$ that yields the *best current terminal iteration* for that $\mu$, that is, since we can continue to ignore discounting, the iteration $T$ that maximizes $W(a, \mu)CT + W[\tilde{a}(T, \mu, a_0), \mu](1-CT)$. This iteration depends, in general, on $\tilde{a}$ and $a_0$ as well as $\mu$.

The argument leading to Proposition 1 is again relevant here. We have that if $\Delta^2 W_t < 0$ on an interval contained in the interval $0 \leqq T \leqq 1/C$, then there is a $T$ that uniquely maximizes $W(\tilde{a}, \mu)CT + W[a(T, \mu, a_0), \mu](1-CT)$ on that interval. This means that for any adjustment process (2) (with strict concavity of $W$) there is, in particular, for each $\mu$ a unique best current terminal iteration among all the iterations that occur prior to overshooting. For the quadratic case there is a unique best current terminal iteration on the entire interval $0 < T < 1/C$.

A natural interpretation[22] of each of these unique best current terminal iterations is as follows: it is that iteration within the appropriate interval at which the *marginal cost* of an additional iteration first exceeds the *marginal gain* of an additional iteration; or, if no such iteration exists in the interval, it is the latest iteration in the interval. The marginal cost of an additional iteration, when $t$ have already been performed, is $C\{W[a(t, \mu, a_0), \mu] - W(\tilde{a}, \mu)\}$, i.e., the payoff foregone by prolonging the interim payoff $W(\tilde{a}, \mu)$ for the time it takes to perform one more iteration. The marginal gain from an additional iteration is $\{W[a(t+1, \mu, a_0), \mu] - W[a(t, \mu, a_0), \mu]\}[1 - C(t+1)]$, the increase in the total payoff enjoyed after the terminal iteration due to postponing the terminal iteration one more time. The condition that the marginal gain exactly equal the marginal cost (a condition not in general met for any integer) is seen to be equivalent to the condition that the first difference of $W(a, \mu) + W[a(t, \mu, a_0), \mu]$ with respect to $t$ be exactly zero.

To apply the marginal-gain-marginal-cost rule in deciding when to stop iterating, the organization must approximate the marginal gain at each iteration $t$ by the preceding marginal gain, since it cannot, at iteration $t$, know the term $W[a(t+1, \mu, a_0), \mu]$ without performing the next iteration. More serious is the fact that to compute the values of $W[a(t, \mu, a_0), \mu]$ and $W(a, \mu)$ requires all of the components of $\mu_i$ of $\mu$. If the process is of the form (4), it is difficult to see how the best current terminal iteration can be selected without depriving the process of decentralization, presumably its main virtue.

If the best current terminal iteration is used (and a constant initial value and interim action) the performance of the process is measured by

$$\pi_3(C) \equiv E \max_{0<T<1/C} \{W(\tilde{a}, \mu)\, CT + W[a(T, \mu, a_0), \mu](1-CT)\}.$$

[22] An analogous interpretation of the best terminal iteration is given by MARGLIN (1963).

We observe that $\mathrm{d}\pi_3/\mathrm{d}C$ is certainly negative, as long as $EW(\tilde{a}, \mu) < EW[a(T, \mu, a_0), \mu]$ for the best current $T$, but that it differs from $\partial\pi_1(T, C)/\partial C$ and from $\mathrm{d}\pi_2/\mathrm{d}C$.

### 4.3. Arrangement C: Constant Terminal Iteration, Constant Initial Value, Interim Action Equal to Preceding Action

In the last two arrangements considered, the organization, following a new environment $\mu$, has to change its action *twice*: once from the previous action to the constant interim action and again from the interim action to the action obtained at the termination of the adjustment process, which is initiated in response to $\mu$. We now consider an arrangement which requires only one change of action and may therefore be useful to organizations whose changes of action must be kept infrequent. The arrangement is also worth studying because it may be a very desirable one once we drop the assumption that successive environments are independently distributed. In this arrangement, the preceding action is continued, after the new environment $\mu$ is observed, until the new action has been generated; the new action is generated by operating the decision process until iteration $T$ ($T$ a constant), starting always at the same initial value $a_0$. (If $T$ is the largest integer not exceeding $1/C$, then there is one action in force throughout each period, namely an action computed in the preceding period.)

The expected total payoff between successive environments again measures performance and is

$$\pi_4(C, T) \equiv \underset{\mu^*, \mu}{E} \{W[a(T, \mu^*, a_0), \mu]\, CT + W[a(T, \mu, a_0), \mu](1 - CT)\},$$

where the expectation is taken over all pairs $\mu^*$, $\mu$. We can immediately note

Proposition 9. *For any adjustment process, the expected payoff under Arrangement C never exceeds the expected payoff under Arrangement A when Arrangement A uses the best constant interim action $\tilde{a}$, both arrangements use the same initial value, and either both arrangements use the same terminal iteration or else each uses the terminal iteration best for it.*

To see this observe that the preceding environment $\mu$ and the action $a(T, \mu^*, a_0)$ is, for a fixed adjustment process, a random variable distributed independently of $\mu$. Therefore, to use the preceding action as the interim action that follows $\mu$ is, in effect, to use a *randomized* interim action following each new environment $\mu$. But consider the general question of choosing an action (out of some set of actions) so as to maximize the expected value of a function of the action and an unknown state of nature. It is well known that if the probability distribution of the possible states of nature is known, and if there exists an action in the set for which the expected value of the function is not less than for any other action in the set, then the expected value of the function cannot be further increased by randomizing over the set of actions. Hence for fixed $T$ and $a_0$ the expected payoff $\pi_1(C, T)$ cannot be improved by substituting for the best constant interim action $\tilde{a}$ a randomized action – in particular, the randomized action obtained from the preceding period.

If the interim action is the preceding action, and if a fixed $T$ and $a_0$ are used, it is *not* true for all adjustment processes, or even for all the processes (2) (with $W$ strictly concave in $a$), that reducing $C$ increases the expected total payoff between successive environments. For it cannot be ruled out that for the chosen $T$ and $a_0$

$$\underset{\mu^*, \mu}{E}\; W[a(T, \mu^*, a_0), \mu] > EW[a(T, \mu, a_0), \mu], \tag{18}$$

i.e., that a $T$ has been picked which yields actions that are, on the average, worse for the environment that initiated the process than for environments drawn at random. If (18) holds, then $\partial\pi_4(C, T)/\partial C > 0$ for $0 \leqq C \leqq 1$. If (18) is false for a given process, however, then $\partial\pi_4(C, T)/\partial C < 0$ and this is true even if the payoff path $W[a(t, \mu, a_0), \mu]$ fluctuates as $t$ increases (i.e., decreases at some iterations and increases at others). For the quadratic gradient-method case, (18) is false.

Finally, we observe that the preceding argument also implies (as noted at the end of Proposition 9) that

$$\pi_5(C) \leqq \pi_2(C) \text{ for all } C, \qquad 0 < C < 1,$$

where $\pi_5(C) \equiv \max_{0 \leqq T \leqq 1/C} \pi_4(C, T)$. If (18) is assumed false for every $T$, $0 \leqq T \leqq 1/C$, then $\mathrm{d}\pi_5/\mathrm{d}C < 0$. In any case $\pi_5(C)$ has a very different shape, in general, than the other functions $\pi_i$, $i = 1, \ldots, 4$.

### 4.4. Arrangement D: Constant Terminal Iteration, Interim Action Equal to Preceding Action, Initial Value Equal to Preceding Action

We briefly consider this arrangement, chiefly because of a distinctive property: discounting can no longer be ignored in measuring the performance of a process. In addition there may be an organizational advantage in the fact that each participant's interim action serves also as his initial tentative action in the adjustment process.

Let $\mu^j$ denote the $j$th of a sequence of successive environments. For a fixed terminal iteration $T$ the total payoff in the interval between the environment $\mu^j$ and the next environment is

$$\pi^j(C, T) = W(a^{j-1}, \mu^j)\, CT + W(a^j, \mu^j)(1-CT),$$

where $a^j$ denotes the action generated by the decision process in response to the environment $\mu^j$, $a^j = a(T, \mu^j, a^{j-1})$, $j = 1,2, \ldots$, and $a^0$ is given. Thus the total payoff between two successive environments is recursively defined. For a given initial environment $\mu^1$, a stochastic process (easily seen to be Markov) generates the sequence of observed total payoffs. The performance of the process under Arrangement $D$ is measured by

$$\pi_6(C, T) \equiv E \sum_{j=1}^{\infty} \rho^{j-1} \pi^j(C, T),$$

where $\rho$ is the discount factor.

An analogous statement to that made in the previous section, about the superiority of a best constant interim action, applies here. An interim action $a^{j-1}$ is taken and the interim payoff $W(a^{j-1}, \mu^j)\, CT$ depends on $\mu^j$, which is unknown when the organization commits itself to the interim action $a^{j-1}$, although its probability distribution is known. The interim action $a^{j-1}$ is a randomized action althought its distribution is far more complicated than the distribution of the randomized interim action considered above. It follows that if $\tilde{a}$ is the best constant interim action, then $\pi^j(C, T)$ is not greater than

$$\tilde{\pi}^j(C, T) \equiv W(\tilde{a}, \mu^j)\, CT + W\{a(T, \mu^j, a^{j-1}), \mu^j\}(1-CT),$$

that

$$\tilde{\pi}_6(C, T) \leqq \pi_7(C, T) \equiv E \sum_{j=1}^{\infty} \rho^j \pi^j(C, T)$$

and also that

$$\pi_8(C) \equiv \max_{0 \leqq T \leqq 1/C} \pi_6(C, T) \leqq \pi_9(C) \equiv \max_{0 \leqq T \leqq 1/C} \pi_7(C, T).$$

## 4.5. Arrangement E: Constant Terminal Iteration, Best Current Local Interim Action, Constant Initial Value

An interesting arrangement, but one that is less routine with respect to interim action than any of the preceding ones, is as follows. After each new environment $\mu$, each participant $i$ takes an interim action which is a function $\alpha_i$ of $\mu_i$, the component of the environment that he observes, but not of any other $\mu_j$, $j \neq i$. Thus the interim actions are decentralized (or "local"), preserving the distinctive virtue of such processes as (5), while yet making some use of the organization's knowledge of the new environment. The chosen functions $\alpha_i$ are to yield a higher expected interim payoff than any other functions $\bar{\alpha}_i(\mu_i)$. If the initial value is kept constant we have

$$\pi_{10}(C, T) \equiv EW\{[\alpha_1(\mu_1), \dots, \alpha_n(\mu_n)], \mu\}\, CT + EW[a(T, \mu, a_0), \mu](1-CT)$$

where

$$EW\{[\alpha_1(\mu_1), \dots, \alpha_n(\mu_n)], \mu\} = \max_{\alpha_1, \dots, \alpha_n} EW\{[\bar{\alpha}_1(\mu_1), \dots, \bar{\alpha}_n(\mu_n)], \mu\}\,.$$

It has been shown by R. Radner (1961) that for the quadratic case, under the assumption of zero correlation between the components of $\mu$,

$$\bar{\alpha}_i(\mu_i) = \mu_i/2q_{ii}\,, \qquad i = 1, \dots, n\,.$$

For the quadratic case, then, we have, under Assumption 2

$$\pi_{10}(C, T) = \tfrac{1}{4}\left(\sum_{i=1}^{n} 1/q_{ii}\right) CT + \tfrac{1}{4}\sum_{i=1}^{n} (q_{ii} - h_{T_{ii}})(1-CT)\,.$$

We observe that $\pi_{10}(C, T) \geqq \pi_1(C, T)$ and that $\partial\pi_{10}/\partial C$ is again negative as long as the expected payoff for the interim action is less than expected payoff for the action generated by the adjustment process at iteration $T$.

### 4.6. Arrangement F: Constant Terminal Iteration, Best Constant Interim Action, Locally Best Current Initial Value

In this arrangement, and in others for which the initial value is chosen in the same manner, the situation may be drastically changed. The initial values is now a *variable* initial value; after each change of environment each member $i$ chooses his initial action afresh as a function of the new $\mu_i$. This means that if a process is defined by a function $f$ in the first-order difference-equation system (1), then using Arrangement $F$ formally requires an addition to the process. The additional step, which precedes the process defined by $f$, is the formulation of the initial actions, each of which has then to be sent to every member who needs it in order to compute his component of $a(1)$. If the process defined by $f$ is temporally homogeneous – as are the price mechanisms that have been proposed – then the augmented process loses temporal homogeneity, unless one formally preserves it by adding some artificial "dummy" actions not effectively entering the payoff function. Unless one does this the operations which each member performs on his current information to obtain his next tentative action are no longer the same prior to every iteration: the operations performed prior to the first iteration are different from the operations after the $t$th and prior to the

$(t+1)$st, $t \geqq 1$. This is not the case when $a_0$ is a constant, as in the previous arrangements.

The sacrifice of temporal homogeneity, or its artificial preservation through dummy variables, would deprive the process of the "decentralized" label given in our definition; it may also be undesirable from the point of view of routineness or for the study of processes most resembling price mechanisms. If one is willing to make the sacrifice, however, then Arrangement $F$ offers a striking possibility: it may become possible to achieve the optimum action $\hat{a}(\mu)$ after a *finite* and perhaps quite small number of iterations while still preserving the main property of decentralization-avoiding the direct transmission of the $\mu_i$. This is the case for the quadratic payoff function and the process (5), at least for certain matrices $Q$. If it is not possible to achieve optimality at a finite iteration in this fashion, it is at least possible (except for every special distributions of $\mu$) to achieve a higher expected value of $W$ at each $T$ than is permitted by a fixed initial value.

Arrangement $F$ requires that we find functions $a_0^{iT}(\mu_i)$ which maximize $EW\{a[T, \mu, a_0^T(\mu)], \mu\}$, where $a_0^T(\mu)$ is the vector $[a_0^{1T}(\mu_1), \ldots, a_0^{nT}(\mu_n)]$. The superscript $T$ indicates that the optimal values for generating the best initial actions generally depend on the terminal iteration $T$. When $W\{a[T, \mu, a_0^T(\mu)], \mu\}$, viewed as a function of $a_0^T(\mu)$ has convenient properties (principally strict concavity) a theorem of R. Radner[23] can be used to determine the required functions $a^{iT}(\mu)$.

In the quadratic case, we see from (12) that the problem may be put: find the vector of functions $a_0^{iT}(\mu)$ maximizing

$$EG_T = E\{\lambda_T' [a_0^T(\mu)] - [a_0^T(\mu)]' S_T [a_0^T(\mu)]\}$$

where $S_T$ is the symmetric positive definite matrix $(I-2hQ)^T Q(I-2hQ)^T$ and $\lambda_T$ is the vector $SQ^{-1}\mu$. Thus $G_T$ has exactly the same form as the function $\mu'[\tilde{a}(\mu)]-[\tilde{a}(\mu)]Q'[\tilde{a}(\mu)]$, the maximization of whose expected value with respect to the functions $\tilde{a}(\mu)$, using the theorem of Radner, yields the best local interim actions of Arrangement $E$. Applying the theorem here,[24] one obtains, under Assumption 2 (zero correlation),[25] that the optimal functions $a_0^{iT}(\mu_i)$ are

$$\hat{a}_0^{iT}(\mu_i) = \frac{\mu_i [i\text{th diagonal element of } (I-2hQ)^T Q(I-2hQ)^T Q^{-1}]}{2[i\text{th diagonal element of } (I-2BQ)^T Q(I-2hQ)^T]} \equiv \bar{a}_0^{iT} \mu_i .$$

[23] The "person-by-person optimality" theorem. See Chapter 10.

[24] For the procedure, see RADNER (1961).

[25] For the case of nonzero correlation among the $\mu_i$ adoption of Radner's procedure is also straightforward.

Using the functions $\hat{a}_0^{iT}(\mu_i)$, the team travels, in $T$ iterations, a greater expected distance toward the optimal payoff $\hat{W}$ than is true for any other rules for determining fresh initial values.

We next ask: For what matrices $Q$ can we find an $h$ such that

$$EW\{a[1, \mu, (\bar{a}_0^T)' \mu], \mu\} = E\,\hat{W}(\mu), \tag{19}$$

so that optimality is achieved in a single iteration?[26] Since for each $\mu$ there is a unique maximizing action $\hat{a}(\mu)$, this condition is met for all distributions satisfying Assumption 2 if and only if $a[1, \mu, (\bar{a}_0^1)'\mu] = \hat{a}(\mu)$ for each $\mu$, i.e., if and only if for every $\mu$

$$\tfrac{1}{2}[I-(I-2hQ)]\,Q^{-1}\mu+(I-2hQ)\,A\mu = \tfrac{1}{2}Q^{-1}\mu$$

or

$$[(I-2hQ)(A-\tfrac{1}{2}Q^{-1})]\,\mu = 0, \tag{20}$$

where $A$ is the diagonal matrix with $i$th diagonal element equal to $\bar{a}_0^1$. This in turn implies that the matrix in brackets equals zero.[27]

Now consider again the equal-interaction matrix $Q$ with ones on the diagonal and $q$'s off the diagonal. After some calculation one finds that (20) is solved (for any $n$) by $h=1/2(1-q)$, for which $\hat{a}_0^{1i} = (1-q)/2[I-(n-1)q^2+(n-2)q]$. In a formal sense the augmented process fulfills both conditions of our decentralization definition (which we restricted, however, to temporally homogeneous processes) and yet for the $h$ just found optimality is achieved after a single iteration (subsequent iterations would merely repeat the same tentative actions). Note that the convergence property has been sacrified, since for $q>1/3$, $h=1/[2(1-q)]$ violates the convergence requirement (14). For this $h$, in other words, there is no longer convergence to the maximizing action for *any* fixed initial value and any $\mu$, which as we saw, is a useful property for some arrangements when a best terminal iteration is to be chosen. But since the initial value is now to be chosen afresh for each $\mu$ the sacrifice is of no consequence.

Just as in Section 4.1, the identical-interaction matrix—a weak case from the point of view of the advantages of process (5) over a centralized process—provides here the most easily obtained illustration of a general point. The point is that optimal local choice of initial value following each environment may considerably improve the performance of a decentralized

---

[26] The vector $(\bar{a}_0^{1T}, \ldots, \bar{a}_0^{nT})$ is denoted $\bar{a}_0^T$.

[27] For specially chosen distributions – e.g., those assigning zero probability to the set of $\mu$'s not on the hyperplane defined by (20) – a weaker condition on $Q$ insures an $h$ satisfying (19).

process. In the case of a gradient-method process, combining such choice of initial value with choice of $h$ (or more generally choice of a vector $(h_1, \ldots, h_n)$, where $h_i$ describes the $i$th member's adjustment at each iteration) provides still further improvement, sometimes permitting optimality at a finite $T$. The condition (20) for optimality at $T=1$ in the quadratic case is satisfied when the interactions display sufficient "similarity" so that $(I-2hQ)(A-\frac{1}{2}Q^{-1})=0$ for some $h$. It seems worthwhile to explore whether or not this is a special case of some more general proposition according to which greater "similarity" of interactions (a property of the payoff function) implies better performance of decentralized processes when one is free to adjust their initial values.

Needless to say, for Arrangement $F$ the increment in the performance of a process as $C$ decreases—the increment in

$$\pi_{11}(C, T) = EW(\tilde{a}, \mu)\, CT + EW\{a[T, \mu, \hat{a}_0^T(\mu)], \mu\}\,(1-CT)$$

as $C$ decreases—is different than for other arrangements (it is greater, in particular, than for Arrangements $A$ and $E$).

### 4.7. Other Possible Arrangements

We have considered arrangements in which the interim action is a constant (arbitrary or best), equals the preceding action, or is the best current local interim action; in which the terminal iteration is a constant (arbitrary or best), or is the best current terminal iteration; in which the initial value is a constant (arbitrary or best), equals the preceding action, or is composed of the best functions of the current local environment. We have by no means examined, even for the quadratic case, all possible combinations of these categories. And other categories, as well as expanded definitions of "arrangement," can be studied. If one expands the definition of arrangement too much, however, one risks leaving the manageable study of a restricted class of processes with each of which any of the possible arrangements can be used; one risks enlarging the inquiry toward the very general problem sketched at the start.[28]

Each arrangement considered, and others, may be of serious interest to

[28] The risk is run, for example, if one adds to the elements defining an arrangement a "terminal operation," to follow the terminal iteration, in which each member uses *all* the information he has acquired through the process thus far in order to choose that new action which is best given that information.

the organization contemplating a proposed adjustment process. For though some arrangements are better than others with respect to the appropriate function $\pi_j$, each has a generally advantageous property: routineness, preserving complete decentralization (as Arrangement $B$ does not), permitting the interim action to become also the initial value, and so on. The exact measurement of these advantages for each arrangement (e.g., the "costs" of changing actions once or twice), and the balancing of these advantages against the appropriate $\pi_j$, would take us into still less explored areas in the study of organizations. Short of such measurement, the comparison of two proposed processes will have to be made for several different arrangements. For any arrangement considered, moreover, a "technology-free" statement of comparison can be made, in which the missing knowledge of the communication and computation technology is precise and perhaps obtainable. We shall briefly illustrate.

## 4.8. Technology-free Comparison of a Decentralized and a Centralized Adjustment Process

Suppose a team with a quadratic payoff function contemplates the process (5) but also contemplates the centralized alternative which we briefly considered in 4.1. If one wished one could formally put the centralized alternative as a temporally homogeneous first-order adjustment process $a(t) = f[a(t-1), \mu]$ in which a central member has an action vector that does not effectively enter the payoff function and other members have action vectors some of whose components do not. The process reaches equilibrium after a small number of iterations, when an optimal action has been attained. In the case of two members (members 1 and 2) plus a central member (member 3) the process might be put, for example, as follows:

$$a_1 = (a_1', a_1''), \qquad a_2 = (a_2', a_2''),$$

$$a_3 = (a_3', a_3'', a_3''', a_3''''),$$

$$W(a_1, a_2, a_3, \mu) = \mu_1 a_1' + \mu_2 a_2' - 2q_{12} a_1' a_2' - q_{11} a_1'^2 - q_{22} a_2'^2$$

$$a_1(t) = f^1 [a_1(t-1), a_2(t-1), a_3(t-1), \mu_1]$$

$$= \begin{cases} (\mu_1, \mu_1) \text{ if } a_3'(t-1) \neq \mu_1 \\ [a_3''(t-1), \mu_1] \text{ if } a_3'(t-1) = \mu_1 \end{cases}$$

$$a_2(t) = f^2[a_1(t-1), a_2(t-1), a_3(t-1), \mu_2]$$
$$= \begin{cases} (\mu_2, \mu_2) \text{ if } a_3'''(t-1) \neq \mu_2 \\ [a_3''''(t-1), \mu_2] \text{ if } a_3'''(t-1) = \mu_2 \end{cases}$$
$$a_3(t) = f^3[a_1(t-1), a_2(t-1), a_3(t-1)]$$
$$= \begin{cases} a_3(t-1) \text{ if } a_1'(t-1) \neq a_1''(t-1) \\ \{a_1'(t-1), \hat{a}_1[a_1'(t-1), a_2'(t-1)], a_2'(t-1), \\ \quad \hat{a}_2[a_1'(t-1), a_2'(t-1)]\} \text{ if } a_1'(t-1) = a_1''(t-1). \end{cases}$$

The process starts with any fixed initial action $(a_{01}, a_{02}, a_{03})$ for which $a'_{0_1} \neq a''_{0_1}$, $a'_{0_2} \neq a''_{0_2}$, $(a'_{0_3}, a'''_{0_3}) \notin M$. Members 1 and 2 merely repeat their environment components twice at iteration 1 while member 3 simply "marks time." Member 3, observing the others' repeated actions, knows it is time to compute the optimal actions and does so, at iteration 2. Members 1 and 2 then observe, respectively, that member 3's first and third action components are now equal to $\mu_1$ and to $\mu_2$ (initially they are not, since they then lie outside $M$, the set of possible $\mu$'s). This is the signal that member 3's second and fourth components are the required optimal values. At iteration 4 equilibrium has been reached; from then on members 1 and 2 repeat their optimal actions (as first components of their action vectors), while member 3 also repeats his action.

Note that the process satisfies condition (ii) of our decentralization definition; if we did not also require condition (i) it would be a decentralized process.

Now let $\bar{C}$ $(0<\bar{C}<1)$ be the time required to complete the iteration at which the optimal actions are in the possession of the appropriate members. If the organization uses such a centralized process it has no effective choice with respect to terminal iteration or initial value, but it does confront choices with respect to interim action, namely *all the choices it confronts if it uses a decentralized process*. Thus suppose the organization plans to use, for both of the contemplated processes, the best current local interim action. For the decentralized process it also plans to use the best constant initial value and the best constant terminal iteration. It must then compare $\pi_{10}(C)$ with

$$\pi(\bar{C}) = \tfrac{1}{4}\left(\sum_{i=1}^{n} 1/q_{ii}\right)\bar{C} + \tfrac{1}{4}\sum_{i=1}^{n} \bar{q}_{ii}(1-\bar{C}),$$

where $(\bar{q}_{ij}) = Q^{-1}$.

Assume now that if the costs of achieving the completion times $C$ and $\bar{C}$ are measured in the proper units and denoted $\varphi(C)$, $\bar{\varphi}(\bar{C})$, then $\pi(\bar{C})-\bar{\varphi}(\bar{C})$, $\pi_{10}(C)-\varphi(C)$ give the organization's expected total "net" payoff between successive environments for the two processes; the quantity $W(a, \mu)$ may now be called "gross" payoff. This is the additivity assumption frequently made in decision problems in which the cost of acquiring information has to be taken into account; without it few such problems would be manageable. The assumption states that the organization ranks alternative choices of adjustment process and information-handling equipment according to expected discounted total net payoff; the additivity assumption is therefore a restriction on the organization's preferences among gambles whose outcomes are gross payoff-completion time-equipment cost combinations.

The organization can proceed to find *conditions on the functions* $\varphi$ and $\bar{\varphi}$ under which the decentralized process yields a higher net payoff than the centralized process. *The statement of these conditions is the required technology-free comparison.* The communication and computation expert can then (in principle) be consulted to determine whether or not the conditions are met. Different arrangements imply different technology-free comparisons.

Some general remarks are now in order concerning the tacit assumption in much current discussion that decentralization (in the sense of retention by individuals of their observations of the environment) is not a virtue but a *necessity*.

However complex the environmental information, there ought to be some amount of time and money which permit it to be gathered in a central place. If necessary, the "device" which performs the transmission may be the temporary physical displacement of each specialized observer from his normal location to the central place. Perhaps a more questionable, but still plausible assertion is that alternative transmission times can be purchased at alternative costs.

Consider the decentralized price mechanisms currently proposed. In several of these schemes each individual's specialized information about the environment is explicitly assumed to be a vector (or matrix) of functions (e.g., the function $g_{ij}(x_i)$ which gives the amount that participant $i$, in charge of activity $i$, requires of commodity $j$ when he operates his activity at level $x_i$). The vector may be an enormously long one and each function in it may take many parameters to identify. But the messages which *are* transmitted in these schemes are also vectors (price vectors, demand vectors) and are generally transmitted many times during the operation of the process (whereas in a centralized scheme the environment vectors would have to be gathered only once in each operation). The difficulties of transmitting the messages which are transmitted as compared to those which are not should be measurable in a precise fashion for a sufficiently well-specified communication technology.

We can briefly illustrate a simple (and extremely clumsy) technology.[29] Suppose all messages transmitted from participant $i$ to participant $j$ in all repetitions of the process belong to a set $P_{ij}$ of $p_{ij}$-dimensional real vectors (this has been the case in the processes we have considered). Now let a *round-off* rule be specified: each coordinate of a message that the process requires to be transmitted is rounded off so as to achieve always a number composed of $D_{ij}$ decimal digits. Let the transmission line from $i$ to $j$ carry ten distinct signals corresponding to the ten symbols of the decimal system. A message from $i$ to $j$ then requires $p_{ij}D_{ij}$ successive signals. The capacity of the transmission line is the number of signals it can transmit per time unit and this determines the time required to send a message. Capacity is continuously variable. If appropriate assumptions are also made about the computing technology, the assumption of our previous discussion (in the present section and in preceding ones) is satisfied; by suitable choice of capacities the time required for each participant – and hence for the organization – to complete an iteration in the decision process $a(t)=f[a(t-1), \mu]$ can be made equal to a specified number $C$.[30]

The costs of achieving alternative transmission capacities, and corresponding information about computation costs, are the missing pieces when one makes a technology-free comparison of centralized and decentralized processes, if the clumsy but simple technology just described is assumed to

---

[29] I am grateful to C. B. McGuire for useful suggestions on matters of technology.

[30] The transmission technology described is very inefficient. Some messages from $i$ to $j$ will in fact occur more frequently than others (the frequency distribution depends, for a given process, on the distribution of $\mu$). Codings can be used that take advantage of this fact so as to require shorter sequences of signals for the more frequently sent messages. The result is that much lower transmission capacities (than in the technology described) suffice to achieve a given *average* iteration-completion time. For this more efficient technology, all our previous discussion would have to be restated so that the number $C$ becomes a random variable whose expected value is chosen. The possibility of transmission inaccuracy (noise) is a further complication.

We note also that if the technology described above is used, the validity of our previous discussion rests on a tacit assumption: that there exist round-off numbers $D_{ij}$ such that all the properties of adjustment processes that we have found are preserved when the messages specified by the original processes are rounded off to $D_{ij}$ decimal digits for each pair of participants $ij$.

obtain. In the absence of such cost information it is by no means clear that the decentralized schemes that have been proposed dominate the centralized alternatives even for the simple technology just described.

## 5. The Case of Serially Correlated Environments

If the probability distribution of the environment at a given time depends on the preceding environments – if the environment is generated by a (nondegenerate) stochastic process – then the performance of a process is much more difficult to measure. Moreover, the same range of choices of interim action, terminal action, and initial value is now open to the organization as in the case of independent environments.

For certain choices, however, it may be possible to draw some conclusions about the performance of a given decision process for a given payoff function from very incomplete knowledge of the environment's stochastic process. We shall give a very simple illustration.

Suppose the payoff function $W$ has the form (3) and some adjustment process $a(t)=f[a(t-1), \mu]$ is used such that $\Delta W[a(t), \mu, a_0]$, the first difference of payoff with respect to iteration number, is positive for all $\mu$, $a_0$, $t$. Suppose that the environmental stochastic process, generating successive environments $\mu^1, \mu^2, \ldots$ has the following property – the martingale property:

$$E\left[\mu^j/(\mu^{j-1}, \mu^{j-2}, \ldots, \mu^1)\right] = \mu^{j-1}.$$

Let a fixed terminal iteration $T$ be used. We shall establish

PROPOSITION 10. *If successive environments have the martingale property, if the payoff function has the form (3), and if the process used yields a positive first difference for payoff, then it is always worse – in the sense of yielding a lower expected sum of discounted total payoffs $\pi^j$ – to use a constant interim action $\tilde{a}$ and to let the initial value also be $\tilde{a}$ than to use the preceding action as the interim action while again using a as the initial value.*

The proof is as follows. Let $\pi^j$ denote the total (undiscounted) payoff in the interval following $\mu^j$, the *jth* environment, when a constant interim action $\tilde{a}$ is used, and let $\bar{\pi}^j$ denote the total (undiscounted) payoff when the interim action equals the preceding action. The term of $\pi^j$ giving the part of the total payoff experienced after the iteration $T$ is identical with the corresponding term of $\bar{\pi}^j$. It suffices to investigate the interim payoff under the two arrangements. We have, for the interim payoff when the interim action equals the preceding action, the conditional expectation

$$\underset{\mu^j/\mu^{j-1},\ldots,\mu^1}{E} \{(\mu^j)' \, a(T, \mu^{j-1}, \tilde{a}) + S[a(T, \mu^{j-1}, \tilde{a})]\}.$$

By the martingale assumption this equals

$$(\mu^{j-1})' \, a(T, \mu^{j-1}, \tilde{a}) + S[a(T, \mu^{j-1}, \tilde{a})],$$

which is precisely the value of $W(a, \mu^{j-1})$ obtained when the process has been operated for $T$ iterations starting with the initial value $\tilde{a}$, and is therefore strictly greater than $(\mu^j)'\tilde{a} + S(\tilde{a})$ – the initial value of $S(a, \mu^{j-1})$ in the same process. Hence for any $j$ and any $(\mu^1, \ldots, \mu^{j-1})$,

$$E(\pi^j/\mu^{j-1}, \ldots, \mu^1) < E(\bar{\pi}^j/\mu^{j-1}, \ldots, \mu^1),$$

which implies the proposition.

## 6. Concluding Remarks

We shall cut short here our survey of the issues that have to be faced in comparing adjustment processes.

We have argued that studying a general problem of optimal design of teams is unlikely to be fruitful for the comparison of specific adjustment processes such as price mechanisms. A more restricted framework is needed. One such framework is provided by the assumption that computation has to cease before a new environment and that between environments only two actions (the interim action and the freshly computed one) are in force. Comparisons among the members of a restricted class of processes, each of which can be used in a number of arrangements, are then possible.[31] For a fixed process, arrangements may differ radically with respect to performance for a fixed iteration time, with respect to change in performance as iteration time is varied, and with respect to the support that one can give to intuitive

[31] Among the specific comparison problems which are not discussed above but can be studied within the framework is the comparison of the Dantzig-Wolfe process for solving ("decomposing") linear programming problems (1961) and the "non-decomposed" standard simplex process. Consider a team which wants to achieve a good feasible solution to a linear programming problem following each new environment (a new environment defines a new problem). Make Assumptions 1 and 2 and suppose that the team adopts Arrangement A, with an always feasible interim action and initial program. Then the condition for the superiority of the decomposed process over the nondecomposed process could be put as a simple technology-free statement if for the $t$th basis obtained (at iteration

statements about the advantage of decentralization and its relation to "externalities" or "interactions".

For arrangements in which the best terminal iteration (constant or current) is to be chosen the classic property of convergence to payoff-maximizing actions was seen to be a useful property if it implies positive first difference and negative second difference of the payoff for iterations in a relevant interval. The usefulness of other classic properties of recently developed decentralized price mechanisms – temporal homogeneity, informational "privacy," and so on – depends in a complex way on payoff function, arrangement, environmental probability distribution, and information technology. Our discussion suggests that it is simply not possible to defend these properties in isolation.[32]

## References

ALMON, C. (1963), "Central Planning without Complete Information at the Center," in G. B. DANTZIG, *Linear Programming and Extensions*, Princeton University Press, Princeton, pp. 462–466.

AOKI, M. (1969), "A Planning Procedure under Increasing Returns," Research Papers, Vol. I, No. 1, Harvard Economic Research Project, Cambridge.

---

$t$) in the decomposed process payoff is not lower than at the $t$th basis in the nondecomposed process. The missing technological information would then have to do with the cost of achieving alternative iteration times in the two processes. If the condition were satisfied and the decomposed process completed each iteration more quickly (for a fixed cost) than the nondecomposed process, the decomposed process would be superior. Unfortunately the condition is not in general satisfied (in fact the reverse of the condition is sometimes true), and no other condition implying a simple comparison has been found.

[32] An alternative approach to that taken here would be to consider all processes that exhibit certain classic properties and that are "satisfactory," in some sense, with respect to a class of payoff functions – they maximize such functions at equilibrium, for example. One might then attempt to show that no satisfactory process outside the class is "informationally more efficient" than any process in the class, where the term in quotation marks is defined in the spirit of the definitions given by HURWICZ (1960): one process is informationally more efficient than another, for example, if it requires of each member the perception of fewer distinct signals (as one passes over the set of possible initiating environments). Such a definition, however, not only provides just a partial ordering of processes but is tied to a restricted information technology (one in which increasing the number of distinct signals perceived is costly, for example, rather than one in which increasing the number of distinct members to whom messages have to be sent is costly). Such a definition, to be workable, may also ignore the costs of computation, concentrating entirely on the costs of transmission. Nevertheless the approach seems well worth pursuing, perhaps in parallel with the one considered here.

ARROW, K. J. and HURWICZ, L. (1960), "Decentralization and Computation in Resource Allocation," in R. W. PFOUTS (ed.), *Essays in Economics and Econometrics*, University of North Carolina Press, Chapel Hill, pp. 34–104.

BARONE, E. (1935), "The Ministry of Production in the Collectivist State," in F. A. HAYEK (ed.), *Collectivist Economic Planning*, Routledge, London, pp. 245–290.

DANTZIG, G. B. and P. WOLFE (1961), "The Decomposition Algorithm for Linear Programs, "*Econometrica, 29*, 767-778.

DAVIS, O. and A. WHINSTON (1966), "On Externalities, Information and the Government-Assisted Invisible Hand," *Economica, 33*, 303–318.

HAYEK, F. (1945), "The Use of Knowledge in Society," *American Economic Review, 35*, 519–530.

HURWICZ, L. (1960), "Optimality and Informational Efficiency in Resource Allocation Processes," Chapter 3 in K. J. ARROW, S. KARLIN, and P. SUPPES (eds.), *Mathematical Methods in the Social Sciences*, Stanford, University Press, Stanford, pp. 27–46.

KORNAI, J. and T. LIPTAK (1965), "Two-Level Planning," *Econometrica, 33*, 141–169.

LANGE, O. (1938), "On the Economic Theory of Socialism," in O. LANGE and F. M. TAYLOR, *On the Economic Theory of Socialism*, University of Minnesota Press, Minneapolis, pp. 57–143.

MALINVAUD, E. (1967), "Decentralized Procedures for Planning," Chapter 7 in BACHARACH and MALINVAUD (eds.), *Activity Analysis in the Theory of Growth and Planning*, Macmillan, London, pp. 170–208.

MARGLIN, S. (1963), *Approaches to Dynamic Investment Planning*, North-Holland Publishing Company, Amsterdam.

MARGLIN, S. (1964), "Decentralization with a Modicum of Increasing Returns," Research Memorandum RM-3421-PR, The RAND Corporation, Santa Monica, California.

MARSCHAK, J. and RADNER, R. (1971), *The Economic Theory of Teams*, Yale University Press, New Haven.

MARSCHAK, T. (1959), "Centralization and Decentralization in Economic Organizations," *Econometrica, 27*, 399-430.

RADNER, R. (1961), "The Evaluation of Information in Organizations," *Proceedings of the Fourth Berkeley Symposium on Mathematical Statistics and Probability*, University of California Press, Berkeley, pp. 491–530.

UZAWA, H. (1958), "Interative Methods for Concave Programming," in ARROW, HURWICZ, and UZAWA, *Studies in Linear and Nonlinear Programming*, Stanford University Press, Stanford.

WEITZMAN, M. (1970), "Iterative Multi-level Planning with Production Targets," *Econometrica, 38*, 50–65.

CHAPTER 13

# THE LIMIT OF THE CORE OF AN ECONOMY

GERARD DEBREU and HERBERT SCARF[1]

1. Introduction. – 2. The core of an economy. – 3. Edgeworth on the limit of the contract curve. – 4. A general limit theorem on the core of an economy.

## 1. Introduction

In an economy made up of agents initially owning certain quantities of commodities and trading with each other, the final result of the exchange process is a new allocation of the total quantities of commodities available. The core of the economy is the set of final allocations that no coalition of agents can, and wants to, prevent. EDGEWORTH (1881) introduced this concept under the name of the "contract curve" and studied the limit of the core under the following conditions. Two agents are said to be of the same type if they have the same preferences and the same initial commodity-vector. Edgeworth proved that, under assumptions to be specified later, in an economy with two commodities and two types of agents, if the number of agents of each type increases indefinitely, then the core of the economy decreases, or stays constant, and tends to the set of competitive allocations. This fundamental result provided the first precise explanation of competitive behavior. Yet, it received little notice for many decades,[2] to a large extent because of the way in which Edgeworth presented his ideas. We shall, as part of this paper, give a detailed account of his contribution.

The concept of the core reappeared in a different form in the theory of games with transferable utility. In this context it was made explicit, received its name, and was studied in 1953 by D. B. Gillies and L. S. Shapley. The connection between Edgeworth's contract curve and the core of a game was

---

[1] We thank Tjalling Koopmans for his comments on an earlier version and the National Science Foundation for its support of our work.

[2] See, however, J. A. SCHUMPETER (1954), pp. 830–831, 984.

then perceived by M. SHUBIK (1959), who called attention to the contribution of *Mathematical Psychics*.

During the last decade several developments have taken place in the study of the core of an economy. The first has consisted in a generalization of Edgeworth's theorem from the case of two commodities and two types of agents to the case of arbitrary finite numbers of commodities and types of agents with convex preferences (SCARF (1962), DEBREU (1963), DEBREU and SCARF (1963)).[3] The behavior of the core of large economies with non-convex preferences was then investigated by L. S. SHAPLEY and M. SHUBIK (1966) in the context of transferable utility, and by K. J. ARROW and F. HAHN (Chapter 8) in the context of nontransferable utility. The limit theorem of DEBREU and SCARF (1963), which will be described in Section 4 of this paper, was extended by J. JASKOLD-GABSZEWICZ (1968) to a class of economies with an infinity of commodities.

A second development began with the proof by R. J. AUMANN (1964) that if the agents of an economy form a continuum, then the core equals the set of competitive allocations, a result for which a different derivation was given by K. VIND (1964). The introduction of a measure-theoretic point of view for the set of agents of an economy is of great importance for models attempting to explain competitive behavior. We do not discuss it further here only because we cannot do so without a mathematical apparatus far more elaborate than the one to which we wish to restrict ourselves in this expository article. We refer instead to the two recent surveys by R. J. AUMANN (1972) and W. HILDENBRAND (1971).

A third direction has been the development of algorithms for calculating a point in the core. In SCARF (1967) a theorem is given, which provides sufficient conditions for the core of an $n$ person game to be nonempty. The theorem applies, in particular, to an exchange economy with convex preferences and the method of proof permits the approximate calculation of a point in the core. The theorem may also be used to demonstrate the non-emptiness of the $\alpha$-core (R. J. AUMANN (1961)) for a game in normal form with convex strategy spaces and quasi-concave utilities. These algorithms are contained in a more general class of numerical techniques which can be used to approximate a fixed point of a continuous mapping of a simplex into itself, and to determine approximate price equilibria in a general Walrasian model (SCARF (1969), HANSEN and SCARF (1969)).

[3] An alternative proof of the main theorem of the last paper was offered by K. VIND(1965).

## 2. The Core of an Economy

Let $\mathscr{E}$ be an economy with $l$ commodities and $m$ agents. Each one of the agents, say the $i$-th one, initially owns a commodity-vector $\omega_i$, an element of the $l$-dimensional commodity space $R^l$. We assume that the commodity-vectors to be assigned to the $i$-th agent are always in $\Omega$, the nonnegative orthant of $R^l$, and that he has preferences among the elements of $\Omega$. This preference relation is denoted by $\precsim_i$ and $x \precsim_i y$ is read "the commodity-vector $y$ is at least as desired by the $i$-th agent as the commodity-vector $x$." The relation $\precsim_i$ has the properties:

(1) for every $x$ in $\Omega$, $x \precsim_i x$ (reflexivity);
for every $x, x', x''$ in $\Omega$, if $x \precsim_i x'$ and $x' \precsim_i x''$, then $x \precsim_i x''$ (transitivity);
for every $x$, $x'$ in $\Omega$, $x \precsim_i x'$ and/or $x' \precsim_i x$ (completeness).

We say that $y$ is preferred to $x$, and we write $x \prec_i y$, when $x \precsim_i y$ and not $y \precsim_i x$. It will be assumed that the preferences of every agent satisfy the following conditions of insatiability (2) and strong-convexity (3).

(2) If $x$ is in $\Omega$, then there is $x'$ in $\Omega$ such that $x \prec_i x'$.

(3) Let $x_1, x_2$ be distinct vectors in $\Omega$ and let $\alpha_1, \alpha_2$ be positive real numbers *adding up to* 1. *If* $x_1 \succsim_i x_2$, *then* $\alpha_1 x_1 + \alpha_2 x_2 \succ_i x_2$.

From this last assumption, we can derive Lemma 1 which will be used in the proof of Lemma 2.

LEMMA 1. *For* $r \geqq 2$, *let* $x_1, \ldots, x_r$ *be vectors in* $\Omega$ *that are not all equal and let* $\alpha_1, \ldots, \alpha_r$ *be positive real numbers adding up to* 1. *If* $x_q \succsim_i x_r$ *for every* $q = 1, \ldots, r$, *then* $\sum_{q=1}^{r} \alpha_q x_q \succ_i x_r$.

*Proof.* We re-index the first $r-1$ vectors in such a way that $x_q \succsim_i x_{r-1}$ for every $q = 1, \ldots, r-1$ and note that for $r = 2$, the proposition is assumption (3) itself. We give a proof by induction making the hypothesis that the assertion is true for $x_1, \ldots, x_{r-1}$.

Observe that

$$\text{(i)} \qquad \sum_{q=1}^{r} \alpha_q x_q = \alpha_r x_r + \left(\sum_{q=1}^{r-1} \alpha_q\right) \left[\frac{1}{\sum_{q=1}^{r-1} \alpha_q} \sum_{q=1}^{r-1} \alpha_q x_q\right]$$

and denote the vector between brackets by $x'$. Two cases may arise:

(a) $x_1, \ldots, x_{r-1}$ are all equal. Then $x'$ is their common value and since all the $x_q (q=1, \ldots, r)$ are not equal, one has $x_r \neq x'$. Moreover, $[x' = x_{r-1}$ and $x_{r-1} \succsim_i x_r]$ implies $[x' \succsim_i x_r]$.

(b) $x_1, \ldots, x_{r-1}$ are not all equal. Then, by the induction hypothesis $x' \succ_i x_{r-1}$. Since $x_{r-1} \succsim_i x_r$, one has $x' \succ_i x_r$.

Thus, in either case, $x' \neq x_r$ and $x' \succsim_i x_r$. It now suffices to apply assumption (3) to equality (i) to obtain $\sum_{q=1}^{r} \alpha_q x_q \succ_i x_r$. Q.E.D.

An allocation for the economy $\mathscr{E}$ specifies the commodity-vector assigned to each agent. Thus an allocation is an $m$-tuple $(x_1, \ldots, x_i, \ldots, x_m)$ of points of $\Omega$, where $x_i$ denotes the commodity-vector assigned to the $i$-th agent. Such an allocation is attainable if the total commodity-vector $\sum_{i=1}^{m} x_i$ assigned to the set of all agents equals the available total commodity-vector $\sum_{i=1}^{m} \omega_i$. Consider now an allocation $(x_1, \ldots, x_i, \ldots, x_m)$. A coalition $S$ of agents *blocks* the allocation $(x_i)$ if its members can redistribute their own initial commodity-vectors among themselves so that every one of them is at least as satisfied as he is with the allocation $(x_i)$ and at least one of them is more satisfied. In symbols, the coalition $S$ blocks the allocation $(x_1, \ldots, x_i, \ldots, x_m)$ if one can find for each $i$ in $S$ a commodity-vector $x_i'$ in $\Omega$ such that

(ii) $$\sum_{i \in S} x_i' = \sum_{i \in S} \omega_i$$

and

(iii) for every $i \in S$, $x_i' \succsim_i x_i$, while for some $i \in S$, $x_i' \succ_i x_i$.

The *core* of the economy $\mathscr{E}$ is then formally defined as the set of attainable allocations that no coalition of agents blocks.

The second term of the comparison with which we are concerned is the set of competitive allocations of the economy $\mathscr{E}$. In a precise manner, the agents of $\mathscr{E}$ are said to behave competitively if (I) total demand equals total supply and (II) there is a price-vector $p$ in $R^l$ such that for every $i = 1, \ldots, m$, *the i-th agent chooses his demand $x_i$ according to his preferences among the commodity-vectors in $\Omega$ whose value does not exceed that of his initial commodity-vector $\omega_i$*. Denoting the value of the commodity-vector $z$ relative to the price-vector $p$ by $p \cdot z$, we can express the italicized part of condition (II) as

(iv) $p \cdot x_i \leqq p \cdot \omega_i$ and $[x \in \Omega$ and $p \cdot x \leqq p \cdot \omega_i]$ implies $[x \precsim_i x_i]$.

Thus an allocation $(x_1, \ldots, x_i, \ldots, x_m)$ is defined as competitive if it is attainable and there is a price-vector $p$ such that (iv) is satisfied for every $i = 1, \ldots, m$.

The asymptotic equality of the core and of the set of competitive allocations is established by Theorems 1 and 2.

THEOREM 1. *Every competitive allocation of $\mathscr{E}$ is in the core of $\mathscr{E}$.*

*Proof.* Let $(x_1, \ldots, x_i, \ldots, x_m)$ be a competitive allocation of $\mathscr{E}$ and let $p$ be the associated price-vector. We first remark that, according to (iv),

(v) $[x_i' \in \Omega$ and $x_i' \succ_i x_i]$ implies $[p \cdot x_i' > p \cdot \omega_i]$.

We also remark that

(vi) $[x_i' \in \Omega$ and $x_i' \succsim_i x_i]$ implies $[p \cdot x_i' \geqq p \cdot \omega_i]$.

The latter statement is correct because there is, by assumption (2), a commodity-vector $x_i''$ in $\Omega$ such that $x_i'' \succ_i x_i'$. Therefore, by assumption (3), for

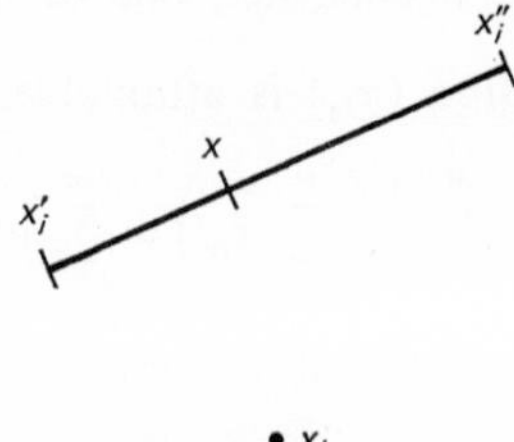


Fig. 1

every point $x$ of the segment joining $x_i'$ and $x_i''$ different from $x_i'$, one has $x \succ_i x_i'$, hence, $x \succ_i x_i$. Consequently, by (v), $p \cdot x > p \cdot \omega_i$. Letting $x$ tend to $x_i'$, one obtains in the limit $p \cdot x_i' \geqq p \cdot \omega_i$.

Suppose now that coalition $S$ blocks the given competitive allocation. For every $i$ in $S$, there is a commodity-vector $x_i'$ in $\Omega$ such that (ii) and (iii) hold. By (vi), for every $i$ in $S$, one has $p \cdot x_i' \geqq p \cdot \omega_i$. By (v), for some $i$ in $S$, one has $p \cdot x_i' > p \cdot \omega_i$. Therefore, $\sum_{i \in S} p \cdot x_i' > \sum_{i \in S} p \cdot \omega_i$, a contradiction of (ii). Q.E.D.

In order to be able to state the asymptotic converse of this theorem we introduce the economy $\mathscr{E}^r$ with $m$ types of agents and $r$ agents of each type. Each one of the $r$ agents of the $i$-th type initially owns the commodity-vector $\omega_i$ and has the preferences $\precsim_i$, where $i = 1, \ldots, m$. An allocation for $\mathscr{E}^r$ is an $mr$-tuple $(x_{11}, \ldots, x_{iq}, \ldots, x_{mr})$ of commodity-vectors in $\Omega$ where $x_{iq}$ is the commodity-vector assigned to the $q$-th agent of the $i$-th type. Therefore, the core is a subset of the space $R^{lmr}$. We will now prove that the core can be represented by a subset of the space $R^{lm}$. An essential simplification will result from the fact this space does not depend on $r$.

The proposition that Edgeworth expressed by saying that "all the field is collected at one point" (EDGEWORTH (1881), middle of page 35) is

LEMMA 2. *An allocation in the core of $\mathscr{E}^r$ assigns the same commodity-vector to all agents of the same type.*

*Proof.* Let $(x_{11}, \ldots, x_{iq}, \ldots, x_{mr})$ be an allocation in the core of $\mathscr{E}^r$ and, for each $i$, denote by $x_i$ the worst of the commodity-vectors $(x_{i1}, \ldots, x_{iq}, \ldots, x_{ir})$ according to the preferences $\precsim_i$. If there are several worst commodity-vectors, indifferent to each other, $x_i$ is arbitrarily chosen among them. Thus one has $x_{iq} \succsim_i x_i$ for every $q = 1, \ldots, r$.

Then let $S$ denote the coalition of $m$ agents formed by taking for each $i$ one of the least privileged agents, i.e., one of the agents to whom $x_i$ is assigned. Since the allocation $(x_{iq})$ is attainable, $\sum_{i=1}^{m} \sum_{q=1}^{r} x_{iq} = r\left(\sum_{i=1}^{m} \omega_i\right)$, from which one obtains $\sum_{i=1}^{m} \frac{1}{r}\left(\sum_{q=1}^{r} x_{iq}\right) = \sum_{i=1}^{m} \omega_i$. In other words, coalition $S$ can distribute its total initial commodity-vector $\sum_{i=1}^{m} \omega_i$ so as to give to its member of the $i$-th type the commodity-vector $x_i' = \frac{1}{r}\left(\sum_{q=1}^{r} x_{iq}\right)$ for every $i = 1, \ldots, m$. Consider a certain value of $i$. If all the $x_{iq}$ $(q = 1, \ldots, r)$ are identical, then clearly $x_i' = x_i$. If all the $x_{iq}$ $(q = 1, \ldots, r)$ are not identical, then, by Lemma 1, $x_i' \succ_i x_i$. Therefore if for some $i = 1, \ldots, m$, all the $x_{iq}$ $(q = 1, \ldots, m)$ are not identical, coalition $S$ blocks the proposed allocation $(x_{iq})$ by giving $x_i'$ to its member of the $i$-th type $(i = 1, \ldots, m)$. Q.E.D.

Thus an allocation in the core of $\mathscr{E}^r$ can be represented by an $m$-tuple $(x_1, \ldots, x_i, \ldots, x_m)$ of points of the space $R^l$ and the core of $\mathscr{E}^r$ can be represented by a subset $C^r$ of the space $R^{lm}$. Obviously, $C^{r+1}$ is contained in $C^r$, for if an allocation belongs to the core of $\mathscr{E}^{r+1}$, it is blocked by no coalition of $\mathscr{E}^{r+1}$ and, in particular, by no coalition having at most $r$ members of each type. Therefore, when $r$ increases indefinitely, the sets $C^r$ form a nested sequence having their intersection as a limit. The characterization of this limit is the problem to which we turn.

### 3. Edgeworth on the Limit of the Contract Curve

The solution offered by Edgeworth is contained in *Mathematical Psychics*, pp. 34–38. In presenting his proof of the asymptotic equality of the core of the economy $\mathscr{E}^r$ and of the set of its competitive allocations for the case of two commodities and two types of agents, we follow his notation and, therefore, abandon in this section the more convenient symbols that we introduced in Section 2.

Initially every agent of the first type owns a positive quantity $a$ of the first commodity and nothing of the second, every agent of the second type owns nothing of the first commodity and a positive quantity $b$ of the second. For the economy $\mathscr{E}$ consisting of one agent of each type, an allocation is represented by the point of the plane $R^2$ with coordinates $(x, y)$ where

$x$ is the quantity of the first commodity assigned to the agent of the second type;

$y$ is the quantity of the second commodity assigned to the agent of the first type.

Therefore, the initial allocation is $(0, 0)$, while an attainable allocation satisfies $0 \leqq x \leqq a$ and $0 \leqq y \leqq b$. The set of points of $R^2$ satisfying these inequalities is a rectangle $E$, the "Edgeworth box." Commodity-vectors assigned to the agents will be denoted by brackets. For the agent of the first type it is $[a-x, y]$, for the agent of the second type it is $[x, b-y]$.

Edgeworth assumes that the preferences of the agents of the first type (respectively, of the second type) are represented by a utility function $F$ (respectively, $\Phi$) with continuous first and second derivatives and such that

$$\frac{\partial F}{\partial x} < 0, \quad \frac{\partial F}{\partial y} > 0, \quad \frac{\partial^2 F}{\partial x^2} < 0, \quad \frac{\partial^2 F}{\partial x \partial y} < 0, \quad \frac{\partial^2 F}{\partial y^2} < 0;$$

$$\frac{\partial \Phi}{\partial x} > 0, \quad \frac{\partial \Phi}{\partial y} < 0, \quad \frac{\partial^2 \Phi}{\partial x^2} < 0, \quad \frac{\partial^2 \Phi}{\partial x \partial y} < 0, \quad \frac{\partial^2 \Phi}{\partial y^2} < 0.$$

In Fig. 2, the indifference curves $I_1$, $I_2$ through the origin for each type of agent are drawn.

The above conditions imply that the preferences of the agents satisfy assumption (3). To see this, consider an indifference curve for the agents of the first type determined by

$$\text{(i)} \qquad F(x, y) = k,$$

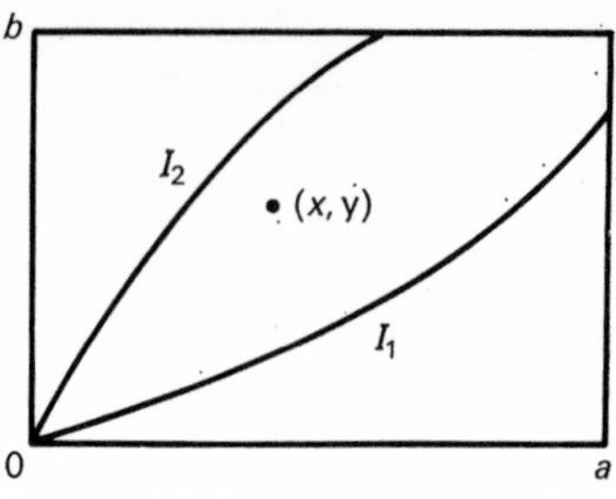


Fig. 2

where $k$ belongs to the range of $F$. There is a function $f$ such that (i) is equivalent to $y = f(x)$. By taking derivatives with respect to $x$ in (i), one obtains

(ii) $$\frac{\partial F}{\partial x} + \frac{\partial F}{\partial y}\frac{\mathrm{d}f}{\mathrm{d}x} = 0\,.$$

By performing the same operation in (ii), one obtains

(iii) $$\frac{\partial^2 F}{\partial x^2} + 2\frac{\partial^2 F}{\partial x \partial y}\frac{\mathrm{d}f}{\mathrm{d}x} + \frac{\partial^2 F}{\partial y^2}\left(\frac{\mathrm{d}f}{\mathrm{d}x}\right)^2 + \frac{\partial F}{\partial y}\frac{\mathrm{d}^2 f}{\mathrm{d}x^2} = 0\,.$$

It follows from (ii) that $\mathrm{d}f/\mathrm{d}x > 0$. Therefore the first three terms in (iii) are negative. Since $\partial F/\partial y > 0$, one has $\mathrm{d}^2 f/\mathrm{d}x^2 > 0$. The function $f$ is strictly convex, which implies (3).

In a similar manner, one can prove that (3) is satisfied for the agents of the second type.

Edgeworth now introduces the economy $\mathscr{E}^r$ made up of $r$ agents of each one of the two types. According to Lemma 2 the core of $\mathscr{E}^r$ can be represented by a subset $C^r$ of the rectangle $E$. Consider an allocation $\alpha = (\xi, \eta)$ that belongs to $C^r$ for every $r$. Let $A_i$ be the set of allocations $\beta$ in $E$ that are at least as desired by an agent of the $i$-th type as $\alpha$. In symbols,

$$A_i = \{\beta \in E \mid \beta \succsim_i \alpha\} \qquad i = 1, 2\,.$$

The central point of the proof (EDGEWORTH (1881), middle of page 38) consists of establishing that

(iv) the convex sets $A_1$, $A_2$ can be separated by a straight line $L$ through 0 in Fig. 3 or in Fig. 4.

Since the allocation $\alpha$ is Pareto optimal for the economy $\mathscr{E}^1$ there is a straight line through $\alpha$ separating $A_1$ and $A_2$ by an argument too familiar to be repeated. Therefore, if $\alpha$ coincides with 0, assertion (iv) is established.

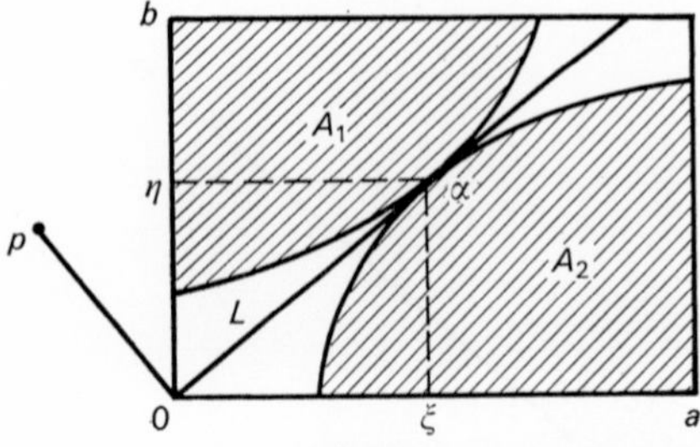


Fig. 3

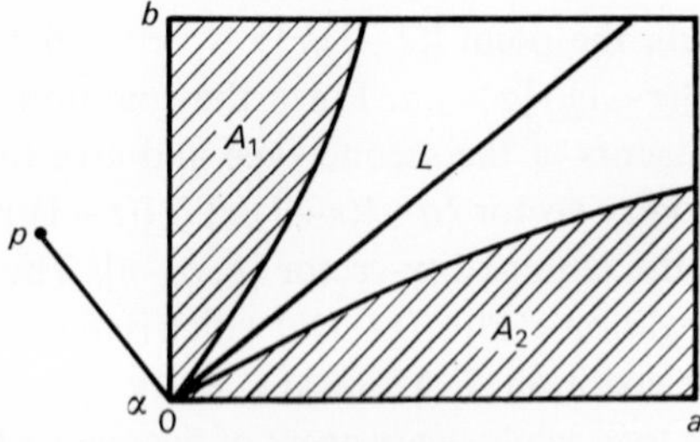


Fig. 4

We now prove that if $\alpha$ is distinct from 0, the straight line through 0 and $\alpha$ separates $A_1$ and $A_2$. Suppose that it is *not* supporting for one of them,

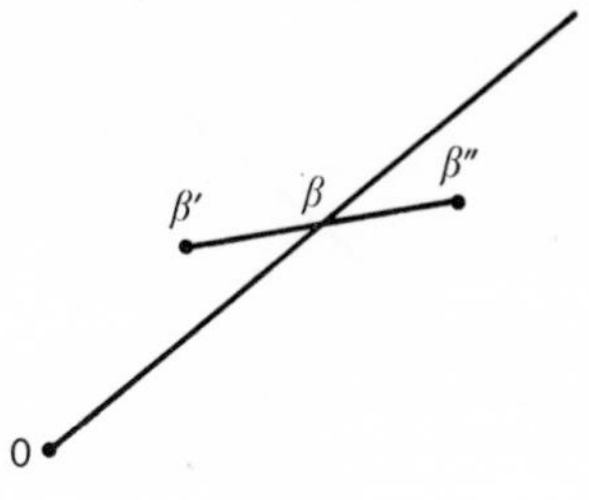


Fig. 5

say $A_1$. Then there are points $\beta'$, $\beta''$ of $A_1$ on different sides of the line 0, $\alpha$. One has $\beta' \succsim_1 \alpha$ and $\beta'' \succsim_1 \alpha$. Consequently, by assumption (3), the point $\beta$

where the segment $\beta'$, $\beta''$ intersects 0, $\alpha$ satisfies $\beta \succ_1 \alpha$. Two cases have to be considered.

(*a*) $\beta$ is between 0 and $\alpha$.

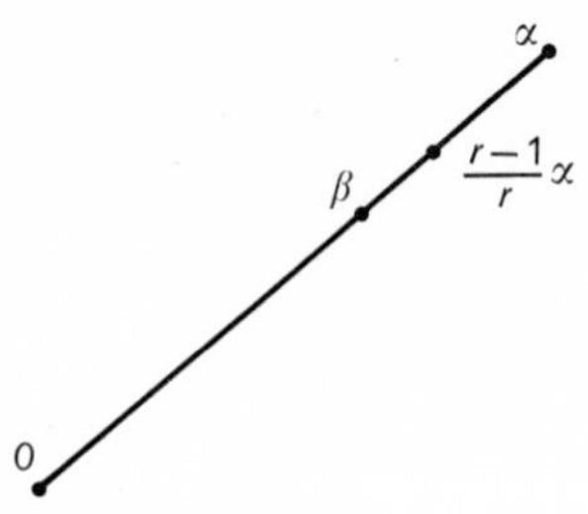


Fig. 6

For $r$ large enough, the point $[(r-1)/r]\alpha$ is between $\beta$ and $\alpha$. Therefore, by assumption (3), $[(r-1)/r]\alpha \succ_1 \alpha$. Form the coalition $S$ with $r$ agents of the first type, $r-1$ agents of the second type and give to each agent of the first type the commodity-vector $\{a-[(r-1)/r]\,\xi, [(r-1)/r]\,\eta\}$, to each agent of the second type the commodity-vector $[\xi, b-\eta]$. The total commodity-vector assigned to coalition $S$ is $[ra, (r-1)b]$ which is the total initial commodity-vector owned by coalition $S$. Moreover, every agent of the first type in $S$ prefers $[(r-1)/r]\,\alpha$ to $\alpha$, while every agent of the second type in $S$ is at least as satisfied with $\alpha$ as with $\alpha$. Consequently, coalition $S$ blocks allocation $\alpha$ in $\mathscr{E}^r$, a contradiction of the hypothesis that $\alpha$ belongs to $C^r$ for every $r$.

(*b*) $\beta$ is not between 0 and $\alpha$.

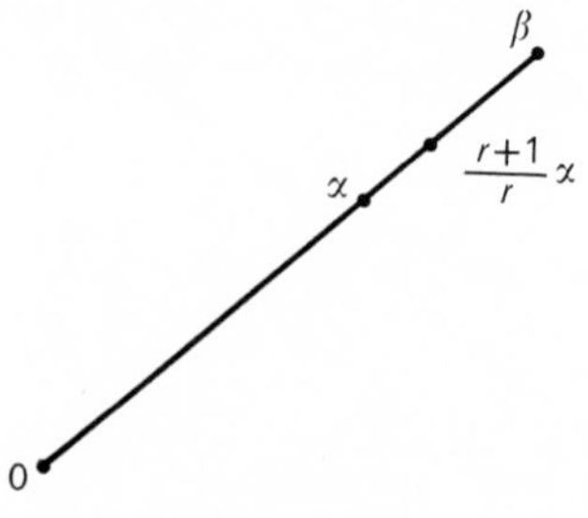


Fig. 7

In this case, repeat the reasoning of (*a*), replacing $[(r-1)/r]\alpha$ by $[(r+1)/r]\alpha$.

Thus the proof of assertion (iv) is complete.

We notice further that

(v) the straight line $L$ is not supporting for $E$.

To establish this assertion, remark that the coalition made up of one agent of the first type does not block $\alpha$. Therefore, $\alpha \succsim_1 0$. However, the utility $F(x, 0)$ is a decreasing function of $x$, hence, $0 \succ_1 (a, 0)$. Consequently, $\alpha \neq (a, 0)$. Similarly, $\alpha \neq (0, b)$.

Since $F$ is decreasing in $x$ and increasing in $y$, one has $(0, b) \succ_1 \alpha$. It follows from this relation and from the continuity of $F$ that all the points of $E$ in a sufficiently small neighborhood of $(0, b)$ are also preferred to $\alpha$ by an agent of the first type. As this neighborhood is contained in $A_1$, which is supported by $L$ from below, the point $(0, b)$ is strictly above $L$. Similarly, $(a, 0)$ is strictly below $L$. Thus assertion (v) is established.

Choose now a price-vector $p$ orthogonal to $L$ as in Figs. 3 and 4. There remains to check that $\alpha$ and $p$ form a competitive equilibrium. Specifically, we must prove that there is no point of $E$ on or below $L$ and preferred to $\alpha$ by the agents of the first type, and no point of $E$ on or above $L$ and preferred to $\alpha$ by the agents of the second type. Let us, therefore, suppose that $\beta$ is a point of $E$ on or below $L$ for which $\beta \succ_1 \alpha$. Actually, $\beta$ must be on $L$ since $\beta$ belongs to $A_1$, which is supported by $L$ from below. Observe that, according to (v), there are points of $E$ in the closed southeast quadrant with vertex $\beta$ that are strictly below $L$. Select one of them $\gamma$ close enough to $\beta$ so that, by continuity of $F$, one has $\gamma \succ_1 \alpha$. Therefore, $\gamma$ belongs to $A_1$ and is strictly below $L$, a contradiction.

In a similar manner, one shows that there can be no point $\beta$ of $E$ on or above $L$ for which $\beta \succ_2 \alpha$, thereby completing the proof of Edgeworth's theorem.

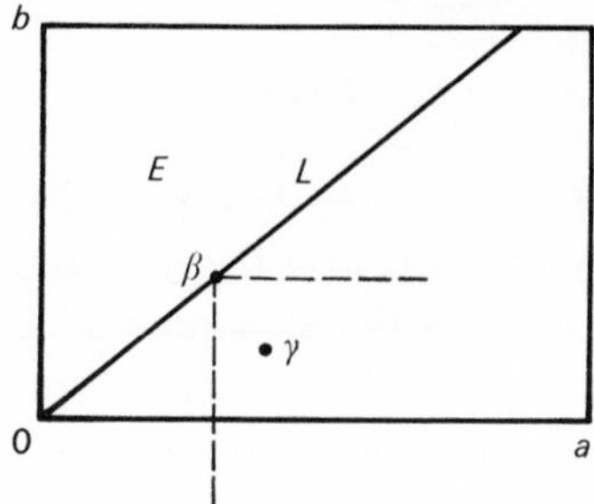


**Fig. 8**

## 4. A General Limit Theorem on the Core of an Economy

We now return to the notation of Section 2 and consider an economy $\mathscr{E}$ with $l$ commodities and $m$ agents. For every $i = 1, \ldots, m$, we make assumptions (1), (2), (3),

(4) the vector $\omega_i$ has all its components positive,

(5) for every $x'$ in $\Omega$, the set of $x$ in $\Omega$ such that $x \precsim_i x'$ is closed.

(4) postulates that every agent initially owns a positive quantity of every commodity. (5) postulates that for any commodity-vector $x'$ in $\Omega$ and any convergent sequence $\{x^q\}$ of commodity-vectors in $\Omega$, if $x^q$ is at most as desired by the $i$-th agent as $x'$ for every $q$, then the limit of $\{x^q\}$ is at most as desired by the $i$-th agent as $x'$.

According to Lemma 2, the core of the economy $\mathscr{E}^r$ consisting of $r$ replicas of the economy $\mathscr{E}$ can be represented by a subset $C^r$ of $R^{lm}$. Let $\alpha$ be a competitive allocation of $\mathscr{E}$. The allocation $\alpha^r$ of $\mathscr{E}^r$ consisting of $r$ replicas of $\alpha$ is competitive for $\mathscr{E}^r$. According to Theorem 1, $\alpha^r$ belongs to the core of $\mathscr{E}^r$. Therefore, $\alpha$ belongs to $C^r$. Denote by $C^*$ the set of competitive allocations of $\mathscr{E}$. When $r$ increases indefinitely, the $C^r$ form a nested sequence and they all contain $C^*$.

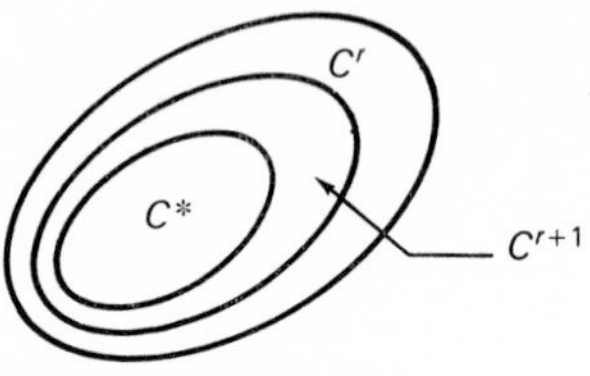


Fig. 9

The limit theorem of Debreu and Scarf (1963), which we now state, asserts that under assumptions (1)–(5) the intersection of the sets $C^1, \ldots, C^r, \ldots$ representing the cores of the economies $\mathscr{E}^1, \ldots, \mathscr{E}^r, \ldots$ is the set $C^*$ of the competitive allocations of the economy $\mathscr{E}$. In other words, $C^*$ is the limit of $C^r$ when $r$ becomes indefinitely large.

Theorem 2. *Every allocation of $\mathscr{E}$ that is in $C^r$ for all $r$ is competitive.*

## References


ARROW, K. J. and F. HAHN, *Competitive Equilibrium Analysis*, Holden-Day, San Francisco (forthcoming).

AUMANN, R. J. (1961), "The Core of a Cooperative Game without Side Payments," *Transactions of the American Mathematical Society*, *98*, 539–552.

AUMANN, R. J. (1964*b*), "Markets with a Continuum of Traders," *Econometrica*, *32*, 39–50.

AUMANN, R. J. (1972), "A Survey of Economies with a Continuum of Agents," paper presented at the Second World Congress of the Econometric Society, Cambridge.

DEBREU, G. (1963), "On a Theorem of Scarf," *The Review of Economic Studies*, *30*, 177–180.

DEBREU, G. and H. SCARF (1963), "A Limit Theorem on the Core of an Economy," *International Economic Review*, *4*, 235–246.

EDGEWORTH, F. Y. (1881), *Mathematical Psychics*, Paul Kegan, London.

GILLIES, D. B. (1953), *Some Theorems on N-person Games*, Ph. D. thesis, Princeton University.

HANSEN, T. and H. SCARF (1969), "On the Applications of a Recent Combinatorial Algorithm," Cowles Foundation Discussion Paper No. 272.

HILDENBRAND, W. (1971), "Measure Spaces of Economic Agents," *Proceedings of the Sixth Berkeley Symposium on Mathematical Statistics and Probability*, L. LECAM, J. NEYMAN and E. SCOTT (eds.), University of California Press, Berkeley (forthcoming).

JASKOLD-GABSZEWICZ, J. (1968), *Cœurs et Allocations Concurrentielles dans des Économies d'Échange avec un Continu de Biens*, Librairie Universitaire, Louvain.

SCARF, H. (1962), "An Analysis of Markets with a Large Number of Participants," *Recent Advances in Game Theory*, The Princeton University Conference, 127–155.

SCARF, H. (1967), "The Core of an N-person Game," *Econometrica*, *35*, 50–69.

SCARF, H. (1969), "An Example of an Algorithm for Calculating General Equilibrium Prices," *American Economic Review*, *59*, 669–677.

SCHUMPETER, J. A. (1954), *History of Economic Analysis*, Oxford University Press, New York.

SHAPLEY, L. S. and M. SHUBIK (1966), "Quasi-Cores in a Monetary Economy with Nonconvex Preferences," *Econometrica*, *34*, 805–827.

SHUBIK, M. (1959), "Edgeworth Market Games," in A. W. TUCKER and R. D. LUCE (eds.), *Contributions to the Theory of Games*, Vol. IV, Princeton University Press, Princeton.

VIND, K. (1964), "Edgeworth-Allocations in an Exchange Economy with Many Traders," *International Economic Review*, *5*, 165–177.

VIND, K. (1965), "A Theorem on the Core of an Economy," *The Review of Economic Studies*, *32*, 47-48.

CHAPTER 14

# ON INFORMATIONALLY DECENTRALIZED SYSTEMS

LEONID HURWICZ*

1. Introduction. – 2. Informational decentralization in nonclassical environments. – 3. Incentive-compatibility.

## 1. Introduction

The purpose of the present paper is to discuss some of the problems that arise in laying the foundations of a theory of economic systems. The study of economic systems can be approached either in the spirit of "positive" science ("what is") or "normative" science ("what should be"). In either case, if the approach is analytical, the essential first step is a formalization of the concept of an economic system.

Informally, we think of an economic system as defined by a set of institutional or behavioral rules that enable us to distinguish, for example, capitalism from socialism, pure laissez-faire from mixed economy, or perhaps, perfect competition from oligopoly. On the other hand, resource endowment, technology, and individual preferences are viewed as given parameters with which the system must cope; the totality of such parameters will be referred to as the *environment*.[1] The symbol $e$ will be used to denote a complete description of an environment; thus to know $e$ means to know completely the initial endowment, the technology, and the preferences. A class of environments will be denoted by $E$. Thus partial (incomplete) knowledge of the environment is represented by the specification of a class $E$ containing more than one element.

At a given point in time, an observer of an economy can characterize it as being in a certain *state* $s$. The state can be described in terms of various "real" activities such as consuming, producing, storing, and also in terms of "informational" activities such as making bids, presenting economic plans, performing calculations, etc. We could imagine giving this observer a

* This work was carried on with the aid of National Science Foundation Grant GS–2077.

[1] We are here thinking of technology and preferences as completely exogenous. Otherwise, only the exogenous components would be treated as environment.

specification so complete of all participants' behavior patterns that, given the knowledge of the environment and of the initial state, he could predict all the future states of the economy. (To simplify discussion, we presuppose for the moment a nonstochastic model, both with respect to environment and to behavior patterns.) The totality of these behavior patterns (as distinct from environment and state descriptions) may be called the economic *mechanism*, and we shall apply the same term even if the behavior patterns have stochastic aspects. We shall use the term *adjustment process* to label a mechanism belonging to a class to be described below.

Among examples of analytical formulations of economic mechanisms one can cite the various dynamic models of market processes (e.g., perfect competition), decentralized planning models (e.g., MALINVAUD (1967), KORNAI and LIPTÁK (1965)), and also models of processes designed to cope with indivisibilities, increasing returns, public goods,etc. (HURWICZ, RADNER, and REITER (1970), MALINVAUD (1970), DRÈZE and DE LA VALLÉE POUSSIN (1969), ARROW and HURWICZ (1960), AOKI (1970), MARGLIN (1969)).

An economic mechanism can be studied with regard to its *performance* in terms of some *welfare* criterion (e.g., Pareto-optimality or some social welfare function) in relation to the environments in which the mechanism operates. In fact, a major part of modern welfare economics deals with a special study of this type, viz., that of the performance of a particular mechanism (perfect competition) in terms of a particular performance (welfare) criterion (Pareto-optimality), depending on whether the environment is "classical" (no externalities, no indivisibilities, technology and preferences convex). Similarly, performance in terms of Pareto or related criteria has been studied for certain mechanisms capable of operating in nonclassical environments (e.g., the "greed process" in HURWICZ (1960a), or the process of HURWICZ, RADNER, and REITER (1970)).

Some models of mechanisms have been formulated for purposes of "positive" science, i.e., in the belief that they provide a useful instrument for the study of observed phenomena. This has, in particular, been the case with regard to both perfectly competitive and monopolistic (including oligopolistic) models. Other mechanisms have been proposed in a normative spirit, a classic example being the Lange model of a decentralized socialist economy. Many have been put forward as objects for study rather than proposals for adoption, but with an ultimate normative objective in mind.

To see whether a mechanism is worthy of serious study, one is led to examine its informational and incentive *feasibility*. On the informational side, the question is whether the mechanism allows for the dispersion of information and limitations on the capacity of various units to process information. On the incentival side, there is the problem whether the rules prescribed by the mechanism are compatible with either individual or group incentives.

Given the feasibility of a mechanism, the issue of its *efficiency* arises. Processing of information uses resources (both capital and operating) and alternative mechanisms may be more or less demanding in this respect.[2] Similarly, incentive-compatibility may involve a system of (positive and negative) rewards and resources to administer them (the enforcement system). To calculate the "net" welfare generated by a mechanism, given the environment $e$, one must take into account the drain on resources by the informational activities (the cost of information processing) and the incentive-inducing activities (the cost of enforcement).

Thus there are two types of "givens" in our problem: those pertaining to the feasibility and cost structure of alternative organizational structures (whether in the informational or incentival sphere) and those pertaining to the economic environment in the narrow sense of the term. In fact, these two types of givens are interrelated, if only because resources used to operate the organization cannot be used for "substantive" purposes.

In simplified form, this can be expressed by defining a function $h(x, q/e)$ which associates the resulting state $s$ with the resources $x$ used for substantive (as distinct from organizational) purposes when mechanism $q$ prevails, given the environment $e$, and another function $b(q/e)$ defining the resource vector required to operate the mechanism $q$. A welfare ordering or function can then be defined on the space of the resulting states. We shall denote by $w = W(s)$ the measure (possibly vectorial) of welfare associated with the state $s$. Thus $w = W[h(x, q/e)]$. (The symbol "$/e$" means "given $e$".)

The fact that, for a given $e$, the resulting welfare $w$ depends on $q$, as well as on the substantively utilized resources $x$, expresses the phenomenon of differential performance of different mechanisms, quite aside from what it costs to operate them. But in fact the operational costs (in resource terms) do differ, so that if the given initial resources are denoted by $\omega_e$, the welfare $w$ generated by the mechanism $q$ in the environment $e$ is given by

$$w = W[h(\omega_e - b(q/e), q/e)]. \tag{1.1}$$

[2] In a more complete analysis, one would also take into account (either on the "cost" or "performance" side) the speed and accuracy of alternative information-processing systems.

(This formulation ignores additional psychological and ideological welfare aspects of the mechanism.) The symbol for initial resources has the subscript $e$ because initial resources constitute part of the specification of $e$. We refer to $\omega_e - b(q/e)$ as the resources available for substantive purposes.

Even aside from resource requirements, the *feasibility* of a mechanism is dependent on the environment, due to both technological and behavioral (preference) considerations. Thus with each environment $e$ one may associate the class $Q(e)$ of mechanisms that are feasible, given $e$. For formula (1.1) to be meaningful, the mechanism $q$ in it should be taken from this class.

Now the normative problem involves selecting a mechanism with only partial knowledge of the environment in which it will have to operate. Such knowledge might, for instance, be expressed (in the Bayesian spirit) as a probability measure on the space of conceivable environments. For the sake of simplicity, however, we shall suppose at this point that the "organizer" only has an *a priori* admissible class of environments $E_0$, without any probabilistic information within this class. We shall further assume that he knows the functions $h$, $b$, and $Q(.)$, i.e., of the dependence of mechanism feasibility on the prevailing environment. He can then find the class of mechanisms feasible over all of the *a priori* class $E_0$, viz., the intersection

$$Q[E_0] = \bigcap_{e \in E_0} Q(e).$$

For any $q$ in this feasible class $Q[E_0]$, and any environment $e$ in $E_0$, he can determine the organizational cost $b(q/e)$, the initial resources $\omega_e$ implicit in $e$, and hence the welfare outcome $w$ as given by (1.1). Thus the normative organizational problem acquires the form that is formally analogous to a statistical decision problem, since the organizer presumably wishes to maximize, for fixed $e$ in $E_0$,

$$w = g(q, e), \qquad q \in Q[E_0], \tag{1.2}$$

where the right-hand side is the same as the right-hand side of (1.1) expressed as a function of $q$ and $e$. If a probability measure on $E_0$ were available to the organizer, he might maximize with respect to $q$ the corresponding expected value $\mathscr{E}_e g(q, e) \equiv G(q)$.[3] In the absence of such "prior" probabilities, the organizer might adopt some principle of decision making under uncertainty, say maximin, over $E_0$ (see HURWICZ (1951)).

[3] $\mathscr{E}_e$ denotes the mathematical expectation with respect to the given probability measure on $E_0$.

It is not yet practical to carry out a complete analysis along the above lines, although the formalization given may be helpful in clarifying various informal arguments concerning the comparative merits of alternative economic systems. At the very least, however, our attention is focused on the main concepts that appear in this analysis, namely, those of the environment and mechanism. Clearly, a prerequisite for progress is the formalization of these two concepts. Both were introduced in HURWICZ (1960a), although not in as general a form as to encompass all cases of interest.

In particular, the environment $e$ was defined as the ordered triple of initial resource endowment, preferences, and technology, $e = \langle \omega, R, Z \rangle$. The mechanism was characterized as an adjustment process, $\pi = \langle f, \phi, \mathscr{M} \rangle$ with a given language $\mathscr{M}$, set of response rules $f$, and an outcome rule $\phi$. Somewhat more general adjustment processes were considered in HURWICZ (1969) and (1971).

The approach used in HURWICZ (1960a) is nowhere near the optimization problem formulated in (1.2). Rather, a subclass of all adjustment processes is defined as *informationally decentralized* if it satisfies certain restrictions with regard to the language and the nature of the response and outcome functions. These restrictions are satisfied by the "usual" (say Walrasian tâtonnement) models of the perfectly competitive process, so that the latter qualifies as informationally decentralized. The intent was to isolate those processes whose *informational* requirements were no greater, and if anything less, than those of the perfectly competitive process, regardless of the *behavioral* nature of these processes. Such a definition could be interpreted in the spirit of informational feasibility, in the sense that an informationally decentralized process is informationally feasible whenever the perfectly competitive process is. (The latter statement presupposes that the feasibility of the computations required by the process, as distinct from possession, transmission, or perception of information, is ignored.) There are two basic notions underlying the restrictions inherent in such a concept of informational decentralization. First, that there is *initial dispersion of information*, with each economic unit processing only partial knowledge of the environment $e$, viz., that of its own component $e^i$ of $e$. Second, that it is impossible to transfer this information to other units in such a way that at some stage of the process some one unit would be, through messages received from others, in possession of complete information concerning $e$ or concerning the proposed actions of all the other units; this can be expressed by saying that it is impossible through communication to centralize dispersed information, i.e., that there is *limited commu-*

*nication.*[4] Thus our concept of informational decentralization takes into account the initial dispersion of information together with the limitations of communication. Both of the latter concepts can be rigorously defined as certain properties of the response functions and of the language used in communication.[5]

---

[4] Both dispersion of information and limitation on communication may be regarded as extreme cases of imperfections in the distribution and flow of information. One way of formalizing such imperfections (see HURWICZ (1971)) is by introducing error variables in connection with both environmental and message arguments of the response functions characterizing the adjustment process. Thus, instead of writing the adjustment equations as, say,

$$m^i_{t+1} = F^i_t(m^1_t, \ldots, m^n_t; e^1, \ldots, e^n) \qquad (i = 1, \ldots, n),$$

we may postulate similar relations but with $m^t_k$ and $e^k$ replaced respectively by, say, $m^k_t + {}^i_m v^k_t$ and $e^k + {}^i_e v^k$, where the $v$'s are random variables representing the errors of perception with regard to the messages received and the environmental characteristics. Dispersion of (environmental) information would then correspond to postulating that the variance of ${}^i_e v^i$ is zero, while the variance of ${}^j_e v^i$, $j \neq i$, is infinite. Similar postulates concerning the joint distribution of the ${}_m v$'s would reflect the limitations on communication. (In the above formula for the adjustment process, the environment $e$ is conceived as described in terms of the $n$-tuple $e = \langle e^1, \ldots, e^n \rangle$, where $e^i$ is the description of the environmental characteristics of the $i$-th unit.)

A further degree of realism can be introduced into the model by making the joint distribution of the error variables dependent on informational activities, associated with different cost levels.

[5] The dispersion of information is reflected in the definition of informational decentralization by a property of the response function which, for want of a better term, is referred to as *privacy-respecting*, viz., that a response function, say, $F^i_t(m_t; e)$ depends on $e$ through $e^i$ only, so that it can be written as $f^i(m_t; e^i)$. (The earlier, even less fortunate, term for this property was "externality," see HURWICZ (1960a).) The function $F^i_t$ tells participant $i$ at time $t$ how to form his next message $m^i_{t+1}$, given the $n$-tuple $m_t = \langle m^1_t, \ldots, m^n_t \rangle$ of messages from the previous period and given the environment $e$. When dispersion prevails, a response function $F^i_t$, which depended on some $e^j$, $j \neq i$, would not be informationally feasible.

As for limitation on the nature of communication, the (1960a) paper required self-relevance of messages and aggregativeness of the response functions. The latter property is trivially satisfied in the examples of the present paper, since these examples refer to cases where the number of participants $n$ equals 2.

In examples of Section 2 below, self-relevance would correspond to what are there defined as proposed-action processes. However, in Section 2, we consider a somewhat broader concept of decentralization in which the meaning of messages is unrestricted (so that self-relevance is not required), but the dimensionality of the messages must be what it would have been under self-relevance, i.e., the same as that of the action space.

Supposing that only informationally decentralized processes are feasible, one could still attempt to attack the problem of optimal mechanism selection stated in (1.2) by restricting the feasible class $Q[E_0]$ to processes that are informationally decentralized. Unfortunately, we run into difficulties. For one thing, little is known in a general way concerning the resource requirements $b(q/e)$ of the various processes. In fact, in traditional economic analysis, e.g., in comparisons of, say, perfect competition with monopoly or oligopoly, these requirements are not analyzed, and only substantive performance is compared. In terms of the notation used in (1.1), the comparison is between $h(x, q'/e)$ and $h(x, q''/e)$, rather than between $f[\omega_e - -b(q'/e), q'/e]$ and $h[\omega_e - b(q''/e, q''/e]$, where $q'$ and $q''$ are two alternative mechanisms, and $x$ the resources available for *substantive* utilization (i.e., not needed to operate the mechanism).

To deal with the question of the welfare index $w$, we shall simplify this phase of exposition by postulating that preferences are expressible through numerical utility functions $U^1(s), \ldots, U^n(s)$ of the $n$ individuals in the economy, each defined on the economy's alternative states $s$. Furthermore, let us at this point postulate complete determinacy of the process $q$ in the sense that, given $e = \langle \omega, R, Z \rangle$ (which includes the specification of the initial distribution of resources, as well as the respective technologies and preferences of the various units) there is a unique outcome in terms of actions (production, resource flow), resource distributions, and consequently, utilities. One may then define $W(s)$ as the $n$-tuple of utilities, say,

$$W(s) = \langle U^1(s), \ldots. U^n(s) \rangle,$$

so that the explicit form of (1.1) would be

$$w = \langle U^1[h(\omega_e, q/e)], \ldots, U^n[h(\omega_e, q/e)] \rangle \tag{1.3}$$

where, in effect, we are setting $b(q/e) = 0$.

---

Furthermore, mathematical regularity (Lipschitzian) properties are imposed to make the dimensionality "genuine."

In both Sections 2 and 3, processes are required to be privacy-respecting. But, in 3, the limitations on the nature of communication are not spelled out explicitly; Section 2, on the other hand, deals with these limitations explicitly.

It is worth noting that by confining ourselves to first-order processes (i.e., first-order difference equation adjustment), we are in fact imposing a limitation on memory, hence, on communication. Even severe restrictions on the nature of communication at any given point in time could be largely circumvented by permitting an accumulation of information over many time periods. Hence some restriction on memory (i.e., order of the process) seems an essential feature of informational decentralization.

As an example, in an environment corresponding to the Edgeworth Box (pure exchange) case, and with $q$ as perfect competition $q^C$, we might consider the outcome to be the competitive equilibrium allocation (assumed unique), say,

$$h(\omega_e, q/e) = c,$$

with

$$c = \langle c^1, \ldots, c^n \rangle,$$

and

$$w = \langle U^1(c^1), \ldots, U^n(c^n) \rangle,$$

where $U^i$ is the utility function representing the (selfish) preferences of the the $i$-th unit.

As a further step, for any mechanism $q^*$, one might adopt a scalar (Bergson-Samuelson Welfare) function, say,

$$\psi(u^{*1}, \ldots, u^{*n})$$

as the measure of the system's performance, so that

$$W[h(\omega_e, q/e)] = \psi(u^{*1}, \ldots, u^{*n}) \tag{1.4}$$

where the $u^{*1}$ is again the utility of the final outcome for the *i-th* unit.

But, perhaps because of known paradoxes in the field of welfare functions, as well as lack of consensus as to a "reasonable" choice of the function $\psi$, the customary approach is in terms of the Pareto optimality of outcomes. Thus, let $Y(e)$ denote the set of allocations that are achievable, given the environment $e$, and $\hat{Y}(e)$ its Pareto-optimal subset. (It is important to note that both the feasible and the achievable sets are defined in terms of $e$, independently of $q$. This corresponds to ignoring the resource and psychological costs associated with the operation of the mechanism.) A basic question asked in welfare economics then is whether the utility image of the outcome defined by (1.3) is maximal, i.e., whether it corresponds to an element of the Pareto-optimal set $\hat{Y}(e)$. If it is, the process is called (Pareto-) *nonwasteful*. One of the main results of welfare economics is that, in the absence of externalities and of local saturation, competitive equilibrium is necessarily Pareto-optimal (see, e.g., KOOPMANS (1957), Proposition 4), i.e., that the perfectly competitive process is nonwasteful. On the other hand, examples have been constructed to show that in similar environments, processes involving monopoly may yield nonoptimal outcomes, i.e., that such a process is wasteful in the sense just defined.

Although, other things being equal, nonwastefulness is an attractive normative postulate, it is by itself inadequate because it does not rule out the possibility that the mechanism would yield outcomes consistently favoring some units at the expense of others. Thus in an Edgeworth Box type situation, a mechanism that would always place a given trader at his origin (i.e., allocate all goods to the other trader) would be nonwasteful when the preferences are assumed strictly monotone! The competitive equilibrium of a private ownership economy (see DEBREU (1959), pp. 78–80) yields a final allocation that is Pareto-noninferior to the initial one, and hence – despite its Pareto-optimality – may not appeal to those whose initial endowments are low.

It is therefore natural to seek a feature of the mechanism that would in some sense equalize the chances of the participants, regardless of their initial endowments. An obvious way to seek such equalization is to admit the possibility of redistribution of the initial endowment (and ownership shares), for instance, by a system of taxes and subsidies (see KOOPMANS (1957), p. 54). Now, with regard to a mechanism characterized by the admissibility of all feasible redistributions, one may ask whether every Pareto-optimal allocation can be attained as an outcome (equilibrium) following some feasible redistribution. (If so, we call the mechanism (Pareto-) *unbiased.*) Again, welfare economics answers this question in the affirmative (see KOOPMANS (1957), Prop. 5, pp. 50–51) for the competitive process with redistributions, provided that the environment is free of externalities and of local saturation, and has a convex technology and convex continuous preferences. (We omit an additional qualification stated in the last sentence of Koopmans' Prop. 5, pp. 50–51.) We shall refer to environments satisfying the assumptions of Koopmans' Prop. 5 (and hence, also 4) as *classical* and denote the set of classical environments by $E_{CL}$. Thus, in our terminology, the competitive mechanism (including redistributions) is unbiased for classical environments.

A further postulate to be considered has to do with the determinacy of the outcomes that result from the operation of the mechanism. It is appealing to demand single-valuedness, but even the competitive process operating in a classical environment may fail to yield it. An example is an Edgeworth Box situation where the indifference curves of the trader have linear stretches and there is a linear segment located simultaneously on the indifference curves of both traders, so that all points of the segment are Pareto-optimal and belong to the equilibrium set for the same price. However, such indeterminacy is not too worrisome because all points of the segment have the same utility, even though representing different physical allocations. Presumably, the participants would be willing to randomize the choice among points of the segment. We shall refer to mechanisms in which the utility outcome is uniquely determined, even though the physical allocations may not be, as *essentially single-valued.* We shall not try to rule out the indeterminacy of allocations as long as utilities are determinate.

On the other hand, there is reason to regard as incomplete processes where the "outcome" is indeterminate even in utility terms, since a further mechanism would be required to resolve the remaining conflict. An example of such an incomplete process would be one yielding as its "outcome" the set of all Pareto-optimal allocations; here both the requirements of nonwastefulness and unbiasedness are satisfied, yet the remaining indeterminacy is clearly excessive.

We shall find it convenient to refer to mechanisms possessing the three attributes just introduced (nonwastefulness, unbiasedness, and essential single-valuedness) as (Pareto-) *satisfactory*. (Note that satisfactoriness is a property of a mechanism, while optimality is a property of an allocation; in our terminology, it would be incorrect to refer to a mechanism as Pareto-optimal.) The two results of welfare economics referred to above (Koopmans' Props. 4 and 5) essentially assert that the perfectly competitive mechanism with redistributions is satisfactory for classical environments. On the other hand, many examples are available to show that this mechanism, generally speaking, fails to be satisfactory in nonclassical environments. (We are not saying that the environment must be classical for, say, unbiasedness, but rather that in Koopmans' Prop. 5 the various environmental assumptions cannot be dispensed with.) Also, as mentioned earlier, mechanisms such as those involving monopoly lack satisfactoriness even for classical environments.

With these well-known propositions of welfare economics as a point of departure, those interested in the normative theory of mechanisms have many options. Some will question whether (Pareto-) satisfactoriness is an acceptable normative postulate, but despite the validity of some objections, we shall not pursue this path. Our purpose will be to see to what extent, with satisfactoriness as the welfare criterion, it is possible to overcome the limitations of the competitive process. In particular, we shall be concerned with two such limitations.

We have already referred to one limitation, namely, the lack of Pareto-satisfactoriness of the competitive process in nonclassical environments. The question then arises as to whether one could design alternative informationally decentralized mechanisms that would be satisfactory even in nonclassical environments. The problem will be discussed in Section 2. Briefly, it appears that is is possible to design such mechanisms for broad classes of environments including those characterized by indivisibilities and nonconvexities, provided externalities are absent. On the other hand, examples are given to show that there may fail to exist informationally decentralized mechanisms guaranteeing satisfactoriness in the presence of externalities.

Another limitation of decentralized processes, including perfect competition, was noted in the presence of public goods – the incentive to misrepresent one's preferences, or perhaps resources and technology. Similarly, incentival difficulties have been pointed out with regard to rules proposed under the Lange-Lerner socialist competitive solution, perhaps because of the nature of the reward structure. Certain aspects of these problems will be examined in Section 3. It will be argued that the incentive toward misrepresentation is also present in a private goods economy except in the "atomistic" case. An example is constructed to show that (in an Edgeworth Box, pure exchange classical environment) not only is there an incentive toward misrepresentation when the competitive mechanism prevails, but that such incentive will appear for a broad class of informationally decentralized Pareto-satisfactory mechanisms. This suggests that there is a fundamental incentival difficulty in reconcilling the two objectives of informational decentralization and unbiased welfare maximization.

## 2. Informational Decentralization in Nonclassical Environments

In this section, we adopt Pareto-satisfactoriness as the performance criterion and abstract from incentival difficulties. We are interested in the performance of informationally decentralized mechanisms in nonclassical environments. Using the concept of informational decentralization of HURWICZ (1960a), we find that the competitive process qualifies as informationally decentralized, but is not Pareto-satisfactory for nonclassical environments. What are the alternatives?

It turns out that the situation is fundamentally different depending on whether externalities are absent ("decomposable" environments) or present ("nondecomposable" environments). For decomposable environments, a number of informationally decentralized mechanisms have been proposed. These include the "greed" process which is Pareto-satisfactory for all decomposable environments but does not in general converge; the stochastic adjustment process in HURWICZ, RADNER, and REITER (1970) which is Pareto-satisfactory for two important categories of nonclassical environments (discrete and nonconvex continuous and converges in a probabilistic sense); KANEMITSU's "inertia-greed" process (1970) which is Pareto-satisfactory and convergent for nonconvex continuous processes; the ARROW-HURWICZ (1960) modified Lagrangean gradient process which converges locally for certain nonconvex (increasing returns) environments. There are also recent contributions listed in the references (AOKI (1970b), DRÈZE and DE LA VALLÉE POUSSIN (1969), HEAL (1969), MALINVAUD (1970)) which are in somewhat the same spirit.

With regard to processes in this category, given that they are informationally decentralized and Pareto-satisfactory for the specified class of nonclassical environments, there still remains the question whether they are informationally as efficient as possible without sacrificing these attributes. The answer depends, of course, on the concept of informational efficiency. In the definition proposed in HURWICZ (1960a), one process is informationally more efficient than another if the formation of messages at each step requires less information (in the sense of a strictly coarser partitioning) about the messages sent at the preceding step. Using this definition, KANEMITSU (1966) showed that the greed process is not as informationally efficient a Pareto-satisfactory process as can be constructed for the class of decomposable environments, although the more efficient *K*-process he constructed differs only slightly from the greed process. It would be interesting, perhaps after introducing other definitions of informational efficiency, to find processes that are maximally informationally efficient with regard to a given class of environments; results of this type do not as yet seem to have been obtained.

When externalities are present (nondecomposable environments), neither perfect competition nor greed and similar processes can claim Pareto-satisfactoriness. In fact, when externalities are of the "nonseparable" type (see DAVIS and WHINSTON (1962)) there may be difficulties in defining such processes without violating the requirements of informational decentralization. Thus one is led to ask whether informational decentralization is compatible with Pareto-satisfactoriness in nondecomposable environments.

What follows is not a general answer to this question, but rather an examination of a suggestive example. The example owes a great deal to the work on quadratic teams by J. Marschak and Radner and also to stimulating suggestions from T. Marschak. Essentially, the result obtained is that, within the class of environments considered, informational decentralization is, in general, incompatible with Pareto-satisfactoriness. However, two points should be noted. On what might by some be considered the negative side of the ledger, the result is very dependent on the precise definition of informational decentralization. To the extent that the definition is controversial, so is the result. On the positive side, however, the result obtained is of interest even in the absence of agreement on the concept of informational decentralization. For what it shows is that the appearance of externalities increases the informational needs of the system, in the sense that, for certain states of information-processing capacity, Pareto-satisfactoriness can be promised if externalities are absent but not otherwise.

*The model.* There are $n$ production units, each characterized by an activity variable $a_i$, ranging over a nondegenerate interval (e.g., all nonnegative reals), a parameter vector $\theta_i$, and an output relation

$$y_i = Y^i(a_1, \ldots, a_n; \theta_i) \qquad (i = 1, 2, \ldots, n).$$

The total output of the economy is the sum $y_1 + \ldots + y_n$. In the examples, we shall confine ourselves to the case where output is one-dimensional and so is each activity variable $a_i$; however, the parameter vector $\theta_i$ will still in general be multidimensional. Furthermore, we shall only treat the case of two production units ($n = 2$), and the output relations will be assumed quadratic in the $a$'s. Without an explicit introduction of the consumers, we shall postulate that optimality is equivalent to the maximization of total output.

*Externalities* are said to be present if, for some $i$, $Y^i$ depends on at least one $j (j \neq i)$; they are *unilateral* if $Y^i$ depends on $a_j$ but not vice versa, otherwise, *bilateral*; they are *separable* if

$$Y^i(a_1, \ldots, a_n; \theta_i) = Y_{i1}(a_1; \theta_{i1}) + \ldots + Y_{in}(a_n; \theta_{in}) \quad (i = 1, \ldots, n).$$

The model can be related to our earlier terminology by noting that it defines a class of environments. The $i$-th unit's environment component $e^i$ is defined by the function $Y^i$ and its parameter $\theta_i$; when the $Y^i$ are required to be quadratic, $e^i$ is completely defined by $\theta_i$. Dispersion of information is postulated in the sense that $\theta_i$ is assumed known to the $i$-th unit and to no other units. For $j \neq i$, the only information available to the $j$-th unit about $\theta_i$ is derived from the exchange of messages specified by the adjustment process to be described below.

The message emitted by the $i$-th unit at time $t$ is denoted by $m_i(t)$. (Since the adjustment process is a form of tâtonnement, "time" is to be interpreted as "computational", not historical.) The response functions are defined by the difference equation system

$$m_i(t+1) - m_i(t) = g^i[m_1(t), \ldots, m_n(t); \theta] \qquad (i = 1, \ldots, n)$$

where $\theta = \langle \theta_1, \ldots, \theta_n \rangle$.
(Thus the response functions are given by

$$f^i[m; \theta] = m_i + g^i[m; \theta],$$

where $m = \langle m_1, \ldots, m_n \rangle$.

The process is in equilibrium at a message $n$-tuple $\bar{m} = \langle \bar{m}_1, \ldots, \bar{m}_n \rangle$ if

$$g^i(\bar{m}; \theta) = 0 \qquad (i = 1, \ldots, n),$$

which is written vectorially as

$$g(\bar{m}; \theta) = 0.$$

Given that the process is in equilibrium at $\bar{m}$, one must specify the outcome function to determine which actions $a_i$ are to be taken. In their most general form, we shall consider ("parametric") outcome functions

$$\bar{a}_i = h^i(\bar{m}; \theta) \qquad (i = 1, \ldots, n),$$

written vectorially as

$$\bar{a} = h(\bar{m}; \theta),$$

with $a = \langle a_1, \ldots, a_n \rangle$.

Outcome functions are called *nonparametric* when $h^i$ is independent of $\theta$. (In HURWICZ (1960), only nonparametric outcome functions were considered.) Now, for the process to be informationally decentralized, it is required that $\theta_i$ replace the $n$-tuple $\theta = \langle \theta_1, \ldots, \theta_n \rangle$ as argument in $g^i$ and $h^i$. Thus, under informational decentralization, the equilibrium and outcome conditions become (omitting the bars over $m_i$ and $a_i$)

$$\begin{aligned} g^i(m; \theta_i) &= 0 \\ a_i &= h^i(m; \theta_i) \end{aligned} \qquad (i = 1, \ldots, n).$$

(This is the "privacy" aspect of informational decentralization.) A particularly simple and natural outcome function is one that identifies messages as *proposed-action* levels, i.e.,

$$h^i(m; \theta) = m_i \qquad (i = 1, \ldots, n).$$

(The so-called *concrete* process in HURWICZ (1960a) is of the proposed-action type, the action being trade and/or production.) The proposed-action outcome function is, of course, nonparametric since here $h^i(m; \theta) \equiv m_i$ and so does not depend on the parameter vector $\theta$.

In considering the possibility of devising an informationally decentralized mechanism, we shall examine the possibility of doing this through a proposed-action process; should this be impossible, by a more general nonparametric process; and, finally, by parametric processes. Thus, a hierarchy of "impossibility" results may be obtained. If someone feels, for instance, that parametric processes are too general to be of interest, he may confine his attention to results relevant in the context of the narrower class of outcome functions.

We shall be dealing with quadratic output functions characterized by parameter values which make them strictly concave, so that first-order differential conditions yield unique optima. These conditions may be written as

$$\sum_{i=1}^{n} Y_k^i(a; \theta_i) = 0 \qquad (k = 1, \ldots, n)$$

where $Y_k^i$ denotes the partial derivative $\partial Y^i / \partial a_k$. When solved for the $a_i$, the first-order optimality conditions will be written as

$$a_i = w^i(\theta) \qquad (i = 1, \ldots, n),$$

or, vectorially,

$$a = w(\theta).$$

A process (defined by the functions $g$ and $h$) is said to be *satisfactory* if and only if the following two conditions are satisfied:

(1) Given $(a, \theta)$ satisfying the optimality relation $a = w(\theta)$, there exists a message $m$ (an $n$-tuple of reals) such that $g(m, \theta) = 0$ and $a = h(m, \theta)$;

(2) given $(a, \theta, m)$ satisfying the relations $g(m, \theta) = 0$ and $a = h(m, \theta)$, it follows that $a = w(\theta)$.

It will be noted that (2) is nonwastefulness while (1) is unbiasedness. Thus the concept just defined is a specialization of Pareto-satisfactoriness to the model at hand. Of course, the Pareto aspect is trivial, since there is no conflict of preferences.

The problem to be investigated is the following. For specified output functions, does there exist a satisfactory informationally decentralized process; i.e., are the functions $g^i$ and $h^i$ (both depending on $\theta$ through $\theta_i$ only),

$(i=1, \ldots, n)$, such that the above conditions (1) and (2) of satisfactoriness hold for all members of a specified class of output functions $Y^i$? It turns out that answers depend crucially on the class of output functions, even among the quadratics. This will be illustrated by considering three examples, always quadratic and always with $n=2$.

*Example A.* Output functions are given by

$$y_1 = \alpha_1 a_1 + \gamma_1 a_2 - (1/2)\, a_1^2$$

$$y_2 = \alpha_2 a_2 \qquad\qquad - (1/2)\, a_2^2 ,$$

with the parameter vectors

$$\theta_1 = (\alpha_1, \gamma_1)$$

$$\theta_2 = \alpha_2 .$$

(This definition of parameter vectors means that the coefficient $\gamma_1$ indicating the impact of the second unit's activities on the first unit's productivity is known to unit 1 but not to unit 2.) In this instance, we have a unilateral separable externality. It is easily seen that the total output $y_1 + y_2$ will be maximized when

$$a_1 = \alpha_1$$

$$a_2 = \alpha_2 + \gamma_1 ,$$

so that these are the optimality relations $a = w(\theta)$.

Now the class of environments represented by Example A can be shown to be informationally decentralizable (*while preserving satisfactoriness*) or nondecentralizable depending on the additional requirements that one may wish to impose on the response and outcome functions. With proofs relegated to the appendix below (pp. 317–20), the following results are obtained for environments and optimality relations of Example A:

(i) Decentralization is impossible with a one-to-one outcome function of the nonparametric type $a = h(m)$; hence, in particular, it is impossible to decentralize through a proposed-action type process where $a = m$; this result has been generalized by T. Marschak to a wider class of environments and optimality relations than those of Example A (see appendix);

(ii) Decentralization is impossible for a nonparametric outcome function $a=h(m)$ (where $m=\langle m_1, m_2\rangle$ and $m_1, m_2$ are real numbers), when $h$ is required to be Lipschitzian and $g$ "quasi-Lipschitzian"[6];

(iii) Decentralization is possible through parametric Lipschitzian outcome functions, with quasi-Lipschitzian response functions, namely, by the following process:

$$g^1 \equiv \gamma_1 - m_1, \qquad h^1 \equiv \alpha_1$$
$$g^2 \equiv 0, \qquad h^2 \equiv \alpha_2 + m_1$$

(the process is parametric because the outcome functions contain the parameters $\alpha_i$, and it is informationally decentralized because $g^1$, $h^1$ do not depend on $\alpha_2$, while $g^2$, $h^2$ do not depend on $\alpha_1, \gamma_1$);

(iv) Decentralization is possible through the following nonparametric, but also non-Lipschitzian, process (where the symbols $p_1(\cdot)$ and $p_2(\cdot)$ represent the two components of Peano's "space-filling curve," see Apostol (1957, p. 396):

$$g^1 \equiv [\alpha_1 - p_1(m_1)]^2 + [\gamma_1 - p_2(m_1)]^2, \qquad h^1 \equiv p_1(m_1);$$
$$g^2 \equiv \alpha_2 - m_2, \qquad h^2 \equiv m_2 + p_2(m_1)$$

(this process is nonparametric, since no parameters enter as arguments of the outcome functions $h^i$; it is informationally decentralized because $g^1$ does not depend on $\alpha_2$, while $g^2$ does not depend on $\alpha_1$, $\gamma_1$; it is not Lipschitzian, in fact not of bounded variation, because the Peano functions $p_i(\cdot)$ lack these properties).

This example is instructive for several reasons. First, consider result (i) as applied to proposed-action type processes. Since communication of this type, with bids, offers, etc., as distinct from some more abstract signals, is often most natural (as in market processes), it is interesting to see that with communication restricted to proposed actions, informational decentralization is incompatible with satisfactoriness. The incompatibility arises from the presence of externality, i.e., the term $\gamma_1 a_2$ in $Y^1$; there would be no difficulty if this term were absent and known to be absent. Furthermore, the incompatibility arises even though the externality is of the very "mild" unilateral and separable type!

[6] We call $g$ "quasi-Lipschitzian" if and only if there exists a positive constant $K$ such that, given $m, m''$, there exist $\theta', \theta''$ satisfying the relations $g(m', \theta')=0$, $g(m'', \theta'')=0$, such that the inequality $\|\theta'-\theta''\| \leqq K \cdot \|m'-m''\|$ holds. (The symbol $\|x\|$ denotes the norm of $x$.) It may be noted that in this example, but not in similar situations involving more parameters, the Lipschitzian property may be softened to the requirement that the functions be of bounded variation.

Once we know that it is impossible to decentralize through a proposed-action process, it is not surprising that the same is true for any outcome function $h$ which constitutes a one-to-one correspondence between actions and messages; for by relabeling actions, we get back to a proposed-action type process. Suppose then that we are willing to adopt a signaling system that is not in a one-to-one relationship to actions, but where the process is still required to be nonparametric. (The latter requirement amounts to specifying that, given the equilibrium message $n$-tuple, an outside agency with no knowledge of the environment could determine the corresponding actions.) Results (ii) and (iv) taken together tell us that decentralization (in the sense of "privacy," i.e., $g^i$ being independent of $\theta_j$ for $j \neq i$) is compatible with satisfactoriness, provided we are willing to use non-Lipschitzian functions.

Now, instead of using non-Lipschitzian functions, one could accomplish the same by the use of a two-dimensional message $m_1$, which would convey to unit 2 the values of the parameters $\alpha_1$ and $\gamma_1$. Thus the Lipschitzian requirement has the effect of making certain that a single real number $m_1$ cannot be used to convey information about two numbers simultaneously. (A simple device, due to Cantor, for performing such a "trick" is to use, say, odd-numbered decimal digits of $m_1$ for the consecutive digits of $\alpha_1$, and the even-numbered ones for those of $\gamma_1$.) If by "genuine dimensionality" of a message we mean the number of numbers it can convey without "tricks," the Lipschitzian requirement simply enforces "genuine" one-dimensional nature of the messages.

It is, of course, legitimate to question whether the requirement of "genuine" one-dimensionality is appropriate as a part of the definition of informational decentralization. But, for our purposes, this requirement is merely an example of the fact that the requirement of "privacy" ($g_i$ depending on $\theta_i$, not on $\theta_j$, for $j \neq i$) is meaningless if there is no accompanying restriction on the process of conveying information between units. In any case, the result (ii) shows that the presence of externalities calls for less restricted information transfers than would otherwise be the case.

It is worth noting that there is a digital counterpart to the Lipschitzian requirement. Thus if we think of a communication process where the accuracy of, say, $k$ digits is required, and communication is by means of $k$-digit messages, it is not possible to transmit two numbers in one message, except by cutting in half the obtainable accuracy (by $k/2$ digits of the message to convey one number and the other $k/2$ for the other number).

The limitation implicit in restricting the "genuine dimensionality" of messages is highly relevant to the original notion of informational decentralization (Hayek, Lange) where the consensus was that it is difficult to transfer the complex information concerning, for example, a firm's production function or a consumer's preference map. On the other hand, the market process generally envisaged involves price and quantity messages, usually interpreted as having the dimensionality of the commodity space. Thus it was, in effect, postulated that messages of lower dimensionality could be conveyed, but those of higher (possibly infinite) dimensionality could not. The above restriction on the dimensionality of the message $m_1$ is in the same spirit, although, admittedly, in a much simpler setting.

Finally, from the point of view of resource cost of communication, it might be reasonable to postulate that the cost of transmission increases with the "genuine dimensionality" of the message. If so, it is again of interest to know that externalities call for increased cost of communication. The alternatives, in situations such as that of Example A, are either sacrificing "privacy" (which might also entail additional costs) or giving up satisfactoriness (i.e., the optimization performance properties).

Since Example A is quite special (a separable unilateral externality), it is natural to inquire whether the phenomena there observed are also encountered in more general situations. In particular, one wishes to know whether, as in Example A (iii), a decentralization using Lipschitzian functions is always possible if one is willing to use parametric outcome functions $h^i(m; \theta_i)$. The answer depends on whether the externality is unilateral. Example B below exhibits such a Lipschitzian decentralized parametric outcome process for the general quadratic unilateral externality. Example C, on the other hand, where the externality is bilateral (though separable), cannot be decentralized even by parametric Lipschitzian functions.

*Example B.* The output functions are given by

$$y_1 = \alpha_1 a_1 + \gamma_1 a_2 - (1/2)\beta_1 a_1^2 - (1/2)\eta_1 a_2^2 - \delta_1 a_1 a_2,$$

$$y_2 = \alpha_2 a_2 \qquad - (1/2)\beta_2 a_2^2,$$

which is a *unilateral* externality, separable if $\delta_1 = 0$ but not otherwise; it is the most general (except for constants) unilateral quadratic externality. It is assumed that unit $i$ knows the parameters whose subscript is $i$, as in Example A. That is,

$$\theta_1 = (\alpha_1, \gamma_1, \beta_1, \eta_1, \delta_1)$$

$$\theta_2 = (\alpha_2, \beta_2).$$

Now the functions to be used by unit 1 have different appearance depending on whether the externality is separable or not (i.e., whether $\delta_1 = 0$). This causes complexity, but does not violate the requirements of informational decentralization, since $\delta_1$ is one of the components of $\theta_1$, i.e., known to unit 1. The functions for unit 2, on the other hand, are the same regardless of separability. We have

$$g^1 \equiv \begin{cases} m_1 - (\gamma_1 - \eta_1 m_2), & \text{if } \delta_1 = 0, \\ \alpha_1 - \dfrac{\beta_1}{\delta_1}(\gamma_1 - \eta_1 m_2 - m_1) - \delta_1 m_2, & \text{if } \delta_1 \neq 0; \end{cases}$$

$$h^1 \equiv \begin{cases} \dfrac{\alpha_1}{\beta_1}, & \text{if } \delta_1 = 0, \\ \dfrac{1}{\delta_1}(\gamma_1 - \eta_1 m_2 - m_1), & \text{if } \delta_1 \neq 0; \end{cases}$$

$$g^2 \equiv m_1 + \alpha_2 - \beta_2 m_2;$$

$$h^2 \equiv m_2.$$

Clearly, $h^1$ is parametric and all four functions are Lipschitzian; informational decentralization ("privacy") is satisfied since each $g^i$, $h^i$ is independent of $\theta_j$ for $j \neq i$. The proof of Pareto-satisfactoriness will be omitted.

The next example has a separable *bilateral* externality, i.e., a bilateral externality of a relatively simple structure. Nevertheless, it can be shown that it is impossible to decentralize it, even with parametric functions, without violating the Lipschitzian conditions. On the other hand, if one is willing to use non-Lipschitzian functions (i.e., violate the "genuine dimensionality" limit on messages), decentralization even through nonparametric outcome functions becomes possible. The proofs are analogous to those of Example A but much more complex, and will not be given here.

*Example C.* The output functions are given by

$$y_1 = \alpha_1 a_1 + \gamma_1 a_2 - (1/2)\eta_1 a_2^2,$$

$$y_2 = \alpha_2 a_2 + \gamma_2 a_1 - (1/2)\eta_2 a_1^2,$$

with unit $i$ knowing parameters whose subscript is $i$, i.e.,

$$\theta_1 = (\alpha_1, \gamma_1, \eta_1),$$

$$\theta_2 = (\alpha_2, \gamma_2, \eta_2).$$

*Appendix*

(i) Example A is not decentralizable through a proposed-action process.

*Proof.* Here $a = m$, hence $g(m, \theta) = 0$ becomes $g(a, \theta) = 0$. It will be shown below that if this process were decentralizable, the latter relation would define a single-valued function, say, $\theta = f(a)$, onto a neighborhood in the $\theta$-space. But this contradicts the optimality relations $a_1 = \alpha_1$, $a_2 = \alpha_2 + \gamma_1$ which show that $\theta = (\alpha_1, \gamma_1, \alpha_2)$ is not uniquely determined by $\langle a_1, a_2 \rangle = a$.

The single-valuedness of $f$ is established as follows. Let $\theta'$, $\theta''$ be two, possibly distinct, parameter vector values compatible with a given value of $a$. Since $g$ is assumed decentralized, $\theta$ enters each $g^i$ only through $\theta^i$, with $\theta^1 = (\alpha_1, \gamma_1)$ and $\theta^2 = \alpha_2$. We thus have

(1) $g^1(a, \theta_1') = 0, \quad g^2(a, \theta_2') = 0,$

(2) $g^1(a, \theta_1'') = 0, \quad g^2(a, \theta_2'') = 0,$

hence also,

(3) $g^1(a, \theta_1') = 0, \quad g^2(a, \theta_2'') = 0$

and

(4) $g^1(a, \theta_1'') = 0, \quad g^2(a, \theta_2') = 0.$

Since $g$ is satisfactory, we have, respectively (by equivalence with the optimality relations),

(1*) $a_1 = \alpha_1', \quad a_2 = \alpha_2' + \gamma_1',$

(2*) $a_1 = \alpha_1'', \quad a_2 = \alpha_2'' + \gamma_2'',$

(3*) $a_1 = \alpha_1', \quad a_2 = \alpha_2'' + \gamma_1',$

(4*) $a_1 = \alpha_1'', \quad a_2 = \alpha_2' + \gamma_1''.$

Hence

$$\alpha_1' = \alpha_1'', \alpha_2' = \alpha_2'', \gamma_1' = \gamma_1''$$

so that $(\alpha_1, \gamma_1, \alpha_2)$ is uniquely determined by $a$.

The following generalization of this result to a wider class of situations than the quadratic two-person output-maximizing team has been provided by T. Marschak. Consider first a two-person organization. Mr. $i$ $(i = 1, 2)$

observes an environment $e_i$ in a set $E_i$ and takes actions $a_i$. The optimality relations

$$a_1 = \hat{a}_1(e_1, e_2), \quad a_2 = \hat{a}_2(e_1, e_2)$$

are to be satisfied. If $\langle g^1, g^2 \rangle$ is a decentralized satisfactory proposed-action process, then $g^1(a_1, a_2, e_1) = g^2(a_1, a_2, e_2) = 0$ if and only if the quadruple $(a_1, a_2, e_1, e_2)$ satisfies the optimality relations. Now if there exist $\bar{e}_1$ and $\bar{\bar{e}}_1$ in $E_1$, $\bar{e}_2$ and $\bar{\bar{e}}_2$ in $E_2$ and actions $a_1^*$, $a_2^*$ such that (1) $\hat{a}_1(\bar{e}_1, \bar{e}_2) = \hat{a}_1(\bar{\bar{e}}_1, \bar{\bar{e}}_2) = a_1^*$, (2) $\hat{a}_2(\bar{e}_1, \bar{e}_2) = \hat{a}_2(\bar{\bar{e}}_1, \bar{\bar{e}}_2) = a_2^* \neq \hat{a}_2(\bar{e}_1, \bar{\bar{e}}_2)$, then there does not exist a decentralized satisfactory proposed-action process.

*Proof.* The following two quadruples (among others) satisfy the optimality relations: $(a_1^*, a_2^*, \bar{e}_1, \bar{e}_2)$ and $(a_1^*, a_2^*, \bar{\bar{e}}_1, \bar{\bar{e}}_2)$. If a decentralized proposed-action process $\langle g^1, g^2 \rangle$ were satisfactory, we would have

$$0 = g^1(a_1^*, a_2^*, \bar{e}_1) = g^2(a_1^*, a_2^*, \bar{\bar{e}}_2).$$

But that would, in turn, imply that the quadruple $(a_1^*, a_2^*, \bar{e}_1, \bar{\bar{e}}_2)$ satisfies the optimality relations, contrary to assumption (2).

[It is easily checked that Example A satisfies conditions (1) and (2) with $e_1 = (\alpha_1, \gamma_1)$, $e_2 = \alpha_2$, $\hat{a}_1 = \alpha_1$, $\hat{a}_2 = \alpha_2 + \gamma_1$, and, for example, $\bar{e}_1 = (5,4)$, $\bar{\bar{e}}_1 = (5,7)$, $\bar{e}_2 = 4$, $\bar{\bar{e}}_2 = 1$, $a_1^* = 5$, $a_2^* = 8$.]

The result extends to $n$-person organizations: if the conditions (1) and (2) are satisfied for some pair of persons and some fixed value of the environments of the other $n-2$ persons, then a decentralized satisfactory proposed-action process does not exist.

Note however that *not every* externality in which one person's optimal action depends on another's environment as well as his own implies nonexistence of a satisfactory decentralized proposed-action process. Thus, e.g., if $E_1$ and $E_2$ are the reals and $\hat{a}_1(e_1, e_2) = e_1 + e_2$, $\hat{a}_2(e_1, e_2) = e_2$, then the process $g^1(a_1, a_2, e_1) = a_1 - a_2 - e_1$, $g^2(a_1, a_2, e_2) = a_2 - e_2$ has the required properties despite the presence of externalities.

(ii) Returning to Example A, we next show that the class of environments cannot be decentralized through a Lipschitzian process with a nonparametric outcome function. The essential step in the proof is the following.

*Lemma.* In a decentralized satisfactory process, the parameter vector $\theta = (\alpha_1, \gamma_2, \alpha_1)$ is a single-valued function, say, $\theta = f(m)$ from the two-dimensional message space of $m = \langle m_1, m_2 \rangle$ *onto* a neighborhood in the three-dimensional $\theta$-space.

*Proof.* Let $\theta'$, $\theta''$ be two, possibly distinct, parameter vector values compatible with a given value of $m$ (at equilibrium). Since $g$ is decentralized and the outcome functions nonparametric, we have

$$\text{(1)}\quad \begin{array}{lll} (1.1) & g^i(m, \theta_i') = 0, \quad a_i' = h^i(m) & \\ & & (i = 1, 2); \\ (1.2) & g^i(m, \theta_i'') = 0, \quad a_i'' = h^i(m) & \end{array}$$

hence also

$$\text{(2)}\quad \begin{array}{ll} (2.1) & g^1(m, \theta_1') = 0, \quad g^2(m, \theta_2'') = 0, \quad a_1^* = h^1(m), \quad a_2^* = h^2(m) \\ (2.2) & g^1(m, \theta_1'') = 0, \quad g^2(m, \theta_2') = 0, \quad a_1^{**} = h^1(m), \quad a_2^{**} = h^2(m). \end{array}$$

Since the process is satisfactory, it follows from the optimality relations that

$$\text{(3)}\quad \begin{array}{lll} (3.1) & a_1' = \alpha_1', & a_2' = \alpha_2' + \gamma_1' \\ (3.2) & a_1'' = \alpha_1'', & a_2'' = \alpha_2'' + \gamma_1'' \\ (3.3) & a_1^* = \alpha_1', & a_2^* = \alpha_2'' + \gamma_1' \\ (3.4) & a_1^{**} = \alpha_1'', & a_2^{**} = \alpha_2' + \gamma_1''. \end{array}$$

(Eqs. (3.1)–(3.4) are obtained respectively from (1.1), (1.2), (2.1), (2.2).) On the other hand, by (1) and (2),

$$a_1' = h^1(m) = a_1'',$$

so that

$$\alpha_1' = \alpha_1'',$$

and

$$a_2' = h^2(m) = a_2'' = a_2^* = a_2^{**},$$

which yields

$$\alpha_2' + \gamma_1' = \alpha_2'' + \gamma_1'' = \alpha_2'' + \gamma_1' = \alpha_2' + \gamma_1''.$$

Therefore,

$$\alpha_2' = \alpha_2'' \text{ and } \gamma_1' = \gamma_1''.$$

Thus $\theta' = \theta''$ and the single-valuedness assertion is proved. The range of the parameter vector $\theta$ has not been restricted in our example. But it is enough to suppose that it varies over some (three-dimensional) neighborhood. Then the satisfactoriness of the process requires that $g(m, \theta) = 0$ have a solution $m$ for every value of $\theta$ in the neighborhood. This establishes the "onto" property of the mapping $f(\cdot)$ in the lemma.

The lemma having been established, it remains to show that the mapping $f$ cannot be Lipschitzian. But this follows from the fact that a Lipschitzian mapping into a space of higher dimension yields an image of Jordan content zero (in the dimensionality of the range space); see APOSTOL (1957), Theorem 10–8, page 257.

### 3. Incentive-compatibility

A mechanism that is informationally feasible may be criticized on grounds of incompatibility with "natural" incentives. That is, participants in the process may find it advantageous to violate the rules of the process. Such violations might involve two or more units ("collusion") or single individuals. In what follows, we shall concentrate on the latter case, i.e., on the problem of *individual incentive-compatibility*.

Analytically, we think of the participants as taking part in an $n$-person noncooperative game, with the response function of the $i$-th individual as his strategy and the utility to him of the outcome as the payoff. A process is defined as individually incentive-compatible if and only if the response functions it prescribes constitute a Nash equilibrium point for this game.[7] The use of utility, as distinct from merely postulating a complete ordering, is not essential, but is adopted for the sake of expository convenience. Also, we shall identify the outcome with the equilibrium allocation generated by the process.

Let the equilibrium of the process $q^*$ be given by the usual relations

$$\overline{m}^i = f^{*i}(\overline{m}^i, \ldots, \overline{m}^n; e^i) \qquad (i = 1, \ldots, n),$$

where $f^{*i}$ is the response function prescribed by the prevailing mechanism $q^*$, and the process is *privacy-respecting* (satisfies the "privacy" requirement) in that $f^{*i}$ depends on $e$ through $e^i$ only. Further, we define the $i$-th *strategy* as the function $g^{*i}$ of the message $n$-tuple $m = \langle m^1, \ldots, m^n \rangle$ given by

$$g^{*i}(m^1, \ldots, m^n) = f^{*i}(m^1, \ldots, m^n; e^i) \text{ for all } m, \tag{3.1}$$

so that $g^{*i}$ is determined by $f^{*i}$ and $e^i$.

Now the *outcome* is a state (say, the equilibrium distribution) $\bar{s}$ given as a function of the equilibrium message $n$-tuple $\overline{m}$,

$$\bar{s} = \phi(\overline{m}).$$

[7] See DRÈZE and DE LA VALLÉE POUSSIN (1969), as well as HURWICZ (1971); the latter contains a somewhat modified version of suggestions initially presented at the Ann Arbor 1968 conference on the comparison of economic systems.

In game theory language, the "payoff" to the $i$-th participant is, therefore,

$$u^{*i} = U^i(\bar{s}),$$

where $U^i$ is the utility function of the $i$-th participant. Indirectly, $u^{*i}$ depends on the strategy functions $g^{*1}$, which may be expressed by the relations

$$u^{*i} = u^i(g^{*1}, \ldots, g^{*n}), \qquad i = 1, \ldots, n.$$

Let us write $g^* = \langle g^{*1}, \ldots, g^{*n} \rangle$ and denote by $g^{*)i(}$the $(n-1)$-tuple obtained from $g^*$ by deleting its $i$-th component $g^{*i}$. Then $g^*$ constitutes a Nash equilibrium over some specified admissible strategy domains $G^1, \ldots, G^n$ if, for each $i = 1, \ldots, n$, the inequality

$$u^i(g^i, g^{*)i(}) \leqq u^i(g^*) \tag{3.2}$$

holds for all $g^i$ in $G^i$.

A mechanism is said to be individually incentive-compatible when the strategies implied by the response rules it prescribes constitute such a Nash equilibrium. It is clear, however, that the Nash equilibrium property of a strategy $n$-tuple $g^*$ depends on the admissible strategy domains $G^i$. Since these domains consist of alternatives to the prescribed rules of behavior, they cannot be regarded as part of the "official" adjustment process. Rather, they are the "natural" alternatives to which participants might resort if it were to their advantage. Are there then any limits to how broad these domains of alternative strategies might be?

To find an answer to this question, let us consider the standard pure exchange (Edgeworth Box) case as the environment, and perfect competition $q^C$ as the mechanism. Thus $e^i$ specifies the initial endowment $\omega^i$, the admissible consumption set $X^i$, and the (selfish) preference relation $R^i$ (represented by the utility function $U^i$). The outcome is the competitive equilibrium allocation $c = \langle c^1, \ldots, c^n \rangle$, together with the corresponding competitive price $p^C$; for the sake of simplicity, this equilibrium will be assumed unique. By $g^{Ci}$ we shall denote the competitive strategy function of the $i$-th participant, given his environmental characteristics $e^i$, i.e.,

$$g^{Ci}(m) = f^{Ci}(m; \mathring{e}^i) \text{ for all } m,$$

with $\mathring{e}^i$ the true environmental characteristic, and $f^{Ci}$ the response function prescribed by the competitive process when the $i$-th characteristic is $\mathring{e}^i$.

The $n$-tuple $g^C = \langle g^{C1}, \ldots, g^{Cn} \rangle$ is therefore incentive-compatible if, on the assumption that all others will abide by their $g^{Cj}$ strategies, no participant

$i$ can profit by departing from his $g^{Ci}$ and adopting some other strategy $g^i$ within the permissible domain $G^i$.

We know, of course, that the opposite situation is the typical one. That is, with a finite number of participants, on the assumption that others will act as price-takers, it will pay a participant to behave monopolistically. If, for instance, traders $2, \ldots, n$ are assumed to behave as price-takers, there will usually exist a price $p^M \neq p^C$ at which $z^2, \ldots, z^n$ will be demanded by $2, \ldots, n$, respectively, acting as utility-maximizing price-takers, and such that $U^1(z^1) > U^1(c^1)$, $z^1 + z^2 + \ldots + z^n = \omega^1 + \omega + \ldots + \omega^n$, so that $z = \langle z^1, \ldots, z^n \rangle$ is feasible. (Note that $p^M$ is not assumed to maximize $U^1(z^1)$, although such maximization is not ruled out.)

If we denote by the $g^{M,1}$ the monopolistic behavior strategy of the first trader, the case where $p^M$ places the first trader at a higher utility level than would $p^C$ is expressed by the inequality

$$u^1(g^{M,1}, g^{C)1(}) > u^1(g^{C1}, g^{C)1(}),$$

so that the perfectly competitive mechanism is not a Nash equilibrium (not individually incentive-compatible) if monopolistic behavior $g^{M,1}$ is in the admissible domain $G^1$.

Suppose, however, that there is a legal requirement to abide by the competitive rules which is enforced insofar as that can be done without violating the participant's "privacy." That is, the enforcement agency has no direct knowledge of the individual environmental components $e^i$, but each trader must be able to justify his observable behavior (bids) as a price-taker's utility maximization.

Since the enforcement agency does not know the first trader's true $e^1$ (to be denoted by $\mathring{e}^1$), he will be able to use a strategy $g^1$ different from that dictated by the response function $f^{C1}$ provided that there exists some (fictitious) $\tilde{e}^i$ such that, for each message $n$-tuple $m$,

$$g^1(m) = f^{C1}(m; \tilde{e}^1).$$

This simply means that the alternative (to price-taking) behavior $g^1$ can be "rationalized" as price-taking behavior for some fictitious specification of the first trader's initial endowment, consumption set, and preferences.

Some fictitious values for $e^1$ might be outside the class of environments for which the process was designed and would not "pass"; we may therefore suppose that the choice of fictitious values for the $e^i$ is restricted to an *a priori* specified "plausible" class $E^i$. In our example, it seems reasonable to select the $E^i$ so that their Cartesian product will yield the class of what we have called "classical" environments. (In the case of pure exchange "classical" means absence of externalities, convexity, and continuity of preferences, and the convexity and closedness of the consumption set.)

In effect, our concept of incentive-compatibility merely requires that no one should find it profitable to "cheat," where cheating is defined as behavior that can be made to look "legal" by a misrepresentation of the participant's preferences or endowment, with the proviso that the fictitious preferences should be within certain "plausible" limits.

It is this notion of incentive-compatibility that seems to underlie the discussion of allocation mechanisms for public goods, as is seen in SAMUELSON's (1954, pp. 388–9) comment in connection with the Lindahl solution, to the effect that "... it is in the selfish interest of each person to give *false* signals, to pretend to have less interest in a given collective consumption activity than he really has...". Similarly, DRÈZE and DE LA VALLÉE POUSSIN (1969) refer to incentives for correct or incorrect revelation of preferences; thus the question is not whether the participants would at all refuse to "play the game," but rather whether they would behave in a way ostensibly consistent with the rules of the process but for a false set of preferences.

We shall see that even when departures from prescribed rules are confined to "plausible cheating" behavior, an important class of mechanisms including perfect competition in nonatomistic[8] economies, turns out to lack individual incentive-compatibility. In such cases, one need not worry whether it is realistic to confine oneself to the (relatively) narrow class of "plausible cheating" alternatives as strategies, since the conclusion of incentive-incompatibility would follow *a fortiori* for a wider class of alternatives.

To summarize then, a privacy-respecting mechanism $q^*$ is *individually incentive-compatible* with regard to individual environment classes $E^1, E^2, \ldots, E^n$ if the strategy $n$-tuple $g^*$ defined by (3.1), where the $f^{*i}$ are prescribed by the mechanism and the $e^i$ are true (equal $\mathring{e}^i$), satisfies the inequalities (3.2) for $i = 1, \ldots, n$ for all $g^i$ such that

$$g^i(m) = f^{*i}(m; \tilde{e}^i), \tag{3.4}$$

with $\tilde{e}^i$ in $E^i$.

Samuelson's above-quoted comment thus implies that the Lindahl

[8] We use the term "atomistic" in the old-fashioned sense, meaning that every participant is infinitesimal as compared with the total market or economy. (In modern measure-theoretic language this case is called "nonatomic.")

solution is not individually incentive-compatible.[9] The question is whether the failure of the various proposed mechanisms for the allocation of public goods to be individually incentive-compatible (in terms of the utility of final allocation as payoff) is peculiar to public goods, or whether it has a counterpart in economies where all goods are private.

In answering this question the crucial distinction is whether the economy is atomistic or not. If it is (i.e., if all traders are infinitesimal), we can agree with Samuelson (*op. cit.*, p. 389) that the competitive process makes it unprofitable to depart from the rules of perfectly competitive behavior when everyone else continues to abide by these rules. But in the nonatomistic case, of which the standard Edgeworth Box situation for a finite number of traders is an instance, the situation is different. We have already noted the well-known fact that in "typical" situations, with the initial endowment not Pareto-optimal, it will be advantageous for a trader to behave monopolistically when others act as price-takers. But this is not sufficient to establish individual incentive-incompatibility according to our definition. To prove absence of incentive-compatibility we must show that when everyone else follows the rules of perfect competition (using their true preferences in utility maximization), it pays the remaining trader to behave in a way that is ostensibly price taking, but with regard to a "plausible" false $e^i$ (that is, false preferences or endowment or consumption set).[10] To be "plausible," this false set $e^i$ must satisfy the classical requirements.

Although we shall not provide a rigorous proof, Fig. 1 suggests that such a false preference map can easily be found. To construct it for $n=2$ and two goods, it is enough to locate a monopoly allocation $z=\langle z^1, z^2\rangle$, $z^i = (z^i_1, z^i_2)$, obtained at a monopoly price $\mathrm{p}^M$, and to construct for trader 1 a false indifference curve (downward sloping, convex to the origin) tangent to the monopoly price line at $z^1$; this will make $z$ into a (false) competitive allocation with regard to $p^M$, which now becomes a (false) competitive price.

---

[9] On the other hand, DRÈZE and DE LA VALLÉE POUSSIN (1969, pp. 28–30) find their mechanism for the allocation of public goods to be individually incentive-compatible. The contrast seems to be due to the local and instantaneous nature of the Drèze-Poussin payoff function, since their criterion is whether $\mathrm{d}u^i/\mathrm{d}t<0$ for a participant departing from the prescribed strategy, while Samuelson implicitly considers the relevant payoff to be the utility of the final (equilibrium) allocation. We adopt the Samuelson payoff assumption in what follows.

[10] One version of the game we imagine the traders to be playing is as follows: each trader picks an indifference map, a price-adjustment mechanism of Lange type is operated until market-clearing equilibrium prices are found, and then each trader collects the value his true utility function takes for the bundle which he obtains at the equilibrium.

It remains to complete the false preference map for trader 1 by a family of indifference curves which would not yield another false competitive equilibrium. That such a completion is possible in a particular case is shown in the Example D below. More generally, to make $[z, p^M]$ into a false competitive equilibrium, it would be sufficient for trader 1 to behave as a price-taker with regard to the (false) utility function given by

$$v = x_1^\alpha x_2$$

with

$$\alpha = (z_1^1 p^M)/z_2^1.$$

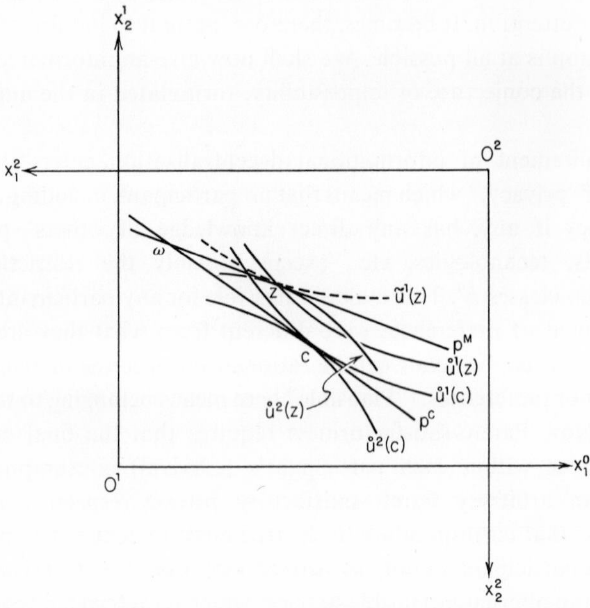


Fig. 1. $\omega$ = initial endowment, $p^C$ = competitive price line, $p^M$ = monopolistic price line, $c$ = competitive allocation, $z$ = monopolistic allocation, $\mathring{u}^i(x)$ = $i$'s true indifference curve through $x^i$, $\tilde{u}^i(x)$ = $i$'s false indifference curve through $x^i$.

(In the formula for $v$, $x_1$ and $x_2$ are the respective quantities of the two commodities obtained by trader 1.) This false utility function has not, however, been checked for uniqueness of equilibria.

Thus in a nonatomistic world perfect competition is not guaranteed to be individually incentive-compatible even for classical environments and with all goods private.

At this point one may be inclined to look for mechanisms other than perfect competition in order to find one that would be individually incentive-compatible, at least for classical (but nonatomistic) environments free of public goods. However, we want the mechanism to be not merely individually incentive-compatible, but also Pareto-satisfactory and informationally decentralized. Some known processes satisfying the latter two requirements (e.g., the greed process (HURWICZ (1960a)), the inertia-greed process (KANEMITSU (1970)), the stochastic adjustment process (HURWICZ, RADNER, and REITER (1970)) can all be shown to lack incentive-compatibility. On the other hand, no process combining the three attributes (Pareto-satisfactoriness, informational decentralization, individual incentive-compatibility) has come to our attention. It becomes, therefore, natural to inquire whether such a combination is at all possible. We shall now give an informal argument in support of the conjecture of impossibility, formulated in the author's 1971 paper.

The requirement of informational decentralization enters through the postulate of "privacy," which means that no participant, including an enforcement agency if any, has any direct knowledge of others' preferences, endowments, technologies, etc., except possibly the restriction to the *a priori* given classes $E^i$. This makes it possible for any participant to act as if his endowment or preferences were different from what they are, provided that his observable behavior can be rationalized in terms of *some* plausible endowment or preferences. ("Plausible" here means belonging to the specified class $E^i$.) Now Pareto-satisfactoriness requires that the final outcome be feasible, hence within each participant's (survival) consumption set $X^i$. Consider an arbitrary Pareto-satisfactory privacy-respecting mechanism and suppose that corresponding to the true environment $e$ the outcome is $s$. Let the first participant's utility associated with $s$ be $u^1 = U^1(s)$ and suppose that there is an alternative feasible state $s\#$ which is preferred by participant 1, i.e., $U^1(s\#) > U^1(s)$. This participant then has the incentive to act as if his consumption set were not the true $\mathring{X}^1$ (which includes $s$) but a smaller false $\tilde{X}^1$ containing only states whose utility for participant 1 is higher than $U^1(s)$. For, if the process is Pareto-satisfactory and privacy-respecting, it will then produce an outcome $s''$ which is feasible with respect to the false consumption set $\tilde{X}^1$, hence more advantageous to participant 1 than the correct outcome $s$ corresponding to the true $\mathring{X}^1$.

(This calculation is predicated on the assumption, implicit in the definition of incentive-compatibility, that other participants continue to follow the prescribed rules of the prevailing mechanism in terms of their true consumption sets, preferences, etc.) The preceding argument would constitute a proof of incentive-incompatibility in all Pareto-satisfactory informationally decentralized (privacy-respecting) processes, if one were willing to accept as "plausible" arbitrary consumption sets $X^i$, even though this implies that the initial endowment $\omega^i$ is far below the survival minimum.

What is particularly interesting about our problem is that a similar impossibility result can be obtained even when participants' falsifications are confined to classical environments, including the convexity of indifference curves, etc. To show this, we shall now confine ourselves to a somewhat narrower class of mechanisms by requiring (in addition to Pareto-satisfactoriness and respect for privacy) that the process always permits each participant to remain at a specified[11] endowment $\theta$; this property, to be called the *no-trade option* is present in the perfectly competitive process; it implies that one can postulate the outcomes to have utility no less than that of the specified endowment $\theta$, since otherwise the process lacks individual incentive-compatibility.

From this point on, we shall carry on the argument in terms of the two-person two-good pure exchange (Edgeworth Box) case. (Because of the negative nature of our claim, this approach is at the very least suggestive of the line of argument for the general case.) Now consider a situation where the specified endowment $\langle\theta^1, \theta^2\rangle$ is not Pareto-optimal and suppose that the allocation $y^* = \langle y^{*1}, y^{*2}\rangle$ generated by a given process has no higher utility for trader 1 than the (unique) competitive[12] allocation $\langle c^1, c^2\rangle$ would have; i.e., $U^1(y^{*1}) \leqq U^1(c^1)$.[13] Assume, furthermore again, that there

---

[11] $\theta = \langle\theta^1, \ldots, \theta^n\rangle$ is some redistribution of the initial endowment $\omega = \langle\omega^1, \ldots, \omega^n\rangle$, such that

$$\sum_{i=1}^{n} \theta^i = \sum_{i=1}^{n} \omega^i .$$

(The symbol $\theta$ used here is unrelated to that of Section 2.)

The interpretation of $\theta$ is that it may arise from some scheme of lump payments and subsidies preceding the tâtonnement phase of the process. By introducing the possibility of a redistribution from the initial $\omega$ to $\theta$, we safeguard the requirement of having an unbiased, hence Pareto-satisfactory process. However, in what follows, $\theta$ plays the usual role of $\omega$; in particular, the various price lines are assumed to go through $\theta$ and the competitive allocation is determined with reference to $\theta$.

[12] Because the environment is assumed classical, a competitive equilibrium necessarily exists.

[13] Postulating this inequality involves no loss of generality, since it necessarily holds for at least one trader.

is a potential monopolistic advantage for trader 1; i.e., there is a feasible allocation $\langle z^1, z^2 \rangle$ and a price vector $p^M$ such that trader 2 would demand $z^2$ if he were a price taker and $p^M$ were the given price, while $U^1(z^1) > U^1(c^1)$.

Let us note that for the class of processes now considered, the outcome must be Pareto-optimal and not below the initial utilities; hence for the case now considered the outcome must be a point of the "core," i.e., of the "contract curve" (that part of the Pareto-optimal curve which is within the lens-shaped area formed by the two indifference curves passing through the initial endowment point). Because the process respects privacy, the relevant contract curve will be the false one if, say, trader 1 plausibly falsifies his preferences, while trader 2 behaves correctly. Hence trader 1 will have an incentive to falsify his preferences if by so doing he can generate a false contract curve all points of which have a higher true utility to him than $z^1$. For the process will then produce an outcome on the false contract curve and trader 1 will necessarily profit, regardless of the particular point chosen on the false contract curve.

To illustrate the possibility of such falsification in a "classical" world, we have constructed the very simple Example D below, in which a false utility function results in a false contract curve all of whose points have a higher true utility for trader 1 than does his competitive allocation. It follows that there are classical environments in which no privacy-respecting Pareto-satisfactory process permitting the no-trade option is individually incentive-compatible. (We are implicitly assuming that communication is limited so as not to nullify the privacy.) Following the example, a somewhat more general result of similar nature is obtained.

*Example D.* (See Fig. 2.) Pure exchange; two traders (identified by superscripts) and two goods (identified by subscripts). Each trader's true consumption set $X^i$ is the nonnegative quadrant of the $x_1, x_2$-plane. The true utility function of each trader $i$ is the same Cobb-Douglas function

$$u^i = x_1^i x_2^i \qquad (i = 1, 2),$$

where the superscript $i$ attached to $x_j$ is not an exponent but merely refers to the $i$-th trader! The specified endowment is in the "northwest" corner of the Edgeworth Box, i.e.,

$$\theta^1 = (0, 1), \qquad \theta^2 = (1, 0).$$

From the symmetry, the Pareto-optimal set is the diagonal of the (here square) box; the competitive price line[14] is the negative diagonal, and the competitive allocation is the center of the square, so $c^i = (1/2, 1/2)$ for $i = 1, 2$.

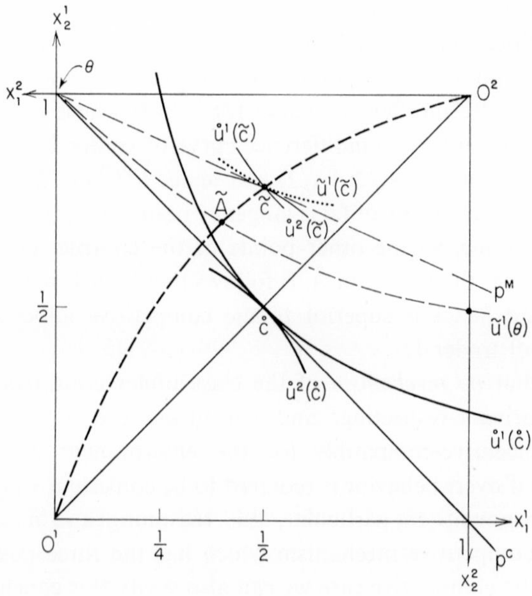


Fig. 2. $\mathring{c}$ = true competitive allocation, $\tilde{c}$ = false competitive allocation, $\tilde{A}0^2$ = false contract curve, $\theta$ = specified endowment, $\mathring{u}^i(x)$, $\tilde{u}^i(x)$ = as in Fig. 1.

Since the true contract curve happens also to be the positive diagonal, all that can be said about the outcome is that it will be somewhere on that diagonal, since nothing more has been specified about the process. Without loss of generality, suppose that this point is either at the competitive point (the center) or closer to the origin of trader 1, i.e., in the lower half of the positive diagonal. Then, assuming that trader 2 will abide by the rules of the process, trader 1 will find it advantageous to use a fictitious utility function

$$v^1 = \begin{cases} x_2^1 - 1/(1+x_1^1), \text{ for } x_2^1 > 0, \text{ or } x_2^1 = 0 \text{ with } x_1^1 \leqq 1; \\ -(1/2), \qquad \text{for } x_2^1 = 0 \text{ and } x_1^1 \geqq 1. \end{cases}$$

It may be noted that, for $v^1 = 0$, the false indifference curve goes through the

[14] The competitive equilibrium is taken with respect to $\theta$, hence the price line goes through $\theta$.

specified endowment point $\theta$ and is otherwise above the competitive price line.

It remains to be proved that this false utility function generates a (false) contract curve whose utility is always higher than the true utility of the competitive allocation $c^1$ which is given by $u^1(c^1)=(1/2)(1/2)=1/4$. Now the lower endpoint $\tilde{A}$ of the false contract curve is obtained from the condition that the false indifference curve for $v^1=0$ whose equation is $x^1= =1/(1+x_1^1)$ is tangent to an indifference curve of trader 2. The coordinates of $\tilde{A}$ turn out to be $(-1+\sqrt{2}, 1/\sqrt{2})$ and hence $u^1(\tilde{A})=.29$, which exceeds 1/4. Furthermore, the locus of false tangency points (i.e., the contract curve) has a positive slope, so the other points of the contract curve have both coordinates higher than those of $\tilde{A}$. It follows that their true utility $u^1$ always exceeds 1/4 and hence is superior to the competitive allocation from the point of view of trader 1.

It follows that *no mechanism* of the class under consideration (Pareto-satisfactory, privacy-respecting, and permitting the no-trade option) is individually incentive-compatible for the environment assumed in our example, even if overt behavior is required to be consistent with some (false) classical environment. In particular, this reasoning and its conclusion is valid for the competitive mechanism which has the three postulated attributes. But in the competitive case we can also verify this conclusion directly by noting that for the above false utility function $v$ the (false) competitive equilibrium allocation for trader 1 is the commodity bundle $\tilde{c}^1=(1/2, 7/9)$ with the (false) competitive price $p=4/9$. Since the true utility $u^1(\tilde{c}^1)$ of the false competitive allocation $\tilde{c}^1$ equals $(1/2)\cdot(7/9)$, and so exceeds the true utility $u^1(c^1)=(1/4)$ of the true competitive allocation $c^1$, it is seen directly that the competitive mechanism is not individually-compatible for the environment of our example. Thus the direct proof is in accord with the general one.

*A generalization.* The preceding example is helpful because one can give an explicit construction of the various points and curves, but it is natural to inquire to what extent it represents a typical situation. Although the problem has not as yet been fully studied, the following generalization of the situation seen in the example is of some interest. We shall assume that the preferences (at least of trader 2) are such that neither good is inferior, and furthermore, that preferences are monotone (at least for trader 1).[15]

[15] Trader 1 is distinguished by the fact that the utility to him of the prescribed allocation is no higher than that of the competitive allocation would have been. As in the example, "competitive" means from $\theta$ as the initial allocation.

The environment is classical with regard to convexity and continuity, so that competitive equilibrium is guaranteed to exist. It is again assumed that there is a monopoly solution $[\langle z^1, z^2\rangle, p^M]$ which is favorable to trader 1, in the sense that $u^1(z^1) > u^1(c^1)$; at $p^M$, trader 2, when acting as a price taker, would demand $z^2$. Finally, we also assume that the monopoly point is an interior tangency point, i.e., a point where the price line $p^M$ through $\theta$ is tangent to some indifference curve of trader 2. This indifference curve may have the equation

$$x_2^2 = G(x_1^2);$$

using the fact that

$$x_j^1 + x_j^2 = \theta_j^1 + \theta_j^2 \qquad (j = 1, 2),$$

this equation may be rewritten as, say,

$$x_2^1 = g(x_1^1).$$

Since $z^1$ is the assumed point of tangency, we have

$$g'(z_1^1) = -\,p^M,$$

and since the $p^M$ price line goes through $\theta$,

$$z_2^1 - \theta_1^1 = -p^M(z_1^1 - \theta_1^1).$$

As a first candidate for a false indifference map of trader 1, we may consider the family of straight lines parallel to the price line $p_M$; the corresponding false utility function can be written as

$$v^1 = x_2^1 + p^M x_1^1 + \beta.$$

Clearly, $z$ is now a point on the false $(v^1)$ contract curve; furthermore, because both goods are noninferior for trader 2, all other points of this contract curve have coordinates that are respectively at least as great as those of $z^1$; since preferences of trader 1 are monotone, all points of the (false) contract curve are superior in terms of the true utility function $u^1$ to $c^1$, hence to the allocation prescribed by the process. Thus trader 1 would find it advantageous to pretend that his utility function is $v^1$ rather than $u^1$.

However, it would be more in the classical spirit to endow him with indifference curves that are strictly convex (to the origin), i.e., a strictly quasiconcave utility function. This can be accomplished by a slight deformation of the straight indifference lines of $v^1$ above. It can be done by slightly "bending" the line going through $\theta$ and $z$, so that the resulting curve is still tangent to the $g$-indifference curve of trader 2, with the point of tangency, say, $w=(w_1, w_2)$, $w_2=g(w_1)$, such that $w_1=z_1^1-\varepsilon$, where $\varepsilon$ is a positive number chosen sufficiently small so that $u^1(w)>u^1(c^1)$, which is possible because of continuity of $u^1$. The new false utility function $v^{1\#}$ will be defined by

$$v^{1\#}=x_2^1+p^M(x_1^1)^\alpha+\beta, \qquad 0<\alpha<1,$$

where $\alpha$ is obtained from the equation

$$-\alpha p^M w_1^{\alpha-1}=g'(w_1)$$

and $\beta$ from

$$\theta_2^1=-p^M(\theta_1^1)^\alpha-\beta.$$

By choosing $\varepsilon$ small enough one can make certain that (at least for a continuously differentiable marginal rate of substitution $u_1^2/u_2^2$ of the second trader) the contract curve of the strictly convex map given by $v^{1\#}$ is arbitrarily close to the contract curve for the linear map given by $v^1$, hence (by continuity of preferences) truly superior to $c^1$ for trader 1. Thus, for the environments and mechanisms under consideration, false "plausible" revelation of preferences is both feasible and profitable, hence individual incentive-compatibility is absent.

One is thus faced with the dilemma of accepting mechanisms that are either not Pareto-satisfactory (with the no-trade option) or not privacy-respecting. If one does not wish to sacrifice Pareto-satisfactoriness, one is forced into making concessions on the side of informational decentralization, specifically with regard to privacy. These concessions will involve the diversion of some resources from substantive uses to the operation of the mechanism – to obtain more information concerning the characteristics $e^i$ of the various individuals, and perhaps, to induce behavior prescribed by the mechanism. In terms of the notation of Eq. (1.1), the resource costs $b(q/e)$ of operating the mechanism[16] are (vectorially) higher than would have been the case if an incentive-compatible informationally decentralized mechanism were possible without the loss of Pareto-satisfactoriness. Consequently, the resources $\omega_e-b(q/e)_I$ available for substantive purposes are lower and hence the welfare possibilities, as measured by the indicator $w$ in (1.1) are (vectorially) less than would otherwise have been the case.

[16] We are again ignoring the psychological cost associated with the loss of privacy and with the enforcement measures designed to compensate for the absence of incentive-compatibility.

To illustrate, suppose that the mechanism initially under consideration is perfect competition, and the environment classical but not atomistic. We know that perfect competition will be Pareto-satisfactory but not incentive-compatible. We may then modify the mechanism by creating an agency whose task will be to acquire information about the individual characteristics $e^i$ of the participants and to enforce price-taking behavior. (This may seem somewhat less fantastic in the context of a Lange-Lerner economy, with the $e^i$ being the technological characteristics of the various producing units.) Assuming that enforcement is successful, the modified system is again Pareto-satisfactory with respect to $\omega_e - b(q/e)$ where $q$ is the modified mechanism and $b(q/e)$ represents the resource cost of operating the agency. Since perfect competition without the agency is incentive-incompatible, hence behaviorally infeasible, it cannot be considered as a realistic alternative to $q$. One could, on the other hand, suppose that there is some imperfectly competitive mechanism $q'$ which is informationally decentralized but not Pareto-satisfactory with regard to resources used for substantive purposes. Supposing for a moment that $b(q'/e) = 0$ we could then compare, in terms of an appropriate welfare indicator $W$, the two expressions $W[h(\omega_e - b(q/e), q/e)]$ and $W[h(\omega_e, q'/e)]$. It is not *a priori* obvious which will be the higher, even though – according to our assumptions – $W[h(x, q/e)]$ would be higher than $W[h(x, q'/e)]$ for any given $x$. In other words, even though $q'$ may be less efficient (in maximizing $W$) in utilizing the resources available for substantive purposes, it may make up for it by not requiring resources to operate the mechanism.

In a more realistic discussion one would recognize that all mechanisms require resources to operate, but the nature of the comparison might be somewhat similar.

The logic of informational assumptions underlying the concept of individual incentive-compatibility may well be questioned. Where do our results concerning the conflict between informational decentralization and incentives depend on the fact that the process is assumed to be privacy-respecting? A partial answer, at least, is obtained by imagining that the $n$-trader economy is enlarged by adding an $(n+1)$-st unit, an enforcement agency whose privacy-respecting response function may be written as $f^{*n+1}(m^1, \ldots, m^n, m^{n+1}; e^{n+1})$. This means that the agency's knowledge concerning $e^1, \ldots, e^n$ would only be derived from the messages $m_t^i$, $i = 1, \ldots, n$, and of the prescribed response functions $f^{*i}$; thus if any of the traders uses a false $e^i$ as an argument in his prescribed response function, there is no way for the enforcement agency to detect this. The same difficulty would arise if the traders themselves were entitled to enforce the prescribed rules of process, say, by suing in court. For here again, by the "privacy" postulate trader $j$ only knows about $e^i$ through the messages $m^i$, hence cannot prove that violation exists as long as a false $e^i$ is drawn from the "plausible" class $E^i$.[17]

In the light of the fact that $j$ does not know the true value of $e^i$, it might seem incongruous that the inequalities (3.2) implicitly contain the true values of $e^i$ in their right-hand members, But this objection loses some of its force if one notes that the functions $g^{*i}$ may be considered as observable in the course of the process, even though $f^i$ and $e^i$ separately are not. Hence, from the Nash solution point of view, the $g^{*i}$ functions seem to be the proper ones to enter the definition of an equilibrium point in a noncooperative game. On the other hand, in view of the known difficulties with this approach to the theory of games, alternative lines of attack should certainly be explored.[18]

## References

M. Aoki (1970a), "The problem of Incentives in the Theory of Planning," paper presented at the Second World Congress of the Econometric Society, Cambridge, England (unpublished).

M. Aoki (1970b), "Two Planning Algorithms for an Economy with Public Goods," Discussion Paper No. 029, Kyoto Institute of Economic Research, Kyoto University.

T. M. Apostol (1957), *Mathematical Analysis*, Addison-Wesley, Reading, Mass.

K. J. Arrow and L. Hurwicz (1960), "Decentralization and Computation in Resource Allocation," in R. W. Pfouts (ed.), *Essays in Economics and Econometrics*, University of North Carolina Press, Chapel Hill, pp. 34–104.

A. Camacho (1970), "Externalities, Optimality, and Informationally Decentralized Resource Allocation Processes," *International Economic Review*, *11*, pp. 318–327.

A. Camacho (1970), "Centralization and Decentralization of Decision-making Mechanisms: a General Model," paper presented at the Second World Congress of the Econometric Society, Cambridge, England (unpublished).

O. A. Davis and A. Whinston (1962), "Externalities Welfare and the Theory of Games," *Journal of Political Economy*, *70*, 241–262.

G. Debreu (1959), *Theory of Value*, Wiley, New York.

---

[17] It may be well to recall that, implicitly, we are assuming restrictions on communication that will make it impossible to "smuggle through" environmental information despite the privacy requirement.

[18] Drèze and de la Vallée Poussin (1969, p. 26), for instance, show that, in their public goods model, minimaxing calls for honest revelation of preferences.

J. H. DRÈZE and D. DE LA VALLÉE POUSSIN (1969), "A Tâtonnement Process for Guiding and Financing an Efficient Production of Public Goods," Discussion Paper No. 6922, CORE, Univ. Cath. de Louvain, Belgium.

T. GROVES (1970), "Incentives in a Team," paper presented at the Second World Congress of the Econometric Society, Cambridge, England (unpublished).

G. M. HEAL (1969), "Planning without Prices," *Review of Economic Studies*, *36*, pp. 346–362

L. HURWICZ (1951), "Theory of Economic Organization," (abstract), *Econometrica*, *19*, p. 54.

L. HURWICZ (1960a), "Optimality and Informational Efficiency in Resource Allocation Processes," Chapter 3 in K. J. ARROW, S. KARLIN, and P. SUPPES (eds.), *Mathematical Methods in the Social Sciences*, Stanford University Press, Stanford, pp. 27–46.

L. HURWICZ (1960b), "Conditions for Economic Efficiency of Centralized and Decentralized Structures," in G. GROSSMAN (ed.), *Value and Plan*, University of California Press, Berkeley, pp. 162–183.

L. HURWICZ (1966), "On Decentralizability in the Presence of Externalities," paper presented at the San Francisco meeting of the Econometric Society (unpublished).

L. HURWICZ (1969), "On the Concept and Possibility of Informational Decentralization," *American Economic Review*, *59*, pp. 513–534.

L. HURWICZ, R. RADNER, and S. REITER (1970), "A Stochastic Decentralized Resource Allocation Process," (unpublished).

L. HURWICZ (1970), "Organizational Structures for Joint Decision Making: a Designer's Point of View," in M. TUITE, R. CHISHOLM and M. RADNOR (eds.), *Interorganizational Decision-Making*, Aldine Press, Chicago (forthcoming).

L. HURWICZ (1971), "Centralization and Decentralization in Economic Processes," Chapter 3 in A. ECKSTEIN (ed.), *Comparison of Economic Systems: Theoretical and Methodological Approaches*, University of California Press, Berkeley (forthcoming).

H. KANEMITSU (1970), "On the Stability of an Adjustment Process in Nonconvex Environments – a Case of the Commodity Space (Strong) Inertia-Greed Process," paper presented at the Second World Congress of the Econometric Society, Cambridge, England (unpublished).

H. KANEMITSU (1966), "Informational Efficiency and Decentralization in Optimal Resource Allocation," *The Economic Studies Quarterly*, *16*, pp. 22–40.

T. C. KOOPMANS (1957), *Three Essays on the State of Economic Science*, McGraw-Hill, New York.

J. KORNAI and T. LIPTÁK (1965), "Two-level Planning," *Econometrica*, *33*, pp. 141–169.

J. O. LEDYARD (1968), "Resource Allocation in Unselfish Environments," *American Economic Review*, *58*, pp. 227–237.

E. MALINVAUD (1967), "Decentralized Procedures for Planning, "Chapter 7 in BACHARACH and MALINVAUD (eds.), *Activity Analysis in the Theory of Growth and Planning*, Macmillan, London, pp. 170–208.

E. MALINVAUD (1970), "The Theory of Planning for Individual and Collective Consumption," outline of a paper to be presented at the *Symposium on the Problem of the National Economy Modeling*, Novosibirsk (Siberian Branch of the Acad. of Science of the USSR).

S. A. MARGLIN (1969), "Information in Price and Command Systems of Planning," in J. MARGOLIS and H. GUITTON (eds.), *Public Economics*, Macmillan, London, pp. 54–77.

T. MARSCHAK (1959), "Centralization and Decentralization in Economic Organizations," *Econometrica*, *27*, pp. 399–430.

J. Marschak (1955), "Elements for a Theory of Teams," *Management Science*, *1*, pp. 127–137.

R. Radner (1961), "The Evaluation of Information in Organizations," in *Proceedings of the Fourth Berkeley Symposium on Mathematical Statistics and Probability*, University of California, Berkeley, vol. I, pp. 491–530.

S. Reiter (1960), "A Market-adjustment Mechanism," Institute Paper No. 1, Institute for Quantitative Research in Economics and Management, School of Industrial Management, Purdue University, Lafayette, Indiana.

S. Reiter (1970), "Informational Efficiency of Resource Allocation Processes," abstract of a paper presented at the Second World Congress of the Econometric Society, Cambridge, England (unpublished).

P. A. Samuelson (1954), "The Pure Theory of Public Expenditure," *The Review of Economics and Statistics*, *36*, pp. 387–389.

## PUBLICATIONS OF JACOB MARSCHAK

### 1923-1971*

1923 "Wirtschaftsrechnung und Gemeinwirtschaft," *Archiv für Sozialwissenschaft, 51.*

1924 "Kautsky und die junge Generation," *Gesellschaft.* (Reprinted in *Erinnerungen an Karl Kautsky*, Dietz, Hannover, 1954).

"Die Verkehrsgleichung," *Archiv für Sozialwissenschaft, 52.*

"Der korporative und der hierarchische Gedanke im Faschismus," *Archiv für Sozialwissenschaft, 52, 53.*

"Faschismus und Reformismus," *Gesellschaft.*

1926 "Die Klassen auf dem Arbeitsmarkt und ihre Organisationen" (with Emil LEDERER), "Arbeiterschutz," "Der neue Mittelstand," in *Grundriss der Sozialökonomik*, Vol. IX/1, J. C. B. Mohr, Tübingen.

"Die deutsche und die englische Elektrizitätswirtschaft," *Der Deutsche Volkswirt.*

"Weltwanderungskongress," *Gesellschaft.*

"Verkehrsmittel und Arbeitsbeschaffung," *Die Arbeit.*

1927 "Die rebellische Konjunkturkurve" (zu Karsten's Hypothese), *Magazin der Wirtschaft.*

"Hohe Löhne und die Volkswirtschaft," *Die Arbeit.*

"Die Ferngas-Denkschrift," *Der Deutsche Volkswirt.*

"Ferngas-Politik," *Gesellschaft.*

"Das Problem der Ferngasversorgung," *Die Gemeinde.*

1928 "Vorbemerkung über empirische Ausbaumöglichkeiten und Grenzen der produktiven Lohnwirkung," in Karl MASSAR (ed.), *Die Volkswirtschaftliche Funktion Hoher Löhne*, Allgemeiner Deutscher Gewerkschaftsbund, Berlin.

"Eine Lohntheorie der amerikanischen Gewerkschaften," *Die Arbeit.*

"Öffentliche Betriebe," in *Wirtschaftsdemokratie*, Allgemeiner Deutscher Gewerkschaftsbund, Berlin.

1930 *Berichte des Enquête-Ausschusses des Reichstags über exportierende Industrien: Pflanzenöle, Margarine, Gold- und Silberverarbeitung, Uhren, Glaswaren, Porzellan und Steingut, Kosmetik, Spielwaren, Ledererzeugung und -verarbeitung, Schuhe, Handschuhe.* Prepared at the Institut für Weltwirtschaft, Universität Kiel, Berlin.

*Die Lohndiskussion*, J. C. B. Mohr, Tübingen.

"Löhne und Ersparnisse," *Die Arbeit.*

"Das Kaufkraftargument," *Magazin der Wirtschaft.*

"Lohntheorie und Lohnpolitik," in L. Heyde (ed.), *Internationales Gewerkschaftslexikon*, Berlin.

"Le problème des hauts salaires," in *Les Documents du travail*, Paris.

---

* Excluding most book reviews and all newspaper articles.

"Zur modernen Interessendifferenzierung," in *Soziologische Studien: Festschrift für Alfred Weber*, Potsdam.

"Zollpolitik und Gewerkschaften," *Magazin der Wirtschaft.*

"Zur Politik und Theorie der Verteilung," *Archiv für Sozialwissenschaft, 64.*

1931 *Elastizität der Nachfrage*, J. C. B. Mohr, Tübingen.

"Was verbrauchen wir," *Die Arbeit.*

"Thesen zur Krisenpolitik," *Wirtschaftsdienst.*

"Problemas del salario", *Sociedad para el progreso social*, Madrid.

"Diskontpolitik," *Der deutsche Volkswirt.*

1932 "Substanzverluste," "Zur Rundfrage über Substanzverluste," "Grössenordnungen des deutschen Geldsystems" (with W. Lederer), *Archiv für Sozialwissenschaft, 67.*

"Lohnsatz, Lohnsumme, Lohnquote und Arbeitslosigkeit," *Soziale Praxis, 41*, 15–17.

"Sozialversicherung und Konsum," in *Volkswirtschaftliche Funktionen der Sozialversicherung*, Berlin.

1933 "Consumption (Measurement)," "Wages (Theory)," in *Encyclopedia of Social Sciences*, New York.

"Annual Survey of Statistical Information: Branches of National Spending," *Econometrica.*

"Volksvermögen und Kassenbedarf," *Archiv für Sozialwissenschaft, 68.*

"Vom Grössensystem der Geldwirtschaft," *Archiv für Sozialwissenschaft, 69.*

1934 "Economic Parameters in a Closed Stationary Society with Monetary Circulation," *Econometrica.*

"On the Length of the Period of Production," *Economic Journal.*

"Pitfalls in the Determination of Demand Curves" (with R. Frisch and W. Leontieff), *Quarterly Journal of Economics.*

1935 "Empirical Analysis of the Laws of Distribution," *Economica.*

1936 *Kapitalbildung* (with W. Lederer), Hodge & Co., London.

"Measurements in the Capital Market," *Proceedings of the Manchester Statistical Society.*

1937 "Limitatiuns of Frisch's Consumption Surface," *Econometrica.*

"Influence of Interest and Income on Savings," "Probabilities and Utilities in Human Choice," in *Cowles Commission for Research in Economics, Third Annual Conference*, Colorado Springs.

1938 "Money and the Theory of Assets," *Econometrica.*

"Assets, Prices, and Monetary Theory," (with H. Makower) *Economica.* (Reproduced in G. Stigler and K. Boulding (eds.), *Readings in Price Theory*, Irwin, Chicago, 1952.)

"Studies in Mobility of Labor" (with H. Makower and H. W. Robinson), *Oxford Economic Papers*, 1, 2, 4.

"Industrial Migration" (with E. Ackroyd), "Occupations," in *Survey of Social Services in the Oxford District*, Barnett House, Oxford.

1939 "Family Budgets and the So-called Multiplier," *Canadian Journal of Economics.*

"On Combining Market and Budget Data in Demand Studies," *Econometrica.*

"The Theory and Measurement of Demand (Henry Schultz)," *Economic Journal.*

"Individual and National Income and Consumption," "Sources for Demand

Analysis: Market, Budget, and Income Data," in *Cowles Commission for Research in Economics, Fifth Annual Conference*, Colorado Springs.

"Personal and Collective Budget Functions," *Review of Economic Statistics.*

1940 "Capital Consumption and Adjustment (S. Fabricant)," "Business Cycles (J. Schumpeter)," *Journal of Political Economy.*

"Peace Economics," *Social Research.*

1941 "Lack of Confidence," "The Task of Economic Stabilization," "Wicksell's Two Interest Rates," *Social Research.*

"A Discussion on Methods in Economics," *Journal of Political Economy.*

1942 "Economic Interdependence and Statistical Analysis," in O. LANGE et al. (eds.), *Studies in Mathematical Economics and Econometrics*, University of Chicago Press, Chicago.

"Identity and Stability in Economics," *Econometrica.*

1943 "Money Illusion and Demand Analysis," *Review of Economic Statistics.*

"Demand Elasticities Reviewed," "Income Inequality and Demand Studies," *Econometrica.*

1944 Introduction (pp. xiii–xxxii), in G. BIENSTOCK, S. SCHWARZ and A. YUGOW (authors), A. FEILER and J. MARSCHAK (eds.), *Management in Russian Industry and Agriculture*, Oxford University Press, Oxford.

"Random Simultaneous Equations and the Theory of Production" (with W.H. ANDREWS), *Econometrica.*

1945 "A Cross-section of Business Cycle Discussion," *American Economic Review.*

1946 "Von Neumann's and Morgenstern's New Approach to Static Economics," *Journal of Political Economy.* (Reproduced in The Bobbs-Merrill Reprint Series in the Social Sciences, S-452.)

"The Economic Aspects of Atomic Power," "Linear Cities" (with L. KLEIN and E. TELLER), *Bulletin of Atomic Scientists.*

Preface (pp. xiii–xviii), in H. MENDERSHAUSEN, *Changes in Income Distribution*, National Bureau of Economic Research, New York.

1947 "On Mathematics for Economists," *Review of Economic Statistics, 29.*

1948 "Statistical Inference from Nonexperimental Observations," in *Proceedings of the International Statistical Conferences*, Washington, D.C.

1949 "Role of Liquidity under Complete and Incomplete Information," *American Economic Review, 39.* (Also in French: *Textes choisis*, vol. I, *Problème, monétaires, Association Internationale des Sciences Economiques*, Dalloz et Sirey, Paris, 1964.)

1950 "Statistical Inference in Economics: An Introduction," in T. C. Koopmans (ed.), *Statistical Inference in Dynamic Economic Models*, Cowles Commission Monograph No. 10, Wiley, New York. (Reprinted in J. M. DOWLING and F. R. GLAHE (eds.), *Readings in Econometric Theory*, Colorado Associated University Press, Boulder, 1970.)

"Rational Behavior, Uncertain Prospects, Measurable Utility," *Econometrica, 18*, (Italian translation in TREZZA (ed.), *Readings on Consumer Behavior*, Milano, 1969.)

"The Rationale of the Demand for Money and 'Money Illusion'," *Metroeconomica, 2.*

*Economic Aspects of Atomic Power* (co-editor with S. SCHURR), Princeton University Press, Princeton. (Also in Japanese, 1954.)

1951 *Income, Employment, and the Price Level*, Augustus Kelly, New York.

"Why 'Should' Statisticians and Businessmen Maximize Moral Expectation?," in

*Proceedings of the Second Berkeley Symposium on Mathematical Statistics and Probability*, University of California Press, Berkeley.

"Optimal Inventory Policy" (with K. ARROW and T. HARRIS), *Econometrica, 19.*

"Comments on Wesley Mitchell's 'What Happens During Business Cycles'," in *Conference on Business Cycles*, National Bureau of Economic Research, New York.

1953 "Economic Measurements for Policy and Prediction," in Wm. C. HOOD and T.C. KOOPMANS (eds.), *Studies in Econometric Method*, Cowles Commission Monograph No. 14, Wiley, New York.

"Équipes et Organisations en régime d'incertitude," in *Colloque International d'Économétrie*, C.N.R.S., Paris.

1954 "Three Lectures on Probability in the Social Sciences," in P. F. LAZARSFELD (ed.), *Mathematical Thinking in the Social Sciences.* (Re-issued 1969, Russell and Russell, New York.)

"Towards an Economic Theory of Organization and Information", "Note on Some Proposed Decision Criteria" (with R. RADNER), in R.M. THRALL, R. L. DAVIS, and C. H. COOMBS (eds.), *Decision Processes*, Wiley, New York.

"Toward a Preference Scale for Decision Making," in M. SHUBIK (ed.), *Readings in Game Theory and Political Behavior*, Doubleday, New York. (Second edition 1964, corrected.)

"Optimal Weapon Systems" (with R. M. MICKEY), *Naval Research Logistics Quarterly, 1.*

1955 "Elements for a Theory of Teams," *Management Science, 1.*

"Norms and Habits of Decision Making under Certainty," in *Mathematical Models of Human Behavior*, Dunlap and Assoc., Stamford, Conn.

"Monnaie et liquidité dans les modèles macroéconomiques et microéconomiques," *Cahiers du Séminaire d'Économétrie, 3.*

1956 "Nature, Amount and Structure of Information, and the Cost of Decision Making," *Behavioral Science, 1.*

1959 "Experimental Tests of Stochastic Decision Theory" (with D. DAVIDSON), in C. W. CHURCHMAN and P. RATOOSH (eds.), *Measurement: Definitions and Theory*, Wiley, New York.

"Efficient and Viable Organizational Forms," in M. HAIRE (ed.), *Modern Theory of Organization*, Wiley, New York. (Reproduced in P. F. LAZARSFELD and N. W. HENRY (eds.), *Readings in Mathematical Social Sciences*, SRA, Chicago, 1966.)

"An Identity in Arithmetic" (with H. D. BLOCK), *Bulletin of American Mathematical Society.*

1960 "Remarks on the Economics of Information," in *Contributions to Scientific Research in Management*, Western Data Processing Center, University of California, Los Angeles.

"Theory of an Efficient Several-person Firm," *American Economic Review.*

"Binary-choice Constraints and Random Utility Indicators," in K. J. ARROW et al. (eds.), *Mathematical Methods in Social Sciences*, Stanford University Press, Stanford.

"Random Orderings and Stochastic Theories of Responses" (with H.D. BLOCK), in I. OLKIN et al. (eds.), *Contributions to Probability and Statistics*, Stanford University Press, Stanford.

1962 "Wladimir Woytinsky and Economic Theory," in *So Much Alive: The Life and Work of W. S Woytinsky*, Vanguard Press, New York.

1963 "Adaptive Programming," *Management Science.*

"The Payoff-relevant Description of States and Acts," *Econometrica.*

*Decision, Information, Organization*, Japan Management Association (in Japanese).

"Stochastic Models of Choice Behavior" (with G. BECKER and M. DEGROOT), "An Experimental Study of Some Stochastic Models for Wagers" (with BECKER and DEGROOT), "Probability of Choices Among Very Similar Objects: An Experiment to Decide Between Two Models" (with BECKER and DEGROOT), *Behavioral Science*. (First article reproduced in W. EDWARDS and A. TVERSKY (eds.), *Decision Making*, Penguin, London, 1967; Italian edition, Boringheri, Torino, 1970.)

1964 "Actual Versus Consistent Decision Behavior," *Behavioral Science*. (More complete version in *Rivista Internazionale de Scienze Economiche*.)

"Measuring Utility by a Single-response Sequential Method" (with BECKER and DEGROOT), *Behavioral Science*.

"Problems in Information Economics," Chapter 3 in C. BONINI et al. (eds.), *Management Controls: New Directions in Basic Research*, McGraw-Hill, New York. (German translation in M. BECKMANN (ed.), *Mathematische Wirtschaftstheorie*, Cologne, 1971.)

1965 "Economics of Language" *Behavioral Science*. (More complete version in *Orbis Pictus*, a volume in honor of D.I. Cizevsky, Eidos-Verlag, Munich; also reproduced in G. FISK and D. DIXON (eds.), *Theories for Marketing-systems Analysis*, Harper & Row, New York, 1967.)

1966 "Economic Planning and the Cost of Thinking," *Social Research*.

"A Remark on Econometric Tools," Foreword (pp. vii–xi) in C. CHRIST, *Econometric Models and Methods*, Wiley, New York. (Expanded version in *Synthese*, 1969.)

1968 "Decision Making: Economic Aspects," in *International Encyclopedia of Social Sciences*.

"Economics of Inquiring, Communicating, Deciding" (Richard T. Ely Lecture), *American Economic Review*.

"Economic Comparability of Information Systems" (with K. MIYASAWA), *International Economic Review*.

1970 "The Economic Man's Logic," in W. A. ELTIS et al. (eds.), *Induction, Growth, and Trade: Essays in Honour of Sir Roy Harrod*, Clarendon Press, Oxford.

1971 *Optimale Symbol-Behandlung: Ein Problem der Betriebs- und Volkswirtschaft*, Bonner Akademische Reden No. 36, Peter Hanstein Verlag, Bonn. (Expanded English version of the above, "Optimal Symbol Processing," *Behavioral Science*.)

"Economics of Information Systems," in M. INTRILIGATOR (ed.), *Frontiers of Quantitative Economics*, North-Holland, Amsterdam. (Also in *Journal of American Statistical Association*, invited paper.)

*Economic Theory of Teams* (with R. RADNER), Cowles Foundation Monograph No. 22, Yale University Press, New Haven.

"Economics of Acting, Thinking, and Surviving," in R. G. GRENELL (ed.), *Essays in Honor of Ralph W. Gerard*, Gordon and Breach, New York.

# REFERENCES


ALMON, C. (1963), "Central Planning Without Complete Information at the Center," in G. B. DANTZIG, *Linear Programming and Extensions*, Princeton University Press, Princeton, pp. 462–466.

AOKI, M. (1969), "A Planning Procedure Under Increasing Returns," Research Papers, vol. I, no. 1, Harvard Economic Research Project, Cambridge, Mass.

AOKI, M. (1970a), "The Problem of Incentives in the Theory of Planning," paper presented at the Second World Congress of the Econometric Society, Cambridge, England (unpublished).

AOKI, M. (1970b), "Two Planning Algorithms for an Economy with Public Goods," Discussion Paper No. 029, Kyoto Institute of Economic Research, Kyoto University.

APOSTOL, T. M. (1957), *Mathematical Analysis*, Addison-Wesley, Reading, Mass.

ARROW, K. J. (1952), "The Determination of Many-commodity Preference Scales by Two-commodity Comparisons," *Metroeconomica*, *4*, 105–115.

ARROW, K. J. (1953), "Le rôle des valeurs boursières pour la meilleure répartition des risques," in *Econometrie*, Colloques Internationaux du Centre National de la Recherche Scientifique, *11*, 41–47, Imprimerie Nationale, Paris; English translation (1964), "The Role of Securities in the Optimal Allocation of Risk Bearing," *Review of Economic Studies*, *31*, 91–96.

ARROW, K. J. (1963), *Social Choice and Individual Values*, 2nd ed., Wiley, New York.

ARROW, K. J. (1965), *Aspects of the Theory of Risk Bearing*, Yrjo Jahnsson Lecture Series, Helsinki.

ARROW, K. J., D. BLACKWELL, and M. A. GIRSCHICK (1949), "Bayes and Minimax Solutions of Sequential Decision Problems," *Econometrica*, *17*, 213–244.

ARROW, K. J., and F. HAHN, *Competitive Equilibrium Analysis*, Holden-Day, San Francisco (forthcoming).

ARROW, K. J., T. HARRIS, and J. MARSCHAK (1951), "Optimal Inventory Policy," *Econometrica*, *19*, 250–272.

ARROW, K. J., and L. HURWICZ (1960), "Decentralization and Computation in Resource Allocation," in R. W. PFOUTS (ed.), *Essays in Economics and Econometrics*, University of North Carolina Press, Chapel Hill, pp. 34–104.

AUMANN, R. J. (1961), "The Core of a Cooperative Game Without Side Payments," *Transactions of the American Mathematical Society*, *98*, 539–552.

AUMANN, R. J. (1964a), "Subjective Programming," Chapter 12 in SHELLY and BRYAN (eds.), *Human Judgments and Optimality*, Wiley, New York, pp. 217-242.

AUMANN, R. J. (1964b), "Markets with a Continuum of Traders," *Econometrica*, *32*, 39–50.

AUMANN, R. J. (1967), "A Survey of Cooperative Games Without Side Payments," Chapter 1 in M. SHUBIK (ed.), *Essays in Mathematical Economics, in Honor of Oskar Morgenstern*, Princeton University Press, Princeton, N.J., pp. 3–27.

AUMANN, R. J. (1972), "A Survey of Economics with a Continuum of Agents," paper presented at the Second World Congress of the Econometric Society, Cambridge.

AUMANN, R. J., and M. MASCHLER (1964), "The Bargaining Set for Cooperative Games," in M. DRESHER, L. S. SHAPLEY, and A. W. TUCKER (eds.), *Advances in Game Theory*, Princeton University Press, Princeton, N.J., pp. 443–476.

BARONE, E. (1935), "The Ministry of Production in the Collectivist State," in F. A. HAYEK (ed.), *Collectivist Economic Planning*, Routledge, London, pp. 245–290.

BAUMOL, W. J. (1959), *Business Behavior, Value and Growth*, Macmillan, New York.

BECKMANN, M. (1958), "Decision and Team Problems in Airline Reservations," *Econometrica, 26*, 134–145.

BECKMANN, M. (1968), *Dynamic Programming of Economic Decisions*, Springer-Verlag, Heidelberg.

BELLMAN, R. E. (1957), *Dynamic Programming*, Princeton University Press, Princeton, N. J.

BELLMAN, R. E. (1961), *Adaptive Control Processes: A Guided Tour*, Princeton University Press, Princeton, N. J.

BELLMAN, R. E., and R. KALABA (1957), "Dynamic Programming and Statistical Communication Theory," *Proceedings of the National Academy of Sciences, 43*, 749–751.

BERNOULLI, D. (1738), "Specimen Theoriae Novae de Mensura Sortis," *Commentarii Academiae Scientiarum Imperialis Petropolitanae, 5*, 175–192. English translation by L. SOMMER (1954), "Exposition of a New Theory on the Measurement of Risk," *Econometrica, 22*, 23–36.

BIRKHOFF, G. (1948), *Lattice Theory*, American Mathematical Society Colloquium Publication, vol XXV (revised edition).

BIRNBAUM, A. (1961), "On the Foundations of Statistical Inference: Binary Experiments," *Annals of Mathematical Statistics, 32*, 414–435.

BLACKWELL, D. (1951), "Comparison of Experiments," in J. NEYMAN (ed.) *Proceedings of the Second Berkeley Symposium on Mathematical Statistics and Probability*, pp. 93–102.

BLACKWELL, D. (1953), "Equivalent Comparisons of Experiments," *Annals of Mathematical Statistics, 24*, 265–272.

BLACKWELL, D. (1965), "Discounted Dynamic Programming," *Annals of Mathematical Statistics, 36*, 226–235.

BLASCHKE, W., and G. BOL (1938), *Geometrie der Gewebe*, Springer, Berlin.

BOHNENBLUST, H. F., L. S. SHAPLEY, and S. SHERMAN (1949), "Reconnaissance in Game Theory," Research Memorandum RM-208, RAND Corp. Santa Monica, Cal.

CAMACHO, A. (1970), "Centralization and Decentralization of Decision-making Mechanisms: A General Model," paper presented at the Second World Congress of the Econometric Society, Cambridge, England (unpublished).

CAMACHO, A. (1970), "Externalities, Optimality, and Informationally Decentralized Resource Allocation Processes," *International Economic Review, 11*, 318–327.

CHAPANIS, N. P., and J. A. CHAPANIS (1964), "Cognitive Dissonance: Five Years Later," *Psychological Bulletin, 61*, 1023.

CHARNES, A., and W. W. COOPER (1961), *Management Models and Industrial Applications of Linear Programming*, Wiley, New York, (2 volumes).

COHEN, J. E. (1962), "Information Theory and Music," *Behavioral Sciences, 7*, 137–163.

DANTZIG, G. B., and P. WOLFE (1961), "The Decomposition Algorithm for Linear Programs," *Econometrica, 29*, 767–778.

DAVIS, O. A., and A. WHINSTON (1962), "Externalities, Welfare, and the Theory of Games," *Journal of Political Economy, 70*, 241–262.

DAVIS, O. A., and A. WHINSTON (1966), "On Externalities, Information, and the Government-Assisted Invisible Hand," *Economica, 33*, 303–318.

DEBREU, G. (1954), "Representation of a Preference-Ordering by a Numerical Function," Chapter 11 in THRALL, COOMBS, and DAVIS (eds.), *Decision Processes*, Wiley, New York, pp. 159-165.

DEBREU, G. (1959), *Theory of Value*, Wiley, New York.

DEBREU, G. (1960), "Topological Methods in Cardinal Utility Theory," Chapter 2 in K. J. ARROW, S. KARLIN, and P. SUPPES (eds.), *Mathematical Methods in the Social Sciences*, Stanford University Press, Stanford, pp. 16–26.

DEBREU, G. (1963), "On a Theorem of Scarf," *The Review of Economic Studies, 30*, 177–180.

DEBREU, G. (1964), "Continuity Properties of Paretian Utility," *International Economic Review, 5*, 285–293.

DEBREU, G., and H. SCARF (1963), "A Limit Theorem on the Core of an Economy," *International Economic Review, 4*, 235–246.

DE FINETTI, B. (1937), "La prévision : ses lois logiques, ses sources subjectives," *Annales de l'Institut Henri Poincaré*, *7*, 1–68; English translation by H. E. KYBURG and SMOKLER (eds.), *Studies in Subjective Probability*, Wiley, New York, pp. 95–158.

DE GROOT, A. (1965), *Thought and Choice in Chess*, Mouton, The Hague.

DE GROOT, M. H. (1962) "Uncertainty, Information, and Sequential Experiments," *Annals of Mathematical Statistics*, *33*, 404–419.

DE GROOT, M. H. (1966), "Optimal Allocation of Observations," *Annals of Mathematical Statistics*, *18*, 13–28.

DIAMOND, P. A. (1965), "The Evaluation of Infinite Utility Streams, *Econometrica*, *33*, 170–177.

DOLEZEL, L., abd R. W. BAILEY, *Statistics and Style*, American Elsevier, New York.

DRÈZE, J. H., and D. DE LA VALLÉE POUSSIN (1969), "A Tâtonnement Process for Guiding and Financing an Efficient Production of Public Goods," Discussion Paper No. 6922, CORE, Université Catholique de Louvain, Belgium.

ECKSTEIN, O. (1960), "A Survey of the Theory of Public Expenditures Criteria," *Public Finances: Needs, Sources, and Utilization*, Princeton University Press, Princeton, pp. 439–494.

EDGEWORTH, F. Y. (1881), *Mathematical Psychics*, Paul Kegan, London.

EILENBERG, S. (1941), "Ordered Topological Spaces," *American Journal of Mathematics*, *63*, 39–45.

FELLER, W. (1968), *An Introduction to Probability Theory and Its Applications*, Vol. I (3rd ed.), Wiley, New York.

FISHBURN, P. C. (1966), "A Note on Recent Developments in Additive Utility Theories for Multiple-factor Situations, *Operations Research*, *14*, 1143–1148.

FISHER, C. (1962), "Linear Programming under Uncertainty in an $L_\infty$-space," ONR Technical Report No. 7, Center for Research in Management Science, University of California, Berkeley.

FISHER, I. (1930), *The Theory of Interest*, reprinted by Augustus Kelley, New York, 1961.

FORRESTER, J. W. (1961), *Industrial Dynamics*, MIT Press, Cambridge, Mass.

GALE, D. (1967), "On Optimal Development in a Multi-sector Economy," *Review of Economic Studies*, *34*, 1–18.

GALE, D. (1968), "A Mathematical Theory of Optimal Economic Development," *Bulletin of the American Mathematical Society*, *74*, 207–223.

GILLIES, D. B. (1953), *Some Theorems on N-person Games*, Ph.D. thesis, Princeton University, Princeton.

GOLDMAN, S. M., and H. UZAWA (1964), "A Note on Separability in Demand Analysis," *Econometrica*, *32*, 387–398.

GORMAN, W. M. (1959a), "Separable Utility and Aggregation," *Econometrica*, *27*, 469–481.

GORMAN, W. M. (1959b), "The Empirical Implications of a Utility Tree: a Further Comment," *Econometrica*, *27*, 489.

GORMAN, W. M. (1965), "Conditions for Additive Preferences," (unpublished).

GORMAN, W. M. (1968a), "Conditions for Additive Separability," *Econometrica*, *36*, 605–609.

GORMAN, W. M. (1968b), "The Structure of Utility Functions, "*Review of Economic Studies*, *53*, 367–390.

GRETTENBERG, T. L. (1964), "The Ordering of Finite Experiments," *Transactions of the Third Prague Conference on Information Theory, Statistical Decision Functions, Random Processes*, Czechoslovak Academy of Sciences, Prague, pp. 193–206.

GROVES, T. F. (1969), "The Allocation of Resources under Uncertainty: The Informational and Incentive Roles of Prices and Demands in a Team," NSF Technical Report No. 1, Center for Research in Management Science, University of California, Berkeley.

GROVES, T. F. (1970), "Incentives in a Team," paper presented at the Second World Congress of the Econometric Society, Cambridge, England (unpublished).

HANSEN, T., and H. SCARF (1969), "On the Applications of a Recent Combinatorial Algorithm," Cowles Foundation Discussion Paper No. 272.

HARSANYI, J. C. (1963), "A Simplified Bargaining Model for the *N*-person Cooperative Game," *International Economic Review*, *4*, 194–220.

HARSANYI, J. C. (1966), "A General Theory of Rational Behavior in Game Situations," *Econometrica*, *34*, 613–634.

HAYEK, F. (1945), "The Use of Knowledge in Society," *American Economic Review*, *35*, 519–530.

HEAL, G. M. (1969), "Planning Without Prices," *Review of Economic Studies*, *36*, 347–362.

HERDAN, G. (1956), *Language as a Choice and Chance*, P. Noordhoff, Groningen.

HILDENBRAND, W. (1971), "Measure Spaces of Economic Agents," *Proceedings of the Sixth Berkeley Symposium on Mathematical Statistics and Probability*, L. LECAM, J. NEYMAN. and E. SCOTT (eds.), University of California Press, Berkeley (forthcoming).

HIRSHLEIFER, J. (1955), "The Exchange Between Quantity and Quality," *Quarterly Journal of Economics*, *69*, 596–606.

HOUTHAKKER, H. S. (1951-52), "Compensated Changes in Quantities and Qualities Consumed," *Review of Economic Studies*, *19*, 155–164.

HOWARD, R. (1960), *Dynamic Programming and Markov Processes*, MIT Press, Cambridge, Mass.

HURWICZ, L. (1951), "Theory of Economic Organization," (abstract), *Econometrica*, *19*, 54.

HURWICZ, L. (1960a), "Optimality and Informational Efficiency in Resource Allocation Processes," Chapter 3 in K. J. ARROW, S. KARLIN, and P. SUPPES (eds.), *Mathematical Methods in the Social Sciences*, Stanford University Press, Stanford, pp. 27–46.

HURWICZ, L. (1960b), "Conditions for Economic Efficiency of Centralized and Decentralized Structures," in G. GROSSMAN (ed.), *Value and Plan*, University of California Press, Berkeley, pp. 162–183.

HURWICZ, L. (1966), "On Decentralizability in the Presence of Externalities," paper presented at the San Francisco meeting of the Econometric Society (unpublished).

HURWICZ, L. (1969), "On the Concept and Possibility of Informational Decentralization," *American Economic Review*, *59*, 513–534.

HURWICZ, L. (1970), "Organizational Structures for Joint Decision Making: a Designer's Point of View," in M. TUITE, R. CHISHOLM and, M. RADNOR (eds.), *Decision-Making*, Aldine Press, Chicago (forthcoming).

HURWICZ, L. (1971), "Centralization and Decentralization in Economic Processes," Chapter 3 in A. ECKSTEIN (ed.), *Comparison of Economic Systems: Theoretical and Methodological Approaches*, University of California Press, Berkeley (forthcoming).

HURWICZ, L., R. RADNER, and S. REITER (1970), "A Stochastic Decentralized Resource Allocation Process," (unpublished).

IBM (1969), *APL/360 User's Manual.*

JASKOLD-GABSZEWICZ, J. (1968), *Cœurs et allocations concurrentielles dans des économies d'échange avec un continu de biens*, Librairie Universitaire, Louvain.

KANEMITSU, H. (1966), "Informational Efficiency and Decentralization in Optimal Resource Allocation," *The Economic Studies Quarterly*, *16*, 22–40.

KANEMITSU, H. (1970), "On the Stability of an Adjustment Process in Nonconvex Environments: A Case of the Commodity-Space (Strong) Inertia-Greed Process," paper presented at the Second World Congress of the Econometrica Society, Cambridge, England (unpublished.)

KELLEY, J. L. (1955), *General Topology*, Van Nostrand, New York.

KELLY, J. L., Jr. (1956), "A New Interpretation of Information Rate," *Bell System Technical Journal*, *35*, 917–926.

KOOPMANS, T. C. (1957), *Three Essays on the State of Economic Science*, McGraw-Hill, New York.

KOOPMANS, T. C. (1960), "Stationary Ordinal Utility and Impatience," *Econometrica*, *28*, 287–309.

KOOPMANS, T. C. (1964), "On Flexibility of Future Preference," Chapter 13 in SHELLY and BRYAN (eds.), *Human Judgments and Optimality*, Wiley, New York, pp. 243–254.

KOOPMANS, T. C. (1965), "On the Concept of Optimal Economic Growth," in *The Econometric Approach to Development Planning*, North-Holland, Amsterdam, and Rand McNally, Chicago (a re-issue of *Pontificiae Aacademiae Scientiarvm Scripta Varua*, Vol. XXVIII, 1965), pp. 225–300.

KOOPMANS, T. C. (1966), "Structure of Preference over Time," Cowles Foundation Discussion Paper No. 206.

KOOPMANS, T. C. (1967a), "Objectives, Constraints, and Outcomes in Optimal Growth Models," *Econometrica*, *35*, 1–15.

KOOPMANS, T. C. (1967b), "Intertemporal Distribution and 'Optimal' Aggregate Economic Growth," Chapter 5 in FELLNER et al., *Ten Economic Studies in the Tradition of Irving Fisher*, Wiley, New York, pp. 95–126.

KOOPMANS, T. C., P. A. DIAMOND, and R. E. WILLIAMSON (1964), "Stationary Utility and Time Perspective," *Econometrica*, *32*, 82–100.

KORNAI, J. and T. LIPTÁK (1965), "Two-level Planning," *Econometrica*, *33*, 141–169.

KUEHN, A. A., and M. J. HAMBURGER (1963), "A Heuristic Program for Locating Warehouses," *Management Science*, *9*, 643–666.

LANCASTER, K. J. (1966a), "A New Approach to Consumer Theory," *Journal of Political Economy*, *74*, 132–157.

LANCASTER, K. J. (1966b), "Change and Innovation in the Technology of Consumption," *American Economic Review*, *56*, 14–23.

LANGE, O. (1938), "On the Economic Theory of Socialism," in O. LANGE and F.M. TAYLOR, *On the Economic Theory of Socialism*, University of Minnesota Press, Minneapolis, pp. 57–143.

LA VALLE, I. (1968), "On Cash Equivalents and Information Evaluation under Uncertainty Part I: Basic Theory," *Journal of the American Statistical Association*, *63*, 252–276.

LECAM, L. (1964), "Sufficiency and Approximate Sufficiency," *Annals of Mathematical Statistics*, *35*, 1419–1455.

LEDYARD, J. O. (1968), "Resource Allocation in Unselfish Environments," *American Economic Review*, *58*, 227–237.

LEONTIEF, W. (1947a), "Introduction to a Theory of the Internal Structure of Functional Relationships," *Econometrica*, *15*, 361–373.

LEONTIEF, W. (1947b), "A Note on the Interrelation of Subsets of Independent Variables of a Continuous Function with Continuous First Derivatives," *Bulletin of the American Mathematical Society*, *53*, 343–350.

LERNER, A. (1944), *The Economics of Control*, Macmillan, New York.

LINDLEY, D. V. (1956), "On a Measure of the Information Provided by an Experiment," *Annals of Mathematical Statistics*, *27*, 986–1005.

MACLANE, SAUNDERS, and G. BIRKHOFF (1967), *Algebra*, MacMillan, New York.

MALINVAUD, E. (1967), "Decentralized Procedures for Planning," Chapter 7 in BACHARACH and MALINVAUD (eds.), *Activity Analysis in the Theory of Growth and Planning*, Macmillan, London, pp. 170–208.

MALINVAUD, E. (1969), "First-Order Certainty Equivalence," *Econometrica*, *37*, 706–718.

MALINVAUD, E. (1970), "The Theory of Planning for Individual and Collective Consumption," Outline of a paper to be presented at the *Symposium on the Problem of the National Economy Modelling*, Novosibirsk (Siberian Branch of the Academy of Science of the USSR).

MARGLIN, S. (1963), *Approaches to Dynamic Investment Planning*, North-Holland, Amsterdam.

MARGLIN, S. (1964), "Decentralization with a Modicum of Increasing Returns," Research Memorandum RM-3421-PR, RAND Corporation, Santa Monica, California.

MARGLIN, S. (1969), "Information in Price and Command Systems of Planning," in J. MARGOLIS and H. GUITTON (eds.), *Public Economics*, Macmillan, London, pp. 54–77.

MARSCHAK, J. (1955), "Elements for a Theory of Teams," *Management Science*, *1*, 127–137.

MARSCHAK, J. (1959), "Efficient and Viable Organizational Forms," Chapter 11 in M. HAIRE (ed.), *Modern Organization Theory*, Wiley, New York, pp. 307–320.

MARSCHAK, J. (1959), "Remarks on the Economics of Information," *Contributions to Scientific Research in Management*, Western Data Processing Center, University of California, Los Angeles, pp. 79–98.

MARSCHAK, J. (1960), "Binary Choice Constraints and Random Utility Indicators," Chapter 21 in K. J. ARROW, S. KARLIN, and P. SUPPES (eds.), *Mathematical Methods in the Social Sciences*, Stanford University Press, Stanford, pp. 312–329.

MARSCHAK, J. (1963), "On Adaptive Programming," *Management Science*, *9*, 517–526.

MARSCHAK, J. (1963), "The Payoff-Relevant Description of States and Acts," *Econometrica*, *31*, 719–725.

MARSCHAK, J., and K. MIYASAWA (1968), "Economic Comparability of Information Systems," *International Economic Review*, *9*, 137–174.

MARSCHAK, J., and R. RADNER (1971), *The Economic Theory of Teams*, Yale University Press, New Haven.

MARSCHAK, T. (1959), "Centralization and Decentralization in Economic Organizations," *Econometrica*, *27*, 399–430.

MCGUIRE, C. B. (1961), "Some Team Models of a Sales Organization," *Management Science*, *7*, 101–130.

MENGER, K. (1934), "Das Unsicherheitsmoment in der Wertlehre, Betrachtungen im Anschluss an das sogenannte Petersburger Spiel," *Zeitschrift für Nationalökonomie*, *5*, 459–485.

MIYASAWA, K. (1968), "Information Structures in Stochastic Programming Problems," *Management Science*, *14*, 275–291.

MORSE, N., and R. SACKSTEDER (1966), "Statistical Isomorphism," *Annals of Mathematical Statistics*, *37*, 203–214.

NASH, J. F. (1951), "Non-Cooperative Games," *Annals of Mathematics*, *54*, 286–295.

NEMHAUSER, G. L. (1966), *Introduction to Dynamic Programming*, Wiley, New York.

RADER, T. (1963), "The Existence of a Utility Function to Represent Preferences," *Review of Economic Studies*, *30*, 229–232.

RADNER, R. (1961), "The Evaluation of Information in Organizations," in *Proceedings of the Fourth Berkeley Symposium on Mathematical Statistics and Probability*, University of California, Berkeley, Vol. I, pp. 491–530.

RADNER, R. (1962), "Team Decision Problems," *Annals of Mathematical Statistics*, *33*, 857–881.

RADNER, R. (1963), *Notes on the Theory of Economic Planning*, Center of Economic Research, Athens.

RADNER, R. (1964), "Mathematical Specifications of Goals for Decision Problems," Chapter 11 in M. W. SHELLY and G. L. BRYAN (eds.), *Human Judgments and Optimality*, Wiley, New York, pp. 178–216.

RAIFFA, H., and R. SCHLAIFER (1961), *Applied Statistical Decision Theory*, Harvard Business School, Boston.

RAMSEY, F. P. (1926), "Truth and Probability," Chapter 7 in F. P. RAMSEY (1950), *The Foundations of Mathematics and Other Logical Essays*, The Humanities Press, New York, pp. 156–198.

REITER, S. (1960), "A Market Adjustment Mechanism," Institute Paper No. 1, Institute for Quantitative Research in Economics and Management, School of Industrial Management, Purdue University, Lafayette.

REITER, S. (1970), "Informational Efficiency of Resource Allocation Processes," Abstract of a paper presented at the Second World Congress of the Econometric Society, Cambridge, England (unpublished).

SAMUELSON, P. A. (1947), *Foundations of Economic Analysis*, Harvard University Press, Cambridge.

SAMUELSON, P. A. (1954), "The Pure Theory of Public Expenditure," *The Reveiw of Economics and Statistics*, *36*, 387–389.

SAVAGE, L. J. (1954), *The Foundations of Statistics*, Wiley, New York.

SCARF, H. (1959), "Bayes' Solutions of the Statistical Inventory Problem," *Annals of Mathematical Statistics*, *30*, 490–508.

SCARF, H. (1962), "An Analysis of Markets with a Large Number of Participants," *Recent Advances in Game Theory*, The Princeton University Conference, 127–155.

SCARF, H. (1967), "The Core of an *N*-person Game," *Econometrica*, *35*, 50–69.

SCARF, H. (1969), "An Example of an Algorithm for Calculating General Equilibrium Prices," *American Economic Review*, *59*, 669–677.

SCHMIDBAUER, P. (1966), "Information and Communications Requirements of the Wheat Market: an Example of a Competitive System," Technical Report No. 21, Center for Research in Management Science, University of California, Berkeley.

SCHUMPETER, J. A. (1954), *History of Economic Analysis*, Oxford University Press, New York.

SEN, A. K. (1971), "Choice Functions and Revealed Preference," *Review of Economic Studies* (forthcoming).

SHACKLE, G. L. S. (1952), *Expectation in Economics*, (2nd ed.), Cambridge University Press, Cambridge.

SHAPLEY, L. S. (1953), "A Value for *N*-person Games," in H. W. KUHN and A. W. TUCKER (eds.), *Contributions to the Theory of Games*, Vol. II, Princeton University Press, Princeton.

SHAPLEY, L. S., and M. SHUBIK (1966), "Quasi-Cores in a Monetary Economy with Nonconvex Preferences," *Econometrica*, *34*, 805–827.

SHAPLEY, L. S., and M. SHUBIK (1969), "On the Core of an Economic System with Externalities," *American Economic Review*, *59*, 678-684.

SHUBIK, M. (1959), "Edgeworth Market Games," in A. W. TUCKER and R. D. LUCE (eds.), *Contributions to the Theory of Games*, Vol. IV, Princeton University Press, Princeton.

SIMON, H. A. (1956), "Dynamic Programming under Uncertainty with a Quadratic Criterion Function," *Econometrica*, *24*, 74–81.

SIMON, H. A. (1957), *Models of Man*, Wiley, New York.

SIMON, H. A., and P. A. SIMON (1962), "Trial-and-Error Search in Solving Difficult Problems," *Behavioral Science*, *7*, *425–429*.

STIGLER, G. J. (1961), "The Economics of Information," *Journal of Political Economy*, *69*, 213–225.

STROTZ, R. H. (1956), "Myopia and Inconsistency in Dynamic Utility Maximization," *Review of Economic Studies*, *23*, 165–180.

STROTZ, R. H. (1957), "The Empirical Implications of a Utility Tree," *Econometrica*, *25*, 269–280.

STROTZ, R. H. (1959), "The Utility Tree – A Correction and Further Appraisal," *Econometrica*, *27*, 482–488.

THEIL, H. (1957), "A Note on Certainty Equivalence in Dynamic Planning," *Econometrica*, *25*, 346–349.

UZAWA, H. (1958), "Interative Methods for Concave Programming," in ARROW, HURWICZ, and UZAWA, *Studies in Linear and Nonlinear Programming*, Stanford University Press, Stanford.

VILLEGAS, C. (1964), "On Qualitative Probability $\sigma$-Algebras, *Annals of Mathematical Statistics*, *35*, 1787–1796.

VIND, K. (1964), "Edgeworth-Allocations in an Exchange Economy with Many Traders," *International Economic Review*, *5*, 165–177.

VIND, K. (1965), "A Theorem on the Core of an Economy," *The Review of Economic Studies*, *32*, 47–48.

VON NEUMANN, J., and O. MORGENSTERN (1944), *Theory of Games and Economic Behavior* (1st ed.), Princeton University Press, Princeton (see also 3rd ed., 1953).

VON NEUMANN, J., and O. MORGENSTERN (1953), *Theory of Games and Economic Behavior* (3rd ed.), Princeton University Press, Princeton.

VON WEIZSÄCKER, C. C. (1965), "Existence of Optimal Programs of Accumulation for an Infinite Time Horizon," *Review of Economic Studies*, *32*, 85–104.

WARD, B. (1967), *The Socialist Economy*, Random House, New York.

WEITZMAN, M. (1970), "Iterative Multi-level Planning with Production Targets," *Econometrica*, *38*, 50–65.

WOLD, H. (1943), "A Synthesis of Pure Demand Analysis, Part II," *Skandinavisk Aktuaritidskrift*, pp. 220–263.

YAARI, M. E. (1964), "On the Consumer's Lifetime Allocation Process," *International Economic Review*, *5*, 304–317.

# NAME INDEX

# SUBJECT INDEX